Paolo Lazzarin

ONE HUNDRED & ONE
Beautiful TOWNS *in Italy*
Food & Wine

RIZZOLI
NEW YORK

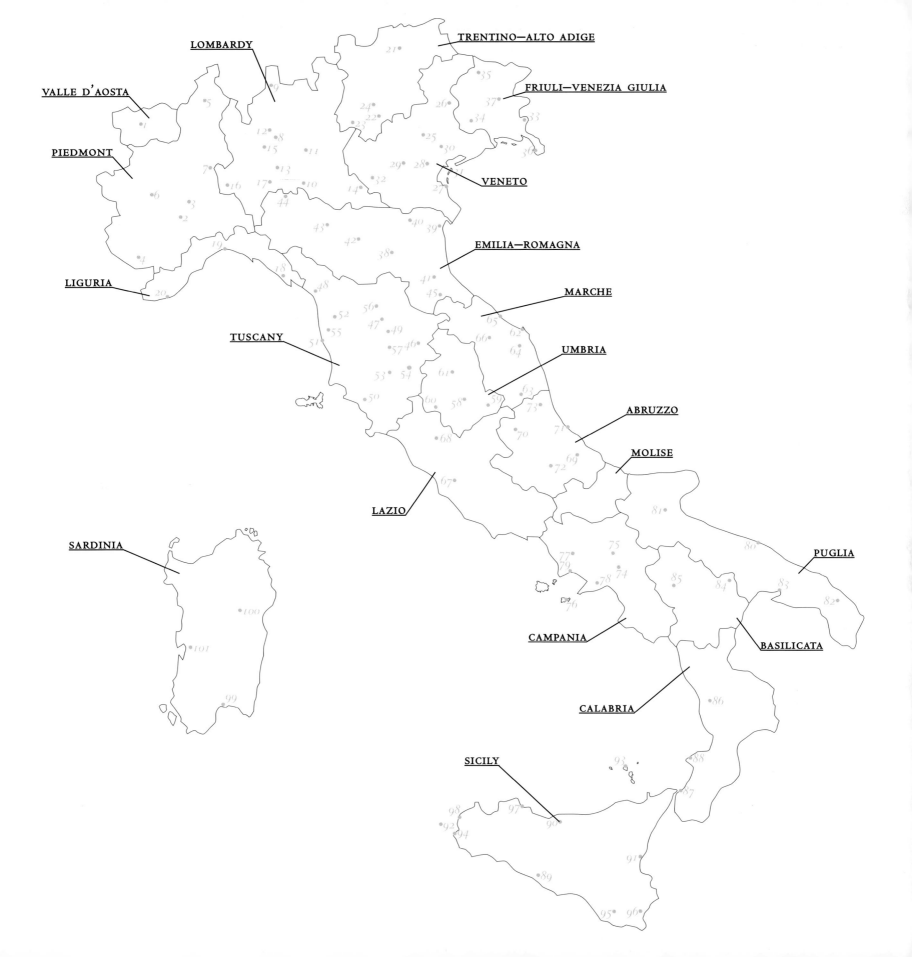

VALLE D'AOSTA

LOMBARDY

TRENTINO–ALTO ADIGE

FRIULI–VENEZIA GIULIA

PIEDMONT

VENETO

EMILIA–ROMAGNA

MARCHE

LIGURIA

TUSCANY

UMBRIA

ABRUZZO

MOLISE

LAZIO

SARDINIA

PUGLIA

CAMPANIA

BASILICATA

CALABRIA

SICILY

REGIONAL CONTENTS

ALPHABETICAL CONTENTS

PREFACE

Giovanni Boccaccio first described the myth of *Bengodi*, the Land of Milk and Honey, halfway through the fourteenth century. In this Promised Land food was never lacking, there were mountains of cheese to season pasta, geese went of their own free will to roast on the spit, vines were bound with savory sausages, and rivers flowed copiously with Vernaccia wine. In the less mythical reality, hunger was a terrible scourge across Italy through the early twentieth century, as it continues to be in many parts of the world, a fact brought to the public's attention in many novels and films—often with piercing irony—by artists such as Aldo Fabrizi, Totò, and Charlie Chaplin and Buster Keaton, their comedic forebears. Appetite was a sign of good health, the possibility of satisfying it proved one's economic well-being, and the overweight were perceived as vigorous and well-off, envied by the many who could not achieve this status, rather than viewed as obese and at risk of a heart attack. The Florentine middle classes were pleased to describe themselves as "fat" to attest their established wealth, and before beginning their sumptuous banquets they exhibited cornucopia-like tables of food outside the palazzo to show off their magnificence to the plebeians—an ostentation likely based more on quantity than quality. Though it certainly cannot be said that the populace had refined culinary taste, it was certainly creative in concocting dishes from very little. Nor can one place blame on the commoners if they did not eat well, considering what cleverly guided their taste; Baldassarre Pisanelli's 1584 book *Trattato della natura de' cibi et del bere* (Treatise on the Nature of Food and Drink), is full of curious suggestions. He authoritatively writes that pheasant "causes asthma in rough people, and the sole remedy is for them to abstain from it, leaving it to refined and noble folk." Today widespread hunger has been conquered, and food is chosen scrupulously, following one's palate and sense of smell, in a search for the savory in a territory of newly appreciated cuisine once considered mere peasant food.

Italy's cuisine and wine are among the world's most prized. Ranking among the top producers of natural food, the national certifications of quality are incredibly nuanced and rigorously controlled. Already by the early twentieth century a *Carta delle principali specialità gastronomiche delle regioni italiane* (Charter of the Principle Gastronomic Specialties of Italy's Regions) was published, followed in 1931 with the first *Guida gastronomica d'Italia* (Gastronomic Guide to Italy) by the Italian Touring Club. The vast variety of Italian food and wine is marvelously rich and historic: sausages from Lucania were imported to the Capitol of the Roman Empire, as were eels from Lake Garda, cheeses from the Vestini Mountains, asparagus from Pozzuoli, stuffed olives from Piceno, and wine from Falerno. Italy's political unification in 1861 may be considered relatively recent, but texts on cuisine have always referred to the peninsula as a whole. The first gastronomic map, drawn by Apicius in the first century AD, was published in his ten-volume treatise *De re coquinaria* (On Cooking). Sixteenth-century papal chef Bartolomeo Scappi, author of a cookbook of recipes rapidly adopted in courts across Europe, collected traditions from all over Italy and thoroughly represented the North, Central, and Southern regions by organizing the chapters around Milan, Rome, and Naples.

The first book of oenogastronomical tourism, however, was probably the *Commentario delle più notabili et mostruose cose d'Italia et altri luoghi* (Commentary of the Most Notable and Incredible Things of Italy and Other Places), written and published by Ortensio Lando in 1548. The adventure starts with Sicilian maccheroni and reaches as far north as the cheeses of the Val Malenco, punctuated by discoveries in each region.

One Hundred & One Beautiful Towns in Italy: Food & Wine includes all of *Italia da gustare*, from the mountainous north to the seafaring south. Following in Lando's legacy, it is an alternative, pleasurable way to discover Italy through the food and wine that are so inseparably woven into its history, culture, and geography.

A view of Longiaru, a beautiful village nestled in the charming Val Badia.

A O S T A

EUROPE'S LOFTIEST VINEYARDS

IN THE SHADOW OF THE HIGHEST PEAKS OF THE ALPS, orderly rows of vines spread across the sun-kissed slopes of the Valle d'Aosta from Pont Saint Martin as far up as Morgex, competing with Switzerland for the record of the highest vineyards in Europe. The inhabitants of the Valle d'Aosta have learned to take advantage of the mountains' scarce resources not only to survive poverty, but to obtain the best this rugged landscape can offer. Aosta owes this to its important place in history, distinguished first by its Roman founders, followed by feudal lords who enjoyed the privileges that came with control of the consular roads of Gaul, a key route connecting the Mediterranean to Northwest Europe. In their wake the Romans left grandiose monuments such as a theater, the arch of Augustus, the Praetorian Gate, bridges, and aqueducts. The feudal lords built castles and fortresses of notable beauty in strategic places in the valley, many of which can still be visited. Not only was the Valle d'Aosta a seat of power in terms of its geographic location, but it was and continues to be famous for its prosciutto (cured ham), which has been produced in Saint Rhémy-en-

The moutainside vineyards of Aymaville.

facing page
Resting on a basket of black bread, the superior *Jambon de Bosses* is best savored with honey and walnuts.

Bosses for centuries. This tiny hamlet at the approach to the Saint Bernard Pass sits at an altitude of over 5,300 feet and is known for a rare quality of prosciutto called *Jambon de Bosses*, a savory ham made from pedigree pigs raised in the area. The local production of *tibias porci* is mentioned in documents from the Great Saint Bernard Hospice in 1397. In a village palazzo the cast iron signs still identify Saint Rhémy as a stopping place for pilgrims, and here the hams are prepared by a method that has been handed down for ages. First the meat is salted and covered with spices (garlic, sage, rosemary, juniper, thyme, and other aromatic mountain herbs), then kept in the "ham room" for two weeks and massaged daily to eliminate all blood and other fluids. It is then washed and covered with coarse ground pepper and left to age for at least a year, so that the meat takes on a sweet, perfumed flavor, savory but not overly salty. Then, if it is considered worthy, the *Jambon de Bosses* is ranked DOP (acronym for Protected Denomination of Origin). Otherwise it is given the name *Bossolein*, indicating a slightly inferior quality. It is eaten with rye bread spread with butter and a drop of honey, accompanied by a glass of young red wine from the Valle d'Aosta.

Recognized as an official "City of Wine," Aosta has given great importance to wine for centuries, as can be seen from the bunches of grapes sculpted into the capitals of the cloister of the collegiate church of Sant'Orso (twelfth century). Among Aosta's wine labels famed beyond the Italian borders is Enfer d'Arvier, a full-bodied red obtained from the vines that owe their name, Inferno, to the fact that the grapes are matured in an amphitheater where the heat in the summer is suffocating. The Blanc de Morgex, also internationally renowned, is obtained from grapes grown in some of the highest vineyards of Europe. It is a dry white, fine and delicate, with a trace of freshly mown hay. Also well worth trying are the Petit Rouge, the most cultivated vine in the valley; the Chambave nero, a red that best typifies the wines of the area; and the Fumin, an ancient enological pearl of the Valle d'Aosta which has been recently rediscovered and refined in *barriques*.

Jambon de Bosses can be bought at the Saint-Rhémy-en-Bosses Cooperative. Local sausages and cheeses are available at the Bottega degli Antichi Sapori, and *fontina* cheese at the Maison de la Fontine, both in Aosta. In nearby Arnad, lard, *mocetta* (cured goat or deer meat flavored with herbs), and juniper *coppa* (cured neck of pork) are richly displayed in Lo Scrigno dei Sapori, the salami factory's shop. Wines, *genepi* liqueur, and *ratafià*, a wild cherry liqueur, are available for tasting and purchase at the wine shop La Cave in Aosta's historic center, and many other fine wines can be sought out at various regional cellars, including the Istitut Agricole Regional, Cooperativa Co.Enfer, and the Cave du Vin Blanc de Morgex.

IIn Valle d'Aosta, according to a *Summa lacticinorum* of 1447, "the cheeses are good and the pastures excellent." To this day the local breed of cows, their summer grazing and winter hay supply, the immediate processing of their fresh milk—which is left to age in caves—and the care with which the cheese forms are made all contribute to the resulting soft and tasty cheeses of great quality. Above them all is fontina, possibly a name inherited from the village of Fontinaz near Saint Martin, or Fontin, near Quart. It is first recorded in the register of the Great Saint Bernard Hospice in 1717, but is certainly of older origin. Current production is controlled by a consortium that bestows the DOP title according to the most rigorous rules governing Italian cheese production. The brand, depicting the stylized shape of Mount Cervino, is placed on the underside of the form and contains the production date and the identifying number of the producer—from 1 to 495 refers to the summer alpine location and from 496 to 999 refers to the cheesemaker. Ageing takes place over a period of roughly three months in dark natural caves with a consistent humidity and temperature. This gives the cheese a thin crust and sweet-tasting, soft, elastic paste that melts easily—a characteristic that renders it ideal for the preparation of the traditional fondue of the Valle d'Aosta.

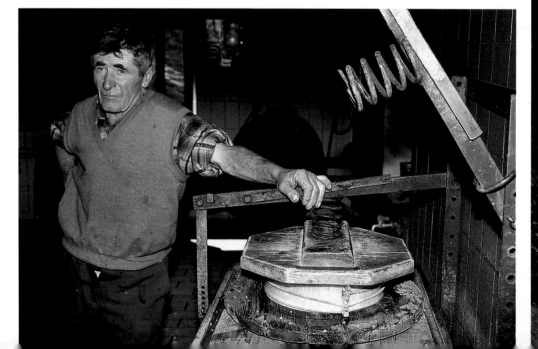

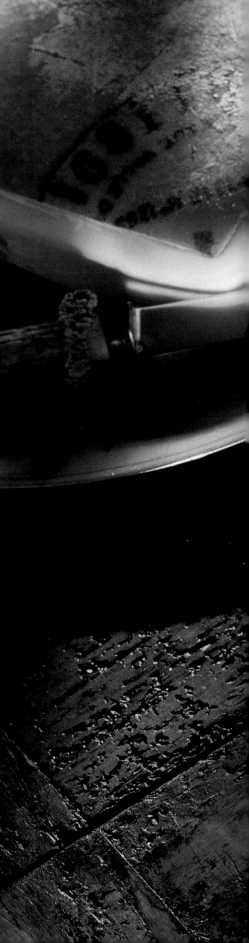

above
The bustling market of the Sant'Orso fair in Aosta.

below
Traditional preparation of fontina cheese in St. Nicolas

opposite
Fondue, the quintessential dish of the Valle d'Aosta, is prepared exclusively with fontina cheese.

A L B A
KING OF WINES, WINE OF THE KINGS

CASTLES THAT ATTEST TO STRENGTH, NOT AGGRESSION, wealth without ostentation, "with sweet curves like the breasts of a young woman, covered with rows of well tended vines." Such is the landscape that frames Alba, a village with a historic center that preserves the town's ancient atmosphere. In autumn, Alba is transformed into a perfumed bouquet of *tartufi di Alba*, the famous truffles of Alba around which a spectacular two-week festival is organized. The air is sweetened with the scent of must (the pulp and skins of fermenting grapes) used to produce Barolo, called the "king of wines and the wine of kings." To drink a good Barolo requires patience. One must wait for at least seven years—or better yet, ten—so the wine has time to fully mature. After the grapes have been pressed, the must remains in the barrel for two to three years, after which it should rest for another four or five years in bottles before it can fully impart its harmony of flavors and intense aromas. Barolo's fame is relatively recent considering the tradition of wine production in the hills of Piedmont. It was in the first half of the nineteenth century that Camillo Benso, Count of Cavour, a statesman who was passionate about wine, employed the French wine expert Louis Odart to improve the quality of

Alba's Cathedral Square.

facing page
A selection of prized truffles, the world's most expensive tuber.

the wines produced on his estate at Grinzane. The grape was called Nebbiolo (meaning cloudy) because of the grayish patina or *pruina* (bloom) covering the mature fruit much like a cloud. To treat the Nebbiolo grapes Odart employed the method used for the Pinot Noirs of Burgundy. This is how Barolo was born and soon became the most popular wine among the aristocrats of Piedmont. King Carlo Alberto of Savoy himself bought a vineyard in Alba and set up one of the most modern wine estates of the time. Barolo, however, is demanding. A good wine improves with age, and a fully mature Barolo cannot be handled like a young table wine. Before drinking the wine, the bottle must be kept in a vertical position for a few days so that the sediment settles on the bottom. Once it has reached room temperature it should be uncorked several hours

before drinking. This ritual is full of suspense, for if the cork is rotten or has let in air that has oxidized the wine, it must be thrown away; but if it is "right" (and this almost always is the case) the wine, like a true gentleman, will be at ease with everything—not only highly flavored game and matured cheeses, but on its own. To fully appreciate Barolo serve it in a large-bowled glass, and in order to let it sufficiently breathe first slowly transfer it into a broad-based decanter.

The pride of Alba, the white truffle (*Tuber magnatum pico*), is a precious tuber that grows in symbiosis with the roots of trees. The truffles are dark and aromatic if they are oaks, lighter and more delicate if near linden or lime trees. They mature mostly in the fall when their scent can be detected by specially trained truffle hounds with a keen sense of smell. The truffle has been appreciated since the times of the biblical patriarch Jacob and Roman statesman Cicero. Emperor Charles V loved them, and the Count of Cavour gave them to diplomats in exchange for certain political advantages. The truffle is eaten raw, cut into very thin slices or shaved and served over hot dishes such as risotto; tagliatelle called *tajarin* (flat-ribbon noodles bathed in butter); fried eggs; *fonduta*, a creamy Fontina-based fondue; and on fresh beef *all'albese* (thinly sliced). Once unearthed, the truffle should only be kept for a little while, wrapped in slightly absorbent paper or stored in a glass jar filled with uncooked rice. Before cutting, each truffle should be carefully cleaned with a brush or damp cloth to remove any soil.

An excellent Barolo that ages well is produced in the hills of Monteforte d'Alba, Castiglione Falletto, and Serralunga d'Alba, and is available in Alba at Fracchia & Berchiella and I Piaceri del Gusto wine shops. Truffles and other traditional products of the region are on sale at the Polleria Ratti. Excellent cheeses are also produced in the surrounding Langhe area, including *tuma dla paja*, a prize-winning delicacy at the 1997 International Fair of Fancy Food in New York, voted best cheese in the world and now sold at the Antica Dispensa in Monteforte d'Alba. In Serralonga d'Alba, Teobaldo Cappellano (tel.+39 0173 613103) produces a Barolo Chinato from a recipe created in the early twentieth century. This has remained a secret ever since, because when Cappellano was asked to export it to the United States he refused in order to avoid making the recipe public.

A S T I
VINEYARD CULTURE

NO CITY IS MORE WORTHY OF THE TITLE "CITY OF WINE" THAN ASTI, whose prestigious school has produced enologists who have taught wine-making in the majority of countries new to the ancient practice, from Chile to South Africa. It is a small city in which the vine and wine represent the backbone of the economy, history, and tradition to such an extent that the fourteenth-century cathedral is called La Vigna (the vineyard) for the garlands of vines sculpted on its columns. Asti is the capital city of Monferrato, emblem of the old, slightly nostalgic Piedmont, and is characterized by loggias under which old shops invite one to peruse their wares and taverns offer fine wine by the glassful. September is the best time to visit, during the Palio festival, when the "Douja d'Or" is awarded to the best wine of the year. On this unique occasion the best wines produced in the region can be tasted. The Basso Monteferrato, stretching north from the city to the Tanaro River and on to the Po, is the region of red wine. This area is home to Freisa, Dolcetto, and Grignolino, but above all it produces Barbera, a strong wine, rich with personality, exported to connoisseurs beyond the borders of the region even in the Middle Ages. Barbera is not, however, a challenging wine, and drinking it should not be

Rows of Pelaverga vines, an ancient grape native to Piedmont.

facing page
Bottles of Asti Spumante.

a rite, nor does it require austere tastings. Paired with dishes of jugged hare and savory slices of salami or pieces of hard cheese, it always rises to the occasion. Not all Barbera grapes, though, become Barbera d'Asti, and only the best are deemed Superiore. These are high-quality wines matured either in special large barrels that are a local tradition or small *barriques* that are a more contemporary fashion. The wine is aged here for at least six months—two years if it is a Riserva—in order to assimilate the wood's essence before it is put into bottles to further refine its flavor.

In Alto Monferrato the most cultivated grape is the small, golden, very sweet white muscatel grown on the hillsides of Canelli, a village dominated by the historic fortress of Gancia Castle. It is used to produce Moscato d'Asti, a wine with a special aroma and fragrance, sweet but not overly so, to be enjoyed young and at the end of the meal with baked desserts. The lively version is Asti Spumante, once the epitome of family parties and celebrations, which has become so famous that it is widely copied. Its aroma and sweet, delicate taste are best appreciated in a champagne glass.

One afternoon in the second half of the nineteenth century, in the Caffè della Concordia at Casale Monferrato, pastry chef Domenico Rossi had the idea of baking a biscuit in the shape of King Vittorio Emanuele II's mustache, perhaps in homage to him. He called them *krumiri*, though no one knows why. These short biscuits made of sugar, eggs, honey, butter, and vanilla became extremely popular and won an award at the Universal Exposition of Turin in 1884. So great was their success that many imitations followed and in 1890 the mayor of Casale Monferrato was forced to certify that "Mr. Domenico Rossi, son of Pietro, is the sole inventor of the so-called *krumiri* biscuit, the recognized specialty of this city." Rossi became a purveyor to the royal households of the Dukes of Savoy and Genoa. Today *krumiri* can be tasted and bought in a shop only a few steps away from where they were invented.

Traditional Asti sweetmeats are available at the Daniella and Giordanino confectionaries, and the unequalled local wines can be tasted at Beato Bevitore. Truffles from this official "City of the Truffle" can be found at the Gastronomia San Secondo, and savory cheeses, such as *robiola* flavored with herbs and flowers, are sold in nearby Roccaverano. A classic goat's milk cheese is made from the native Roccaverano breed, and Fucci Formaggi sells high-quality *robiola* from select pastures recognized for their excellent milk and cheeses.

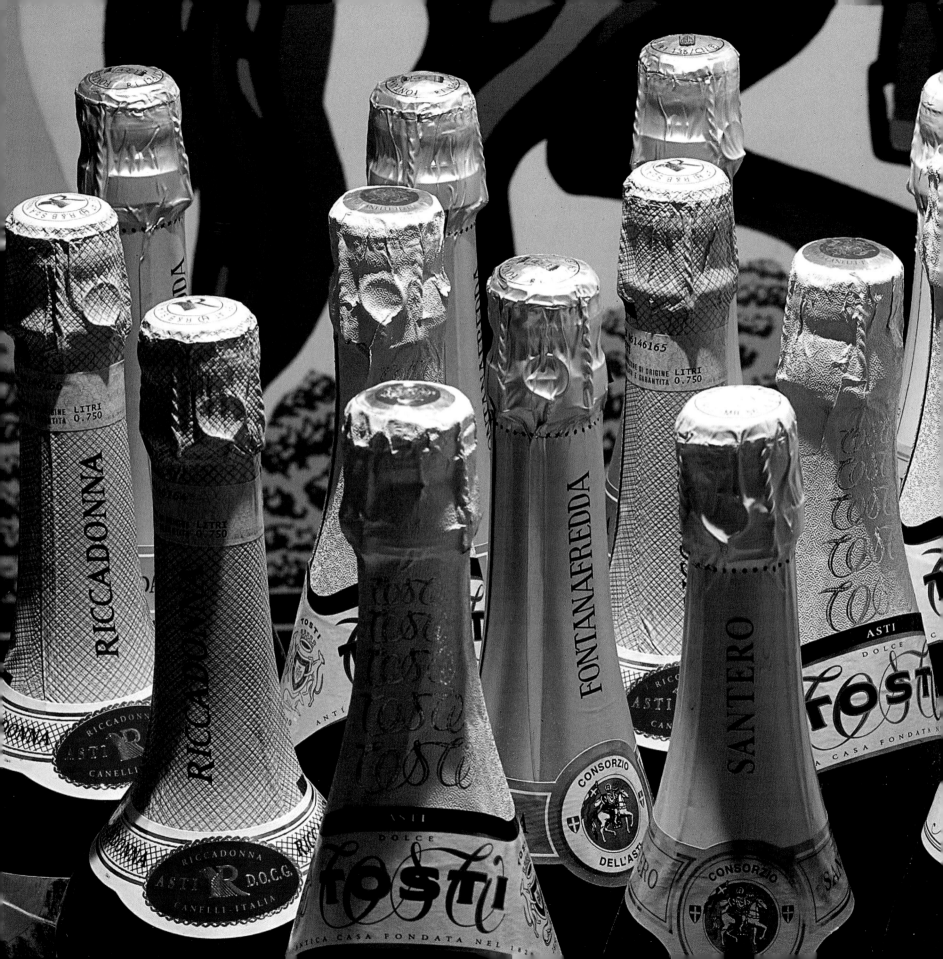

C U N E O
AT THE ALPINE VALLEYS' FEET

THE VALLEYS DESCENDING FROM THE MARITTIME ALPS flanking French Provence are heavy with the scent of woods and pastures, and flow with clear streams that beckon visitors to enjoy nature reserves rather than typical tourist centers. Cuneo catches all in a warm embrace; in the past the city defended the valleys from barbarian invasions, and it now protects them from the equally bothersome incursions of factories and mass tourism. Though Piedmont's hills are famous for their great wines, the valleys are just as celebrated for their cheeses. *Castelmagno* and *Bra* cheeses are still produced in a strictly traditional way. The latter is named after the town where it used to be aged, and today it is still made from mountainside cows' milk as it was in the fourteenth century and sold either hard or soft, depending how long it has matured. Hard *Bra* is made from skimmed milk and matured for at least six months to perfect its strong, tangy flavor. Because it grates well there is a steady market for it in neighboring Liguria, where it is used instead of Sardinian ewe's milk cheese to make pesto. *Bra* has been popular in the United States since the nineteenth century, travels well, and is best served with a full-bodied, fruity wine such as Barbera d'Asti. In contrast, soft *Bra* is made of whole milk, soaked in brine for forty-eight hours, and left to age for six weeks, resulting in a compact buttery form with a slightly sweet and aromatic flavor that pairs well with Dolcetto di Dogliani and similar fruity red wines with good acidity.

A savory selection of Murazzano cheeses.

facing page
An intricate distillation apparatus at the Museum of the Regional Wine store in Grinzane Cavour.

Castelmagno is a truly noble and historic cheese that has been produced for over a thousand years from the milk of cows grazing on the sandy pastures rich in *evax* flowers around the Sanctuary of San Magno in upper Val Grana. Legend has it that in the eighth century a local prelate took two wheels of *escarum*, as it was then called, to the court at Aix-la-Chapelle. He advised Charlemagne to eat the dark part around the crust as well as the rest of the cheese, and from then on *Castelmagno* was always at the Emperor's court. Today only three thousand forms are produced a year, and the cow milk is enriched with some ewe and goat milk before a lengthy ageing and consequent sale. It is crumbly and grainy in the mouth, tastes of mountain herbs, and is best served with a well-aged Barolo or related red wine.

Early each morning in Neive a long queue forms in front of the Levi Distillery. Each patient soul waits to buy several bottles of this famous newspaper-wrapped grappa, and there is no other way to obtain it, as Romano Levi, the distiller, hasn't any telephone. Despite the fact that he is nearly eighty years old, every morning from September to May he rises at five o'clock to light the fires under the old stills his father left him sixty years ago. His is one of the very few distilleries left in the world employing this method, after which the grappa is barrel-aged for a couple of years. Once it is mature, holding the bottles between his knees, Levi pours the grappa through a funnel into bottles he then corks by hand. All this adds to the grappa's singularity, but the labels are his real masterpiece. Drawn by hand on paper torn from the most varied sources, they are applied one by one with a brush, making poetic gifts of words and images for all who buy his grappa.

Over two hundred types of cheese are available at the Non Solo Toma shop in Cuneo, including Piemonte's best traditional products. Superior *cuneesi al rum* cakes are baked by the Arione confectioner, and Levi grappa, along with a vast selection of wines, is available at Liquor Center in the heart of the city. To taste and buy Dolcetto, oenological standard-bearer of the area, it is best to go to the Grica di Dogliani wine shop in the historic district. *Droneresi al liquore*, a liqueur-laced confection, and the Elixir of the Val Maira are available in Dronero from the historical Galletti confectioner.

DOMODOSSOLA
ALPINE FLAVORS

THE OSSOLA VALLEY LEADS TO THE IMPORTANT SIMPLON PASS, and although through the ages it has been crossed and re-crossed by the Gauls, Romans, Spanish, and Austrians, it has managed to jealously guard its own rural architecture and traditions, including its cuisine. Perhaps because of the barren land and *infames frigoribus Alpes* (the "infamous freezing Alps" as the Roman historian Titus Livius described them), the food is both imaginative and inviting. Having resisted all attempts at change to suit modern tastes, its appeal lies in its ancient roots. The ageless black rye bread baked in Coimo is a tradition, as is the cured goat's meat "violin" from Val Formazza, which has been playing the same tune for centuries. Modern gourmets appreciate *Bettelmatt* cheese just as much as their seventeenth century predecessors did, and the same earthenware pots are still heated on wood stoves to prepare it. A number of cheeses are produced in the Ossola valley but *Bettelmatt*—which takes its name from the mountains of the upper Val Formazza at the foot of Bättelmathorn (Chamois Peak)—with its delicately distinctive flavour, is probably the best known outside the region. There is only a very limited milk production from the cows that graze on the local Alpine herbs, and particularly from a cow known as "the little brick," which gives the cheese its particular shade of yellow. The region's cured meats are also well worth savouring, particularly the small salami from the Val Formazza, Trontano's smoked ham, Varzo's salted

A veritable cornucopia of culinary heritage from the Val d'Ossola.

facing page
Alpine refuges in Val Formazza.

donkey meat, and Valle Antrona's cured goat leg prosciutto dubbed the *viulìn*, sliced very thinly and served with buttered rye bread. In addition to the omnipresent maize flour *polenta*, there is an infinite variety of soups and broths, ranging from a simple mixture of bread cubes fried with bacon and onion in broth served at all hours in the Vigezzo valley's wine shops, to a soup made from dried goat's meat and pork in the Val Formazza. A special springtime dish is a delicious blend of wild flowers and leaves including nettle, spinach, chicory, violets, lamb's tongue, xylem, sorrel, and watercress turned into an unforgettable soup. Autumn is the time for creamed pumpkin, and every lunch ends with the Val Formazza's famous coffee—which even women used to drink before starting their morning chores—of sugar dissolved in a glass with a little grappa, hot coffee, and half an inch of thick cream floating atop it all.

Early documents reveal that vineyards were planted high in the Ossola Valley and that the wine had to be exported to Switzerland because Lombardy and Venetia imposed too high a duty on it. The main grape was, and still is, Nebbiolo, from which Prunent and Bruschett wines are produced. The latter is very dry, excellent with the local cheeses and cured meats, whereas the former has innumerable admirers. Luigi Veronelli, one of Italy's leading wine experts and Prunent's strongest supporter, described it as a beautiful, smooth, elegant wine. It shouldn't be savored until at least two years old, as it ages very well (it has been known to keep well between eighty and one hundred years), is considered mature between four and twelve years, and is best served with game and aged cheeses.

Bava, the historic wine shop in Cannobio, offers a careful selection of wines and traditional products that attract gourmands from all around Ossola and Lago Maggiore. Coimo black bread, popular with restaurants, can be bought fresh from the oven at the Conti bakery, and prosciutto and salami of pork and venison can be bought at the Macellerie Crosetti in Crodo or in nearby Formazza. Castagna, in Ornavasso, offers many fine cheeses, including *bettelmatt* and *maccagno* cheeses from the Val Vigezzo.

T U R I N
ROYAL COFFEE AND CAKE

TURIN IS THE ONLY ITALIAN CITY DIVIDED BY THE PO RIVER, and the waters lend a touch of poetry to the austere *Augusta Taurinorum*, founded by the Romans in the first century BC in a key strategic position for communications with Gaul, and of which the orderly geometry of the roads remains today. Beginning in the eighteenth century the reign of the Savoy family turned Turin into a great European city, making it the administrative capital of the Kingdom of Italy and enriching many of the city's already sumptuous buildings, including the Mole Antonelliana, which has become the symbol of the city; the Royal Palace and Duomo, which now houses the Holy Shroud; the Science Academy that houses the Egyptian Museum, the world's most important collection outside Cairo; and finally the arcades of the historic center, which showcase the traditional cafés and confectionary shops.

The local indulgence, the *bicerin*, is prepared with coffee, chocolate, and milk served hot in a chalice-shaped glass, and can be enjoyed at the eighteenth-century Caffé al Bicerin on Piazza della Consolata. The *giandujotto* was invented at the Prochet Gay confectionery on Piazza San Carlo, and is a traditional chocolate shaped like a slice of orange made of sugar, cacao, and the sweet hazelnuts of Piedmont. Although it now seems a rather rich sweet, according to local legend *giandujotto* was invented in a period of great difficulty, when there was a shortage of cacao because of the stringent blockades Napoleon imposed on the region, so at the beginning of the nineteenth century some confectioners put their minds to inventing a way to overcome this shortage, and this slightly chocolate, mostly hazelnut treat was their splendid solution.

The *caramella* treat was born in Turin. Had it been created in Tuscany it would have been called *pasticca*, or tablet. Sugar refined from sugarcane imported from the colonies was melted in a copper pot over a low flame and flavored with extracts of fruit or herbs, after which it was removed while still boiling with a ladle and poured, drop by drop, onto a marble surface on which it rapidly became transparent and hard. This is the way *bottoni di prete* (priest's buttons), sweets that the Savoy senators used to melt in their mouths before undertaking a speech, are still made today. These candies were long reserved for the noble classes, and only halfway through the nineteenth century, with the industrial extraction of sugar from beets, did they become popular. Lollipops are another innovation of Turin's confectionary creativity; large, round, colorful, and held atop a wooden stick, when these *lecca-lecca* first appeared they were dubbed *Gianduja* for their resemblance to Piedmont's traditional theatrical mask.

The nineteenth-century Mole Antonelliana, symbol of the city, dominates Turin's skyline.

facing page
Window of a café in Turin.

In 1786, in a workshop on Piazza Castello, Benedetto Carpano inaugurated the rite of the vermouth aperitif, a sweet wine flavored with mountain herbs based on a recipe deposited in the *Pharmacopea Taurenensis* in 1763. This recipe has very ancient origins, and in Greece in the fourth century BC there existed a *vinum absinthiatum* whose invention is attributed to Hippocrates, the father of medicine. Vermouth became an immediate success and the example of Carpano was followed by Martini, Cinzano, Gancia, and Cora. A full quarter of the wine exported from Italy today is vermouth. Then in 1870 Punt e Mes was born, a bitter version of vermouth, named after the way a stockbroker ordered it, requesting in dialect *un punt de vermouth e mes de china*, one part vermouth and half quinine.

Bicerin, the local "little glass," is served in almost all the cafés. It is a tradition in Piazza della Consolata at the café of the same name, where the chocolate toasted sandwich is an unforgettable treat, or at the Café San Carlo, frequented by Alexandre Dumas'. Sweetmeats can be bought at Stratta, a favorite of statesman Camillo Benso, Count of Cavour, or at Baratti & Milano. Grissini *stirati* are prepared in all the bakeries, and those of the Lampiano bakery, just outside the city, are excellent. Tasty salami and cheeses are available at Montagna Viva.

The Savoy are responsible, even if indirectly, for the invention of the *grissino* bread stick that acts as ambassador of Turin throughout the world. Long, thin, and irregular, the *grissino stirato* (pulled) was born from the deformation of a small loaf of bread lengthened and narrowed to look like a little stick. In dialect this was called *ghersa*, which then morphed into ghersin, little *ghersa*. Some people maintain that it was created to cure Duke Vittorio Amedeo II, who suffered from ill health and was subject to frequent food poisoning, while others claim it was due to the lack of flour in wartime, or the avidity of the bakers, as the *gherse* were sold by numbers and not by weight and thus became thinner and thinner each day. In any case, the grissini of Turin, *stirati* (pulled) or *rubatà* (rolled), are made with an elastic dough of flour and water kneaded by hand for a long time, resulting in grissini that are very thin, very long, and very light, curving and acquiring a lovely golden color when baked in a wood-burning stove. There are two ways to shape them; the most traditional is to lift a ball of dough and lengthen it by shaking it rhythmically between one's hands while distancing them, while the thinner and longer *rubatà* grissino from Chierese is made by rolling the dough as though one were preparing gnocchi. They are eaten with appetizers, soups, and plates of salami and cheese.

left
Chocolate truffles
*in the central
pasticceria*
Stratta.

above
Turin's inimitable
grissini, the
most famous
breadsticks
round the globe.

below
The arcades of
Piazza San Carlo
frame the *pasticceria*
Stratta.

VERCELLI
A LAND OF WATER

THE SEA OF RICE FIELDS SURROUNDING VERCELLI MAKE FOR A MOST UNUSUAL LANDSCAPE that changes with the seasons, with vast mirrors of sky-blue water framed by narrow dykes reflecting the farmhouses and grand poplar-lined avenues. Even though rice has been grown in the leeched soil between the Elvo and Sesia rivers for centuries, and rice was a dietary staple of patients at the hospital of Sant'Andrea in Vercelli as far back as 1250, the landscape has not always been as it is today. The main changes to the land were wrought by Cistercian monks who reclaimed it and set up a vast network of irrigation canals—one of the largest in the world. This changed the geography and economy of the region, and rice cultivation spread from Piedmont all through the Po River valley, but it was not an easy conquest. Stagnant water brought malaria, and although important chefs appreciated rice it was certainly not welcomed in all kitchens. Rice has always divided Northern and Southern Italy, and has never won its war with the more southern pasta. In the nineteen-thirties the National Rice Board was formed and launched a campaign to convert the skeptics, including mobile kitchens that were dispatched throughout Italy offering free plates of risotto to all.

A heavenly view of Vercelli's rice fields.

facing page
Vercelli's inhabitants maintain, quite justly, that their rice makes a superlative risotto.

There is no shortage of nuanced rice recipes; it makes excellent risotto, is very good in soup, and goes well with meat, fish, vegetables, cooked nettles, escargots, oranges, wild strawberries, pork liver, chocolate, milk, and wine. There is a tendency today to divide rice into just two categories—long or round grain—but in Vercelli the original names of the various categories are still respected. Carnaroli and Baldo are large grains particularly suitable for risotto, as the grains do not stick together during cooking; Arborio is used a great deal in Lombardy, where the risotto is creamier; Sant'Andrea is perfect for soups, salads, and fritters. The most popular dishes around Vercelli are risotto prepared with *cossett*, the thighs of small frogs, risotto *al Barolo*, a local recipe even if the wine comes from afar, which turns the rice a dark violet, and *ris an cagnon*, rice dressed with butter and the local Toma cheese. *Panissa* (or *Paniscia* in nearby Novara), a thick soup emblematic of harvest time made with *borlotti* beans and local salami, was the staple dish of the young women who harvested the rice.

A local proverb maintains that "rice is born in water and dies in wine," and there is certainly no shortage of wine on the hills north of Vercelli. The most beloved is Gattinara DOCG, a very old wine that was enjoyed at the court of King Charles V. Produced in a small section of the eponymous area, one of the official "Cities of Wine," it has a beautiful garnet color tending towards brick, and the violet bouquet grows more acute with aging. The standard wine is aged for three years, while the Riserva rests for four, and it is dry, harmonious, and has a slightly bitter aftertaste. Ghemme, another rare grape, as it is grown on a mere five hundred square acres of vineyard, is very similar to Gattinara and equally appreciated. Both these wines are best served with substantial pasta or rice dishes, red meat, and aged cheeses. Also worth tasting are Bramaterra, Sizzano, Fara, and Boca, the other DOC wines produced along the banks of the Sesia River.

Rice can be bought at the Ferraris farm in Bianzè, and in addition to the various varieties of rice at the Lodigiana farm in Ronsecco you can buy ready-to-cook packages of risotto with mushrooms, leeks, or peppers, as well as homemade rice flour, grissini, and biscuits. In the Pastino shop of Livorno Ferraris there are many varieties of rice biscuits: *Livornesi* of pure rice with cacao and spices, *Noccioriso* of rice flour and hazelnut, *Risaiole* made with cream of black and red rice. Superior wines can be bought at Cantalupo in Ghemme or at Antoniolo in Gattinara.

BERGAMO
CHEESES OF THE OROBIE ALPS

FROM THE SURROUNDING PLAINS UPPER BERGAMO looks as though it has been drawn on the foothills and curtained by the spectacular profile of the Orobie Alps. Bordered by natural beauty, the nearby valleys are home to a great variety of cheeses produced to feed a region particularly partial to them. At mealtime in Lombardy a cheese plate is often the first item put on the table and the last to be removed. Even in the past, when nobles and the rich middle classes considered cheese a mere sustenance for the poor, and it was viewed suspiciously by doctors who were perplexed by its fermentation, at the banquets of Bergamo's aristocracy cheese was savored on its own and used to flavor soups that would have otherwise been "insipid, unpleasant, and bland." All sorts of cheeses were served: fresh and matured, fatty and lean, cheese from sheep's and goat's milk, with fruit if aged and mixed with sugar if creamy. Typical meals included *provole in carrozza* (a relative of provolone served warm on toast), biscuits with gorgonzola, or mozzarella with truffle slices. These days all taboos—smell, unsightly crust, mold, dubious patches of odd colors, yellow-tinted edges, and even worms—have fallen away. The most emblematic cheese from Bergamo's surroundings is *Taleggio*, which comes from the eponymous valley. Believed to date back as far as Roman times, Taleggio was served at the banquet in celebration of Pope Clement VI ascendancy to the papal throne in 1344. Despite this honor Taleggio was not a cheese born with noble intentions, but was a product of the desire to make use of leftover milk. Taleggio's otherwise uniform consistency is softer toward the outside, where it matures first, with a thin pink crust that should be only lightly scraped. In the shepherds' huts of Alta Val Brembana, one of the most unspoiled gems near Bergamo, summer is the season of *Formai de mut*, a mountain cheese made from cows' milk. Toward summer's end cheese forms are brought to the valley and aged for periods of two to six months, resulting in a distinctive cheese with a nuanced taste and a hint of pastoral herbs. *Cadolet* is a soft and delicate cheese from the long-horned goats of the Orobie Alps. *Agrì di Valtorta* cheeses differ from valley to valley: *Bernardo* comes from the alpine slopes of Clusone; *Orobico stracchino*; *Strachtund*, with its blue-green veins punctuated by small holes; *Branzi*; and sundry other cheeses found only in small dairy shops of the many secluded valleys.

A rich selection of *caprini* cheeses.

facing page
The Colleoni Chapel presents the eye with innumerable striking details.

Wine has been produced in the land bordered by the Adda and Sebino rivers since Roman times. In the village of San Lorenzo there is a temple dedicated to Bacchus, the Roman god of wine and intoxication. Bergamo's wine was even produced in such quantities that it was exported, and appreciated so much that during the synod of 1783 there were complaints that the eighty-seven local inns attracted more people than did the churches. Among those of note is the Valcalepio Rosso, aged over twelve months, six of which are spent in oak barrels, or three years if it is a Riserva. The bouquet is intense and the dryness reminds one of black cherries. Another is the Valcalepio Bianco, delicate and fruity, that pairs well with fish dishes or stands on its own as an aperitif. The Valcalepio Moscato Passit is a late-harvest wine produced in limited quantities with selected grapes that are dried before fermentation, and demands such precise growing conditions that in some years it cannot be produced at all. It is a wine for meditation, better enjoyed on its own even if some would advise tasting it with fine pastries or gorgonzola cheese.

A fine Valcalepio Rosso wine is made in the cellars of Medolago Albani in Trescore Balneario, and other regional wines can be bought at the Enoteca del Borgo, which proudly carries 2000 labels from all over Italy. The Cantina Chel del Formai is a wine shop with the best wines to accompany various cheeses and mustards, and the Vineria Cozzi is one of the most characteristic shops of the Upper City. Valligiani cheeses may be tasted at Ol Formager, one of the best Italian specialists, and two typical desserts prepared in Bolzano, the Donizetti cake and the *polenta e osei*, can be bought at the Jean Paul confectioner.

CHIAVENNA
GOING TO THE *CROTTI*

ALONG THE SPLUGA ROAD BETWEEN LAKE COMO AND THE MEZZOLA PLAIN lies a world that still lives by its traditional values and is "extraordinarily cordial to strangers," as goes the nineteenth-century saying. One is almost inevitably invited to visit the *crotti*, natural caves piercing the ravines among the rocks of an ancient landslide, many of which have been transformed into inns and restaurants. Owing to the ideal conditions of the *sorèl*, an air current at a constant temperature between forty-five and fifty degrees Fahrenheit, the *crotti* are perfect ageing places for the local wines, cheeses, and salami. Among the most prized salami is the *violino*, made from the haunches and shoulders of goat, deer, or chamois, with a dense, dark red meat that emanates the musky and spicy aroma of the wild. Not only is the violino shaped like a musical instrument, but it is also carved as a violin would be played; the paw is grasped with the left hand, keeping the leg firm under the chin, and the knife in the right hand is used like the bow of a violin. Presented whole at the table and sliced only when it is ready to be tasted, tradition requires that once it has been started it must be finished in the same sitting. To obtain the best violino the haunch must first be cleared of nerves and cleaned, then dried and put in

The *violino di capra*, Valchiavenna's traditional variety of prosciutto.

facing page
The renowned Crotto Ombra restaurant.

brine, where it should be kept for one or two weeks, with an occasional massaging and seasoning with spices (the traditional mixture is of cloves, juniper berries, laurel, coriander, pepper, and garlic). After a second cleaning and an additional nerve removal the meat is massaged before it is slightly smoked with larch- and pine-wood and subsequently placed in the *crotti* to age for at least three months. The violino is best enjoyed with a character-filled red wine such as the Valtellina Superiore.

Brisaola, forerunner of the Valtellina's famous bresaola, was also born in the Valchiavenna. Both of these fine meats are named for the *brisa*, a very salty bovine gland, and are simply salted meat requiring no cooking or grinding that whets the appetite with its shades of intense red. Brisaola is made from cuts of beef or horsemeat cleaned of all traces of fat, tendons, and other impurities, and is therefore the lean salami par excellence. Every good producer has his own special recipe for the brine of salt, pepper, and natural herbs in which the meat is marinated for a couple of weeks to impart its characteristic aroma. After one to four months of fresh air ageing it is eaten when the meat is still soft, accompanied with a red wine from the Valtellina such as the Inferno.

The extraordinary terraced vineyards that produce the wine Leonardo da Vinci called "very potent" have brought the Valtellina into the exclusive group of world heritage sites protected by UNESCO. Today the *retica vite*, a grape cited by Latin poet Virgil in his *Georgics*, has been supplanted by the noble nebbiolo. From this local variety of nebbiolo dubbed "chiavennasca" come the various Valtellina and Valtellina Superiore red wines such as Inferno, Sassella, Grumello, and Valgella. In both name and taste the most distinguished regional wine is Sfursàt (Forced), whose name recalls the ancient practice of "forcing" the grapes, a method by which the best grapes were dried on grates in well-aired rooms. This special technique results in a strong wine of great character, usually above 14 percent alcohol. As an important wine it should be tasted in big *ballon* glasses warmed in the palm of the hand before sipping.

Marino wine shop has a selection of the best wines of the Valtellina, and is on Via Dolzino in the city center. Many wines can be tasted at the Hotel della Posta di Montespluga, the highest wine shop in Italy at over five thousand feet of altitude. *Bresaola* and other salami can be found in town at the Tognoni butcher, and the *violino* of goat meat, lamb, or venison can be found at the Casa della Carne in Lanzada, together with venison *bresaola* and *malenca*, a typical beef of the Valmalenco. The Casa del Formaggio carries excellent cheeses, and authentic *bitto* cheese, which can be aged for many years, is available at Ciapponi in Morbegno. Dishes worth tasting in local restaurants include *pizzoccheri* pasta, *sciatt* fritters, *polenta taragna*, and *costine al lavec*, ribs cooked in an earthenware pot.

right
Pizzocheri pasta at the Bitto Fair, a festival named after the Valtellina's most prized cheese.

below
An enticing selection of the Valtellina's finest cheeses.

opposite
Assorted local wines of the Valtellina.

A typical mountain valley cannot but excel in the art of cheesemaking, and the people of the Valtellina most likely learned some secrets from the Celts after they were driven northward from the plain of the Po River by the Romans. The term *bitu* (eternal) comes from the Celtic and it seems that the name Bitto comes from here; archetypal cheese of the Valtellina, Bitto can be kept for a very long time. Forms that have been aged for ten years are brought to the autumn Fiera del Bitto (Bitto Fair) at Morbengo. Supply always falls short of the high demand, as this cheese is produced only during the summer—in a few shepherds' huts in the Valley of Bitto, within the Park of the Orobic Alps—and is rather difficult to find outside this very limited area of production. The forms are brought down to the valleys and left to age in the *crotti* or in deep cellars, and periodically turned and polished with cloths soaked in olive oil to keep the cheese soft even after years of ageing. A complimentary cheese to the Bitto is the Valtellina Casera, which was historically produced only in winter. *Casera*, from the Latin *caseus*, is the house where the forms are worked and aged. It is a soft, sweet DOP (Protected Denomination of Origin) cheese, and the flavor intensifies with age. It should be eaten with *bresadella* rye bread and accompanied by a glass of red Valtellina Riserva.

CREMONA
SPICY MEETS SWEET

THE TALLEST BELL TOWER IN ITALY, THE UNIQUE *TURASS* OF CREMONA rises three hundred sixty feet above the Po Valley's flat horizon. Its terracotta bricks stand in one of the most magnificent squares in Italy, and to make quite sure that its architect would never build another, the planner was thrown from the top of the tower upon its completion. The *Turass* is the symbol of Cremona, a city of art surrounded by fertile plains,

rich canals, springs, and fields of grain and maize flanked by giant elms. The Cremonese insist that *torrone*, one of its two gastronomic delights, is named after the famous tower, despite the food historians who claim that it is derived from *Turun*, a hard Arab almond biscuit. Regardless of its nomenclature, the Cremonese are in no doubt that the *torrone* nougat was created for the wedding feast of Francesco Sforza and Bianca Maria Visconti in 1441. Made of a fine almond, honey, and albumen paste, it was shaped like the famous tower to celebrate the union of two great families, and certainly put Cremona on the gastronomic map. The court presented it to the dukes of Milan and the rich burghers indulged to the extent that not even a law limiting its consumption could stop them. To this day the wedding anniversary is celebrated on November 13, the feast of Cremona's

The Piazza del Comune, with its beautiful romanesque Baptistery, is illuminated by night.

facing page Mostarda di Cremona, a colorful triumph of candied fruit and mustard.

patron, Saint Omobono. Over the centuries the local pastry chefs have amused themselves by adding new flavors such as vanilla, mint, cedar, orange, rose, clove, nutmeg, cinnamon, coffee, chocolate, pine nut, pistachio, and anise. In addition to the classic hard white *torrone* they produce a celebrated soft chocolate-covered nougat.

Mostarda di Cremona, a candied fruit in a sugary syrup flavored with mustard seed, is the city's other great claim to gastronomic fame, now even more renowned than *torrone*. During the Middle Ages and the Renaissance this local delicacy was famous throughout Europe for its lengthy conservation. Though it is principally a fruit spread, it is called mustard because it was originally made just after the grape harvest when wine must was boiled, concentrated, and seasoned with tangy mustard seeds from the plant that grew wild all over the Mediterranean. A method perfected in the nineteenth century is still used to produce *Mostarda di Cremona*, which is exported throughout the world, considered the finest fruit mustard, and pairs exceptionally well with boiled meats, *cotechino* sausage, cooked ham, and both fresh and aged cheeses, especially *mascarpone*, a creamy, rich fresh cheese.

The province of Cremona is the largest producer of Grana Padano, the famous hard cheese served grated on pasta or eaten in slivers that plays a key role in the Lombard economy. Its invention is attributed to Cistercian monks from the Abbey of Chiaravale near Milan in the year 1000. Their aim was to produce a very hard cheese that travelled well and lasted. Its success lies in its ageing process of twelve to twenty-four months, its characteristically grainy quality, and its large seventy-seven-pound forms. Though originally always grated, it is now popular served in slivers with well-structured red wines such as Brunello di Montalcino or a vintage brut from Franciacorta.

The Catullo wine shop carries excellent vintages, and at the wine shop Cremona all kinds of delicacies such as salami, cheese, nougat, and mustard can be bought to accompany wine. Excellent cheese and butter come from the Soresina dairy, and Mazzini has an excellent selection of cheeses. Nougats and mustards should be bought at the elegant and historic Lanfranchi confectioner, who also prepares delicious sculptures in sugar. Organic mustards made of fruits complete with their rind are prepared by Luccini in Cicognolo. In local restaurants the pumpkin *tortelli* and *marubini ai tre brodi*—ravioli of beef, veal, pork, and sometimes also chicken and salami in three kinds of broth—are both unforgettable dishes.

ERBUSCO
LAND OF BUBBLES

FRANCIACORTA, THE GREAT AMPHITHEATER-SHAPED MORAINE SOUTH OF LAKE ISEO, has historically been an important vineyard area; today, however, it is the uncontested capital of top quality "bubbly." It is named for the fact that it has been a "tax free" zone since the thirteenth century when the Cluniac monks reclaimed the land and planted the first vineyards, earning the freedom from government duties as a reward.

Franciacorta's fine wine is poured by hand at the Bellavista Company.

facing page
The stunning alpine crown surrounding the Lake of Iseo.

Erbusco is the most important town in the area, and lies at the foot of Mount Orphan, named thanks to the fact that it is the only peak on the surrounding flat plains. The mountain's sunny slopes are covered in vineyards, and a beautiful sea of vines and magnificent scenery punctuated by occasional villas extends all the way up to Lake Iseo. The sixteenth century villas are well worth visiting, not to mention the fourteenth century Villa Cattuich and the nearby medieval castles. Bornato is a rare example of a renaissance villa built within the ramparts of a medieval fortress, and Palazzo Carmagnola is a superbly imposing palazzo built upon an earlier fifteenth century fortress. The charming village of Iseo lies along the lakeshore, and a ferry sails from here to Montesola's delightful, unspoilt fishermen's villages which ha preserved their winding lanes, little gardens, and fishing nets hung out to dry along the shore.

There are several DOC wines from Franciacorta, and all are well worth attention. The still white wine is ideal with fish and delicate white meats, while the red wine is best served with red meat and cheeses. After ageing in vats for two years, the Reserve is a deep red, dry, aromatic wine with a fruity bouquet. Surprisingly light, the rosé is brilliantly colored and very suitable for drinking throughout a meal. Above all, however, the sparkling DOCG wines are by far the most appreciated. Made from Chardonnay, Pinot Bianco, and Pinot Nero, they are created with precisely the same process as the famed champagne wines, and this gives them their characteristic long lasting and fine sparkle. For two to three months they are gently rolled by one-eighth of a rotation on *pupitres*, specially designed wooden racks. From harvest to market the entire process takes twenty-seven months, eighteen of which are spent fermenting in the natural yeasts. The special vintages are kept in the yeast for thirty months, and when they enter the market after thirty-seven they have their characteristic intense bouquet of bread, dried fruit, spice, and delicate aromas. The various types of sparkling wines from Franciacorta are labelled Non Dosato, Extra Brut, Brut, Satèn, Sec, Demi Sec and Rosè.

The local cuisine is based chiefly on fish from the lake, and numerous small restaurants along the shore and on the island offer the most popular specialties, including grilled sardines, stuffed oven-roasted tench, and *bigoi co le àole*—one of the simplest and tastiest local dishes. *Bigoi* are a type of large fresh homemade spaghetti made in the usual way, but instead of being rolled out the dough is pushed through a special hand press. It emerges in the shape of fat spaghetti that is then either boiled immediately or left briefly to dry. Every household used to have a pasta press on the kitchen's center stage, but today they have become fairly rare. *Àole* are a type of small chub caught in the lake and dried in the sun. After drying they are either bottled in oil and later grilled or kept in brine and until ready to be served with a rich plate of pasta.

Wine is available from many cellars in the area, including Bellavista, Cà del Bosco, and Cavalleri. Besides the wine at the Cellars of Franciacorta, many other local products are on sale. Fish and many other specialties are served in the restaurants overlooking the lake, and Franciacorta's traditional beef in oil, tripe, and kebabs of chicken and other poultry is an excellent dish. In Montisola, near Cure, salami is prepared with a recipe that has not changed for centuries: in winter, with the waning moon, the pig is slaughtered and a mince is smoked in an old cellar with bare stone walls and a vaulted roof.

LECCO
LAKE COMO'S FISH
AND HOMEMADE CHEESE

LAKE COMO FORMS AN INVERTED Y IN THE FOOTHILLS OF THE LOMBARD ALPS, atop which stands Lecco, the city of Alessandro Manzoni's *I promessi sposi* (*The Betrothed*), one of the pivotal works of Italian literature. Anyone convinced that the book's setting was in the author's imagination should visit the ruins of Fra Cristoforo's convent at Pescarenico, Lucia's house at Olate, or the Zucco promontory en route to Germanello, where in a chapel of Don Rodrigo's castle the Bravi set their ambush. These places introduce the Valsassina, where Renzo Tramaglio, the bridegroom-to-be, stopped to eat cheese. His snack was probably Quartirolo, already popular in the tenth century as *stracchino quadro*, or square cheese, a name descriptive not only of its square shape but also the milk from which it was made from—that of *stracche* cows, exhausted after returning from their summer alpine pasture. Another explanation is that in autumn the cows were forced to graze on *quartirola* grass, which grew only sparsely after the third reaping of the hay. Today this cheese is produced throughout the year and only briefly aged for five to thirty days, resulting in a sweet, aromatic, soft cheese. *Taleggio*, named after the village near Bergamo, has been produced in Valsassina for

Boats on the beach of Lecco, along the southeastern fork of Lake Como.

facing page
The Valsassina's unmistakable cheeses: robiola, quartirolo, and caprini.

centuries from cave-aged milk of the *stracche* cows, and was cited in the twelfth century as an article for barter. Many other cheeses come from the Lariani mountains: *Fiorone della Valsassina*, soft and smooth; *Conca*, named after the *conche*, shell-shaped copper pans in which it is left to rest during production; *Caglio*, made from mixed cow, sheep, and goat milk; *Pressato*, aged for a long time; *Robiola della Valsassina*, a soft cheese with a most delicate taste; and *Zincarli*, a ricotta typically seasoned with salt, pepper, and garlic.

Of the many fish populating lake Como the most important is *agone*, a species of freshwater pike that is cleaned and dried in the sun or marinated in oil and lemon juice, fried, and served with a sauce of butter, vinegar, and anchovy fillets. In the past the *agone*'s innards were used to prepare what is now a very rare dish, the *curadura*, a delicacy cooked slowly in a pan until it becomes a slightly bitter cake eaten with toasted polenta. Tench (a relative of carp), is the base ingredient of another typical dish, Lariana soup, or is filleted and braised with onions and potatoes. A traditional appetizer is soused lake fish, fried and immersed in a marinade of vinegar, oil, and wild thyme from the Tremezzo Riviera. *Alborella* and *vairone* are local names for small fish of the carp family dried in the sun without even being gutted.

South of Lecco there is a little oasis in the heart of the Brianza, a regional park unspoiled by cement, which was once a holiday resort for the elite of Milan, who built many luxurious villas. The protected area stretches from the valley of the Curone River to Montevecchia, a modest hill near the village of Merate covered with hardwood forests and vineyards on sun-drenched terraces. The most widespread vines are Sauvignon, Merlot, and Cabernet, but some producers have returned to cultivating the green Verdèa grape—which produces a fruity, light white wine—and the Marzemino. The Pincianel or Mustranel cultivar was highly praised by nineteenth-century Milanese poet Carlo Porta and twentieth-century writers Gianni Brera and Mario Soldati, and is still produced in some cellars.

Lavarelli and dried *agoni*, two excellent local fish, are available at Ceko il Pescatore, and the best places to go for cheese are the direct sales offices of the many producers of the Valsassina, including goods from the Cademartori cheesemaker in Introbio. A great number of products prepared with local berries and wild herbs, such as jams, jellies, syrups, herbal grappas, herb tea, and medicinal herbs can be bought at the Cascina Coldognetta. Abbinamento Sapori e Sapere in Monza is a well-supplied wine shop worth a visit.

LODI
MILAN'S VEGETABLE GARDEN

IN 1158 BARBAROSSA, EMPEROR OF THE HOLY ROMAN EMPIRE, built the city of Lodi (*Laus Nova*) on the banks of the Adda River after the Milanese had destroyed nearby Old Lodi (*Laus Pompeia*), founded by the Romans in the first century BC. Thanks to the resources of the fertile plain of the Po River, the city grew large and prosperous within one hundred years, but was still subject to the Milanese who treated it as a mere larder from which the finest vegetable and dairy produce could be taken. As larders go it was highly organized, with clever, natural refrigerators called *giazzère*—round, domed constructions completely covered by a thick layer of earth for ideal insulation. The cold room was reached through a series of long, low tunnels where foodstuffs packed with snow and ice were kept fresh through the summer. Some *giazzère* have been restored and can be visited in a park south of the Adda.

A costumed parade during Lodi's annual Palio dei Rioni festival.

facing page
An attractive basket of fresh vegetables seduces one's appetite.

Today Lodi is an important center for the production of cheese, from *Grana Padano* (worthy competitor of *Parmigiano Reggiano*) to *Provolone, Quartirolo, Pannerone, Crescenza*, homemade *Mascarpone*, and *Granone*, which is then scraped into thin shavings called *raspadura* and eaten by hand accompanied by grapes and a fine white wine. The fabulous Gorgonzola, founding member of the blue-veined cheeses, has a sweet, creamy, unmistakable taste, and is named after a town north of Lodi, where it seems to have been discovered by chance in the twelfth century when the town was under the Visconti's protection. It is essentially a *stracchino* cheese which developed the now characteristic blue-green mold after being prepared in a rather unorthodox manner, and can be sweet and creamy with very little mold if aged under sixty days, or more consistent and sharper when aged between ninety and one hundred days.

The place of honor at table belongs to the *frittata*, omelets with onions or wild asparagus, and to the *ruspant*, courtyard animals including chickens, capons, guinea fowl, and turkeys, boiled or roasted and stuffed with chicken liver and crushed *amaretti* (apricot-pit macaroons) that give them a special taste. The first course is minestrone with rice and fresh vegetables from the garden—which in summer is full of wild herbs, poppy leaves, chicory, nettles—and meat or pumpkin ravioli with *amaretti* in capon broth. Among the main courses to try are San Bassan tripe, prepared for the January 19 holiday of the patron saint, and meatballs that are the delicious result of country folks' parsimony, prepared with boiled or roasted mincemeat leftovers ennobled by cheese, sausage, cabbage, or eggplant.

San Colombano, an ancient village between the Lambro and Olona rivers, sits atop a semi-circlular outcrop of the Apennines in the alluvial plain of the Po River. The town's two hills have been baptized Colline di San Colombano and Collina Milanese, and with their few hundred hectares of vines form the border of Lombardy's vineyards. The village is an official "Città del Vino" where Barbera, Croatina, and rare grapes are cultivated from which some very well-balanced red wines are made. These can be either sparkling or still wines, fairly full-bodied and dry, with a classic bouquet. The Rosso DOC San Colombano red can be aged up to three years, but is better savored young and fresh within its first year accompanying white meat-based dishes.

Isola di Caprera, a restaurant on the street of the same name, serves savory traditional dishes. De Toma wine shop has a good choice of Lombard wines, and good cheeses are available at the Bottega Casearia. Angelo Croce in Casalpusterlengo is specialized in the production of Gorgonzola, a cheese originally named after the town just outside Milan where herds returning from the mountains were gathered. The characteristic of this cheese is that it is bored with thick needles on all its sides to provoke the fermentation of *penicillium glaucum*, and *Granone*, another fine local cheese, is produced at the Zucchelli dairy in Orio Litta.

MANTUA
CUISINE OF THE GONZAGA

MANTUA'S LONG AND GLORIOUS HISTORY REACHED AN UNPARALLELED MAGNIFICENCE during the rule of the noble Gonzaga family, who governed from the second half of the fourteenth century through the early eighteenth century. The dukes brought not only eminent artists to their court—Raphael, Mantegna, Giulio Romano, and Pisanello among them—but also summoned the most famous contemporary cooks who concocted opulent dishes with the lush agricultural resources of the lakes surrounding the city. Thus was born an original, sumptuous, refined, yet popular cuisine; from the wine carriers came the *maltagliati*, a broad, flat pasta; from the rice huskers came *riso alla pilotta*, with sausage; and from the fishermen came rice and *strangoli* pasta. This cuisine spread to the nearby regions thanks to Bartolomeo Stefani, a cook from Bologna who served the Gonzaga and in 1662 published *L'arte di ben cucinare*, or *The Art of Good Cooking*.

Pumpkin *tortelli* is the representative dish of Mantua, with a unique taste due not only to the quality of the pumpkin, but also the *amaretti* and mustard elements. The origin of their name is uncertain; some say it comes from *torta,* or cake, because they look like little cakes, while others maintain it comes from the fact that the pasta is *torta e ritorta*, twisted and turned. Mantua's pumpkins have always been highly appreciated, and in the past the seeds were planted in little pots kept on house or stable windowsills, and once the seedlings were sufficiently sprouted they were transplanted to a heap of manure behind the stables. Each autumn there was a competition to see who could collect the biggest pumpkin. *Riso alla pilota* is another essential dish of Mantua's cuisine, and is a key part of the city's history, eaten by commoners though it also appeared on the tables of the elite. It was said to give strength to the *pilattori*, workmen who worked the *pila* (mortar). The rice was put into a huge mortar, and consequently crushed with a great mechanical pestle to separate the rice from the husks, a process that required a great deal of strength. The rice was then seasoned with a generous amount of butter, sausage, and *grana* cheese. *Riso alla pilotta*, neither risotto nor soup, is poured in a cone shape into a pot and only partially covered with broth. Other courtly dishes that have stayed the test of time are the drum-shaped *timballo* of fettuccine served with pigeon, an almost cosmopolitan dish in that its name comes from the Arabic term for the mold which forms it; *maccheroni alla Gonzaga*, pasta seasoned with dried fruit, an original recipe from the seventeenth century; and *luccio* (*Esox lucius*, a freshwater fish) in an anchovy sauce served hot or cold is one of the most popular local appetizers.

Preparing the fresh pumpkin filling for ravioli.

facing page
Mantua's incessantly bustling Piazza delle Erbe.

The Colli Mantovani, hills north of the city with an ideal vineyard soil, are ancient moraines of the Garda glaciers, and traces of today's vines can even be found in ancient dwelling sites in the area. Today DOC white, red, and rosé wines of mixed grapes are produced: the white is delicate and pleasant, to be enjoyed young with fish dishes; the red, and its variant Rubino, has a pleasant aroma and slightly bitter taste, and is best savored young, within its second year of ageing; the rosé and the Chiaretto, made from red grapes with a partial vinification in white, are wines for the whole meal; Lambrusco is made from a single variety of grape and is worth tasting in any of its sparkling, dry, or sweet varieties; Cabernet and Merlot, both wines of great character, are well adapted for ageing and are typically served with meat dishes and cheese assortments.

The classic Mantuan pumpkin *tortelli* are prepared with a mustard of fruit and vegetables soaked in a syrup of water and sugar flavored with mustard, and the traditional mustard of pears or honey can be bought at Tamerici in San Biagio. Also worth tasting are the white watermelon mustard accompanied by lard, the prune mustard with roast pork, and others excellent with cheese. Salami is available at Lusetti in Suzzara, and pumpkins and other fresh vegetables are available at Rinascita in Goito. Local wines can be purchased at the Re Carlo Alberto store in the town center.

MILAN
HOME OF PANETTONE

THE MILANESE ARE TOO BUSY TO ENJOY THE BEAUTY OF THEIR CITY; between past mechanical industries and today's fashion industry they have always rushed day and night to keep up with ever-accelerating times, and so they pay little attention to the grandiose Castello Sforzesco and Duomo, leaving both monuments, along with strolls in the Galleria Vittorio Emanuele and along da Vinci's canals, to the tourists. Even the confectioners' shops and the Teatro alla Scala built during the Risorgimento seem to have lost their appeal, even if they still have their velvet upholstry and crystal chandeliers. Panettone was born here and has become the most widespread Italian cake, mainly eaten at Christmastime, and exported even to Harrod's in London, temple of everything delectable in the world. The origins of panettone date back to pagan times, though it was then adapted to the Christian Christmas, and it is a mixture of "great breads" enriched with honey and dried fruits for holiday occasions. Several legends aggrandize its past: Antonio, an apprentice to the pastry cook of the Sforza dukes of Milan, had to make a cake in a great hurry, and not knowing what else to do he mixed a dough with everything he could find and served his "pan di Toni" at the table. Then there is the story of Ughetto degli Atellani, a falconer of Ludocivo the Moor, who managed to win the favor of the beautiful baker's daughter Adalgisa by preparing an elegant bread richly stuffed with candied fruit.

Panettone is made with flour, eggs, milk, butter, raisins, candied fruit, and vanilla, kneaded together three times and left to rise naturally for hours and hours in order to make it more digestible and long lasting. It is a little taller today than it was at the end of the nineteenth century in the Biffi and Cova *offellerie* (pastry shops), both then and now the most elegant cafés. It became world famous thanks to a competition between two Milanese confectioners in the nineteen-twenties: Angelo Motta, who made it rise in height by wrapping it in a cylinder of oven paper, and Gino Alemagna. Out of the panettone they created two confectionary industries of immense fame, and one now has a choice between the inexpensive, high-quality commercial product, or the local artisan's loaves, which are more expensive but also unique. The truly magnificent taste cannot be fully enjoyed unless it is slightly heated so the butter in the mixture relaxes. According to tradition many Milanese eat it on February 3, the holiday of San Biagio, as Christmas leftovers lightly toasted and sprinkled with confectioner's sugar, and panettone is traditionally enjoyed with a sparkling Moscato or a small glass of sweet vermouth.

Milan's Duomo acts as monumental backdrop to the equestrian statue of King Vittorio Emanuelle II.

facing page
Panettone has risen from a Milanese tradition to the archetypal cake of Italy.

In 1867 Gaspare Campari inaugurated the Caffè Campari in the Gallerie Vittorio Emanuele II in Milan beside the Duomo. From the bar he offered his clients his own creation, "bitter all'olandese," a bright red, bitter aperitif received with great enthusiasm by the clients who immediately named it Bitter Campari. This nonpareil drink spread around the globe, and Gaspare's recipe is still a secret, though we do know that the aroma comes from an herbal infusion of roots, fruits, and various plants, its bitterness comes from quinine or the peel of bitter oranges, and its red color was once created by cochineal but is now artificially added. Bitter Campari is an excellent aperitif diluted with a dash of soda and decorated with a slice of orange, and is also the base for many cocktails and long drinks.

The cuisine of Milan is constantly being reevaluated, and the best restaurants are those that have not abandoned tradition, such as Il Berti, on the ramparts of Porta Nuova since 1866; Il Boecc, a dive that dates back to the times of the poet Carlo Porta and the Carbonarist conspiracies; the Antica Trattoria della Pesa, and the prestigious Savini in the Galleria Vittorio Emanuele, that for more than a century has prepared the excellent refried *risotto al salto* as an after-theater dinner following operas at La Scala. At Al Less one can taste many boiled meats with appetizing and unexpected sauces—even ice cream. *Panettone* can be bought at the famous Sant'Ambroeus confectionary, and an aperitif at Cova in Via Montenapoleone is an essential part of any visit to Milan.

Milan is Italy's only true metropolis, a city where the most diverse gastronomical offerings have come together and traditions seem to have vanished in favor of the newer "Tuscan cuisine" of the restaurants that have invaded the city since World War II and taken the place of the Milanese, who have abdicated in favor of heterogeneous ethnic food. A second glance, however, uncovers an unexpected reality, with many dishes that are a key part of Milanese culture prepared at home and in some restaurants. The most notable is the *casseula*, stewed meat and cabbage served with polenta, and saffron *risotto* toasted in butter with additional fresh saffron added after cooking to preserve its fine aroma. After the flame is turned off the rice is stirred, folded with a knob of butter, and complete with a sprinkling of grated *grana* cheese. It should be served *all'onda*, soft and creamy, and can also be served as a side dish accompanying *ossobuco*, stewed veal's thigh. *Nervitt sui scigull*, veal cartilage with onions, is a traditional appetizer, as is warm *cotechino*, spiced sausage with onions in vinegar. A Hapsburg inheritance, on the other hand, is the veal cutlet breaded and fried *alla milanese*. Soups with rice are also widespread, enriched with vegetables, seasoned with bacon and pork sausage, and served cold in the summer. Mixed boiled meat with mustard or horseradish is also a menu favorite; less widespread are *mondeghili* meatballs and *busecca*, tripe cooked with white Spanish beans, once very popular in Milan.

left
Glass and iron elegantly arch over the great octagonal center of Galleria Vittorio Emanuele II, the salon of Milan.

above
Veal cutlet *alla milanese*, served strictly on the bone.

right
Rice with golden saffron.

47

MORTARA
LEGACIES OF JEWISH CUISINE

MORTARA'S ANCIENT ROMAN ORIGINS ARE PRESERVED IN THE QUADRILATERAL STREETS of its historic center, its medieval agricultural and commercial prosperity is visible in the farmsteads and stately houses around its old gothic parish, and its goose meat salami and prosciutto are a legacy of the Sforza government. A key initiative of Ludovico Sforza, "the Moor," an enlightened fifteenth-century Duke of Milan, was to set aside much of the surrounding plains to raise geese. Lomellina, a town between the Po, Ticino, and Sesia rivers, was a vast marsh until the eleventh century, when Cistercian monks drained the area, planted wheat and rice, and began raising pigs and steer. Ludovico Sforza fostered the establishment of a Jewish colony here, and because their religion prohibited pork, he set them to raising geese for meat that conformed to their beliefs. Geese are easily raised and, much like the pig, none of the animal goes to waste, so almost every farming family kept at least one goose in the courtyard. Salami and prosciutto were made from the choicest meat, while the remaining pieces were conserved in salt or marinated in brine and put into lard-filled vats used later for cooking.

One of Mortara's many working farms, surrounded by rice fields.

facing page
Sausages of goose, pâté, and foie gras are some of the many unique delights of Mortara.

Before the geese were sacrificed the women would hold them stomach-side up between their knees, pluck the light and precious down, and sell it for a good sum to merchants who passed from farmhouse to farmhouse collecting it. A lean salami is still prepared in Lomellina from the breast of the bird, but the renowned "goose salami of Mortara" is a synthesis of both Jewish and Catholic cultures, mixing the lean meat of the goose with porcine bacon stuffed into the neck or skin of the bird's body. This salami can be enjoyed either cured or cooked in a double boiler, and other choice goose delicacies available only here include bite-sized raw prosciutto, cooked prosciutto, galantine in aspic, and paté. For their final week of life the geese of Lomellina are fed only maize, and are raised also to prepare *foie gras* destined for the most refined tables. The local *Ficatum* is liver of geese fed solely dried figs, and many local restaurants offer menus exclusively based on goose from appetizer to dessert. Breast of goose with watercress and goose with rice are worth tasting, as is goose stuffed with dried prunes, apple, roasted chestnuts, hazelnuts, sausage, and bacon.

Products made from goose are available at the Corte dell'Oca, together with classic handmade salami, prosciutto, *foie gras*, and *Ficatum*—goose fed with dried figs. In the dining room next door local dishes of goose and rice are served. At the San Giorgio farm in Sartirana the Prince d'Autriche Martin Carlo Amedeus produces an exquisite duck pâté and, of course, goose pâté. Local dishes can be sampled at the Guallina restaurant in the hamlet of the same name in the nearby countryside.

Lomellina is surrounded by rice fields, irrigation ditches, and springs—an ideal habitat for frogs. Because they were easy to catch and cost nothing, in the past frogs were an important part of the diet of farmers here. Today they remain a local gastronomic specialty, but have become a pricier dish for discerning palates, and because pesticides have eliminated mosquitoes and other insects the frogs feed on, restaurant owners often have to use imported frogs. They are generally fried in batter, served bathed in wine with assorted vegetables, or as delicious *ris e ran*—either a risotto prepared with frog broth and decorated with frogs' legs or a soup of rice and boneless frog.

PAVIA
A BUNCH OF GRAPES
BETWEEN THE RICE FIELDS

JUST SOUTH OF THE PO RIVER THE RICE FIELDS SURROUNDING PAVIA come to an end and the hills of Oltrepò appear on the horizon. The Oltrepò Pavese between the Staffora and Versa rivers is one of the most important wine growing areas of Italy. Great as it is, this enological fame should not overshadow the history and art of medieval villages like Casteggio and castles like the Visconti castle of Canneto or the Dal Verme castle at Zavatterello. The fortress of Pietra de' Giorgio was built in 1012, but became famous with the founding of the first Italian cooperative wine growers' association in 1904. In the village of Torrazza Coste fewer than fifteen hundred inhabitants own and look after two hundred small winemaking companies. Santa Maria della Versa is probably more famous for its *spumante* than for its seventeenth-century sanctuary for which it is named. The only thing said of the fourteenth-century tower of Rovescala is that a market was once held at its base. Nearby vineyards grow predominantly red grapes such as Barbera and Croatina (known locally as Bonarda) that flourish in the exposure to the sun low on the hills. Cultivation of white grapes, however, is expanding; Italian Riesling is planted on the eastern slopes where the temperature range is more moderate than on the western slopes, along with grapes for *spumante*. The reds—Oltrepò Pavese Rosso, Barbera, and Bonarda—are best consumed young at cellar temperature, a guideline that applies to both still varieties and the region's more common sparkling, "vivacious" wines. They are not overly demanding wines, but are very pleasant, and can be enjoyed with any dish: first courses with sauce, boiled meat, game, risotto, cheeses and salami. The Pinot Nero, a unusually elegant, well-structured red with a bouquet of blackcurrant, cherry, dried flowers, and undergrowth, is also served at cellar temperature with game and aged cheese.

The red wines Buttafuoco (spitfire) and Sangue di Giuda (blood of Judas), intriguing both in name and taste, are made from a mix of the black grapes of the Oltrepò: Barbera, Croatina, Ughetta, Pinot Nero, and other rare grapes that grow sparsely on the bunch and are cultivated in the area. Buttafuoco is produced in both still and sparkling varieties, while Sangue di Juda is exclusively sparkling with a clear ruby red color and sweet fragrance best served with jam-based desserts and sharp cheeses. A prominent place among the whites is reserved for the *spumante*, served as an aperitif or with a meal of fish, as well as for the Italico and Rennano Rieslings that accompany lean appetizers, vegetables, and fish.

The great cloister of the Certosa di Pavia.

facing page
A view of the vineyards in the Oltrepò pavese.

Zuppa pavese is a quick, simple soup made with a slice of stale bread sautéed in butter, covered with grated Parmesan cheese and broth, all topped by a very fresh egg. It was prized at the court of France, which helped spread its fame, and a legend based on historic fact claims that in 1525 French King Francois I de Valois was defeated by the people of Pavia and fled into the countryside, where his hunger stopped him at a farmhouse to ask for food. He would accept anything, with the stipulation that it was served immediately, so to honor his important guest the farmer poured a boiling broth already warmed at the fireplace over a slice of toasted bread generously covered with grated cheese and added a whole egg, being careful not to break the yolk. This soup was so beloved enough that the recipe, with a few variations, has been exported to other regions of Italy and even to areas of France and Spain.

The best wines of the Oltrepò Pavese are available at La Cantina wine shop in the heart of Pavia, where there is also a wide selection of regional and national delicacies. Wine can be bought at the Cantina Sociale cooperative in Santa Maria della Versa, and the Antica Osteria del Previ in the old village is a good place to eat. Since the twelfth century the Malaspina Counts, who owned the lands of the Oltrepò, offered their guests the *salame di Varzi*, which is still prepared from the best parts of the pork and can be bought at the artisan sausage workshop Thoga di Cecima. The best dessert in Pavia is the *torta Paradiso* available from the Vigoni confectioners.

CINQUE TERRE
IN SEARCH OF THE
MYTHIC SCIACCHETRÀ

THE THIN CRESCENT OF THE LIGURIAN PROVINCE COMES TO AN END IN THE SOUTH at the elegant and evocative peninsula of Portovenere, which separates the Tyrrhenian Sea from the peaceful *Golfo dei Poeti* (Poets' Gulf), part of the sea named after a group of nineteenth-century intellectuals (Shelley and Byron among them) who were enchanted by the scenery. Just above it is the Cinque Terre Park, a length of coast declared a world heritage site by UNESCO. Riomaggiore, Manarola, Corniglia, Vernazza, and Monterosso are the five villages—each a world unto itself, hence the name the "Five Lands"—which cling to a precipitous coastline. The fascinating landscape, with steep, craggy cliffs emerging from the cobalt blue sea, is filigreed with vines aligned on narrow terraces supported by ageless stone walls built by workers who carried boulders up in wicker baskets on their shoulders. This is where Sciacchetrà, a rare vintage wine, symbol of the Cinque Terre and bound to the area as none other, was born and grew to become the pride of Ligurian and Italian winemaking. There are just over forty acres of vines, from which only one cellar is organized on a commercial scale. A few other private cellars manage to produce little more than three thousand bottles a year, and they are jealously guarded for years until they have reached full maturity. Given this wine's preciousness it is indeed blasphemous that the European Union proposes to liberalize the use of such a mythic denomination, together with another sixteen prestigious Italian wines, and allow it to be used outside this particular area. Sciacchetrà is an ancient, aristocratic, hard-to-find wine, and amphorae of Vernaccia of Cornelia have even been unearthed at Pompeii. It seems that the name comes from the Ligurian dialect's explanation *sciac e trac*, "press and pull," a straightforward description of how the wine is made by pressing the grapes and removing the marc immediately so that the must does not take on an excessively deep color. *Sciac e trac* also describes the staggering gait of a slightly inebriated person. Sciacchetrà is a DOC wine obtained from grapes left to dry on grating until November, a resting period during which the grapes are consumed by noble molds that are most productive in stormy seasons when the sea beats harshly against the cliffs. After two years of ageing the still young wine is put into bottles where it can stay for twenty to thirty years, improving in character with each turn of the calendar. Its color is a beautiful gold with amber reflections, and the bouquet is fruity and spicy—apricot and acacia honey ease its travel from the nose straight to the heart. It is a celebratory wine for grand occasions and also used historically for medicinal purposes.

Bottles of Sciacchetrà.

facing page
The promontory of Corniglia, surrounded by hills of olive trees and vineyards.

Squid pâtè is a speciality of Portovenere and much appreciated by the *zavorristi*, men who went through the shallow waters and along the strand of gulf collecting stones for ballast used in fishing the surrounding sea. As they worked they disturbed many squid, and there must have been an abundance, given that these squid in turn managed to stir the imagination of D. H. Lawrence, author of *Lady Chatterly's Lover*. While he was staying on the gulf of La Spezia in 1913 Lawrence wrote a letter to a friend describing an octopus that had grabbed hold of the bell rope of a church, suddenly ringing it. Local sailors beat the little gulf squid on the rocks, then with mortar and pestle grind them into a paste mixed with capers, parsley, oil, garlic, and black pepper used as a spread for bread.

Cinque Terre white wine and Sciacchetrà are available at the Cooperative of Riomagggiore, the Baroni di Lerici wine shop, Pasini, and at Buranco in Monterosso. Freshly fished octopus can be found at the Cerone grocers in La Spezia, and the best anchovies of the Mediterranean, fished in the marine park of the Cinque Terre, are preserved with salt and can be bought at the Cooperativa Punta Mesco in Levanto, which also offers local oil, wine, and honey.

GENOA
TRADEMARKED FOCACCIA

DESPITE ITS PORT AND SEAFARING HISTORY, GENOA ISN'T FOND OF FISH, as it was among the first Italian cities to produce pasta commercially, and boasts more about its invention of *pansoti e zembi* (stuffed ravioli) than any of its fish dishes. Making the best of a bad job, the Genoese transformed ordinary bread into the flatbread for which they are famous, overcoming the challenge of baking good bread in the damp sea air, where the yeast reacts poorly, the loaf's interior remains soggy, and the crust is not crisp. Centuries ago—the first written reference is dated 1312—local bakers developed a flatbread eaten straight out of the oven, enhancing its flavor with lavish splashes of extra virgin olive oil and salt. Today it is difficult to find a Genoese who doesn't start the day with a slice of fresh *focaccia* from the local baker, enjoying another slice for an afternoon snack and another with his aperitif, assuring that the sumptuous smell of baking bread permeates the streets throughout the day. To really discover the city pay a visit to the narrow streets behind the port, where the *carrugi* (deep alleys) never see sunlight and are lined with tall houses accessible only by seemingly endless, narrow stairways. Venturing within this area is worth the trouble because only here can one breathe in the maritime atmosphere, with artisans' shops selling curious wares amid the scents of the local turf's food blending with breezes of surf. Thanks to their great inventiveness the Genoese managed to build not only Italy's most important port along a narrow strip of land, but also wide roads that climb up the surrounding hills to noble palaces and magnificent churches. After absorbing the historical roots of the city in the port's narrow alleys it is well worth taking the funicular from Largo Zecca to Righi to enjoy the panorama.

In 1996 the association of Genoese bakers decided to protect themselves from poor imitations of their product, which had become famous far and wide, and they formally trademarked their flatbread. Its dimples make it instantly recognizable, as the bakers press their fingers into the dough as they spread it in the baking pans and within these little depressions the extra virgin olive oil and sea salt settle, imparting its unique flavor and texture. Some bakers flaunt tradition and cover the *focaccia* with thin slices of zucchini, eggplant, ham, and mozzarella, but there are a few more standard additions, including chopped sage or black olive paste kneaded into the dough, and sailors' girlfriends are held responsible for adding a thin layer of raw sliced onions to the dough before baking, thereby warding off any potential paramours.

The Bigo, designed by Genoese architect Renzo Piano for the 1992 Expo celebrating the 500-year anniversary of America's discovery.

facing page
Typical Ligurian focaccia.

Wines can be tasted and bought at Migone, the oldest wine shop in Genoa, and *focaccia* can be bought at almost every bakery in the city, though it is particularly good at Patrone and Bisanti bakeries. At Recco the typical *focaccia* is made of two soft, thin sheets filled with *stracchino* cheese, while at Voltri it is thinner and cooked directly on the oven hotplate dusted with corn flour. Liguria was also one of the first Italian regions to produce dry pasta, many types of which can be bought in Genoa at the artisan pasta maker Il Primo Piatto.

The narrow Polcevera River that flows through Genoa and enters the sea between Sampierdarena and Cornigliano is merely thirteen miles long, perhaps less if one considers that it is called Riccò at its source under the Giovi Pass. It is, however, long enough to bestow its name on a valley where DOC wines of high quality and low quantity are produced. The white, red, and rosé Polcevera are well worth trying, as are the Bianchetta Genovese and Vermentino, two straw-colored, dry, delicate sparkling whites savored young with appetizers and fish. Coronato is another sparkling white that goes well with fish or throughout a meal, and in Valpocevera an excellent strong, sweet, flavorful white Passito dessert wine is produced.

IMPERIA
TRIUMPH OF THE BAROQUE

CURIOUSLY, THE SYMBOL OF LIGURIAN CUISINE IS NOT FISH, as one might expect, but basil pesto, which grows along the region's thin strip of land. Its most celebrated dish, *capon magro*, is probably the most sumptuously baroque dish in all Italy. Because their corner of the Tyrrhenian Sea has never been rich in fish, a cruel destiny forced the Ligurians to the difficult task of farming the precipitous mountainsides. Along the narrow terraces supported by ancient stone walls they have always managed to grow extraordinarily tasty vegetables, grapes for several prestigious wines, and olives with a delicately scented, well-flavored oil.

The fountain of Piazza Dante.

facing page
Key ingredients and utensils for the ideal pesto.

One would never guess that *capon magro* (lean capon) was originally a peasant dish. It was called the *capponata dei galliotti*, as it was originally fed only to the rowers who waited in the ship's hold while ancored at port. Made of ship's biscuits, fava beans, dried chestnuts, salted cod *baccalà*, and cured dolphin meat, it was the daily rations of the men who ferried goods and people out to the ships anchored in the harbor. Today, almost as though to debunk the Ligurian reputation for parsimony, it is one of the few dishes where no expense is spared, and is a synthesis of all the best that land and sea can provide. The recipe became codified in the best local kitchens in the mid-nineteenth century. A large pyramid is constructed of biscuits dipped in vinegar and water and covered with a layer of diced vegetables including artichokes, celery, potatoes, carrots, and green beans dressed in parsley, garlic, capers, pine nuts, and anchovies. This is covered with a layer of fine fish fillets and seafood. The entire mound is garnished with olives, quartered hardboiled eggs, scampi skewers, peeled shrimp, half shell oysters, and lobster. The ingredients vary with what the sea seasonally has to offer, but inevitably make for a breathtaking and mouth-watering spectacle

The preparation of pesto, on the other hand, follows strict rules. Only the smallest and most tender leaves of a basil originally imported from the Near East may be used. They are then pounded together with garlic, olive oil, pine nuts, and grated Sardinian pecorino cheese, all of which are ground with a boxwood pestle in a marble mortar—electric mixers are strictly forbidden. These rules were established by the association formed to defend genuine pesto from the innumerable poor imitations made with the wrong leaves and improperly called Genoese Pesto. Pesto is ideally paired with *trofie*, small swirls of homemade pasta, and *trenette*, a pasta similar to linguine, and is also wonderful in the local *menestrun dei cadrai*, a soup that used to be rowed out to ships in a sort of floating restaurant kitchen so the crews could enjoy a change from their usual hardtack and *baccalà*.

Olive pâté, a relatively new creation made from the black Taggiasche olives grown on hillsides of the western Riviera, is a soft, delicately flavored cream that enjoyed an immediate success. The olives are soaked in an alkaline solution to sweeten them, put in brine, pasteurized in small ovens, pitted, chopped very finely, and seasoned with salt, extra virgin olive oil, basil, and rosemary. The pâté is then either served on rounds of toast or used as a pasta sauce, and is particularly popular with *trenette*. The best Taggiasche olives, spared from the oil mill, are bottled whole in brine or their own oil and seasoned with chili pepper, orange zest, or oregano.

Rossese di Dolceacqua wine is produced on the estates of Giuncheo di Camporosso and Alessandri in Ranzo. Ligurian olive oil, fragrant, delicate, and protected by the denomination "Riviera Ligure," is available at Baita in Borghetto d'Arroscia, where they also prepare an excellent olive pâté. Quality organic oil, DOC wines, fruit, and vegetables are available at the Maccario farm in Dolceacqua, where there is also a small inn. At the Streghe shop in Triora honey, jams, mushrooms, vegetables, and various sauces are offered for tasting and purchasing.

Rossese di Dolceacqua is a red wine as fresh, light, and pleasing as the land where the vines are grown, surrounding a castle overlooking the sea close to the French border. Official documents from the early twentieth century mention it, but the Rossese is an ancient vine with Medieval origins, if not even older roots. It may have been a Docletto brought here by merchants from Piedmont en route to France. Rossese has undoubtedly always been prized, and Andrea Doria, the fifteenth century condottiere from Genoa, had it served to his fleet on special occasions. French Emperor Napoleon Bonaparte took it with him on his Italian campaign, Farnese Pope Paul II put it in his soup. It is a clear ruby red color, has a bouquet of raspberry and black cherry, and a fresh taste. Typically not refined in wood, it is ready to drink in the spring following the harvest, and if aged it becomes darker in color and more full-bodied, reaching an alcohol content of at least 13 percent, thereby achieving the rank of Superiore.

above
A modern interpretation of the classic *capponata dei galliotti*.

right
Terraced inland vineyards of Dolceacqua.

opposite
The Isnardi oil mill, one of Oneglia's great *frantoi*, has preserved its old olive press.

BRESSANONE

VESTIGES OF THE HAPSBURG EMPIRE

THE ALTO ADIGE OR SÜDTIROL, FORMERLY PART OF THE AUSTRO-HUNGARIAN EMPIRE, was ceded by Austria and annexed to Trentino after World War I, thereby joining the then recently unified Italy. Bressanone lies in a strategic position within a wide and fertile valley, surrounded by high mountains but blessed with a temperate climate. It was the bishopric of the county, and as spiritual capital of the region Bressanone was the last bastion of Northern European culture in Italy to withstand the Mediterranean influences brought by merchant and military caravans as they slowly spread up the valleys of the Adige and Isarco rivers. The region has resisted, firm in its convictions, and still manifests every aspect of its life with pride, from its language to its style of dress and management of community life. Food and wine are no exception, even though some concessions have been made to the more "Mediterranean" pasta. Speck (a flavorful bacon), black bread, sauerkraut and an infinite array of other dishes are reminders of the Hapsburg Empire, and not only by their names. The regional emblem is sauerkraut, and it is still prepared in the traditional way by the local farmhouses; fresh cabbage is cut into thin strips with a very sharp knife and placed in layers in a wooden tray with rock salt, cumin, juniper berries, and coriander. The

Bressanone's Piazza del Duomo.

facing page
Savory or sweet, Alto Adige's classic rye bread often features fennel, poppy seeds, or cumin.

tray is then covered with a wooden lid weighted down with heavy stones, and after a few days the mixture begins to ferment. After about a month of fermentation, punctuated by periodic draining of the excess liquids that form, it is ready to be used in soups or as a side dish. Sauerkraut was historically appreciated not only in these valleys but also taken on long sea voyages because the bacteria produced during fermentation aid a healthy digestive tract flora, and its high content of vitamin C protected sailors from scurvy.

A particularly rich variety of bread is prepared in the Alto Adige. Invariably served at table and also used to thicken soups, the traditional black bread is a base of rye flour and wheat. There is also the *Schüttelbrot* or "shaken bread," similar to rye bread but crunchier; *Vorschlag*, a round loaf made of wheat flour; and *Paarl*, from the Val Venosta, made of rye flour and yeast cooked in paired loaves. In the past, if one member of a couple died, only one half was prepared. *Paarl* is often seasoned with cumin, fennel, or anise, and even with *Trigonella caerulia*, a type of clover cultivated in kitchen gardens. A special bread-based dish, *Knödel*, is prepared with stale bread softened with water or milk and mixed into a paste further flavored by speck, cheese, onions, spinach, or mushrooms.

During his travels through Italy, Johann Wolfgang von Goethe described the landscape from Bolzano to Trento thus: "Beside the river and on the slopes of the hills the plantations are so close together, so mixed, that it seems one would suffocate the other. Pergolas of grapes, maize, mulberry, apple, pear, quince, walnut...." The wines produced here deserve ample space in the best wine shops. Lagrein, the most well known, is a full-bodied red with a bouquet of mixed berries. It is refined in *barriques* and generally improves with age. The Lagrein vine has been cultivated in Alto Adige since the seventeenth century, but until recently only the Kretzer wine, a modest rosé, was made from its grapes. Kalterer See, a wine produced near the Lake of Caldaro from a cultivar, was never greatly appreciated given its almost viscous sweetness, but thanks to the ability of many producers this wine has recently gained a previously unheard-of importance among the wines of Alto Adige.

Vinus in Bressanone has an excellent selection of Alto Adige wines, and they can also be found at the cellar of the nearby Novacella abbey in Varna. *Speck* and salami made from the local breed of pigs can be bought at Shanung, and the authentic black bread of the friars, called *Ur Paarl nach Klosterart*, is sold in Val Venosta at Zerzer. For a demonstration of the richness of traditional Tyrolean dishes one must try the "elephant dish" served in the historic inn of the same name in Bressanone, a reminder that Hannibal stopped here to rest his elephants. This is an excellent place to go in large groups, because enormous trays are served with every kind of meat, resting on a base of pilaf rice and accompanied by an equally rich assortment of side dishes.

In Alto Adige speck is still made in the traditional manner from pigs reared on the local farms. First, the hides are branded as a guarantee of their high quality by a consortium of producers. The haunch is then opened, deboned, and marinated in a brine of sea salt and spices whose exact composition is a well-guarded secret. The ingredients can include laurel, juniper berries, pepper, nutmeg, cinnamon, and coriander. The choice meat is then left to drain on inclined wooden boards, rotated periodically, smoked, and aged. In the past they were hung in farmhouse fireplaces, though today they are smoked cold in special rooms with a maximum temperature of twenty degrees centigrade for about ten days, during which the meat is infused with the aroma of the wood (usually maple and beech with branches of juniper or pine). The ageing process takes about five months and requires particular care, as the meat must be kept in well-aired rooms at a constant temperature. The cold climate of Alto Adige is ideal and perfectly preserves the meat's nonpareil tenderness. Speck is, naturally, part of the afternoon snack in Alto Adige, a cold dish including *Schüttelbrot*, speck, cheese, smoked bacon, pickles, fresh small tomatoes, and onions in vinegar, accompanied by beer or one of the local wines.

left
Black bread, beer, and speck on pewter plates: a typical *spuntino* of Tyrolean cuisine.

A local waters the geraniums that have always decorated the houses of Alto Adige.

A wine shop's unique sign.

LAVARONE
FRUITS OF THE FOREST

ASIAGO IS ONE OF MANY WELL-KNOWN CHEESES PRODUCED ON THE HIGH PLAINS around Trento and "imported" to the city from nearby Sette Comuni. There are also cheeses from the past, such as those made in Vezzena, a shepherds' hamlet a few miles from Lavarone, which Austro-Hungarian Emperor Franz Joseph insisted on having at his table every day. Vezzena is the epitome of traditional cheesemaking in the Trento area, and the *M* branded on the form indicates that the cheese was produced exclusively with milk from these mountain pastures, a flavor quite distinct from winter milk from the stables where the cows are fed with hay. The high plains of Trento are essentially a world unto themselves, a vast territory covered with meadows whose inhabitants carry out traditional activities and are proud of the thick forests scattered throughout the area. Near Lavarone, for example, a gigantic two-hundred-and-twenty-year-old pine called *Avéz del Prinzep* (the prince's pine tree) has been preserved; its trunk is one hundred sixty feet tall, thirteen feet in circumference, and even Sigmund Freud, father of modern psychoanalysis, loved to meditate in its shade. After the devastation of the First World War nature has returned to once again reign supreme, though traces of vestigial trenches and roads testify to the strategic importance of this territory bordering Austrian Trento and Italian Vicenza from a military point of view.

A beekeeper carefully checks the hives.

facing page
Within the classic form the cheese begins to take on its characteristic shape

An imposing system of fortifications called "le sette fortezze dell'Imperatore" (the Emperor's seven forts) span a line of nineteen miles, and even though they are almost in ruins each can still be visited. Fort Belvedere, the only one that has been restored, now houses a war museum.

On the high plains there are still approximately fifteen shepherds' hamlets that remain active during the summer months, although most of them have been converted into tourist inns and only supply milk to the dairies in the valley below. Vezzena cheese is produced from June to September in eight thousand forms a year in the cooperative dairy of Lavarone, with milk from Rendene cows raised on the pastures belonging to only two of the hamlets—Cortesin and Meillegrobbe. After seven months of ageing it becomes an excellent cheese, maintaining its buttery consistency and giving off a perfume that changes according to the period of pasture. June, for example, gives off a delicate scent of garlic. When left to mature more than a year it becomes a nutritious and easily digestible hard cheese typically grated into local soups and pasta.

The vast meadows and pastures of the high plains around Lavarone are an ideal place for agriculture carried out with biological methods and modern techniques. To economize the scarce energy of bees during the winter months they are placed in controlled hibernation, and honey from bees' visits to both red and white pines, rich with trace elements and enzymes, is then made. *Millefiori* (one thousand flowers) is a mixture of nectar from wild flowers ideal for treating anaemia, while *monoflora* (one flower) is also in great demand—especially the dark, unique flavor of chestnut, and the rarer rhododendron honey, which is light and delicate but very difficult to produce, as the hives must be taken up to high altitude. Practically the only sweetener used until the seventeenth century, honey is featured in recipes for desserts and savory cheeses, and also has pharmacological uses, while resourceful artisans use the leftover beeswax to make candles.

Vezzena cheese is available at the cooperative dairy in Lavarone, and Puzzone di Moena, the other great cheese typical of the Trentino, characterized by an intense flavor and aroma, can be bought at the dairy at Predazzo. Paternoster farm in Vigo di Ton produces dozens of different honeys and other products with a honey base, including mountain pinecones, dried apples, and almonds.

RIVA DEL GARDA
BISHOP'S WINE

IN THE HIGHLANDS LAID OUT LIKE A CROWN JUST NORTH OF RIVA DEL GARDA some vineyards produce Vino Santo (Holy Wine), the apotheosis of Trentino's winegrowing tradition. This unique, sweet wine has an ancient, noble history. One theory about its name is that it refers to the fact that the grapes were pressed during Holy Week, and was traditionally called the wine for Mass. Another, perhaps less credible, hypothesis is that the name derives from the Greek *xantos* (yellow, the color of the wine), a reminder of the ancient origins of the vineyard on the Aegean island of Santorini, where late harvest wines have been produced for millennia. During the Council of Trent local bishops already used a sweet white wine from Calavino, a village by the lake of Toblino, in their Sunday functions. Only in the early nineteenth century, however, were precise documents kept recording the wine production in the cellars of Castel Toblino of a Vino Santo ordered by the counts of Wolkenstein for themselves and the Viennese court. The Vino Santo of Trentino is produced from Nosiola, the only grape native to the region, which a mere ten percent of the region's vineyards cultivate because only the sparse bunches are gathered, as it is essential that the grapes grow distant from each other so that air can circulate around them. To avoid bruising they are then carried by hand to the cellar, where they are left for six to seven months on the traditional *arele*, a grate exposed to the afternoon lake breezes. No other grape destined to make wine is left to dry for so long; the bunches are examined repeatedly, and the grapes that go bad are removed. Those that form the "noble mold" *Botrytis cinerea* are kept, as they give the wine its characteristic taste similar to the aristocratic French Sauterne. After pressing, which still takes place over Easter, it is put into *barriques* where it refines slowly for at least six to seven, and often ten, years of ageing. Bottle ageing enhances its flavor, and it is at its best when drunk after ageing for at least ten to fifteen years. The mature wine is dense, amber colored, with a definite and persistent fruity aroma. It is sweet, clean, full-bodied, and ideally tasted in little sips as though it were a noble wine, gradually revealing all its aromas. It gives its best either alone or served with desserts such as apple strudel and tarts, with blue-veined cheeses such as Gorgonzola, or with *foie gras*.

Castel Toblino rises on a rocky spur piercing the waters of Lake Garda.

facing page
Nosiola grapes are harvested in great wicker baskets after they have been left to mature on the vine.

Carne salada is a special meat born in Alto Garda Trentino, where it is eaten with beans dressed in oil, vinegar, and raw onion. It has certainly been prepared for ages and at the beginning of the eighteenth century some families at Tenno began to commercialize it. It is the meat from the leg of veal, cut into pieces of about two and a quarter pounds, and put in layers in a large pot, traditionally wood or terracotta, seasoned with salt, pepper, garlic, juniper, rosemary, sage, and laurel and kept in a fresh place. The spiced meat is kept pressed for a week, a splash of white wine is added to keep it soft, and it is left to age for an additional twenty days. Sometimes lightly smoked, *carne salada* is tender, tasty, and usually eaten raw in thin slices with a drizzle of extra virgin olive oil and a dash of fresh lemon.

Vino Santo del Trentino can be tasted and bought at Pisoni, a small cellar that also produces excellent table wines, or at Pedrotti in Cavedine. The traditional dish of *carne salada* is served at Bertoldi in Riva, and Panesalame, in the historic center of town, is an ideal place to pause and eat local delicacies accompanied with a good choice of wines.

TRENTO
TYROLEAN GOLD

TRENTINO TAKES FIRST PLACE IN ITALY FOR THE PRODUCTION OF *SPUMANTE* WINES. About five million bottles a year are exported all over the world, and the prince of the region's wines is the important-sounding Teroldego Rotaliano produced north of Trento, where the vine unique to this tiny area yields impeccable results. Local tradition maintains that the name comes from *Tiroler Gold* as it was called at the court in Vienna, where it was used to improve thinner wines, imparting body. When it was no longer used to improve other wines it began its career of increasingly flattering appreciation, and is now recognized as the extremely delicious wine that it truly is. Its color is an intense ruby red with violet reflections, a fruity bouquet, and full, dry flavor with a slightly almond aftertaste. It ages well and improves in character up to ten years after harvest, and its success is certainly due to the quality of the grapes and the skilled wine masters of Trentino, educated at the Agrarian Institute of San Michele all'Adige, one of the best wine schools in Europe. The peculiarities of the Val Lagarina, a fertile and generous land crossed by the Adige River and covered by wide swathes of vineyards and orchards that constitute the region's great wealth, also contribute to this wine's distinct character. Teroldego is not the only great wine of the area, and finds Marzemino, another pearl of Trentino winemaking, in close company. Marzemino comes from a noble vine imported by the Venetians at the beginning of the sixteenth century from Marzemin, a village in Croatia, and it found its ideal habitat in the Val Lagarina. A fine and harmonious wine, it is brilliant ruby red, with a pleasantly delicate bouquet of violets and fruit. The best vintages are refined in oak barrels, but never excessively aged, spending a maximum of three to four years gaining character.

Neptune's Fountain in Trento's Piazza del Duomo.

facing page
Apples are sliced and placed to dry beside a fire.

The relatively recent Rebo is a DOC wine, magically made only in 1948 by Rebo Rigotti, a researcher at the Agrarian Institute, by cross-pollination of Marzemino and Merlot flowers. The production of Rebo began to spread in the sixties, but it is now so much in demand that the producers never satisfy their customers. This wine is enjoyed young, and has the refined quality of Marzemino tempered by the intensity of a Merlot. Nosiala is a white wine derived from a unique vine of the same name, the oldest of the white grapes. It is fine and balanced, light yellow in color, with a concentration of velvety flavor, and a delicate, fruity bouquet. A summery wine best consumed young, it is also excellent as an aperitif and with fish dishes.

The petite Val di Non produces almost half of all the apples in Italy, and the methods of cultivation here are so refined as to render pesticides and herbicides unnecessary. The most widespread varieties are the Renetta Canadese, with a rust colored skin, and Golden Delicious, with a yellow gold skin and reddish reflections on the sun-kissed side. The flesh is sweet, juicy, and crisp. Delicious Stark is dark red, while the Imperatore apple is also very well known for its sweet-and-sour taste and is particularly adapted for use in the kitchen and in desserts, much like its relative the Ida red, originally from North America. Granny Smith is compact and juicy, spotted yellow green in color and pleasantly sour like the Elstar, while the red Gloster, oblong in shape towards the flower, has a delicate taste, and the Jonathan, warm green and pink, is sweet and aromatic.

The traditional wine shop for locals is Grado 12, established by Bruno Lunelli, owner of the famous Ferrari spumante. In one of the most beautiful piazzas in Italy, facing the Duomo, in a thirteenth-century palazzo, is the Scrigno del Duomo, a wine shop and restaurant that offers the best wines of Trentino. Organic apples are sold at the Valentini farm at Tassullo. *Lucanica*, the best of the regional salami, can be found at the Mattei grocer, and is used in thousands of ways: raw in sandwiches, cooked on a hot plate and served with polenta, used to flavor the *canederli*, or in the *tonco del pontesel*, a stew with toasted wheat.

BASSANO

A WHITE PRINCE CONQUERS THE SUN KING

THERE IS A WORLD-FAMOUS CHARACTER OF WHICH THE CITY OF BASSANO IS PROUD. Known as the "White Prince," it is a hearty white asparagus with a delicate taste and slightly bitter flavor. So soft from the tips to the stem that it is called "mangiatutto" or eat-it-all, it became famous during the Council of Trent in the mid-sixteenth century, when the bishops began to appreciate it and praised it in France, so much so that it became a favorite of Louis XIV, the Sun King. Naturally it is not the only pride of this village at the foot of the Veneto Alps. The center of Bassano's livelihood and history is the Ponte Vecchio, said to have originally been built by condottiero Ezzelino da Romano in 1228. Although destroyed many times by the flooding of the Brenta River and by war it was always rebuilt, and since 1569 each reconstruction has followed the simple and elegant structure designed by Andrea Palladio. The wooden, roof-covered bridge leads to the city's main treasures: its Alpine Troops museum and grappa distillery. It is not by chance that in order to get to the museum of the Alpine Troops one has to pass the Taverna del Ponte, where the local grappa is served.

The *Asparagus officinalis*, a lilylike plant of Mesopotamian origin, was offered to the gods by the Egyptians five thousand years ago and was later savored by the ancient Romans (Pliny the Elder describes its cultivation in his *Naturalis historia*). During the Middle Ages the asparagus practically disappeared, but knowledge of its particular growth process was preserved in monasteries, from whence it reappeared in the Renaissance. This local delicacy has been grown in the countryside around Bassano since time immemorial. Here the earth is rich with sand and gravel, supplying good drainage and elasticity, characteristics that enable the asparagus to grow without stringy stems. Its distinct white color is due to the fact that during cultivation it is constantly *rincalzato*, a process by which the tips are shielded from daylight as they sprout from the ground. Even the slightest exposure to sunlight, allowing photosynthesis to occur, de-classifies them. The white asparagus of Bassano is in season from St. Joseph's Day (March 19) to that of St. Anthony of Padua (June 13). Local restaurants serve it blanched and seasoned with a sauce of minced hard-boiled egg, extra virgin olive oil, vinegar, and salt and pepper, but there are many ways to prepare it: Germany's first chancellor Otto von Bismarck preferred the asparagus with fried eggs. They also give a delicate yet decisive flavor to risotto, omelets, soups, purées, and even desserts and ice creams. A white wine that is neither too acidic nor too perfumed is the ideal accompaniment.

The Nardini distillery, located near the Ponte Vecchio, was opened in 1779 and is the oldest distillery in Italy. Grappa, transparent as water and as hot as fire, was once the "water of life" that drove away evil, soothed fatigue, and boosted immunity against colds. It is the quintessential Italian distilled spirit. Once drunk only by peasant men, today it is imbibed in the houses of the upper classes. The quality of the grappa depends on the marc (dregs, pulp, and skins) of the grapes, on the type of grape it comes from, and the methods of distillation. Young grappa, clear, 40 to 45 percent alcohol, is the most popular, while a Riserva is aged in oak barrels. The single-grape grappas, made from the marc of an exclusive type of grape, have become increasingly successful over the last few years, and there are also many varieties of grappa infused with natural flavors now on the market.

Grappa can be tasted and bought at the Grapperia Nardini by the Ponte Vecchio, or at Poli in Ferracina, where there is also a museum of grappa. Asparagus can be tasted at Bonotto in Hotel Belvedere, which has been in business since the fifteenth century and is not far from the old city walls, or at the Trattoria Al Ponte.

left
The Veneto's white asparagus bears a seal of guarantee declaring its provenance.

facing page
Bassano's famous Ponte Vecchio.

BELLUNO
VALLEY OF THE *GELATIERI*

HIDDEN DEEP IN THE HEART OF THE BELLUNO DOLOMITES, THE VAL DI ZOLDO specializes in the preparation of world-famous homemade gelato. The village is located in the "valley of the gelato makers," though this was out of sheer necessity, not mere choice. The Dolomites are currently the most popular mountain destination in the world, and feature fantastic landscapes that inspire writers and poets. Seeing this landscape one understands why in 1920, when the Red Guides of the Italian Touring Club published a book on this region, it was presented as the *Guide of Marvels*. Before the Dolomites were discovered by tourists, however, these hostile mountains with scarce resources forced their inhabitants to emigrate in search of a better life, which the people of the Val di Zoldo, or *Zoldani*, did as well.

Belluno, with the impressive Dolomites as backdrop.

facing page
An apple sumptuously dressed with plum gelato.

It was the Chinese who invented gelato, if one is to credit a recipe based on fruit mixed with snow dating back to four thousand years ago. Refreshing drinks were appreciated almost everywhere in the ancient world. *Granita*, a water-ice or sherbet so popular in Greece in the fifth century BC that Hippocrates warned against the possible damage it could cause to an overheated body, was a mixture of fruit and honey with ice. To prepare sorbet in imperial Rome the emperors had ice brought from Etna, where there was a temple reserved for the sale of snow, and it was also served to the bathers in the *Thermopolia* of Pompeii. In the sixteenth century Florentines produced the first Italian gelato, and its unstoppable success began when Catherine de' Medici, queen of France, introduced it to the courts of all Europe. In 1686 Procopio Coltelli, a Sicilian living in Paris, opened the famous *Café Procope*; frequented by nobles and intellectuals, it was the first *café glacier* to offer an incredible variety of *granita*, gelatos, and sorbets. Even King Louis XIV had a weakness for gelato, and by the nineteenth century this icy treat had become a mandatory dessert at every banquet. Abraham Lincoln had it served on April 10, 1865, to celebrate the Civil War victory over the Confederates, and George Washington bought himself a machine to prepare it at home. Homemade gelato's worldwide diffusion took hold at the beginning of the last century and is owed to the people of the Val di Zolda. Today *gelaterie* (gelato parlors) run by *Zoldani*, are found all over Europe, Japan, South Africa, Peru, China, and wherever gelato is prepared—in innumerable flavors and presented in imaginative confections.

The *Phaseolus vulgaris* white bean was introduced to the valleys of Belluno by the humanist Pietro Valeriano, who in 1532 had received the seeds as a gift from Pope Clement VII. Thereafter the bean's fame spread quickly, and at the beginning of the eighteen hundreds many specialized varieties were being cultivated and brought as far as Venice. Lamon, a village near Feltre with a particularly mild climate, has been classified as a protected geographic area, indicated with an IGP label on its authentic products. Here the beans are cultivated on a plateau using ecological methods. They are similar to the normal borlotti or cranberry bean, and share the same pink stripes, but their skin is thinner and more tender. Four varieties are grown: *spagnolit* is the smallest, round and tasty and often used in soups; the *spagnolon* is larger, oval in shape, and eaten in salads; the *calonega* has a slightly flattened shape and is also cooked in soups; the *canalin* has a thicker skin that makes it ideal for purées.

All the gelato parlors of the Val di Zoldo prepare homemade ice creams in dozens of flavors—vanilla and chocolate, fruit, and other produce in season—and they are served in cones to be eaten on the street or at the table in elaborate bowls in specialties like "strawberry cups" and "spaghetti eis." Special gelato can be tasted at the Al Soler confectioner in Pecol, at Bar Centrale in Forno, or at Pelmo di Dont. Local beans are sold at the Al Fagiolo d'Oro inn in Lamon; *pendole*, slices of lamb or beef smoked with juniper or beech wood, and *pastin*, pork and beef minced and seasoned with white wine and spices, can be found at the Dal Mas butcher in Pecol.

CHIOGGIA
FISHING IN THE LAGOON

THE VENETIAN LAGOON IS THIRTY MILES LONG, nine miles wide, and occupies almost 25,000 acres between the Brenta, Bacchiglione, and Sile rivers. Half of the area is subject to the tides and the other half is "dead lagoon," nearly stagnant but very much alive with fish. Fish and all sorts of crustaceans are caught in this basin, and many pilchards inevitably prepared soon thereafter *in saor*. A delicacy of the bars and restaurants bordering the lagoon, these tiny fish are coated in flour, fried, layered into a terracotta dish, and covered with sautéed onions drizzled with white vinegar. If kept fresh, *sarde in saor* can last a week, and are savored as an appetizer or light meal.

Chioggia closes the southern end of the lagoon, and its fish market is one of the most important in Italy. The majority of the fish goes straight to the restaurants of Venice where, thanks to the omnipresent tourists, more fish and seafood are consumed than in any other Italian city. The sale of fish at the Chioggia market, however, involves a ritual incomprehensible to those unfamiliar with it. Unlike most other fish markets, trades are not directed by an auctioneer, but follow an ancient tradition by which the buyer whispers his offer in the fisherman's ear to avoid being overheard. If the price is acceptable, the fisherman nods; if it is too low, he audibly insults the customer, thus letting other potential buyers know that his catch is still available. In the past fishing at Chioggia was done with *bragozzi*, typical flat-bottomed boats adapted to the shallow sandy waters of the lagoon, with colorful sails that brighten the town's Vena canal on holidays. Along the canals of Borgo San Giovanni, the fisherman's district where the market is also held, hang the *vieri*, wooden crates containing *moleche* or crabs (*Carcinus aestuarii*). The moleche, very widespread in the Mediterranean, are partial to the low waters of the lagoon, and for centuries the fishermen of Chioggia have caught them in the spring and autumn when they lose their carapace and are particularly tender. They are gathered in nets and the *gransi mati*, those which will no longer molt that season, are thrown back into the sea. The *spiantani*, which will molt within a couple of days after capture, and the *boni*, ready in one or two weeks, are sorted and stored in separate crates. To cook them, the back is first pierced with a knife to drain the excess seawater, then they are rolled in flour and thrown into boiling oil in which their soft, raw, green flesh is transformed into a succulent, crispy, sweet, bright red morsel with a subtle hint of algae.

Fishermen's boats afloat in the Vema Canal of Chioggia.

facing page
Fried *moleche*—local crabs served with white polenta.

Vegetable farming is to Sottomarina and the coast of the Lusenzo lagoon what fishing is to Chioggia—a rich livelihood. Lettuce, red chickory, peas, beans, artichokes, eggplant, carrots, and onions all flourish here. The chicory called *rosa di Chioggia* (rose of Chioggia) is also grown here, and is distinguished from other radicchio by its reddish blue leaves tightly curled into a compact ball. The pumpkin known as *barucca* is wide and squat, and reminds one of the Turkish ambassador's turban in a famous painting by Vittore Carpaccio. This squash's pulp is an intensely flavored bright orange and is eaten either roasted, steamed with pickled vegetables, or prepared in the oven, covered with sugar and cinnamon and doused in hot or cold milk. The barucca's seeds don't go to waste, and are savored after drying in the sun or in an oven. Traveling merchants who used to sell chestnuts and cooked pears invariably sold these seeds as well.

Soft shell crabs and other fresh fish are available at the Chioggia Cooperative, and the Gatto restaurant in the market area serves typical local dishes such as *broeto*, risotto with *go*, *bibarasse in cassopipa*, and stewed clams. Another little restaurant called La Taverna, despite its vaguely mountain-like décor, is well worth a visit, as is the hundred-year-old Garibaldi in Sottomarina, an elegant, family-owned restaurant. Country produce such as the *suca baruca* pumpkin can be bought at the market beside the Canale della Vena.

PADUA
BEAUTY'S LUCK

THE PADUA HEN, WITH ITS FRIVOLOUS, FLICKERING TUFT OF PLUMAGE, is undeniably beautiful. Until a few years ago it had all but disappeared, overwhelmed by the competition of chickens more adapted to intensive breeding, and survived only on a few local farms where they were lovingly reared. Their attentive caretakers showed them at competitions for their elegant demeanor, the richness of their multicolored plumage, and the unmistakable tuft crowning their heads. This renewed admiration was a stroke of luck that facilitated a return to traditional breeding methods, granting the hens a vast space in which to roam and feeding them exclusively whole grains. It wasn't long before the Padua hen, whose authenticity is now guaranteed by its own trademark, began to reappear on the menu of almost all the city's restaurants as the queen of second courses. Its fine meat is distinguished from average battery hens by its flesh, which is firm but not hard, and pink like that of a pheasant, rather than the pale white supermarket chickens. It is most savory prepared *alla canevera*, with the delicate balance between the apples' sweetness and the citrus's sourness blending into an aroma of the exotic spices imported by the historic seafaring Serenissima Republic of Venice. This recipe calls for the whole hen (those between six and twelve months old are most suitable for the table) to be stuffed with fruit, vegetables, spices, salt, and confectioner's sugar and tightly tied around a thin

Closeup portrait of a proud Paduan hen.

facing page
The double row of statues in Prato delle Valle, surrounding the oval Isola Mennia.

bamboo cane (*canevera*), which allows the excess liquids to evaporate during cooking. It is then wrapped in a cloth sack or, more traditionally, pig's bladder, placed on its head in a pot of salt water with the *canevera* at the top, and simmered for at least two hours over a low flame. The dense broth that forms while it slowly boils is then poured over the meat when served at the table. If what the locals say when faced with a generously supplied table, "*ghe n'è per sete padovani*" ("it's enough for seven Paduans") is true, then the hen is not the only delicacy worth tasting in Padua. The list of specialties that appear on menus throughout the city is long, beginning with a risotto *ricco* prepared with twenty-two ingredients even when meat was a luxury eaten only on holidays. Stuffed *anatra muta* (duck hunted in molting season) is delectable, as are capons, and *falso parsuto*, a delicate and unmistakably tasty petite goose prosciutto.

The plains just outside the gates of Padua extend up to the Colli Euganei, a unique group of gently rounded hills with an ancient volcanic origin. Poet Giosuè Carducci described them as "gentle and serene," and the ancient villages Este and Arquà Petrarca are tucked away within green forests amid knolls that have held cultivated vineyards since ancient times, cited even by the Latin poet Martial. However, only since 1960 have high-quality wines been produced here. The DOC wines of the Colli Euganei, including vintages such as Superiore, are simply called Bianco and Rosso, or Chardonnay, Pino, Cabernet, and Merlot; there are also more authentic wines worth a patient search, like the Moscato Sirio, Veneto's only indigenous Muscat wine, which many admirers prefer over Piedmont's more widespread Moscato Bianco for its greater aroma.

Paduan hens are on sale in many poultry shops or available from the breeders themselves—La Fattoria in Ciottà and I Sapori di Corte. There are also many restaurants where wine tasting takes place, including Bastioni del Moro in Padua and Dotto di Campagna in Ponte di Brenta. Fine wines can be tasted and bought at Angelo Rasi in the city center, and interesting discoveries can be made at Tomanin in nearby Montagnana, an old hamlet famous not only for its long encircling wall, which is still intact, but also for its sweet, delicate prosciutto, celebrated every year in May with a fair that attracts buyers from far and wide. Outside of the fair, it can be bought at Fontana Prosciutti.

SANDRIGO

GADUS MORHUA ALLA VICENTINA

TECHNICAL BOOKS DEFINE *GADUS MORHUA* AS A PLUMP, greyish fish that lives in the cold waters of North America, Greenland, and Northern Europe. Its schools swim open-mouthed in order to catch anything that comes in their path, consuming enough so that by the age of five the average fish is over two-and-a-half feet long. Its life span is twenty years, but only if it manages to escape ending up in one of the million tons of this fish caught each year. *Gadus* is the common cod, and though it is not very prized as a fresh catch, preserved varieties, including *baccalà* (salted) and *stoccafisso* (sun-dried), have their own niche within Italian cuisine. The differentiation between *baccalà* and *stoccafisso* is universally the same except in the area of the Triveneto—Friuli Venezia Giulia, Trentino Alto-Adige, and the Veneto regions—where they are named vice-versa. From Friuli to Sicily it is widely used, and there are many ways of preparing this fish to accentuate its unmistakable taste and strong personality. Many popular dishes include raw cod, while one of the most typical northern recipes is *baccalà alla vicentina*, cooked in milk with garlic and served with polenta.

Villa Rotunda, Palladio's masterpiece, and the world's most famous villa, near Vicenza.

facing page
A chef in Sandrigo crushes *stoccafisso*, the initial step in preparing *baccalà alla vicentina*.

Careful preparation of the fish is key for all successful dishes. Once the fins are removed the fish is soaked in cold water for two days; its spine is then removed, it is bisected, returned to fresh water, and while it is submerged the scales are removed. It is then cut into large pieces that are washed, tenderized by hand, put back into water for another two days, rinsed well, left to drip on an inclined surface, and pressed under heavy weight for one night. Only after this elaborate treatment is the cod ready for cooking.

Italy is the chief importer of the best cod exported by Norse fishermen from the North Sea. This compact and savory fish was first brought to Venice in 1432 by captain Pietro Querini, who had taken refuge on the small Norwegian island of Rost in search of shelter from a storm, and while there he filled his ship's hold with a cargo of dried cod. The Venetians, however, had plenty of fresh fish and therefore disdained the dried variety, leaving the peasants to adopt this woody fish in their recipes, and the inhabitants of San-drigo in particular helped spread its fame around the region. This village just north of Vicenza is considered today the capital of *baccalà*, and in recognition of this the king of Norway recently made a gift of Rost to Sandrigo's venerable Confraternity of *Bacalà alla Vicentina*, who have re-baptized the island Sandrigoia.

The mustard of Vicenza differs greatly from others of a similar name. Its recipe calls for pieces of candied fruit (including peaches, cherries, and apricots) and a precise amount of mustard added to a base of creamed quince and sugar. Historically the mixture was much stronger, as required by the original recipe, but today it is made into an aromatic, rather than spicy, sauce. This allows the people of Vicenza to put their mustard on practically everything, bringing a unique contrast to fatty, savory, and sweet dishes. It is used to flavor boiled meats, sharp cheeses, pig's trotter with lentils, omelets, and also with *pandoro* sponge cake and Christmas *panettone* with whipped cream.

The place to go for *baccalà alla vicentina* is the Antica Trattoria Due Spade, the historic premises of the Venerable Confraternity of Baccalà. It is an old stable with a portico that has been turned into a welcoming restaurant. Excellent liqueurs of Vicenza are available at Carlotto in Valdagno or the Capovilla farm in Rosà, where they distill varieties of wild pear, blackberries, elderberry, and dogwood.

TREVISO
THE EDIBLE FLOWER

RADICCHIO, OR RED CHICORY, IS TREVISO'S NOBLEST EMBLEM—an edible flower, child of winter, cultivated in a restricted area around the springs of the Sile River, and honored with the coveted IPG seal of approval. Its inimitable, slightly bitter taste is like spring water, and it has become a delicacy now exported even to American and Japanese markets. Its unmistakable character is the result of a forced whitening process performed immediately following the harvest. This method requires that the farmers keep the roots for as long as possible in the winter, storing them in damp stables and cellars under straw with very little light. Considered a vegetable of the poor for many centuries, radicchio has now become a delicacy for even the most discriminating palates. Cooked or raw, it is excellent when eaten on its own and adds an aristocratic elegance to all dishes it accompanies. It can be found in pâtés, sauces, grappa, conserved in oil, and even in *panettone*.

The famous *radicchio rosso di Treviso*, red chicory of Treviso, is the late summer crop, noted for its tightly crinkled leaves forming winding, elegant gothic shapes. The leaves' borders are a deep carmine red fringing an alabaster white stalk, and it is prized for its firm and crisp consistency free of secondary, stringy fibers. Rather different from the radicchio harvested in late summer, the early harvest begins appearing in markets in September rather than December, and though it also grows in compact, crinkled bunches, the leaves are thinner on a wider stalk, and the white stalk spreads in ribs far into each leaf.

Oca in onto is another delicacy of the winter months. First used as a substitution for pork in the Jewish communities, this recipe made the most of the entire goose, which could then be preserved for months. On the feast of St. Martin in early November, geese were eaten to celebrate the end of the harvest season; the leftovers were cut into pieces, the fat removed, and the meat was covered with salt for a few days and lightly roasted. It was then put into terracotta or glass dishes and layered with pieces of meat, melted goose fat, and laurel leaves. This was used to season pasta and bean soup, or was eaten as a main course with stewed red peppers, a touch of horseradish, and polenta. It is still made today, but is difficult to find because the few producers sell it under different names, as the term *in onto* (in fat) inadvertently discourages many contemporary consumers.

Piazza dei Signori with the Palazzo dei Trecento and the Municipal Tower.

facing page
The coutless ways to prepare radicchio di Treviso.

The *Gioiosa Marca Trevignana* surrounding Treviso is a sunny, amicable land that offers visitors innumerable beauties and delicacies, and above all is known for its Prosecco, a light, lively, perfumed white wine enjoyed young and cold on festive and many other occasions as an aperitif, to quench one's thirst in the hot summer afternoons, or with an entire meal. Produced on the hills north of Treviso between Valdobbiadene and Conegliano, prosecco is sold in still, sparkling, and *spumante* versions. The first, dry and aromatic, is ideal with many dishes, such as *radicchio* and *soppressa* sausage, a typical local dish. The sparkling version has a fine consistency of bubbles and lends itself to every occasion, while the *spumante* undergoes a more refined production (Brut or Extra Dry), and can be served for the whole meal—except for sweet desserts—and on grand, celebratory occasions. Prosecco di Cartizze, produced in a very small area of Valdobbiadene, is particularly sought after.

Prosecco, including the excellent Treviso DOC, can be tasted in all the town bars, as well as in wine shops and restaurants, and can be purchased from the producers Drusian and Bisol. *Oca in onto* is found at the Monfragon inn in Afranta, and *radicchio di Treviso* is served at the Bottegon and Antico Portico restaurants; it can also be bought at the Savi greengrocer in Silea, a business that prepares a variety of incredible products with edible flowers, from grappa to desserts. A complete list of the wine producers of Ormelle can be obtained from the Plavensi Association to help plan tastings.

VENICE

HARRY'S BAR

ONE CANNOT LEAVE VENICE WITHOUT A TRIP TO HISTORIC HARRY'S BAR on Calle Vallaresso, a little backwater just around the corner from crowded St. Mark's Square that is as unique as Venice itself. No words suffice to describe Venice, the fascinating *grande dame* of the Adriatic who manages to deal with an ever-increasing tide of visitors from around the globe. Walking through the narrow streets and tiny squares that lead to the Rialto Bridge and St. Mark's Square one breathes in the poetic atmosphere and singular spirit of *La Serenissima*, rubbing against walls that carry the patina of centuries touched by thousands of ancestors. A long moment spent admiring the elegant stores and the artisans' unchanged shops will last forever in memory.

Glimpse of a characteristic Venetian canal.

facing page
A window of Harry's Bar, described in Enrest Hemingway's *Across the River and Under the Trees*, and where the author had his own table.

Harry's is not an "in" place. It has been above and beyond fashion's fickleness ever since Giuseppe Cipriani opened it in the 1930s, and it has changed very little since. Legend has it that during the American Depression Cipriani was barman at the nearby Hotel Europa-Britannia. Among his customers was a young American student by the name of Harry Pickering who passed all day and every night at the bar running up huge bills. Cipriani lent him the money to pay his debts and buy passage home on a ship with the ten thousand lire he had been saving to buy his own bar. However, Cipriani chose his benefactor with great luck, and a few months later Mr. Pickering returned to Venice to repay his debt in spades. The two men decided to open Harry's Bar with the money, and it became an immediate success, gaining great popularity with local society and visiting celebrities. Everyone from the Dutch, Greek, and Spanish royal families to writers, artists, and bankers visited it. The Rothschilds, Guggenheims, Aristotle Onassis and Maria Callas, Charlie Chaplin and Barbara Hutton, not to mention Prince Charles and Princess Diana, have all wined and dined there.

Cipriani invented simple but inspired drinks that everyone loved immediately, including the Bellini (Conegliano Prosecco with white peach nectar), Rossini (Prosecco and strawberries), and Tiziano (Prosecco with sweet grape juice). Equally inspired and unique at the time was his carpaccio appetizer, a plate of finely sliced fresh beef dressed with lemon, oil, and shavings of parmesan cheese that he created to cure Venetian noblewoman Amelia Nani Mocenigo's anemia in the 1950s. Named after the Venetian Renaissance painter who was famous for his bright reds, today various types of carpaccio are enjoyed worldwide.

Two of the many famous Venetian desserts are *zaleti* (round yellow biscuits mentioned in Carlo Goldoni's plays), and *fritole* (fritters of deep-fried batter flavored with currants, pine nuts, and lemon or orange zest sprinkled with vanilla flavored sugar). *Fritole* were sold in the streets by the men who fried them, and they became so important that the fryer-vendors formed a corporation in the eighteenth century. Despite the fact that today *Pandoro* is considered the number-one cake of Verona, it originally came from Venice. *Pandoro*, meaning golden cake, was named when the Republic of Venice was at the height of its splendor and seemed sprinkled from head to toe with gold dust. Shaped like the cross-section of a Christmas tree whose eight points form a star, it is now sprinkled with confectioners sugar before slicing and served with a sweet dessert wine.

Typical Venetian
sweetmeats can be
bought in many of
the confectioners in
the city, including
Rosa Salva near
Piazza San Marco,
Puppa on Calle dello
Spezier, and
Marchini. Caffè
Florian is an
obligatory stop
where many desserts
can be tasted, and
one should not miss
a stop at the *bacari*,
where Venetians
gather for the
traditional *giro di
ombre* glasses of
wine and savor the
popular dish of
sardele in saor, part
of the traditional
dinner of the Feast
of the Redeemer,
which can be tasted
at the Aciugheta.

For centuries Venice has been the inspiration for the cuisine not only of its former territories but all across Italy and in the European courts. It was the cradle of gastronomical publishing, the authority on cuisine, and was the pioneer market for intriguing products such as spices imported from the Near East. Today fresh fish and seafood arrive daily at the Rialto market from the Adriatic and the Venetian lagoon. Some fish are difficult to find anywhere else, and seafood has a naturally important place in the local cuisine. Excellent risotto can be tasted in the city's restaurants, with *gò* (goby), octopus ink, *granseole* (crabmeat seasoned with oil, salt, parsley, and garlic), *moleche* (little soft-shelled crabs fished in spring) dipped in a bath of beaten eggs and fried, octopus, or *bisati in tecia* (steamed eel). *Sarde in saor*, a particularly good appetizer or light meal, is a traditional Venetian recipe whereby sardines are cleaned, fried in oil, then left to soak in a sauce of fried onions, vinegar, sugar, pine nuts, and raisins. The Venetian table is just as rich in the fruits of the earth, and vegetable gardens on the lagoon's islands and on the *terra ferma* have always been lovingly cared for. Proof of this is that the most widespread soup in Venice, rather than one with a seafood base, is *risi e bisi*, served particularly in the summer when the peas fresh from the vegetable gardens are used for the broth. *Figà* (veal liver) is also a beloved dish, cooked with an equal amount of onions, served *radeselo* (wrapped in pork intestine and sautéed), or *garbo e dolce* (in slices covered with flour, breadcrumbs, and egg sautéed and sprinkled with vinegar and sugar).

opposite
The old *procuratie*— the government officials' dwellings—and the historic Café Florian.

above
Venice's carnival would not be the same without the mirth-inspiring *fritole*.

below
Interior of a *bacaro*, the typical Venetian tavern.

VERONA
CAPITAL CITY OF WINE

VERONA WAS NOT ONLY ONE OF THE FIRST CITIES TO BECOME PART of the "City of Wine" association, but has long been the recognized capital of wine by merit and qualification, as one would declare in an official competition. The surrounding hills and countryside are home to some of the greatest cooperative wine growers' associations in Europe, and its fairgrounds annually host Vinitaly, the world's most important wine exposition. This great heritage is mostly that of the Valpolicella, a splendid county for the wealth of its vineyard, vegetable, and cherry cultivation. The slopes of the Lessini Mountains descend toward the plain of Verona and are caressed by the breezes of Lake Garda and Monte Baldo, both of which mitigate the cold harshness of winter and the torrid summer heat, creating ideal conditions for the excellent grapes and fine wines that have been produced here from time immemorial. This valley's name derives from the Latin *vallis polis cellae*—the valley of the many cellars—and traces of grape seeds have been found in the archaeological remains of Bronze Age thatched-hut settlements. The well-ventilated climate likely inspired the Romans to dry the grapes from which they produced *Acinatum*, an ancestor of the modern Recioto, which has always been the most char-

Verona's Arena, the best-preserved Roman amphitheater.

facing page
Grapes are laid out on shelves in the drying room before their metamorphosis into wine.

acteristic local wine. The name may derive from *recia*, the top of the bunch, as only the best bunches of grapes are chosen, those that are very healthy, perfectly ripe, and appear sparsely in the bunch, allowing the air to pass freely around them. They are left to dry in special well-ventilated trays or in rooms where the humidity and temperature are controlled, and are kept here for at least one hundred and twenty days. In January and February the dried grapes are pressed, and the must obtained is put in small *barriques* or large oak casks for at least two years. Recioto is a sweet wine, but it was discovered that when subjected to prolonged fermentation the sugar turned into alcohol and produced a strong, dry wine called Amarone, meaning "rather bitter." It has a bouquet of raspberry and cherry, great character and body, and a high alcohol content of at least 14 percent. Amarone was produced for the first time in local cellars at the end of the 1930s, but it officially appeared on the market with the label Recioto Amarone Riserva del Nonno, *annata* (vintage) 1950, from the cellars of Bolla. Historically, it is a young wine, but it is now considered one of the best. A remarkable 80 percent of the production is sold abroad, and almost half of this in the United States and Canada.

Isola della Scala, just south of Verona, is the capital of the *vialone nano veronese*, a small-grained rice ideal for risotto, as well as in vegetable casseroles and with meat, snails, fish, cheese, or sausage. Rice has been cultivated in the low plains surrounding Verona since the sixteenth century, but the *vialone nano* was introduced to Italy only in 1937. To be worthy of the certification of IGP it has to go through a lengthy process: twelve plants, chosen for characteristic perfections, are cultivated separately from the others, and their grains, which must also be perfect, are sown separately, and so on. Only after four generational cycles can it be deemed true *vialone nano veronese*, cultivated in a strictly limited area free of all pesticides and herbicides. Live carp are set free in the flooded rice paddies to keep the water clear of insects and weeds. This exquisitely fine rice is best when tasted in the classic *risi e bisi* with fresh peas, a typical dish halfway between a hearty soup and the more standard risotto.

Recioto and Amarone of the Valpolicella can be bought at the cooperative cellars in Valpantena, from producers Allegrini and Masi, or tasted in town at the Chicchetteria Veneta. The *riso vialone nano* rice dish is available at the historic Ferron rice producer on the Isola della Scala; *zuppa scaligera*, boned pieces of pigeon, turkey, and chicken placed on stale bread well dusted with *grana padano* cheese; *pastissada de caval*, braised horsemeat marinated in red wine and spices; and *bollito con la pearà*, a sauce prepared with broth, spices, breadcrumbs, butter, salami, pepper, and ox marrow, are all available at the 12 Apostoli restaurant and the Trattoria Al Calmiere.

GORIZIA
COLLIO'S NOBLE WINES

THE HILLS OF EASTERN FRIULI SURROUNDING GORIZIA ARE HOME to the production of great white wines with an unparalleled softness and delicacy. For centuries wine and vineyard deeds have been traded outside the Venetian-era walls and in the large Piazza della Vittoria, and there is a beautiful view of the landscape from dominant Borgo Castello, the old city center. This world-famous region is called Collio Goriziano, and the rarest of its exquisite wines is Picolit, an evocative, elegant white of poetic tastes and aromas derived from small bunches of tiny, transparent grapes that give the wine its delicately sweet flavor and high alcohol content (over 15 percent). Picolit is savored alone in small sips after two or three years of ageing. There is a broad choice of regional white table wines: the dominant vine is Tocai Friulano, a crisp, dry, golden wine served with fish; Ribolla pairs well with freshwater fish and young cheeses; Riesling is best with appetizers and dairy dishes; the delicately aromatic Sauvignon also accompanies omelets and flans, and the Verduzzo di Ramandolo concludes the meal along with dessert.

North of the city are the vineyards of Josko Gravner, an eccentric character who produces Ribolla Gialla, Breg Bianco, Rosso Gravner, and Rujno Rosso Riserva. Though they have many admirers, these wines are rarely served in restaurants because they lack perfect transparency. Birds, rather than insecticides, keep the vines clear of pests, and Mother Nature alone decides when a given vine should die and be replaced; there is no steel, plastic, or fiberglass in the cellars—only great Slovenian barrels of oak. Great amphorae of terracotta are used for fermentation after being coated in beeswax and buried with only their necks emerging from the earthen floor. Gravner brought these containers from the Caucasus, where the wine is made just as it was five centuries ago. Special amphorae are handmade for the sole purpose of containing wine, and two months of work goes into them before they are fired in a kiln. The grapes are pressed gently with an old torque to avoid extracting too much of the crushed skins, resulting in a clean must with very few dregs which is then put directly into the vessels. After several months of ageing, and during a waning moon, the wine is poured into the casks without filtering. These unfiltered wines maintain essential enzymes and bacteria, both fundamental components of any wine's character, and no sulfur dioxide, yeast, or clarifiers are added.

The Castle of Gorizia on its prominent hillside, dominates the entire city.

facing page
A plate of Montasia *frico* borne in triumph.

The *gubana* made its first appearance in public in 1409, when it was offered to Pope Gregory XII during a visit to Cividale. It is a richly perfumed sweetmeat from the valleys of the Natisone, and symbolizes the hospitality of the Friulani. This bread that peasants offered their guests as a sign of friendship and good wishes is still prepared today according to the ancient recipe; dough is stuffed with twenty-one ingredients, including dried fruit, pine nuts, raisins, prunes, dried figs, bits of chocolate, spices, and liqueurs. The thick sheet of dough is then rolled and folded into itself, forming a characteristic spiral. The name *gubana* comes from the Slovene *gubat* (meaning "to fold"), and this delicacy is eaten sliced, drizzled abundantly with grappa, and savored with a sweet, white, well-balanced wine such as Verduzzo di Ramandolo.

The regional wine shop La Serenissima in Gradisca specializes in local wines and is the best place for tasting and buying. The Cormons cellar has planted the *Vigna del Mondo* on their land, and these vineyards have more than 450 vines from five continents, from which they make the Vino della Pace, the wine of peace, which is presented to all visiting heads of state. *Gubana* of Gorizia can be found at La Golosa confectioners, and for restaurants that occasionally serve ancient Roman recipes consult *www.madeinfriuli.com*.

PORDENONE
AT THE CELLAR DOOR

AN OLD FRIULI TRADITION STILL ALIVE TODAY IS CALLED *andar per frasche*, "going to the bushes," referring to the signs posted as advertisements along the street. *Frasche* are neither taverns nor inns (though they do provide salami and cheeses to accompany wine tastings), but cellars where one can taste the wine and take it home for bottling. This is a springtime rite that dates back to the dominion of the Austro-Hungarian Empire, when Empress Maria Teresa issued a decree allowing producers to sell their wine directly to the public. *Osterie* (taverns) are also customary meeting places, and serve not only wine, but delicious home-cooked meals of gnocchi or polenta with *frico* (mountain cheese sautéed in butter, oil, or lard) on market days. One goes to a tavern for a *tajut*—a mid-morning pause for a traditional glass of Tocai and hardboiled egg— to drink a glass of wine and converse with friends after work, or for the common Sunday round of card games. Many local delicacies pair well with the perfumed *Grave* wines: *musét*, the most typical salami of Friuli, is a type of *cotechino* sausage made with meat from the pig's head seasoned with salt, pepper, various herbs, and eaten with polenta and *broade* (red turnip fermented with grape marc and cooked with lard, garlic, and onion); *pendole*, tasty strips of smoked sheep, deer, or beef muscle; *petuzza* (also *peta* or *pitina*) from the mountain valleys north of Pordenone is a mixture of sheep, goat, deer, and chamois meat seasoned with salt, pepper, garlic, wild fennel, juniper berries, and mountain herbs rolled in corn flour and smoked. Today *petuzza* is refined with pork and eaten raw, with its casing intact, in slices, blanched in vinegar, or browned in butter and onions served on a slice of toasted polenta. Among the cheeses, Montasio is made in the mountain hamlets; Salato, either soft or hard, is typical of the Valcellina and named after the method of marinating it in brine for long periods of time; flavorful Asìno, produced here since the early seventeenth century for the tables of Venice and Trieste's nobility, takes its name from the village of Pieve d'Asio, and is fresh, soft, delicate, and spongy.

Corso Vittorio Emmanuele, Pordenone's main thoroughfare.

facing page
A well-earned culinary pause in the bushes punctuates a hard day's work.

Unique vines grow on the alluvial plains of the Meduna and Tagliamento rivers, including Verduzzo and Refosco, named for its distinctive stalks that take on a pinkish color when the grapes ripen. Refosco produces a full-bodied, ruby red wine best savored within two years of age with meat dishes accompanied by cheese, while Verduzzo is a golden yellow with a slightly tannic taste, consumed young with fish dishes. Verduzzo di Ramandolo DOCG, produced in a small area north of Udine, is a rare and aromatic barrel-refined dessert wine. Distinguished by its flavors of apricot and chestnut honey, it is a great relaxation wine, and is typically consumed with San Daniele prosciutto, figs, Montaperta lard, Nimis salami, Montasio cheese, smoked trout from the Cornappa River, and sausage from Cividale.

To find the *frasche*, follow the signs which can be found at Montereale (Agribene), Tauriano (Fentinel) Pinzano (Florutis), and San Vito (Bianchi). La Torre, in Spilimbergo, is found one of the oldest wine shops of Friuli, where interesting wines can be tasted, and where there is also a selection of typical local products. La Primula, a wine shop in San Quirino, offers a complete range of Friuli wines accompanied by tasty local, light meals and *spuntini*. The wines of Grave are well represented in the restaurant Novecento in Casarsa della Delizia.

SAURIS
THE LEGENDARY WOLF

FAMILIES IN FRUILI OFTEN RAISED PIGS FOR SALAMI AND PROSCIUTTO to last the winter months or to sell at market. These meats were prepared by the *purcitar*, a butcher and main protagonist of the "pig festival," a ceremony with precise rituals in which everyone took part and children were exempted from school in order to attend. In the mid-nineteenth century festivals Pietro Schneider from Sauris, nicknamed "Wolf," was held in such esteem for his work as a butcher that he even signed his prosciutto.

Sauris has always been famous for the local artisans' salami, and is known in particular for its sweet, lightly smoked prosciutto. The microclimate of sparkling valley air facilitates the yearlong ageing process in this village of wooden houses with long balconies tucked away high in the Carnic Alps. It can be reached from Ampezzo by following the narrow gorge excavated by the Lumiei cascade that opens up into a wide basin of meadows and forests surrounding a shining lake. Had a fire at the end of the nineteenth century not destroyed the archives of the parish, it might have been possible to reconstruct the history of pig farming in this Austrian enclave. Smoked speck is produced abundantly here, and an informed guess would suggest that smoking meat to preserve it was introduced in the thirteenth century, when a Carinthian community settled here, bringing along its religious and gastronomic traditions. The local dialect still carries a strong German influence. It was not entirely by chance that Pietro "Wolf" was from Sauris, and a century later his grandson, Beppino Petris, began making his first prosciutto in the village, though at the time he didn't even have his own shop in which to work. Initially he managed to produce only about fifty, but they were so good that over the span of two decades he quickly expanded into the domestic and export markets. Today the Wolf prosciutto producers make fifty thousand pieces annually, not counting one hundred pieces of speck, *culatello, ossocollo*, salami, lard, and *pancetta* and *guanciale*, two varieties of bacon. All are prepared according to the old recipes and preserve the high quality that made Pietro Wolf famous, thanks to the land's grass and fruit on which the animals grow healthy in the open air, and thanks also to the wood used in the smokehouse which imparts a unique foresty flavor.

The main church in Sauris di Sopra.

facing page
Prosciutto is regularly checked in the well-controlled aeging room.

Each spring the meadows of the Carnic Alps are rich with *racid de mont*, a wild mountain chicory. Its scientific name is *Cicerbita alpine*, and in May it sprouts tender violet seedlings across the Alpine slopes as soon as the snow has cleared, hence it is also called *radic da glaz* or *radici de levina*—both references to the melting snow. It can only be harvested in the wild for a brief period of two weeks, and is rigorously controlled in Friuli, where no more than two pounds can be collected in one day. In neighboring regions, such as the Veneto, picking it is completely forbidden. As soon as it is collected the radicchio is blanched with a drop of vinegar, white wine, salt, and a pinch of sugar. The liquid is then drained, the leaves are cooled on cloths that are constantly changed so that the vegetable stays dry, and it is served in extra virgin olive oil, garlic, and chili pepper. *Radic de mont* is eaten as a *stuzzichino* (light meal) on small pieces of toast or as a side dish with salted meat, deer prosciutto, speck, and venison salami.

Wolf, the producer of prosciutto, is located in Sauris di Sotto. There is another small prosciutto producer called Petris & Polentarutti in Sauris di Sopra, and their products can only be found in a few shops throughout the region. The small Alla Pace inn outside town was converted from an ancient palazzo and is where prosciutto, *speck*, salami, and hearty local dishes are served. *Radic di mont* is prepared by Eliana Solari in Prato Carnico, and can also be found at the Arta Tur Consortium in Arta Terme.

93

TRIESTE
ONE HUNDRED WAYS TO SAY COFFEE

ANYONE WHO APPROACHES THE BAR AT ONE OF THE SEVERAL FAMOUS, historical cafés in Trieste thinking that simply requesting an espresso is a sufficient order will quickly become disoriented as they realize that of one hundred clients no two ask for the same thing. One may order it *alto* (tall), *basso* (short), *ristretto* (concentrated), *caldo* (hot), *bollente* (boiling hot), *freddo* (cold), *con panna* (with cream), *con latte caldo* or *freddo*

Aerial view of the nineteenth-century seaside castle of Miramare.

facing page
The dark wood of the bar at Café San Marco preserves the atmosphere of another era.

(with hot or cold milk), *corretto con grappa* or *anice* ("corrected" with a splash of grappa or anise liqueur), with a sprinkling of cocoa powder, in a glass, in a large cup, shaken, and many other ways. Each of these preparations has a code name that only the people of Trieste can decipher. This rich variety exists despite many already implicit guarantees, as espresso served in Italian bars must conform to a set of regulations: the blend must include beans of different origin, be certified by the National Institute of Italian Espresso, and be ground only at the moment of brewing; the coffee must pour from the spouts in precisely twenty-five seconds and fill half the cup, thereby maintaining the best aromas, fats, and proteins contained in the blend. For proper espresso the cup must be well heated, the liquid should be pitch black, and the cream that forms on the surface should have a rich brown tone.

Coffee first appeared in Trieste in the fifteenth century, and was imported from the Middle East. Abyssinian shepherds were the first to notice its stimulant properties when their goats became particularly vivacious after having eaten the red beans of a plant called *kif* or *koffe*. *Coffea arabica* spread from Ethiopian plains across the Arab countries, where the Koran forbids alcohol but does not mention coffee. The beans were made drinkable by roasting, grinding, and pouring boiling water over the resulting powder—thus the first coffee was born over one thousand years ago and spread across the Middle East in a short time, reaching the Mediterranean by the beginning of the fifteenth century. The term *moka* derives from the eponymous Yemeni port where the fresh green coffee beans were loaded into ships that traveled to ports throughout Europe. The main distribution centers for Northern Italy were Venice and Trieste. In Venice, during the short span of two city administrations, ten coffee dealerships opened under the first, and fifteen under the second administration. Coffee nevertheless remained the drink of infidels, and it was only at the end of the sixteenth century that Pope Clement VIII decreed it an acceptable Christian beverage.

Fine coffee can be enjoyed in all the old cafés of the historic center, many of which are more than a century old. The elegant Caffè Tommaseo has been a meeting place for famous people for over 150 years, while locals frequent the San Marco and Pirona confectioners for dessert. Wines of the Carso can be bought at Parovel in San Dorligo; cheeses from Zbogar in Sgonico, and the Daneu restaurant in Opicina serves traditional local dishes.

North of Trieste, toward Gorizia and the Slovene border, the Carso plateau extends over a limestone area that is geologically quite singular. This series of karst formations includes funnel shaped basins, sinkholes, large fissures, and grottoes created by the water's slow erosion. The DOC wines of this area include Istrian, Malvasia, and Terrano. Malvasia was most likely imported from Greece in the fourteenth century and spread with excellent results, producing a well-balanced, fruity, pleasant-tasting white wine typically enjoyed young with appetizers, fish dishes, eggs, and fresh cheese. Terrano, indigenous to Istria and closely related to Refosco, is an intense ruby red wine with a characteristic aroma of raspberry and violetand low alcohol content, and is best consumed within a year of harvest accompanied by the cuisine of the Carso.

The dishes of the Carso have roots in Austria and the Slavic countries. *Jota* is a popular soup of cabbage, potato, beans, smoked pork skin, and ribs. Historically a typical peasant's first course, today it appears even in *haute cuisine*. Slavic *cevapcici* are fresh sausages of pork, beef, or lamb diced and sautéed. Prune gnocchi, of Austrian origin, are large potato dumplings stuffed with dried plums, first boiled and then sautéed. Regardless of their sweetness these dumplings are served as a first course seasoned with melted butter and sugar. Goulash is Hungarian in origin and includes pieces of beef stewed with paprika and other strong spices. It is typically served as a main course with a side of boiled potatoes, and when cooked longer it is served as a soup. *Lepre alla boema*, Bohemian-style hare, is a legacy of the Hapsburgs and is stewed over a slow fire with spices and sugar diluted in white wine vinegar. The archetypal *Carsolina* soup prepared in many restaurants is a hybrid of Roman *stracciatella* egg-drop soup and *passatelli* of Romagna; flour is gradually mixed with whipped eggs to form consistent little spheres that are then fried in butter and boiled in broth. The ideal way to discover the Carso and its delicacies is to follow the indications of leafy branches along the roadside, bunches of natural herbs placed to signal the *osmizze*—bars or cellars where local products can be tasted and bought. *Osmizza*, from the Slovene *osmica*, means eight, indicating the period of eight days during which, based on a 1784 decree, farm businesses were allowed to sell their produce: wine, fruit must, bacon, *porcina* of boiled mixed pork meats with horseradish, and *ossocollo*, a kind of pork sausage. Genuine cheeses produced with the traditional methods of the Carso are marked with the word *Moisir*, meaning "my cheese" in Slovene.

top
Shin of veal with potato *chifeletti*.

left
A little cup of coffee holds a monumental flavor.

Piazza Unità d'Italia,
the largest seaside
square in Europe.

UDINE
REGINA POLENTA

POLENTA IS A HEARTY CORN-BASED DISH VERSATILE ENOUGH TO PAIR WELL with practically everything, and it is so well rooted in Italy's mountain cuisines that it is incredible to think that it was only introduced after the discovery of the New World. Documents prove that maize was cultivated in the Tehuacàn Valley of present-day Mexico in five hundred BC and that the Mayans venerated it as a divinity. After landing in the Caribbean, Christopher Columbus made reference in his diaries to vast fields of a type of grain called *mahis*. He brought seeds to Europe, and when they reached Italy they were called *granoturco* because of their similarity to a type of grain imported from Turkey and the Near East, but for several years it remained unpopular and was grown only for animal fodder. It had a fate similar to that of the potato, which was considered merely a decorative plant until finally used to prepare bread and dumplings, and the tomato, which had to wait many years before appearing on the table.

The former Piazza delle Erbe, now Piazza Matteotti, is transformed into a busy market during the day.

facing page
Polenta, poured onto a platter, is still cut with wire as it always was.

Imported by Venetian merchants, corn arrived in Friuli in the mid-sixteenth century; a hundred years passed before it was prepared for human consumption, and it probably saved the local population from starvation during a terrible famine. While Native Americans often boiled or grilled corn whole on the cob, Europeans ground it into flour. Initially this flour, like that of chestnuts, fava beans, and chickpeas, was made into gruel. However, gradually the recipe called for a thicker and thicker paste, until it could be carried by hand and taken to the fields or forests as a portable meal for the workers. It was also a very popular dish consumed in front of the kitchen hearth, and even today runny cornmeal is referred to as "famine food."

To make a good polenta one pours course-grained corn flour into simmering water in a large copper pot and stirs the mixture with a wooden spoon until the water has been absorbed and the mixture falls away from the sides of the pot, a process that can require up to an hour. The loaf is then laid on a wooden surface and covered with cloth for a few minutes before being cut with a thin string. Beholding the polenta straight off the stove—smoking, tender, grainy, and appetizing—one's eyes brighten as at the sight of a golden sun. It is eaten straightaway while still warm with cream, dried beans, fresh vegetables, or rich meat stews. It is perfect as *frico*, made with a soft cheese and fried until hard and crispy, or turned into a thick cake. *Frico* even made it into the *Guinness Book of World Records* when a group of cooks from Udine prepared a serving that weighed over six hundred pounds and was fried in a nine-fooot-diameter pan.

San Daniele in Fruili is one of very few places in Italy allowed to produce a DOC prosciutto. It obtained this honour thanks to its ideal location on the right bank of the Tagliamento River in an area ventilated by both thin mountain air and a touch of sea breeze. This prosciutto may only be produced from the fresh meat of certified pigs raised in the Po River valley, and must be cured in the traditional way. All excess skin and fat is removed, the slices are then salted in proportion to their weight for several days, after which they are pressed to extract any remaining fluids. The meat is then hung to dry for at least ten months, during which it acquires a special flavor, enhanced when served with ripe melon or figs.

All the beers made by the Birrificio Udinese microbrewery are well worth tasting. Prosciutto and other local products can be bought at the Bottega del Prosciutto di San Daniele, part of the group of the *Città dei Sapori*, or at Coradazzi, which makes prosciutto and also offers tours of their facility. Local dishes with polenta can be ordered at the Alla Vedova restaurant, and the grappas and acquavit so important in Friuli can be bought, though not tasted, at the Casa degli Spiriti.

BOLOGNA
ACADEMICS AND EPICURES
UNDER THE ARCADES

THERE ARE THOSE WHO CLAIM THE TWO LEANING TOWERS OF THE ASINELLI AND GARISENDA families as the emblems of Bologna, but these in reality are only the most visible aspect of its bygone medieval past. The numerous arcades are what truly characterize the city, embracing every street and square in the historic center and continuing even beyond. The arcades of Bologna are a functional as well as a decorative architectural element, assuring there is no need for an umbrella when one goes shopping or stops to chat. They are the places where the domestic interior and the public exterior fuse, transforming the entire city into one great salon and providing a meeting place for both intellectuals and gastronomes. The University of Bologna was one of the first in Europe, dating back to the eleventh century, and thanks to its special position in the heart of a richly fertile land the students and faculty have perfected the pleasure of passing time together talking at tables under the arcades' shelter.

Tagliatelle were born in Bologna, and the measurements of this popular form of pasta were special enough to be preserved on file at the Chamber of Commerce. Anywhere from one-eighth to one-quarter inch wide and very thin. They are claimed to have been invented in 1501 by master Zefirano, cook at the court of Giovanni Bentivoglio, Lord of Bologna, who hosted the wedding banquet for Lucrezia Borgia and Alfonso d'Este. The tagliatelle were crafted to resemble the noblewoman's long hair, and are traditionally served with a red sauce (*ragù*) of lightly sautéed meat and vegetables and simmered for a long time over a gentle flame. This may seem a simple recipe, but the preparation of a truly exquisite Bolognese *ragù* is a veritable entrance exam for admission to the Olympus of great cuisine.

Although *lasagne* did not originate in Bologna they have been adopted by the Bolognese as the archetypal oven-prepared first course. Latin writers, Cicero and Horace among them, sung their praises, and in his book *De re coquinaria* (perhaps the first cookbook) Apicius describes a timbale enclosed within *làgana*, a pasta that the Romans had discovered in Lucania. The Bolognese interspersed flourishes of egg, spinach, and their *ragù* between sheets of pasta laid layer upon layer in a pan. These flavors are then harmonized with a final layer of grated Parmesan cheese and *béchamel* (a white sauce invented by French chef Louis Béchamel in the seventeenth century), which turns a splendid golden brown in the oven.

Fettucine bolognesi, the grand tradition of egg-based pasta.

facing page
Piazza Maggiore with the Fountain of Neptune, or the Giant, in the background.

Bologna is one of the renowned "Città del Vino" (Cities of Wine). Cradled between the Lambrusco area to the north and the Sangiovese to the south, the terrain around Bologna encompasses vast vineyards of Cabernet, Sauvignon, Merlot, and Pinot. More traditional grapes, such as the white Pignoletto and Montuni (or *montù*), heirs of the *Bononiae vina*, predate these newer arrivals by ten centuries. The Pignoletto dei Colli Bolognesi is a pale yellow-green white wine, delicate and dry, to be tasted cold and young (never more than a year old), and served with each course of the meal. The Montuni, on the other hand, comes from the plains of the Reno River and has a straw-yellow tint with a rather dry and well-balanced flavor. It should also be enjoyed cold during its first year in either its sweet or sparkling version.

Among the city's many wine shops and inns the Enoteca Italiana is centrally located and specializes in regional wines. Fresh pasta is available from Paolo Atti, which has been in business for over a century, or from Dolce Sana or Come Una Volta, and traditional Bolognese cuisine can be savored at the Biagi restaurant. *Mortadella*, named for the fact that it was seasoned with myrtle—so typical of Bologna that it is known simply as bologna in the United States—is available in six varieties depending on the meats used: pork and beef, identified with the letters S and B, is available at Tamburini. At Castelmaggiore, Guido Fini Zarri, former producer of the famous Oro Pilla liqueur, distills the best artisan brandy in Italy, as well as nocino, a walnut liqueur, acquavit, and cherry brandy.

COMACCHIO
EELS OF THE PO DELTA

THE PO RIVER DELTA, ENCOMPASSING AN AREA THAT EXTENDS NORTH from the valleys of Comacchio to the mouth of the Brenta River, constitutes the largest basin of brackish lagoon water in Italy. It stretches for miles laced with an intricate system of canals and lochs that regulate the tidal ebb and flow, and its waters teem with eels and clams. Now a protected area within the Natural Preserve of the Po Delta, it is a zone of intense public interest visited by many tourists and bird-watchers who can see more than two hundred species of migratory and local birds, including woodcocks, sea swallows, egrets, plovers, swans, and flamingos. A visit to the Museo delle Valli is recommended; to get here, take a boat from the Foce station, and float slowly down the canals past typical fishing huts with thatched roofs built on strips of artificial land or on stilts. Each hut has fishing nets by its side, and has remained relatively unchanged for centuries, primitive at first sight but very functional, with bow nets that capture the fish and eels as they swim toward the sea each autumn. More than five thousand tons of clams are collected annually in the area of Basso Polesine, and at Scardovari, in the inner lagoon, clam fishing is still done by hand with special rakes. Eels, however, are the true queens of the delta, able to live in both freshwater and saltwater environments, enjoying an epi-

A typical dish of Comacchio eels served with grilled polenta.

facing page
The seventeenth-century Tre Ponti are the symbol of Comacchio.

cally well-traveled existence worthy of Homer's *Odyssey*. These eels begin life in the Sargasso Sea, a basin in the Atlantic Ocean between the Antilles and the Azores. The Gulf Stream transports them as far as the Strait of Gibraltar, where they enter the Mediterranean, take up residence at the mouths of rivers, and stay for eight to twelve years before returning to their birthplace to spawn and die. Little more is known about their peripatetic existence. They are fished in the Valli di Comacchio with an ingenious system of connected chambers. There are more than fifty ways eels can be prepared: grilled, roasted, braised, stewed, with sauce, as a sauce for pasta, in a delicate risotto, or with the classic recipe of the *casoni* (fishing huts) with chopped vegetables and red wine. The *capitone* (adult female eel) is the typical Christmas dish in Emilia. Elvers, the young eels, called *cieche* (blind, though not actually so) because they are easy to catch, are another delicacy.

The wines of the Bosco Eliceo (named after *elce*, a reference to the holm oak, an area also called Gran Bosco della Mesola), a great forest near the Valli di Comacchio, have been famous for centuries. Tradition maintains that the principle vine, a golden grape called Fortana, was imported from Burgundy by Duchess Renata of France, wife of Ercole II d'Este, the Duke of Ferrara, who had it planted in the estate of Pomposa, a Benedictine abbey. It produces a red wine with a moderate alcohol level, served young with salami or fish from the vales of the delta. Aside from the Fortana, in the thin strip of land between the mouth of the Po di Goro and the outlet of the Reno River, so-called sandbar wines are produced: reds from Merlot and Sauvignon, with intense color and aroma, and whites from Trebbiano and Malvasia grapes. Today all the DOC and IGT wines produced between the Po Delta and as far south as Ravenna and Ferrara take the name of Bosco Eliceo.

Eels and other fish from the Valli can be found at Trepponti fishmonger, and many typical products of the delta can be bought at the Bottega di Anna Fantinoli. The Manifattura dei Marinati prepares traditional marinated eels of the Valli di Comacchio, cooked on the spit and placed in a brine of water, vinegar, and salt of Cervia. Barcaccia serves eel and other specialties, such as the typical *risotto alla canarola*, which used to be cooked by the men who gathered the marsh reeds, putting the rice in a pot with beans and dried fish and leaving it to cook until their return. Fine local wine is available at the Cento al Wine Bar Vino.

FERRARA
BREAD OF THE ESTE COURT

STROLLING ALONG THE STREETS OF FERRARA IN THE MORNING on the way to visit the imposing Este Castle, one is often overtaken by the pleasant smell of fresh bread being baked. The temptation to enter a bakery is impossible to resist, and one inevitably emerges with a *coppia* to munch on while taking in the palazzos that display the power of the families that lived there—the Schifanoia, the Massari, and the dei Diamanti, among others. In Ferrara, the so-called City of Bread, bread is sacred. Tradition dictated that it had to be eaten with the right hand, the one with which one makes the sign of the cross, and it was believed to be an indispensable food, to such an extent that during periods of famine the saying at court was "if there is no bread we shall have to eat meat." Until a few decades ago every family had an oven in the courtyard of the house, a little temple around which the children and elderly gathered to assist the "celebrant" who baked the bread once a week, often even less, depending on the economic means of the family. The *intorto e ritorto* bread of Ferrara is mentioned in a passage describing a banquet offered in 1536 for the Duke of Este by a gentleman called Giglio, in an era when problems of mere subsistence had been overcome and the people could dedicate themselves to the pleasures of a more sumptuous life. It was during this time that *coppia* bread was born and soon became a symbol of Ferrara's bakery tradition. A central loaf with two little curved and pointed horns, *coppia* was a work of art, light, fragrant, and widely imitated.

A glimpse of the Castello Estense.

facing page
Bread of Ferrara, *la coppia*, enjoyed here for the past five centuries.

The art and science of eating well, a special legacy of the Dukes of Este, is still alive today. *Salama da sugo*—a sausage defined by many as a mystic experience—is so treasured by the people of Ferrara that they cannot have a celebration without *salamina* on the table. Lorenzo the Magnificent officially thanked Duke Ercole I for having received it as a gift, and flattering comments about it have been made by actress Greta Garbo, composer Pietro Mascagni, and poet Gabriele D'Annunzio. Ferrara's *pasticcia di maccheroni* has very noble, old origins. It is a pie of flaky pastry filled with butter, cheese, white ragout, béchamel sauce, and truffles. Among the desserts inherited from the Este court the best known is the *pampepato*, whose recipe dates back to 1600, when the nuns of the Corpus Domini convent used to prepare it for the nobles and prelates. It has the shape of the priestly skull cap and is made of flour, sugar or honey, almonds, powdered chocolate, a twist of orange, mandarin oranges, lemons, candied fruit, cinnamon, and cloves, all covered with melted dark chocolate.

According to legend it was cruel-hearted Lucrezia Borgia who invented *salama* at the beginning of the sixteenth century, but documents prove this specialty was made around Ferrara at least a century earlier. When sliced it looks like a heart cut in two, and is a paste of minced pork marinated in a full-bodied red wine mixed with brandy, salt, black pepper, and various spices in doses that every cook keeps secret. After it is packed into a porcine bladder and aged for a year, to cook it one must first carefully and delicately clean it of any mold, wrap it in a cloth bag, and place it in a pot of water, keeping it suspended above the bottom. It is then cooked on a low flame for six to seven hours, and eaten in moderate portions (because it is quite strong and aromatic) with mashed potatoes or polenta.

All of the traditional salamis of the region can be bought from Mario, who also supplies detailed instructions as to how to cook the *salama al sugo*. With a reservation, he will also cook and garnish it with mashed potatoes. Ricci bakery produces many kinds of fresh bread, as well as *pampapato al ciocolato*, the typical dessert of Ferrara, and *garganelli*, *strozzapreti*, and other types of pasta. Trattoria Volano, simple and traditional, serves the classic dishes of Ferrara.

FORLÌ
THE PLEASURE OF KNEADING DOUGH

IF ONE WERE TO ATTRIBUTE TO THE ANCIENT ROMANS a foresight they certainly lacked, it could be said that with the via Emilia they created the first gastronomical route in Italy. The thousands of delicacies to be had from the hills of Piacenza to the coast of Rimini, passing through Parma, Reggio, Modena, Bologna, Forlì, and Cesena could indeed overwhelm one's senses with delight. All of these towns share the pleasure of preparing fresh pasta, and working the dough with a rolling pin is a daily rite. The ritual of pasta preparation has remained unchanged over the centuries and still concludes with the phrase "May God bless you, and may you break," referring to the fact that a supreme result is guaranteed only if the yeast breaks on the surface after the dough has rested overnight. Every day local housewives form a pile of flour on the marble table of their kitchens, mixing it with a careful dose of eggs to prepare all kinds of pasta: *tagliatelle, lasagna, cappelletti, tortelli, strozzapreti* ("priest-stranglers," an alternative name for ravioli which only an anticlerical people could coin). The egg-free dough used to prepare light tidbits becomes various kinds of flatbread: *piadina, guscione, crescentina, gnocco fritto*—all taking the place of plain bread and filled with ham and cheese for a treat between meals. Each

The rolled pastry preceds the many different sizes of tagliatelle.

facing page
The recently restored Rocca, citadel of Caterina Sforza, also known as Rivaldino.

of these is uniquely flavored, enriched by the strong personality of lard or bacon fat—favorites in Romagna, the region that divides Italy in two, separating the northern butter-based dishes from those of the south, which rely on extra virgin olive oil. The *piadina* of Romagna is a yeast-free dough rolled into a large plate-shaped disk and cooked on slabs of stone (or *tigelle*, which in nearby Modena give their name to the local variety of *focaccina*). Once baked this flatbread is folded in half to form a half moon and stuffed with prosciutto, roasted vegetables, and *raviggiolo*, a tender, fresh cheese. Had John Montagu, Earl of Sandwich, known of *piadine* he would certainly have saved himself the trouble of inventing those inconsistent and deathly pale sandwiches with which he kept up his strength while he played cards. *Crescentina* is made with the same dough as *piadina* but includes yeast and bakes into half-centimeter-high disks. It is cooked in the *tigelle* between two chestnut leaves, then filled with chopped garlic, rosemary, and lard. The same dough is used for the fried *gnocco*, then cut into little squares, fried in lard, and eaten while extremely hot.

Sangiovese—a clear, brilliant red wine with an aroma of violets and a slightly bitter aftertaste—is native to this region and served young throughout an entire meal. Its name comes from Mount Giove, a hill near Sant'Arcangelo di Romagna, but according to tradition the name (*sanzvès* in dialect) derives from *Sanctus Zeus*, Roman mythology's Jupiter. Albana takes first place among the whites in any of its dry, sweet, or sparkling varieties. Another legend claims that Galla Placidia, daughter of fifth-century Holy Roman Emperor Theodosius, stopped at Bertinoro, sipped some sweet Albana and said it was worthy of "berti in oro," (being served in a golden chalice) thereby renaming the village. *Pagadebit* (meaning "pays debts") earns its name from the firmness of its grapes, which even in bad years guaranteed the production necessary to pay the debts of the vineyard. It has a straw-yellow color, the delicate, grassy aroma of Hawthorn blossoms, and is served young with *capelletti* and *passatelli* pasta in broth.

An excellent Sangiovese wine is produced by Braschi in Mercato Saraceno and Celli in Bertinoro. *Piadina* can be found in many stalls along the roadside in town and in the countryside, and can be bought at Dimensione Pasta di Forli and from the Lucci brothers in Cesena. Piadine with *squacquerone* and local Romagna wine can be savored in Cesena at Casa Romagna, along with other typical products. *Squacquerone* is a soft, sweet cheese that should be eaten very fresh, and is available at the Pascoli di Savignano dairy in Rubicone.

MODENA
A TROVE OF DELICACIES

WHEN DINING IN ANY OF THE RESTAURANTS BETWEEN THE SECCHIA and Panaro rivers one must be of a rare unluckiness to have an average meal. In this era of rediscovered gastronomical treasures, Modena, the "sacred city" of Italian cuisine, is the richest and most tempting trove, critical even of nearby and equally rich Parma, which it considers too Francophile in its approach to many dishes. Countless books have been written describing the breadth of Modena's recipes, and none fail to mention "king *tortellino*." This little golden whorl of stuffed dough is cooked and served in a broth—one tablespoon per *tortellino*—of beef, chicken, or capon dotted with drops of delectable golden oil. This classic of local cuisine would never be served with a tomato or cream sauce, which would be seen as a tasteless resignation to the dictates of French cuisine. As legend has it, *tortellini* were invented by Pope Alexander V's cook in 1330, although another story claims their creator was an innkeeper looking to replicate Venus's navel in pasta. The art of their preparation is a secret handed down from mother to daughter, and their taste comes chiefly from the hands of the woman who kneads them "with cold hands and a warm heart," because if pressed between warm hands the edges would open while boiling. Dough is prepared and cut into squares a few centimeters across, a ball of meat and Parmesan cheese is placed in the center, and all is folded into a triangle with the edges firmly sealed together. Then, holding the longest side between thumb and index finger, with a refined touch the triangle is spun around the index finger of the other hand, firmly uniting the two corners with a pinch.

Another fundamental dish of Modena's cuisine is the *zampone*, pig's trotter stuffed with seasoned mince-meat of a flavorful consistency and eaten with lentils or mashed potatoes. *Zampone* should not be confused with *cotechino*, a plebian dish created using everything including the pig's skin to give substance to the meat; in the past it was considered a low-quality dish, but fortunately today is more greatly appreciated. *Zampone*, on the other hand, is refined using the best pieces of pork, and was already prized in nineteenth-century Paris, London, and Vienna. Its mythical birth dates back to the 1511 siege of nearby Mirandola, when the citadel's inhabitants, surrounded by the troops of Pope Julius II, decided to save what little pork was left by stuffing it into the animals' own trotters.

A vigilant stone lion guards the Duomo of Modena.

facing page
A selection of both dry and fresh homemade pasta.

Nocino is a liqueur of an infernal color but heavenly flavor, and is the nectar of a tree torn between sacred and profane: the walnut is not only dedicated to Jupiter and symbolizes prosperity, but also denotes the meeting place for a witches' Sabbath. Nocino was most likely invented in Modena, where it is still prepared by hand, and a commission of producers meets annually to award the best liqueur. The walnuts are traditionally collected at dawn on the feast of Saint John on June 24 while not yet ripe, with green, tender, dew-covered husks. They are shaved into fine flakes and set to soak in a bottle of pure alcohol, twenty-one walnuts per liter of alcohol, with cloves, cinnamon, and sugar, then put in the sun for forty to sixty days. After refining in a dark cellar for a year or so, it is corrected with spices and sugar, resulting in a mahogany colored tonic.

The Giusti delicatessen is probably the oldest in Europe, founded in 1598, and is where various cold meats and *zampone* are made by hand. There is a small restaurant next door with only four tables that serves the products of the shop and some other local dishes. Traditional balsamic vinegar is available at the Producers' Consortium or from the Galli vinegar producer. Homemade tortellini and fresh pasta can be bought at the Divina Pastella, one of the few shops that still distinguish between the tortellini of Modena and those of Bologna.

A tasting spoon for balsamic vinegar.

During the Middle Ages a "vinegar syrup" was produced in Modena and used as a medicine that "could waken the dead." It gained such an excellent reputation that Pope Boniface III, in order to present a bottle to Emperor Henry II, built a silver-trimmed carriage to carry the flask. The traditional balsamic vinegar of Modena is not made from acid wine, but comes instead from the must of Trebbiano grapes warmed on a gentle flame until it becomes a dense, dark brown syrup. A splash of wine vinegar is added to prompt fermentation, and the concoction is then left to age for two years in an attic where it is subjected to swelteringly hot summers and freezing cold winters. These extreme temperature changes reduce the liquid's volume—from one hundred down to only two liters—but still it is not ready. Only after it has aged for at least twelve years can it be sold as "Traditional Balsamic Vinegar of Modena," and if it ages for another thirty to fifty years it continues to improve. Each vinegar cellar contains many barrels of various dimensions and woods— oak, chestnut, cherry, ash—and the vinegar is poured from one barrel to another in order to acquire a more nuanced aroma with each new wood. The final barrel is the smallest, holding only ten to fifteen liters, and from here the vinegar is bottled in small doses and immediately replaced with younger vinegar awaiting its turn to mature. The so-called balsamic vinegar now widely produced commercially is merely common vinegar with artificial flavor and coloring added.

A sip of traditional balsamic vinegar at the local Vinegar Consortium.

PARMA
AN AWARD-WINNING TRIO

PARMA, HOME OF COMPOSERS GIUSEPPE VERDI AND ARTURO TOSCANINI, and stage to the most famous names in lyric opera, is also keeper of Italy's most famous gastronomic jewels: *grana padano* cheese, prosciutto of Langhirano, and *culatello* of Zibello. The *dolce di Parma* holds the uncontested honor of world's best prosciutto, and comes from south of the Via Emilia between the Parma and Taro rivers, where the last

The Piazza del Duomo, with the Gothic bell tower and Baptistery.

facing page
Cutting Parmigiano Reggiano—an operation requiring skill and experience.

breath of the Versilia wind dies down, calming its salty spirit and acquiring the aroma of the Apennines' chestnut forests. This air is ideal for the sixteen to eighteen months of requisite ageing of the raw ham or prosciutto, whose name is derived from *prosciugato*, meaning "dried." Langhirano, birthplace of prosciutto, is hidden within these forests, and aside from the air its secret lies in a passionate perfectionism. The pigs are raised with care and almost wholly deprived of salt so that the meat stays sweet and delicate.

Culatello, the quintessence of prosciutto, is made with the central part of the de-boned pork loin on the banks of the Po River at Zibello. The meat of lesser quality is removed, leaving the most succulently tender part, which is then covered with salt, white wine, and various herbs absorbed during an energetic massage. The piece of meat is consequently stuffed into a pig's bladder and tied, giving it the classic pear-shaped form. The fourteen-month ageing process gives it the final touch, perfecting the flavor and aroma; the summer air dries it, while the damp winter mists of the Po keep it tender. This marinade, massage, and maturation set the *culatello* head and shoulders above the rest, and first slice is always a surprise. The pigs also determine the quality of the ham, and must be small, of native breed, black with red markings, fed exclusively natural products, and often left to range freely and eat the acorns among the oaks.

Parmigiano Reggiano is a prestigious cheese, often imitated but never equaled, and is now strictly protected by its own consortium. It comes from the valleys of the Enza River, between the provinces of Parma and Reggio Emilia. Its secret lies first and foremost in the quality of the milk, which comes only from local farms, followed by a slow natural maturation process completely free of preservatives, colorants, and anti-fermentative chemicals, resulting in a convincing yet subtle aroma. It is wonderful on its own at the end of a meal, as an accompaniment to an aperitif, with fruit, or in salads, but most importantly it improves the taste of soup, pasta, and risotto dishes.

The people of Romagna, considered generous but a bit boastful, say that in their region the traveler is offered Sangiovese wine to slake his thirst, while in Emilia he is offered water. In truth, the wines of Emilia are more abundant than those of Romagna, including the Gutturnio of Piacenza, Malvasia of Parma, and finally the Lambruschi of Modena, Reggio, and Parma. Lambrusco is a recently developed wine, no more than fifty years old, and should not be confused with the older Fortana that it reflects in taste. It is a light, sparkling wine well adapted to the open character of the people of Emilia because it is a talk-inducing wine one may drink in excess without clouding the brain or other serious consequences. Some are snobbishly disdainful of Lambrusco, but it does seem to be ideally suited to the local cuisine; what but a sparkling Lambrusco di Sorbara could rise to the occasion when paired with a quivering, glutinous *zampone*? Certainly no Barolo or Brunello could withstand such a juxtaposition of flavors.

Agrinascente, located not far from the exit for Fidenza on the A1 *autostrada*, produces and sells its own DOP Parmesan cheese, and it is also possible to tour the premises to see the cheese being made. Parmesan can also be found at the Casa del Formaggio in Parma together with a vast assortment of cold meats. *Culatello* and other pork delicacies such as *salame di Felino*, *spalla cotta* of San Secondo, and *fiochetto*, can also be bought from Gino Fereoli in Langhirano or from the Boutique della Carne in Zibello, an official "City of Flavors." Typical products of the region can be tasted at the Davoli wine shop accompanied by the local Lambrusco.

PIACENZA
GENEROUS COUNTRY HOSPITALITY

A PANEL PAINTING IN THE CIVIC MUSEUM OF PALAZZO FARNESE IN PIACENZA greets visitors with a quote in dialect that reads, "Gentlemen, you all are welcome," a phrase that aptly conveys the simple, hospitable, generous character of the city's people. Facing both the plains and mountains, Piacenza has a dichotomous nature—one face is that of a many-towered sentinel keeping the waters of the Po at bay, while the other is a showcase for the city's rural surroundings, scattered with ancient villages of rare beauty rising gently into the Apennines. The culinary tradition of Piacenza is based on a few select, genuine ingredients prepared with great ability and, above all, with immense love. There were once seventy-seven typical dishes for the city's feast days, but the farmers had to be satisfied with *pisarei e fasò*, little gnocchi made of flour and bread crumbs flavored with a mixture of seven beans, or at most *anolini di stracotto* (stew-filled pasta), rice balls, or *tortelli* with oxtail, dishes still offered in restaurants all over the city. Alternatively, the poor had to take advantage of rainy days to send their children out in search of snails that were then cleaned by putting them into wire baskets hung outside for a few days, covered in corn flour, washed with water and vinegar, and cooked in boiling water. Stewed

The Baroque bronze statue of Ranuccio I Farnese in the city center's Piazza dei Cavalli.

facing page
Aeging sausages are strung up in dark, dry cellars.

with oil, vinegar, salt, pepper, corn flour, assorted chopped vegetables—including onion, parsley, celery, and carrot—and boiled for at least two hours a day for three to four consecutive days, they were then left to rest in a closed pan for a few hours until mealtime. The classic shelled snail, which is much more flavorful than its farmed counterpart, is gathered in the open countryside and mountains on rainy days, and in Bobbio one can still taste them with a slice of hot polenta accompanied by a light, aromatic white wine. Piacenza's cuisine, however, is still based primarily on pork. Medieval paintings in the church of San Savino in Piacenza and in the abbey of San Colombano in Bobbio show pigs being slaughtered, a sacred rite. *Pancetta* is the central part of the pig's ventral fat, treated with natural herbs and spices that are then scraped away. Salami is made with lean mincemeat and lard seasoned with natural herbs and spices, kneaded, and stuffed into a pig's bladder. *Coppa*, however, the favorite of all Piacenza's salami, is taken from the pig's neck muscles, salted, seasoned, massaged, and aged for six months so the meat acquires its characteristic pink color.

Piacenza has been an official "City of Wine" since 1987, but has been a de facto capital of winemaking since ancient Roman times; Senator Pisone was accused of alcoholism, Licinius Sestulus recommended it to calm the soul, and a silver goblet along with a statuette of a drunken Hercules *Bibace*, both of the Roman era, have recently been unearthed. Goblets were called *gutturnia*, and Gutturnio, the standard-bearer of Piacenza's wines, is a lively, dry red made from Barbera and Bonarda grapes with a classic wine bouquet. It is ideal with risotto, pasta, roasted white meat dishes, and, naturally, salami. The local red wines made straight from Barbera grapes (dry and generous) or Bonarda (pleasant and slightly tannic) are all DOC, and among the white wines, Ortrugo (made from native grapes), Monterosso della Val d'Arda (dry and delicate), and the sparkling Malvasia di Candia (either sweet or dry) are all worth tasting.

The communal wine shop at Castel Arquato offers a wide selection of wines from the area surrounding Piacenza, and one can also go directly to the producers, such as the Viticoltori Arquatesi or the cellars of Cantine Malaspina. Salami and cured meats can be bought from Grossetti in Trevozzo or at the La Rocca delicatessen in Castel Arquato. Some of the most representative dishes of the region are prepared by Ra Ca Longa in Bobbio: *pisarei e fasò*, snails, *anolini*, *turtei*, *bomba di riso*, *tripe a la Piacentina*, mule stew with polenta, boned duck, turkey stuffed with chestnuts, roast *coppa*, and ragout of horse meat are all worth a taste.

SOGLIANO
AL RUBICONE CHEESE

SOGLIANO AL RUBICONE, A VILLAGE OF ANCIENT ROMAN ORIGIN in the Apennines of Romagna, has a centuries-old tradition of cheese making. Its specialty, *la fossa* (hole), is a hard cheese named for the technique of ageing it in holes dug out of the tufa rock. The whole village participates in its production, though the origins of this ritual remain shrouded in mystery. The most popular legend claims that in 1494, in order to prevent everything in their town from being sacked by the armies of Ferrandino, heir to the throne of the Kingdom of Naples, the peasants of Sogliano hid their cheese forms behind the archway tiles in holes that were then sealed with plaster. When the invaders left, the villagers uncovered their cache and were pleasantly surprised that the cheese had acquired a special taste and was much more easily digestible, so they decided to repeat and refine the practice. Sogliano already had a tradition of digging large ditches (nine feet deep and six feet wide) not only to preserve grain, but to protect it from mice, thieves, and above all from the Saracens who conducted frequent raids along the Adriatic coast. This practice of burying goods dates back to the Roman era, and was used to conserve food from summer harvests for use throughout the winter months. The cheese destined for this special ageing is made of sheep's milk, in small forms weighing from twenty to sixty ounces, and aged for eighty to one hundred days. Tradition dictates that the ditch be dug in August and the "disinterment" take place on November 24, the eve of the feast of Saint Catherine. Amid the oxygen-free tufa walls of these ditches the cheese ferments, acquiring a special taste, delicate and then more decisive with age, rich with aromas of undergrowth and mushrooms, with a slightly bitter aftertaste. When the forms are removed they are no longer the perfect cylinders they were, misshapen by the weight of being stacked atop one another, and the crust and cream are nearly indistinguishable after softening during ageing. *Fossa* cheese is best eaten with a drizzle of honey, a small slice of fruit gelatin, a sprinkling of balsamic vinegar of Modena, or with *savor*—a fruity sauce of boiled grapes, pears, apples, and almonds. Ideally accompanied by a full-bodied red wine such as Sangiovese del Rubicone or Castelli Sammarinesi, it also pairs well with late harvest dessert wines or dry Marsala.

Cheese during its aeging process in caves.

facing page
Forte della Rocca, the Fortress of San Marino, looks toward the hills of Sogliano al Rubicone.

A large selection of *fossa* cheeses is available at the Casa del Formaggio, but in town, which is an official "City of Flavors," there are many producers who sell it directly. Gianfranco Rossini boasts the most ancient caves, while the Fosse Pellegrini have set up a museum of *fossa* cheeses with photographs and old utensils and receive visitors in a cellar that feels like a medieval prison. Valentini in San Marino is a great wine shop with over 3,000 wine and liqueur labels; their policy is to moderate their prices, and they offer a good selection of the fine wines of this little republic.

On the slopes of Mount Titano, just a few miles from the Valle del Rubicone, rise the towers surrounding the fortress of San Marino. Covering roughly thirty square miles, tiny San Marino is proud of its heritage as the most ancient republic in the world, founded around the eleventh century and completely independent since the fifteenth century. The mountain slopes facing the Adriatic have been dedicated to wine production for hundreds of years, and today there are about three hundred producers belonging to the consortium protecting the traditional wines of San Marino. The most representative wines are Brugneto, which is principally Sangiovese, Biancale, and Moscato Spumante. Additionally, there is an excellent barrel-aged San Marino Riserva; Sangiovese, Rosato, and Bianco of the Castelli Sammarinnesi; sweet Moscato; sparkling white Grilèt; Chardonnay; white Sangiovese; and the Riserva del Titano Brut Spumante are all worth a taste.

The central Italian countryside acquires an unmistakable color after the wheat harvest.

AREZZO

THE WHITE BULLS OF THE VAL DI CHIANA

THE *CHIANINA*, NATIVE TO THE PORTION OF THE VAL DI CHIANA south of Arezzo, is the most valuable and oldest cow breed in the world. The "white bull" is the name given to the majestic snow-white Etruscan bovine of the first century AD, so beautiful that it was honored in processions and sacrificed to the gods during their most important ceremonies. Strong and muscular in build, with a china-white coat and black

Piazza Grande, or Piazza Vasari, where the Antiques Fair and the Joust of the Saracens takes place.

facing page
The noble Chianina cattle impatiently wait to be led to pasture.

extremities, the white bull is bred for its decidedly superior quality of meat, which the Tuscans say is salty (it is also very flavorful, lean, and light red in color). Under constant supervision by the *butteri* (cowboys) on horseback, the *chianine* are free-range animals left to graze in vast pastures that include forests of Mediterranean shrub and pine groves. This special breeding, with traditional methods and rigorous medical controls of the animals sent to slaughter, is an absolute guarantee for the consumer. The meat is of the highest quality and is used to prepare the famous *bistecca alla fiorentina*, Florentine steaks, the meat on the bone to which the Tuscans are famously addicted, so much so that there was nearly a popular uprising when a prohibition law was passed as a consequence of the "mad cow" epidemic. The *fiorentina* steak used to be called *carbonata* because it was cooked on a grill over charcoal from the wood of the Maremma, and later came to be called "bistecca," a distortion of the English word "beefsteak." Legend holds that in 1565 spits of roasted ox were given to a crowd on Piazza San Lorenzo in Florence. The English people in the gathering loudly demanded some of the meat, calling out "beefsteak," and the Florentines changed the name to bistecca. Cooking the *fiorentina* is a ritual of precise rules. First, the meat must be in one T-bone piece at least three fingers (seven centimeters) high and include the filet. It is then grilled over hot coals or olive-wood embers for seven minutes on each side and seven minutes in vertical, resting on the bone. Attention must be paid not to pierce the meat, so that none of the flavorful juices escape. Salted only after it has been cooked, it can be brushed with a marinade of oil, rock salt, and herbs, and must be cut with a sharpened, non-serrated knife.

It is said that King Charles V introduced beans into Tuscany and today, apart from the common *cannellini* and *toscanelli*, rare varieties such as *coco nano* and *zolfino* are cultivated here. The *zolfino* is known as the *fagiolo del cento* (the one hundred bean), because it is planted on the hundredth day of the year. It is also known as *burrino*, because it melts in the mouth like butter. Cultivated between the Arno and Pratomagno rivers on poor, arid soil because it doesn't grow well around stagnant water, it is small and round, with a pale yellow skin, and a delicate and creamy texture. The *zolfino* should be boiled slowly in a terracotta pot filled to the brim with water for three to four hours. At one time the farming families would put the pot on for the whole night under the ashes of the wood fire where the bread had been cooked, or they would fill glass jars three quarters to the top and place them on a layer of ash beside the fireplace to slowly cook.

The *fiorentina* pairs well with warm Tuscan white beans seasoned with an intense extra virgin olive oil, salt, and pepper, all served with a slice of homemade bread. The accompanying wine should be a purebred Tuscan red, moderately aged and well balanced.

Fiorentina steak on the bone from the Chianina breed of bulls and other cuts of meat can be bought from various producers who sell directly to the public at their farm shops. Among them are Romani, outside Arezzo, and Belucci, in Badia Tebalda. In Arezzo's historic center it can be bought from the Barelli butcher, who also offers a good selection of cold meats, lard, and cheeses. The Falconiere restaurant at San Martino, near Cortona, serves a perfect *fiorentina* steak with traditional *cannellini* beans. Restructured from a seventeenth-century Tuscan villa, it is an elegant eating place that also has rooms to host guests overnight.

CARMIGNANO
TO CHIANTI AND BACK

AN EXCELLENT RED WINE IS PRODUCED ON THE HILLS OF MONTALBANO, between the Ombrone and Arno rivers, in the midst of Chianti country. Fifty years ago it was legitimized as Chianti, and twenty years ago it separated itself from the "Great Family" of that more recognized wine, reclaiming its natural origins and again taking its true name—Carmignano. As opposed to its famous relative, the prevalent grape used to produce Carmignano is Cabernet grown in vineyards that were planted in the sixteenth century by Catherine de' Medici, queen of France. Some of the older wine growers still call it *uva Francesca*, a distortion of its French origin. Traditionally bottled on September 29, the feast of the patron saint, Carmignano's color is a bright ruby red tending toward garnet as it ages, and its flavor tastes slightly of violets without the grassy aftertaste that characterizes Chianti. Carmignano is aged for two years, one in oak or chestnut casks, and at least three years for the Riserva, which requires an additional two years of ageing in the bottle. It is traditionally served with roasted meat, game, noble fowl, and matured cheeses. Its history is belived to date back to the Etruscans, and it was already famous in the fourteenth century; "The wines of Carmignano are excellent," wrote medieval chronicler Domenico Bartolini. The wine merchants of Prato and Florence were prepared to pay one florin per *soma*, approximately seventy-five liters—four times the price of the wines most in demand at that time. Three hundred years later, in his eulogy *Bacco in Toscana*, writer Francesco Redi has Bacchus himself extol its virtues. In the nineteenth century this distinctive red wine was considered one of the best of Tuscany, thanks also to the fame granted it a century earlier by Cosimo III de' Medici, Grand Duke of Tuscany, who was most impassioned about wine. In paintings hung in the Medici Villa at Poggio a Caiano painter Bartolomeo Bimbi depicted dozens of different grapes hanging in bunches from a ceiling, labeled by a series of didactic ornamental scrolls. The Grand Duke almost always presented a bottle or two of Carmignano when he held court throughout Europe, and was particularly fervent in giving this gift to Queen Anne of England even though it was thought to travel badly, especially on long voyages. In 1716 a decree proscribed the area of production and established precise rules for the grape harvest. The producers safeguarding the quality of the wine pay more attention to this decree than to the rules of the DOCG limiting the area of production to just over forty acres—one of the smallest consortia in terms of size—in the townships of Poggio a Caiano and Carmignano, where there is also an interesting wine museum in the basement of the Palazzo Comunale.

The serene harmony of the Tuscan countryside.

facing page
Grapes destined for Vin Santo are dried on grills in airy rooms.

Prato's famous confectionaries are unparalleled; the classic *cantucci* can be found all over Tuscany, but the local *brutti e buoni* (ugly and good) are not to be missed. They are dark colored, hard, rough little biscuits with a wavy shape and unique almond essence. *Mangia e bevi* (eat and drink) are soft, sweet flatbreads filled with mint and cedar syrup. Prato peaches are tiny, round cakes made in two half circles of pastry dipped in alkermes liqueur and filled with custard cream or chocolate. The *berlingozzo* is also round and soft, with vanilla and orange essence. *Pan di ramerino* (rosemary bread), a soft, sweet roll made here since the Middle Ages, courageously blends the flavors of grapes and rosemary within a shiny, nut-brown crust.

The wine shop Su Pé i Canto in the main square of Carmignano was once an old coal cellar and has been recently renovated by the Alderighi family. There is a selection of almost all the wines of the area, which can be bought or tasted with *crostini*, tongue and onions, or chocolate. In addition to Carmignano wine, the Barco Reale, produced from the same grapes, should be sampled, as should the Vin Ruspo rosé, a fresh, sparkling wine to be consumed as an aperitif when very young with salami. Vin Santo, dry or sweet late-harvest wine, is aged three or four years in small barrels and then for much longer in bottles. The typical sweetmeats of Prato can be tasted and bought in the Mattei historic biscuit bakery, where *cantucci* were invented.

COLONNATA

RICH MEALS AMID MARBLE QUARRIES

THE APUAN ALPS FORM A LIMESTONE MASSIF THAT FLANKS THE APENNINES just west of the Lunigiana, a historic area named for the mysterious city of Luni, whose ancient remains lie just a few miles from the Tyrrhenian Sea. This mountain range is famous for its incomparable marble, which has been sought after by the most famous sculptors, and is also noted for the lard produced in the village of Colonnata. This unique lard, which was formerly the favorite food of local quarrymen, is now treasured by gourmands. Colonnata is hidden among the quarries of Carrara, and lies atop one of the oldest and richest veins of pure white statuary marble. The ancient Romans excavated here beginning in the first century after discovering the Canaloni massif and remaining entranced by its exquisitely fine-grained marble. Known as *vetrino*, this smooth and remarkably strong stone is used to make *conche*, the hand-carved, shell-shaped basins in which the lard is left to age. Fresh lard, from the layer of adipose tissue just beneath the skin of the pig's back, arrives from September through May from nearby Emilia, where only the haunches are used for prosciutto—leaving the rest of the animal and its lard, which requires prompt use within of few days of slaughter, for others to take care of. Once cleaned of residual fat, bristles, and other impurities, the meat is cut into squares that are then layered in the *conche*, rubbed with coarsely chopped garlic, aromatic herbs, and natural spices. When all basins are full they are sealed tight and reopened only six or ten months later, after the constant temperature and high humidity have aided the production of brine, an indispensable part of successful maturation, as it infuses the lard with a unique flavor. Because of its high nutritional value, rich in vitamins and essential fatty acids, lard was once used chiefly as an accompaniment or treatment for other foods—meats were typically coated in lard to flavor and soften them. Today it is consumed raw, cut into very thin slices with toasted bread, and it melts in the mouth. An unlikely yet very savory combination pairs it with a drop of acacia or chestnut honey from the Lunigiana, the first and only DOP honey in Italy. It was appreciated for centuries, as it was the only sweetener before the arrival of commercially refined sugar, and Charlemagne deemed this honey so important that he required all local landowners to also act as honey-harvesting beekeepers, and strictly punished anyone caught stealing honey.

Sculptors test themselves with marble in Carrara's main piazza.

facing page
Chianti wine and Colonnata lard make an excellent lunch at Locanda Cervia.

Porcini muschrooms abound in the forests surrounding the mountainous Passo della Cisa gap, and are possibly the only fungi in the world to receive the honor of IGP status. Many varieties are collected between May and late autumn's first snow: *Boletus aestivalis,* distinctively flavorful, is collected until September; the sweet and delicate *pinicola* and *aereus* mature in late summer, as does the perfumed and subtle-tasting *Boletus edulis.* Porcini can be prepared in many ways, with the youngest ones, locally known as champagne corks, best enjoyed raw in salads, while the firm tops of the more mature mushrooms are prepared *alla genovese*, with garlic and parsley. The last harvest is usually diced and swiftly sautéed over a high flame with oil, parsley, and garlic, or added to meat sauces and polenta, and is an ideal accompaniment to risotto or tagliatelle pasta. Many local restaurants serve a soup combining chestnuts and porcini, a curious delicacy well worth tasting.

In the Lunigiana area every product has its own taste, which differs from village to village, and each has a precise name: lamb of Zeri, *panigaccio* flatbread of Podenzana, cake of Erbi, *marocca* (bread made of chestnut and wheat flour) of Casola, *Bigliolo* beans, *Treschietto* onions, *Binotto* apples, and Vermentino wine from the Colli di Luni. A vast wine selection is available at Bosco in Pontremoli. Fresh and dried mushrooms can be purchased from the Giogallo cooperative in Pontremoli, and lard is offered in the best grocers' shops all over the peninsula; in Colonnata it can be bought straight from the producers La Conca and Guadagni.

FLORENCE
RENAISSANCE CUISINE

SINCE THE MIDDLE AGES FLORENCE HAS BEEN MOST ATTENTIVE and hospitable to visiting merchants, travelers, noblemen, and monarchs. In the fourteenth century there were statutes dictating the behavior of hosts towards their guests in order to maintain decorum. Among the forbidden behaviors were, for example, placing laid tables along the street, offering bread or wine in a loud voice, inviting passersby to eat, drink, or stay the night. In the fifteenth century the Medici made the city magnificent and brought the art of good cooking to the courts of Europe, where the food had been abundant but rough, emphasizing quantity over quality. Most meat was boiled, roasted, and coated in spices to cover its unappetizing smell and taste. Florentine cooks, however, developed simple recipes using choice products with care, refined the presentation at table, and invented new dishes, including ice cream.

In the 1990s, during the celebrations of the centenary of Lorenzo the Magnificent's passing, careful historical research brought many Renaissance recipes to light which were then published, bought by many restaurants of the city and surroundings, and are still offered today. Examples are the *torta inbalconata*, a "balcony cake" with almonds, walnuts, raisins, and dates, and the *antico peposo*, a peppered leg of rabbit with apples whose recipe is attributed to sculptor and architect Filippo Brunelleschi.

Florentine cuisine has remained sober and flavorful, with no hint of spaghetti or maccheroni, which are replaced by *pici* or *pappardelle* that better absorb the local sauces. Tripe is typically Florentine and considered the best of the peasant dishes; used in ancient Greece and Rome in sausages, from the Middle Ages to the present day it is key in the gastronomy of many Italian regions because it is nutritious and inexpensive. This kind of food has been reevaluated, and today *trippista* stalls sell bread rolls filled with tripe just as they did two centuries ago.

Salami also has an old tradition, beginning with the *finocchiona*, the most famous of the Tuscan sausages, prepared with *pancetta* from the pig's belly, coarsely minced and seasoned with wild fennel, pepper, salt, and red wine. It is briefly matured for three months, has such a soft consistency that it is also known as *sbriciolona* because it melts in the mouth, and is eaten either with homemade bread and fresh fava beans or with flatbread brushed with extra virgin olive oil and salt.

The Ponte Vecchio arching the Arno River at sunset.

facing page
The art of transforming food into fine cuisine dates back to the Medici and beyond.

Chianti Frescobaldi can be bought from the producers in their cellars in Nipozzano or from the family wine bar in Florence. A visit to the Pinchiorri wine shop should not be missed, as it is affiliated with a restaurant that has one of the best cellars in the world—a true monument to the best Tuscan and international labels. Traditional Tuscan cuisine is available at Del Fagioli, a rustic trattoria, or at Vecchia Bettola, with its marble-topped tables and copious flasks of Chianti payable according to the amount consumed.

Henry VIII, who reigned in England in the sixteenth century, was certainly not the person to delegate important decisions to others; rather than taking a mistress, he had no fewer than six wives, nor did he leave the selection of wine to others, and in the archives of the Florentine Marquis of Frescobaldi there are orders for wine personally signed by the king. The Frescobaldi family, originally from the Val di Pesa, is today one of the oldest wine dynasties, producing wine on the hills around Florence, among which the most prevalent is, naturally, Chianti. The historic estate of Castiglioni where it is produced south of the city is even mapped in the Uffizzi gallery as it appears in the 1331 will of Berto Frescobaldi. Wine is also produced at the castle of Nipozzano, built in the tenth century and now transformed into a cultural center, the castle of Pomino, and several others.

GROSSETO
MOUNT AMIATA'S CHESTNUTS

AT THE TERMINUS OF MAREMMA'S ROLLING HILLS STANDS THE UNMISTAKABLE profile of Mount Amiata, whose ancient volcanic slopes are densely wooded with stately chestnut trees. Hidden within the mountain are abandoned mercury mines that are now a museum and precious Longobardian abbeys. Autumn is the best season to visit, when the broad yellow foliage plays in the sun's rays and the wind shakes the branch-es, causing the ripe chestnuts to fall to the ground with a faint thud, a sound that was music to the ancestral mountain dwellers' ears, as it meant the possibility of surviving the winter. The ancient Greeks called the sweet, energy-rich chestnuts Jupiter's acorns, and for central Italians they are an important, natural, healthy staple. Historically, chestnuts belonged to any- and everyone; even those who did not own a tree were per-mitted to collect them along the boundaries of others' properties, and after each har-vest the poor freely gathered the remains, which explains the common saying that every husk contains three fruits—one for the owner, one for the harvester, and one for the poor. The chestnut forests of Mount Amiata cover a surface of more than five thou-sand hectares of excellent-quality red chestnut fruit prepared in many different ways: *bucchiate* are peeled, cooked, and flavored with fennel; *brodolose* are roasted, peeled,

The gentle hills of Tuscany's Maremma.

facing page
By the first frost chestnuts are gathered beside the fire for roasting.

and boiled until they form a soft cream; *castrate* are cut in two and roasted over an open fire in a slotted pan; *castroni* are skinned and boiled with fennel; *suggioli* are boiled with the skin; *vecchiarelle* are dry chestnuts boiled with laurel. In preparation for the winter months the chestnuts are dried in a rustic shed beside the house, roasted on reed grates over a low, constant flame, and ground into a fine powder. Before grinding they are put into a sack and beaten to separate the dried fruit from the husk, and are then milled to pro-duce a sweet flour with which the *castagnaccio*—a flat cake flavored with rosemary, pine nuts, and wal-nuts—is prepared. The *fiandolone* is a bread made with chestnut and wheat flour, and even chestnut polen-ta was once savored with ricotta, smoked herrings, steamed cod with onions, sausage, or sweetbreads.

Wild boars roam throughout Italy and are often hunted to control their population density and spare valuable crops from the damage they wreak. In Maremma the boar has always been part of the landscape hunted for its excellent meat. Today most *cinghiale*, whether wild or bred in captivity, are a cross between the native breed and larger breeds imported from central Europe. Sausages of all sorts are prepared from boar meat: salami, ham, and the typical *coppiette*—dried and smoked bars of meat flavored with salt and chili pepper. There are many other recipes in which the meat's gamey flavor is sweetened with various ingredients, including tomatoes, pine nuts, candied fruit, and even cacao.

The Giovannino delicatessen in Pitigliano produces and sells excellent wild boar meats, including a rare *culatello*. The Tuscan Maremma, land of the boar, is also that of the *bottarga*, the smoked grey mullet of Orbetello with which many rich dishes are prepared, and this specialty can be found at the Orbetello Pesca Lagunare cooperative. *Acquacotta*—stewed onions, tomatoes, and basil poured over a slice of stale bread—is the traditional dish of the Maremma, and is the simple soup of the local cowboys and charcoal burners. It is made exceptionally well in Montemerano at Caino, who also distributes it in bottles to the best regional grocers.

LIVORNO
A PLETHORA OF RECIPES FOR *CACCIUCCO*

ONE OF THE FEW AUTHENTICALLY TUSCAN FISH RECIPES is the *cacciucco alla livornese*, a type of soup that corresponds to the character of this anarchic, cosmopolitan, and thoroughly unconventional city. Livorno's inhabitants even refer to themselves as *cacciucco*, a mixture. A concise description should suffice to convey this city's vitality: in the historical center there are churches and temples of almost all religions; in Italy's most liberal city there is the world's only monument acknowledging slavery (*I Quattro Mori*); in the restaurants the red mullet of the Tyrrhenian Sea alternates with North African couscous, whose preparation is never the same and depends on the mood of the cook; and in the best restaurants the black squid ink risotto, contrary to all reasonable culinary laws, is sprinkled with grated parmesan cheese. To define *cacciucco* as a fish soup is too limited, even if it resembles a soup, as it is a mixture of various ingredients, a synthesis of the many recipes for fish soup that have been imported from all over the world. The etymology derives from the Turkish *kuzuk*, meaning small, because it is prepared with the bits and pieces of fish. In the sixteenth century it was made with the least prized fish—even the leftovers—and was given to the oarsmen chained in boats' galleys. Today less use is made of the bits and pieces, fewer heads, and more valuable fish and shellfish are used. Each piece is cooked by itself and mixed together only at the moment of serving, poured onto a slice of unsalted bread in the bottom of the plate, then covered with a hearty sauce. To make the best *cacciucco* one should go to the Livorno fish market where squid, rock octopus, *palombo* (dogfish), *scorfano* (black scorpion fish), shellfish, shrimp, and prawn are sold along with delicious suggestions on how to cook it (opinions differ from stall to stall). *Cacciucco* is served in virtually all local restaurants, as tradition dictates with a young red wine. Should you happen to overindulge in the wine, simply order a *persiana* at the end of the meal, and you will receive a green liqueur with a refreshing anise and mint base. If, however, you are only passing through en route to Sardinia, while waiting for the ferry you can have a guided boat tour of the *fossi*, a network of navigable canals that crisscross the seventeenth-century quarter called Venezia, one of the oldest districts of the historic center. Here one can also taste the traditional patty of garbanzo bean flour generously covered with pepper, ordering it the way the old inhabitants used to by requesting a *cinque più cinque*, five lire worth of patty and five of bread.

I Quattro Mori monument in honor of Ferdinando I de' Medici.

facing page
Caciucco, a sight for sore eyes ready to feast.

The Coast of the Etruscans stretches south of Livorno, scattered with ancient villages, famous beaches, and dynamic, qualified vineyards. These include Castagneto Carducci, where Sassicaia is produced, a red wine of Cabernet Sauvignon grapes grown along the tall and straight lines of cypress trees of San Guido that were the subject of many poems by Giosuè Carducci. Sassicaia has been sold only since 1970, but it immediately became a mythic wine all over the world, bringing with it many other wines of the area. All are worthy of a prominent place in any notable wine shop, such as the *enoteche* of Val di Cornia and Suvereto, at the base of the medieval Campiglia Marittima, an area that has become the standard-bearer of the new direction of Tuscan wine making. Various whites and reds should be tried with each meal, and at the end the Ansonica Passito and the Aleatico Passito are excellent dessert wines.

The Trattoria Galileo is an excellent place to taste the authentic fish cuisine of Livorno, and Cantina Nardi, originally a wine shop, also serves red mullet with tomatoes in a fish soup, accompanied by a good selection of wine. The Gambero Rosso in San Vincenzo is one of the best cellars in Italy, and its innumerable labels are complemented by excellent food. The San Guido farm in Castagneto Carducci, along the Wine Route of the Etruscan Coast, is where Sassicaia was first made, and Borsi liqueur producer, who makes a moderately alcoholic quinine liqueur with a strong personality, is also nearby.

LUCCA
A MOST DISTINGUISHED OIL

THE EXTRA VIRGIN OLIVE OIL PRODUCED IN LUCCA is one of the best in Italy, and is used by knowledgeable tasters as a term of comparison to determine the taste and acidity of other oils. It is so famous that even the Concise Oxford English Dictionary has an entry: "Lucca oil: a superior quality of olive oil." However, the olive of this region was not born to please the palate, and was originally used in the textile industries.

In the fourth century Lucca imported olive oil from Puglia for the processing of wool, but the expense and the difficulty of transporting the oil forced the Tuscans to produce oil from the olives of their own hills, and it was chiefly the Medici who encouraged the cultivation of olive trees by giving part of their lands to local peasants with the understanding that they were to grow grapes and olives. This mixed cultivation of vineyard and olive grove characterized the Tuscan landscape until a few decades ago. Lucca oil is bright and transparent, golden in color, with a full-bodied taste and a light aroma of almonds, apples, or artichokes. If the oil comes from olives close to the seashore it is more delicate and rounded, while the olives of the hillsides, which grow at lower temperatures, result in a stronger, fruitier oil. The quality of oil depends on its oleic acid content, which must be between one-fifth and one-half of 1 percent, and each oil's characteristics depend on the cultivar, the terrain, the climate, and the harvest period. The color is given by the age of the pressed olives; greener oil comes from younger olives that are not yet fully mature. Early autumn is the best time for harvest, when the fruit has not fully ripened so the olives have not become completely black, but remain partially green. They are most easily picked by hand, the higher branches reached with stepladders, and the trees should not be beaten with sticks or raked, as this may break the branches or damage the fruit. Additionally, the olives should not fall to the ground and thus be mixed with fruit that has fallen before its time or contains impurities, and for this reason nets or sheets are placed under the trees during harvest. The fruit is then deposited in small nesting crates, never in big containers that might bruise it or start fermentation early. The olives are then taken to the press as quickly as possible, preferably within twenty-four hours, where they are washed, the leaves are removed, and they are pressed with stone mills. The resulting paste obtained from a second cold press is then filtered to extract the oil. The must obtained from the pressing is collected and clarified through decanting or filtering to eliminate any residues still in suspension.

Piazza dei Mercanti recalls the long business tradition of this small town.

facing page
Olives ready to provide Italy's finest extra virgin oil.

The hills around Lucca produce wines that were prized by the ancient Romans, who built a "wine road" that crossed the hill of Montecarlo and connected the Via Cassia with the Via Romea. Today local cellars offer many white and red DOC wines, but especially worth trying is the wine that poet Giovanni Pascoli used to drink. He lived in Garfagnana between 1895 and 1912, and was a great lover of food and wine. He frequently went to Ponte di Campia, to the Ritrovo del Platano (Sycamore Sanctuary, as he himself named it) on the banks of the Serchio River, where he would eat a simple meal accompanied by the wine of the Fiattone hills at the foot of the Apuan Alps. The same wine was rediscovered and called Melograno (Pomegranate), and today it is still possible to taste it at the same inn and eat the dishes that were dear to the poet, such as *vinata di neccio* (chestnut flour and red wine), *zuppa di faro* (spelt soup), and *il piatto pascoliano*, a dish named after the poet which includes savory tortes, salami, and cheeses.

Excellent olive oil is available from Le Camelie farm in Pieve di Compito, while wine is sold at the Vigna del Greppo farm in Montecarlo, and both olive oil and wine are made and sold at the Maionchi farm in Tofori. Spelt wheat can be bought at the Garfagnana Produce Consortium in Castelnuovo Garfagnana, which is also home of the Chestnut Growers' Association of Garfagnana, where one can buy chestnut flour with which to prepare *necci*, the typical flat bread to accompany salami and ricotta, and *castagnaccio* with olive oil, chestnuts, and orange peel.

Farro, or spelt wheat, is the oldest grain used in cooking. Ancestor of all cereals cultivated today, it was the staple of entire Mediterranean populations for over two thousand years. Probably introduced in Italy by the Greeks in the sixth or seventh century BC, the ancient Romans used it to prepare *puls*, a basic dish used to feed entire legions of soldiers. In Garfagnana spelt has long been cultivated, and was polished in ancient stone mills and used to make bread, pasta, desserts, and above all soups, to which the locals attribute their excellent physical condition—a hypothesis confirmed by nutritionists who maintain that spelt contains antioxidants that delay the ageing process and provides essential vitamins and minerals. Compared to other types of spelt in commerce, that of Garfagnana is more tender and floury, does not need too much soaking in water before use, and cooks in a much shorter time. *Zuppa di farro* with beans and chickpeas is an excellent typical dish served over a slice of toasted Tuscan bread. Some bakers in Garfagnana still make potato bread, a reminder of times when there was a shortage of grain. This bread is made with mashed potatoes and grain flour, resulting in a particularly soft, tasty loaf that keeps for a long time. It is eaten with the typical salamis of the Garfagnana, *mondiola*, *biroldo*, *lardo*, and *guanciale*.

above
Farro is the hearty grain at the base of many Tuscan recipes.

right
Olives are harvested manually with the help of great nets.

MONTALCINO
ANCESTOR OF THE *SUPER-TUSCANS*

LIKE SONS OF A PROLIFIC NOBLE FAMILY, MANY VALUABLE RED WINES are being born in Tuscany, some of them still resting in cellars awaiting discovery. All are descendants of Brunello di Montalcino, now more mythic than any other simple wine, which many people strive to have grace their tables. If Chianti is the most famed Italian wine outside the country's borders, Brunello is the most prestigious, acting as Italian ambassador of exclusive quality. Clemente Santi invented this fine red in 1865 and presented the first vintages at the exhibition of Siena in 1870. His first challenge was to make pure wine from the grapes, discarding the traditional methods used in the Chianti region that often included even white grapes, the second was deciding upon a long maceration and lengthy ageing in oak barrels, techniques that resulted in a strong, velvety wine with extraordinary personality. Ferruccio Biondi-Santi, agronomist, enologist, and Santi's nephew, then perfected the technique and in 1888 obtained the first official recognition for a choice red wine obtained from propagated Sangiovese *grosso* vines, winning flattering appreciation. Biondi-Santi also codified requirements to guarantee a wine's quality; the present DOCG rating confirms the principles of traditional production around Montalcino and the exclusive use of a single variety of Sangiovese grape. Since then, for decades and with perseverance, the producers who had created the wine built up its image, with an intelligent promotional campaign and modern marketing criteria, until it became the most famous wine in the world.

Brunello is a ruby red tending to garnet with a characteristic and intense aroma, hinting at scents of undergrowth, aromatic woods, and berries. It is a dry, slightly tannic, well-balanced, robust, and persistent wine, truly exceptional when aged for five years (six for the Riserva), with a minimum of two years in oak barrels and six months in bottles. According to expert wine critic Mario Soldati it can "mature to infinity and get better all the time." Brunello is the classic wine for red meats, roasts, and game, though the ideal marriage is with spit-roasted thrush, a specialty celebrated in Montalcino each fall. The best recent years are 1995 and 1997, and this wine is important enough to have earned a museum dedicated by the Colombini family and set up on their Fattoria dei Barbi estate, where there is also a comfortable inn where one can taste the region's typical dishes and buy salami, oil, and cheese in addition to the requisite wines.

The castle walls of Montalcino remain almost entirely intact.

facing page
In the cellar, before tasting, the scent of the wine indicates its superior quality.

The La Fortezza wine shop and bar, in one of the fourteenth-century towers of the fortress in Montalcino, carries all 125 labels of local Brunello, as well as rare vintage wines such as Biondi Santi Riserva '55, Casebasse Riserva '83, and Salvioni '87. Apart from the olive oil and wine, cheese and salami are available for tasting. A vast selection of Brunello and Super-Tuscan wines is available at the Osteria del Vecchio Castello in Pieve San Sigismondo, one of the best restaurants in the area.

Broths and soups abound in Tuscan cuisine, and though they are often frugal peasant recipes, many have recently been reevaluated in restaurants across the country. *Acquacotta*, the most famous, is prepared with onion, celery, and tomato sautéed in olive oil, diluted with boiling water, seasoned with salt and chili pepper, and poured into the bowl over a slice of homemade bread. *Ribollita*, named for the fact that it is prepared, left to rest, and put back on the fire the next day, is a typical winter vegetable soup based on beans and black cabbage seasoned in the plate with a drizzle of oil instead of grated cheese. *Pappa con il pomodoro* is another poor man's soup that has become famous, prepared only with water and fresh tomatoes flavored with oil, garlic, basil, salt, and pepper.

MONTEPULCIANO

THE NOBLEST WINE

IT IS DIFFICULT TO DETERMINE IF THE EPITHET "NOBLE," which has accompanied Montepulciano's wine since the seventeenth century, is due to the nobility of the land, the vine, the wine, or the lineage of connoisseurs who sought it out. In order to maximize the value of the local hill wine the best stock of Sangiovese, known as *il prugnolo gentile*, was chosen. The eclectic author Francesco Redi in his book *Bacco in Toscana* (Bacchus in Tuscany) describes Montepulciano as "King of all wines," and according to the papal cupbearer it was deemed "perfect in both winter and summer." Vino Nobile di Montepulciano is a ruby red tending to garnet color, intensely perfumed, dry, and well-balanced. It is aged for two years in barrels (three years for the Riserva) and refined for six months in bottles. It can be served throughout the meal, pairs well with *pici al ragù*, a spaghetti-like pasta dish with a tomato-based sauce, and does equally well with the grilled *fiorentina* steak. Obtained from the highest quality grapes in the vineyard, there are still people who plant the vines by extremely historical methods. One of these techniques, *a settonce,* dates back to ancient Roman times and requires division of the land into equilateral triangles. The vine shoots are placed at the apex of every triangle, left to grow to a height less than the triangle's side length, and the ends are tied so that each

An overhead view of the town with its narrow, constantly intersecting, labyrinthine streets.

facing page
Vin Santo is an ancient wine, and the Avignonesi continue to produce it using traditional methods.

plant takes on the shape of a little oil lamp, as they refer to it locally. The Avignonesi family of Montepulciano employs this system in the family palazzo designed by the architect Vignola, and Le Capezzine estate, between Montepulciano and Cortona, produces a Vin Santo Occhio di Pernice with the same *prugnolo gentile*. This Vin Santo (named "eye of a partridge") is among the best in the area. Of the various explanations for the name Vin Santo or Holy wine, none have been proven factual, and the most interesting one takes us back to fifteenth-century Florence, where the bishops of the Roman Catholic church met with those of the Greek Orthodox persuasion in a failed attempt to unify the two churches. Legend has it that when the Greek Orthodox bishops tasted the Tuscan wine made from late-harvest dried grapes they said that it resembled the wine of Xantos, or that it was yellow—both Greek terms would have sounded the same to foreign ears. The Italian bishops liked the term because it sounded like *santo* (saint) and decided it was the appropriate name for the wine, which was also used for Mass. The Occhio di Pernice is a great wine when savored alone, but it can also be served with desserts that are not too sweet, as well as strong cheeses. It can be sipped with *cantucci* (almond-based Tuscan biscuits) or *Fochi* biscuits.

Pecorino Toscano DOP, recognizably branded with the initials TP, is the most characteristic and widespread cheese in the region. It has been made by shepherds since Etruscan times, and has graced the tables of princes and popes. Depending upon its ageing, the interior cheese can be soft and therefore best savored in slices at the table, or hard and ideal for grating over pasta and soups. In a land so oenologically rich it was inevitable that the cheese would sooner or later end up in the wine casks, and so the barrels used to refine the Vino Nobile di Montepulciano are then used to age Siena's Crete pecorino cheese. At the end of the conventional ageing process the forms are put into little oak barrels that previously held wine, and for another three months the cheese undergoes a second fermentation that results in a violet shade, a smooth consistency, and a hint of wine and grape skins.

Vino Nobile can be bought directly from the producers at the Le Capezzine farm or at the Consortium of Vino Nobile of Montepulciano's wine shop in Piazza Grande, which exclusively carries the Vino Nobile di Montepulciano produced by the member companies of the consortium, including almost all producers in the area. Pecorino cheeses, both fresh and aged, *fossa* cheese, and cheese wrapped in chestnut leaves under grape must or ashes are all available at the Cugusi dairy on a farm built at the end of the nineteenth century; the dairy also has a shop in the village.

P I S A
ALL TUSCANY IN A BREAD BASKET

IN TUSCANY BREAD IS UNIQUE, IRREPLACEABLE, AND OMNIPRESENT at each table and beside all kitchen stoves. Dante Alighieri, the first great poet of Italian literature, was a Ghibelline by both conviction and convenience, and as a follower of the Emperor's secular power in 1302 was banned from Florence upon the papal Guelphs' rise to power. While exiled in Ravenna he was forced to beg for hospitality, and he remarked at the time, "How salty is the bread of others." This was Dante's first taste of salted bread, because Tuscan bread is intentionally saltless in order to accompany, but not interfere with, the region's highly flavored dishes. From town to town bread is often made with slightly different flours and other ingredients, but the crisp-crusted, porous-centered loaf of homemade bread keeps Tuscans company throughout the day. For breakfast a slice spread with butter and honey is dipped in milky coffee, the mid-morning *fettuta*—a relative of bruschetta—is a slice of toast drizzled with extra virgin olive oil and rubbed with garlic, tomato, and salt, and in the afternoon one tops the bread with a savory slice of prosciutto or enjoys a buttered piece of bread dusted with sugar and dipped in wine. An integral part of all dishes with a vegetable base, a slice of bread is put in a bowl of soup before it is served, is grated over homemade *pici* (spaghetti), accompanies beans, soaks up the sauce left in a plate, and is indeed the very soul of every dish. At the end of a meal bread makes an encore performance with a plate of pecorino cheese, dried figs, and fresh grapes.

All ingredients of the Tuscan kitchen, in their wonderfully wide variety, grace the tables of Pisa. Wine and extra virgin olive oil top the list, but there are also specialties unique to this city. Until a few years ago the Arno River teemed with *cèe*, the tiny "blind" eel alevin used to prepare omelets or sautéed in oil with sage. They are a unique specialty but, given their rarity, fishing them is now prohibited and it is very difficult to find them in restaurants unless they are imported. Other local specialties include boar from the surrounding mountains used chiefly for sausages, white truffles of San Miniato, porcini mushrooms of Valdera, and pecorino cheese of Volterra, which is treated with olive or oak ashes (to keep it soft and prevent mold formation) and aged in wooden barrels to preserve its singular taste and perfume.

A rustic lunch of bruschetta drizzled with olive oil and paired with a glass of Chianti, polished off by cantucci with Vin Santo.

facing page
The white Duomo at sunset.

Bacchus wine shop offers many Tuscan labels, and excellent salami are sold at Falaschi in San Miniato and Giusti in San Giuliano Terma. Pralines are a specialty at the De Bondt chocolatier, and Morelli, the pasta factory of San Romano since 1860, produces a singularly scented and fragrant pasta. They use the germ of the wheat, which is usually left out to make the pasta last longer, and dry it at a very low temperature.

Pisa is a great producer of DOC wines, from Chianti to Montescudaio, from Vin Santo Occhio di Pernice to Bianco Pisano di San Torpè, which has been produced on the Pisan hills since time immemorial but has only recently been rediscovered and given this name, a reminder of a Christian martyr beheaded in Pisa, his body abandoned on a rudderless boat and found on the French coast in the village now named for him—St.-Tropez. This fine white wine is produced with Trebbiano grapes and has a straw yellow color, vine-like aroma, delicately well-balanced taste, and is served young with appetizers, fish soups, shellfish, and eels. The dessert variety, San Torpè Vin Santo, comes from the same grapes selected, dried, and aged for four years in small *barriques*.

PISTOIA
CHOCOLATE VALLEY

Monsummano Terme, Agliana, and Pontedera are just a few of the towns around Pistoia where many artisans produce chocolate of the highest quality, thereby giving the region the nickname Chocolate Valley, though chocolate is only one of their many specialties. Amid one of the few Tuscan landscapes not known for gently rolling fertile hills, Pistoia is the industrious heart of a region that specializes in artistic and industrial commerce. The mythical Vespa, first Italian *motorino*, was born at Pontedera during the early post-war boom years, Prato has been an important center of textile production and commerce since the Middle Ages, and Pistoia itself boasts of a rich financial past, today tending more toward industrial and agricultural activities, including its famous floral nurseries. At Monsummano the *Cioccolosità*, an exhibition that brings together the best Italian master chocolatiers, is held in January. Andrea Slitti works wonders here; according to the prestigious *Chocolate Companion* guide he is one of the world's best chocolate makers, and his tablets of GranCacao, with cocoa concentrations between sixty and one hundred percent, can convince even the most cynical chocolate skeptic to convert. His chocolate drinks flavored with cinnamon and chili pepper are

A balustrade of the Gothic Baptistery provides a great view of the Piazzetta della Scala and its fruit and vegetable market.

facing page
Cocoa beans and their precious powder.

almost impossible to resist. In Agliana artist Roberto Catinari sculpts chocolate into animals and other whimsical forms; his rose oil chocolates flavored with Vin Santo and Barolo fortified with quinine are also famous. In Pontedera the chocolatier Amedei produces single-cocoa chocolates with such a decisive and persistent taste that they leave the mouth with an insatiable desire for more. Porcelana, the most famous of these refined chocolates, is obtained from a very ancient, rare seed grown only on small Venezuelan plantations. Amedei has secured exclusivity on this cocoa bean's exportation so it can produce a truly unique chocolate, and has also ensured rights to export Theobroma ("food of the gods") and Chuao beans, which were originally from the Amazon forest around the Upper Orinoco River but are now cultivated on a small plantation in the Venezuelan Caribbean reachable only by sea. In order to produce the first bars of Chuao Amedei tried thirty-one different recipes, finally settling on a twenty-day ageing period. Forastero is the world's most widespread cacao, sixty percent of which comes from Africa, and produces up to thirty tons of beans per two-and-a-half acres of crop. Chuao and Porcelana, on the other hand, produce a mere 330 pounds, but their rarity carries an unequaled flavor.

Amedei in Pontedera is one of the pillars of the Chocolate Valley. Arte del Cioccolato in Agliana is a small store with an equally small workshop that produces 100 different types of chocolate. Slitti, in Monsummano Terme, world champion of sculptures in chocolate, is located in a former coffee factory, and offers a wide selection of wines and liqueurs to compliment the chocolate. Cioccolato & Company is an elegant shop in Massa, and Cozzile serves chocolate specialties. Local Pistoia wine can be tasted at Baldo Vino, along with savory cheeses and Tuscan salami.

The Val di Nievole lies just west of Pistoia and produces unique DOC wines from both ancient native and recently imported vines. The white, produced with Trebbiano grapes (but also with Malvasia, Canaiolo Bianco, and Vermentino), deserves particular attention. It is light yellow, has a slight wine aroma, is dry and well-balanced, sometimes slightly sparkling, and is best drunk within one year with appetizers, fish dishes, or fresh and sweet cheeses. Vinsanto, a dessert wine, is produced from the same grapes, specially selected, dried, and aged for three to five years in small barrels. It has a rich amber color, intense perfume, dry and slightly bitter aftertaste, and an alcohol content of up to seventeen percent. It can age in bottles for four to five years and is drunk cold at the end of the meal or with chocolate.

SIENA
HOME OF CHIANTI CLASSICO

THE CHIANTI AREA IS A SEA OF HILLS BETWEEN SIENA AND FLORENCE covered in vineyards and olive groves so well tended they look like gardens—a landscape so sweet and steeped in history that half the world has fallen in love with it. In the sixties there were so many British residents that it was dubbed "Chiantishire" by the Italian press, but since then its fame has spread through the whole of Europe and much

Aerial view of Piazza del Campo with its characteristic shell shape.

facing page
A parish church surrounded by vineyards at Castellina in Chianti.

of the United States, Australia, and New Zealand. Today the Germans love it so much that they call it "Chiantiland," and Chancellor Kohl's political opponent Oskar Lafontaine's party was nicknamed "Frazione Toskana." Naturally, this area in the heart of Tuscany became famous initially for its wine; with its production of nearly three million liters of DOCG wine per year, Chianti is the most famous wine in the world. It is also considered the most convivial, though unfortunately very poor imitations are often sold as Chianti. A local wine called Vermiglio first appeared in a notary's act dated 1398, and since the seventeenth century has been exported in its characteristic straw-covered flasks that prevented breakage. In 1716 the Grand Duke of Tuscany, Cosimo Medici III, passed a law to protect its name, and inevitably such an important wine entered the art world. Following the example of winegrowers of the Veneto, important Tuscan winegrowers asked distinguished artists to design their labels.

The various denominations of Chianti—Colli Fiorentini, Senesi, Aretini, and Pisani—all obtained the coveted DOC distinction in 1967, and twenty years later this was increased to a DOCG rating. The qualities that all share are their ruby red color, scent of violets, and dry, harmonious flavor that grows velvety with age. Since 1932 a vintners' association has protected Chianti, only allowing wine produced in the Chianti Classico area to bear the mythical black rooster on its label. This lucky symbol was born of a legend dating back to the thirteenth century, when Siena and Florence were constantly at war. They finally decided to establish a border by racing two horsemen directed toward each other's city in the early morning upon the cock's crow. Siena chose a white rooster as its signal to depart, and Florence a black one; the former took great care of their bird and fed it well, while the latter starved theirs. As a result the black rooster began crowing with hunger long before daybreak, while the well-fed white rooster slept until well after dawn. Thus the two horsemen met at Fonterutoli, a village only fourteen miles from the gates of Siena.

Cinta Sinese (Sienese Belt) is a native breed of pig named after the pale band around its circumference just behind the front legs, and is so distinct it is easily spotted in the medieval art works in which it appears, such as the fresco in the civic museum of Siena, the floor of St. Sebastian's Church, and the chapel fresco of Casanova di Ama. Its breeding is controlled by the *Compagnia della Cinta*, with whom all piglets must be registered and certified at birth. The pigs are allowed to roam freely in the area's woods and pastures, and particular attention is paid to their well-being. They are then turned into special meats including cured prosciutto, *spalla* (shoulder), salami, air-dried *guanciale* (jowl), lard, *capocollo* (neck), *soppressata* (hard salami in sweet and spicy varieties), and the traditional *buristo*, a savory Tuscan speciality made from parts of the head and cooked blood.

There is an excellent selection of Chianti wine at the Enoteca Italiana wine shop in the seventeenth-century Medici fortress, which includes a wine bar that stretches along corridors and vaulted rooms, and is also a center of cultural life in the city. Another broad selection of wines is on display at Il Salotto wine shop in Colle Val d'Elsa. Cakes and other confectionery splendors are made at Le Campane, and sausages and salami from the Cinta Sinese breed of pigs are available at the Antica Salumeria Salvini in Pisa. In nearby Panzano, Dario Cecchini is the only pork butcher who prepares the"tuna of Chianti," a meat of suckling pigs, called *lattonzoli*, cooked in *vin brusco*—the remains of the pressed Chianti wine—and preserved in olive oil, a curious process which results, unexpectedly, in a tuna-flavored meat.

right
Cantucci to dip into Vin Santo.

below
Chianti in its traditional straw-wrapped flask.

Siena's celebrated cakes and biscuits have a distinctly Middle Eastern quality, probably because of the merchants who for centuries passed through Siena on their way north and south. Siena's pastry chefs are so proud of their *panforte* and *panpepato* (flat and spicy fruit cakes) that they were even bestowed a patron, Saint Laurence. *Ricciarelli* (lozenge-shaped biscuits), were called simply "little marzipans" until the nineteenth century, in reference to their almond-based dough. Although not very elegant to look at, they were always offered to important visitors, and according to legend when Sigismund of Luxemburg visited in 1432 they were covered in a very fine layer of gold, which improved their appearance without changing their flavour. They are made of sweet and bitter almond flour (particularly the small but very tasty almonds of Avola called *pizzute d'Avola*) mixed with sugar and egg white. Because they are always prepared by hand, no two are ever exactly alike, and the almond oil helps keep them soft for several days. They are typically served at dessert with a good local Vin Santo.

right
Ricciarelli fresh out of the oven.

MONTEFALCO
EXORCISM WINE

SAGRANTINO, THE CHIEF WINE OF MONTEFALCO, is called *sacro* (sacred) because it was used not only for important occasions, but also in the rituals of an exorcist who lived in the nearby caves and sprinkled victims of demonic possession with the wine to banish the evil spirits. In memory of these rites *Scacciadiavoli* (devil-banisher) is the name of the Pambuffetti brothers' estate, part of which is the large cantina built by prince Boncompagni Ludovisi in 1880 following the model of the French estates in Bordeaux.

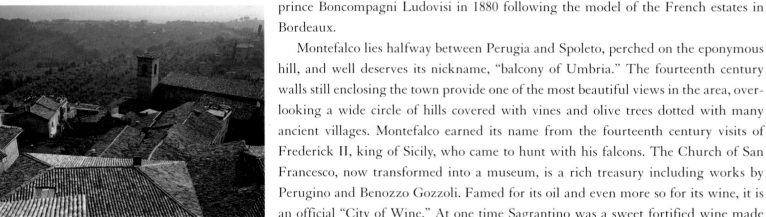

Montefalco lies halfway between Perugia and Spoleto, perched on the eponymous hill, and well deserves its nickname, "balcony of Umbria." The fourteenth century walls still enclosing the town provide one of the most beautiful views in the area, overlooking a wide circle of hills covered with vines and olive trees dotted with many ancient villages. Montefalco earned its name from the fourteenth century visits of Frederick II, king of Sicily, who came to hunt with his falcons. The Church of San Francesco, now transformed into a museum, is a rich treasury including works by Perugino and Benozzo Gozzoli. Famed for its oil and even more so for its wine, it is an official "City of Wine." At one time Sagrantino was a sweet fortified wine made from grapes dried on grates and enjoyed with sweetmeats at the end of the meal. This wine is still produced with a complete respect for tradition, and in the Palazzo Santi-Gentili a few steps from the main square stands the Centro Nazionale Vini Passiti, a unique institution for late harvest dessert wines. Much more well-known today, however, is the Sagrantino secco, a dry red wine with a strong taste, intense ruby red color, nose of blackberry, aroma of prune and cherry, and spicy taste which best accompanies dishes of game and hard cheeses. It is aged for at least thirty months, including twelve months in small wooden barrels, and it can be enjoyed immediately or aged longer in bottles for several more years, allowing the tannins to soften its edge. DOCG since 1992, Sagrantino is a wine of great personality, produced exclusively from vines brought to Umbria long ago by Franciscan friars from Asia Minor. It is appreciated around the globe and has been very successful in the last decade, making Montefalco an obligatory stop for wine lovers. The twenty-five-year-old Caprai is one of a select circle of wines available only in the world's best enotecas, and has received the prestigious Three Cups distinction for the past six years in addition to earning its producer the Oscar of wine.

A view of the hilltop village from the tower of the Palazzo Comunale.

facing page
Only 100% guaranteed Sagrantino grapes produce a bottle of Montefalco Sagrantino.

The ancient Greeks and Romans were probably familiar with wild celery, as documents prove its roots and leaves were used for various applications in the fifth century BC, but it was not used for human consumption until the Middle Ages, and only in the second half of the nineteenth century did large-scale cultivation begin. Cardinal Valenti, Bishop of Rimini, had it planted on the plains between the via Flaminia and the Clitunno River when he founded the Congregational Consortium of Water for the reclamation of the Clitunno area. The black celery of Trevi has particular characteristics, with dark green, very long stalks free of fibrous strings. The villagers claim that if eaten raw it can reawaken amorous appetites, and whether it is an aphrodisiac or not, a very crowded black celery festival is still celebrated annually on the third Sunday of October and attests to its popularity.

Montefalco is an official "City of Flavors," and here, in an ancient building facing the Palazzo Comunale in the center of town, stands the Federico II wine shop, an ideal place to taste a fine glass of wine, with outdoor tables in the summertime. Mundi, the pork butcher, is in the same piazza, and the wine and salami perfectly compliment one another. Bottles of Sagrantino can be bought at Scacciadiavoli and from other cellars of impeccable reputation, such as Val di Maggio-Caprai, and the Trevi farm produces the local black celery specialty and an excellent olive oil.

NORCIA
THE BLACK DIAMOND

PRINCE OF GASTRONOMICAL PRIDE IN NORCIA IS THE BLACK TRUFFLE *(Tuber melanosporum cittadini)*, known as the black diamond of Norcia. For more than forty years, each February it has been the main exhibit of a market fair that draws the largest attendance of similar fairs in all Europe. This treasure is the delicacy of ancient Northis (meaning fortune), built long before the arrival of the Romans beside the marshes of a fertile plateau, protected by an amphitheater of mountains. The gateway to the city is called Vetusta Norcia and attributed to Gregory the Great. The city was formerly known for its wool and jewelry, as birthplace of Saint Benedict, and for the ability of its butchers, who were expert in the castration of both pigs and aspiring opera singers, crafting the male soprano voices in particular. Today it is visited for its medieval architecture—which has fortunately survived many earthquakes, though the earthquake of 1859 destroyed six hundred buildings—for the beauty of the surrounding landscape (especially the protected park of the Sibillini mountains), and for its wonderful salami and truffles.

A field of sunflowers in sunny Umbria, the green heart of Italy.

facing page
Black truffles of Norcia are gathered near oak, chestnut, and holm oak trees.

The truffle has been a culinary keystone for at least five thousand years, ever since the Babylonian kings ordered it to be sought out in the sands of the desert. It has always been the object of curiosity, stimulating scientists and philosophers and fostering the many legends and myths created around it. The truffle's true identity has been in dispute for a long time: in ancient Greece the black truffle was the fruit of Aphrodite, goddess of love, because it supposedly had aphrodisiac powers; the philosopher Theophrastus believed that it was the child of rain and thunder, and the historian Plutarch said it derived from the fusion of earth, water, and lightning; the naturalist Pliny the Elder classified it as a "callous of the earth," a distinction that remained until the eighteenth century. We now know that the black truffle of Norcia is a round underground fungus, dark brown in color, sometimes tending to violet, with whitish veins, and a surface covered in wartlike marks. Its scent is aromatic and its taste delicate—it is also called the sweet black truffle. This morsel grows in the forests of oak in the Valnerina, in places practically free of undergrowth and called witches' circles. In the kitchen it is used to give aroma to dishes that do not have a strong or characteristic taste, and is therefore never served with cheese. It is used to season pasta, rice, stuffing, and as a pâté on toast. Unlike the truffle of Alba it is not eaten raw, nor is it truly cooked; it should just be gently heated with attentive care to bring out its finest flavors.

Prosciutto has been made in Norcia for more than a thousand years, and today the city can boast the coveted IGP distinction. Local prosciutto is salted, contains a fair amount of spices, and is typically pear shaped, with a dense meat to be cut into fine slices with a very sharp knife. In order to earn the name Antico di Norcia the leg must first be dried, smoked for eight months, and aged for an additional year. "Pocket" prosciutto is a piece of thigh stuffed into the pig's skin, and the typical salami of Norcia include *budellaccio* (intestine cured with salt and fennel seeds and dried on the hearth), *capocollo* (the upper part of the animal seasoned with salt, pepper, garlic, and coriander), *norcinetto* (small salami seasoned with salt, pepper, and garlic), and *corallina* (finely minced meat cured with salt, pepper, garlic, and marinated in wine).

Norcia, an official "City of Flavors," is famed for its truffles, which can be bought fresh in season or preserved from Ciliani and other pork butchers of the village. La Madia Regale in Ponte Sargano specializes in making sauces, pickles, pastas, and pâtés, and the most prized lentils in Italy are grown on the nearby plains of Casteluccio, at over 4000 feet of altitude. Small and green, with a high protein content and trace minerals, these lentils are so tender they do not need to be soaked before cooking, and should only be boiled for twenty minutes. They can be bought at the Cooperativa Agricola Il Casteluccio, where they also sell spelt wheat, organic barley, and chick peas.

ORVIETO
IN ETRUSCAN CELLARS

ONE OF THE MOST FAMOUS, OLDEST ITALIAN WHITE WINES IS THAT MADE IN ORVIETO. The Etruscans carved deep cellars out of the tufa cliffs atop which the town is perched, and fermented the wine there for many months, with the stone imparting a sweetish residue and pleasantly mellow taste. Orvieto white has been appreciated ever since, was highly acclaimed by the ancient Romans, and in the medieval period was an object of wealth, entrusted to vineyard caretakers who would protect the plants and wine production throughout the year. Luca Signorelli, the master who painted the chapel of San Bizio in the city's cathedral, was given as much Orvieto wine as he wanted as he worked, and in Pinturicchio's contract commissioning the frescoes in the Duomo of Siena the artist stipulated access to "a supply of Orvieto wine without limitations." In Rome, Pasquino, the statue hung with signs and statements that gave a satirical voice to the people against the city's abusive rulers, could not but praise Pope Paul V for the inauguration of the Acqua Marcia aqueduct, so he hoped for "as happy a miracle as if the water were to become the wine of Orvieto."

Orvieto DOC Classico is traditionally the smooth one, with a light straw yellow color, delicate and pleasant perfume, dry taste, and typical touch of sweetness from the noble mold *(Botrytis cinerea)* that forms on the grapes in the autumnal dampness, just as it does on the celebrated French Sauternes. Today, however, a dry version is also produced locally, as is a red Orvieto Rosso, full-bodied and best served with game. Orvieto is an official "City of Wine," but also organizes gastronomical events aimed at protecting traditional dishes, and schools for tasting to train people's palates to the unique flavors and aromas. Wine and food meet in the archetypal dish of Orvieto, the *gallina 'mbriaca*. This recipe of the old agrarian community, a legacy of when the sharecropper would go on Mardi Gras to do his duty and give two hens to the owner of the land. He naturally chose the oldest and toughest birds, but to refuse the gift would have been rude, so the chefs of the *padron* invented a recipe to render the meat edible. The hen is bathed in wine, covered in oil, garlic, and salt, diced, and marinated in Orvieto wine with vegetables and herbs a day before it graces the table. The following day it is slowly cooked for four hours on a low flame in a terracotta pot covered with a sheet of oven paper under the lid and kept closed tight by a weight.

The facade of the Duomo seems a richly decorated curtain.

facing page
An antique instrument for distillation.

Among the many caves carved into Orvieto's cliffs, there is one that contains the Mulino di Santa Chiara, the olive press of Saint Claire in one can see an almost industrial organization, with very orderly arranged containers for the olives, basins for the oil, and stalls for the animals that moved the large basalt grinding stones. It is said to have pressed olives from the time of the Etruscans through the seventeenth century. Orvieto's extra virgin olive oil, together with its wine, has always been thought to be the best in Italy, and since 1988 it has carried the ranking of DOP, an honor extended across the region of Umbria but subdivided into areas based on the characteristics of the territory and the olive cultivar. The commonest variety in the Orvieto hills is the *leccino*, which produces a delicate, fruity extra virgin oil.

The Enoteca Regionale Umbra wine shop, in the cellars of the former convent of San Giovanni, is such an interesting place that guided tours are organized through the underground passages dug out of the tufa. The Vinosus wine shop, on the central Piazza del Duomo, with a terrace that overlooks the surrounding hills, is also fascinating, and its excellent kitchen is always open for *spuntini* and hearty meals. Wine can also be bought from the producers, such as the Le Velette farm, and at the Titignano farm's excellent olive oil is available in addition to their wine.

PERUGIA
THE INDUSTRY BORN OF A KISS

THE PERUGINA CHOCOLATIER IS KNOWN ALL OVER THE WORLD, particularly for its *Baci* (kisses) made of dark chocolate with a chocolate and hazelnut filling. They are simple and satisfying, but above all they are a message of love, in both their name and in the tiny paper scroll hidden inside the wrapping that contains phrases and poetic quotes for lovers.

The elegant Fontana Maggiore is the central attraction of Piazza Grande.

facing page
Perugina's Bacio—a line of love with each chocolate.

This love affair with chocolate dates back to 1907, when Francesco Buitoni, son of the eponymous pasta magnate, married Luisa Spagnoli, and together with his father-in-law, Annibale, founded the Perugina Chocolate and Confectionary factory on Corso Vannucci in Perugia for the production of candied almonds and other sweet delights. Credit for the invention of the *Bacio* is attributed to Spagnoli, the popular fashion designer who in 1922 suggested that the hazelnuts left over from the preparation of other sweets should be used. Its immediate commercial success was due also to the packaging, which depicts two lovers under a starry sky designed by the popular illustrator Seneca, whose inspiration was Francesco Hayez's painting *The Kiss*. This mythical little chocolate has directed the development of the Perugina company for the past hundred years, and is the main exhibit in the firm's historic museum, which can be visited in the factory at San Sisto, where one discovers that it was originally called *Cazzotto*, punch, instead of *Bacio*.

The Eurochocolate festival is held in Perugia each October and attracts almost a million producers and tourists from around the globe. During the fair chocolate sculptures can be admired in every corner of the city, and all kinds of chocolate can be tasted—dark, milk, white, buttered, drinking chocolate, hazelnut chocolate, and large solid bars or tiny sweets. A stay at the Etruscan Choco Hotel in Via Campo di Marte is obligatory; all the furnishings are inspired by cacao, the cocoa bean, and its derivatives. Perugia's *Compagnia del Ciocolato* is a nonprofit organization that promotes the spread of chocolate and encourages new creations. The recent invention of chocolate with black truffles comes from Norcia. Seminars and conventions are held in addition to cooking classes and gastronomic weekends centered on chocolate, and the company works with public offices and the European Union to institute strict regulations protecting quality chocolate free of palm oil and other impure additives. The association's charter states that chocolate consoles the afflicted, is a greater stimulant than coffee, offers serenity to the soul, improves creativity, relaxes the nerves, and facilitates sleep.

Torgiano is a medieval village at the confluence of the Tiber and Chiascio rivers. Wonderful red and white DOC wines are produced here. The white, clear, fruity, and pleasantly acidic, is drunk young with appetizers and fish dishes, while the red is ready for tasting only a year after it has been bottled, and is best with meat and game dishes. Torgiano Riserva DOCG is the most famous of all Umbrian wines, made from Sangiovese and a few other native grapes, resulting in an elegant, full-bodied wine that perfectly accompanies red meat and ages quite well. Torgiano is an official "City of Wine," and in what was once the storeroom of the Palazzo Graziani-Baglioni on the farm belonging to the Lodigiani family there is an interesting Museum of Wine, which presents a historical panorama of vine growing, beginning in the Middle East more than two thousand years ago and running up to the present viticulture in Umbria.

Baci and other chocolate candies made by Perugina can be had in all the city's confectionary shops. Delicious homemade cakes and chocolates are available at the historical Sandri confectioner, founded on Corso Vanucci in 1860, and the traditional *torcolo* of San Costanzo, a doughnut-shaped biscuit, can be bought at nearby Alunni; the sweet's patterned surface decoration symbolizes the gates of the city. Products typical of the region are available at Geofoods, and wine can be tasted and bought at the Enoteca Provinciale, in an antique palazzo with vaulted brick ceilings and period furniture.

A N C O N A
FLAVORS OF THE ADRIATIC

ANCONA'S *BRODETTO* IS A SOUP JUSTLY CELEBRATED ABOVE ALL ITS OTHER TRADITIONAL DISHES, so much so that an academy of brodetto was founded with the goal of strictly monitoring the preparation of the dish so that it adheres to the original recipe. Equally widespread in the city is the *stoccafisso*, a dried cod that comes from the cold seas of Northern Europe and hasn't even a distant relative among the fish of the Adriatic.

The small region of the Marches stretches along one hundred miles of coastline encompassing nine major fishing ports and Ancona, its capital, has made fishing its standard-bearer to which it dedicates an annual fair unique in Italy and one of very few in Europe. Ancona's fleet consists of 130 motor trawlers, 50 *vongolare* boats for mollusk fishing, and 30 additional little boats that tourists can rent for an entire day and help with the work on board, releasing the nets and separating the catch. Fishing is an ancient tradition that owes its history to the rich variety of fish, shellfish, and mollusks that abound in the sea. *Garagoj*, a spiny-shelled murex, is a delicacy that Ancona's ancestors not only ate with pleasure but

Ancona's Mole Vanvitelliana, once a leper house, is now a museum.

facing page
Fishermen returning with their catch.

from which they also extracted a vivid purple dye for their clothing. The local *brodetto* was originally a soup made from unsold fish; at the end of each day every motor trawler has fish and shellfish that are not quite the best quality or too small for the market, and with these the fishermen prepare a dense soup, adding only a little seawater, vinegar, and olive oil. The soup's flavor differs according to the season and the fish left in the nets, and its preparation is always a challenge for the cook, who has to cleverly unite many diverse tastes. The recipe also varies from one port to another, and in Ancona it is traditionally prepared using anywhere from nine to thirteen different kinds of fish, shellfish, and mollusks. This mixture is slowly simmered with onions, tomatoes, parsley, garlic, oil, and vinegar. Slightly departing from strict tradition, today one can also add high-quality fish, fresh vegetables, and spices.

Stoccafisso is prepared with cod and various vegetables, herbs, tomatoes, potatoes, olives, and anchovies. The pieces of fish are first soaked for several days to revive their flavor then placed in a terracotta dish on dried canes or branches of rosemary stripped of its leaves. They are then sprinkled with Verdicchio wine and cooked for about three hours on a lively fire followed by an additional hour baking in the oven. It is served with Verdicchio from the hills of Jesi or, as tradition prefers, with a young Rosso Conero.

The Rosso Conero is a ruby red wine with a pleasant bouquet, dry, well balanced, slightly tannic, and full-bodied. It is aged at least two years before drinking and pairs well with rich food, stuffed pasta, and meat dished. At Numana, on the opposite slopes of Monte Conero, the Fattoria Le Terrazze produces a Rosso Conero DOC of great quality from pure Montepulciano grapes, as well as Chaos, a red IGT of international fame refined for a year in *barriques*. The owner, a serious fan of Bob Dylan, dedicated a wine to the singer-songwriter, calling it Vision of J. He presented Dylan with a gift of six bottles when he was in Italy for a concert and after some time, together with thanks, he received a proposal to produce wine together. For the time being he makes a custom wine for him called Planet Waves.

The Boccon Divino restaurant, near Piazza Plebiscito, serves excellent local dishes, and Emilia, a restaurant in nearby Portonovo, specializes in fish dishes and has a beautiful terrace overlooking the Adriatic. Those who love fish in all its varieties must visit the Salumeria Ittica Anikò in Senigallia, where all kinds of marinated, cooked, and canned fish can be bought, along with sauces to accompany fish dishes, "sausages" of mackerel, tuna, salmon, grouper, eel, and even sushi. Good local wines can be bought at the Mimotti wine shop on the outskirts of the city, or at the Le Terrazze farm.

ASCOLI PICENO

BETWEEN MOUNTAIN AND SEA

STAR OF SEVERAL TYPICAL DISHES OF THE PICENO AREA IS A TYPE OF PEA WITH A FLAT, tender pod and tiny seeds. Because they are eaten whole they've been nicknamed "mange-tout," and are locally called *taccole*. One of many gifts of the self-sufficient vegetable farming of a hard-working, land-venerating sharecropping society, they are usually blanched in boiling water and stirred into a pan with butter and tomato.

Piazza del Popolo, Palazzo dei Capitani, and the Church of San Francesco.

facing page
Only Ascolane olives will suffice for this pleasant pause.

Regional lore claims that a woodpecker, sacred bird of the ancient Roman god Mars, indicated to the Umbri—shepherd and farmer ancestors of today's population—the ideal place to settle, in the foothills of San Marco and at the confluence of the Castellano and Tronto rivers. History has since left an accumulation of villages with medieval castles and towers, including Ascoli, with its Roman ground plan, the Augustan bridge, and the arches of Porta Gemina on the Via Salaria—all ancient constructions still in use. The medieval aspects blend harmoniously with the austere travertine monuments and grand buildings that rise around the town's heart between Piazza dell'Arengo and Piazza del Popolo.

Here the land's produce has always held a key place at table, and the vegetables have been especially important since the first half of the sixteenth century, when the doctor and naturalist Costanzo Felici published *Dell'insalata e piante che in qualunque modo vengono per cibo all'homo* (Regarding Salad and Plants That Somehow Become Food for Man). This was one of the first Italian books of botanical science, and is filled cover to cover with culinary and health advice written in the form of a letter to the famous humanist Ulisse Aldovrandi, spiritual father of contemporary naturalists. The text describes cultivated and wild plants and herbs that, "without any shame whatsoever," could be brought to table, and not just the tables of the poor, but also to accompany sumptuous dishes in the houses of noblemen. Many of these herbs still grow wild on the nearby hills, and some are cultivated intensely, including various salads, artichoke, fava beans, zucchini, capsicum chili peppers, and eggplant. Of all these riches the most famous and highly exported is stuffed olives made with the Ascolana variety of olives, the best table olives in the world, praised by Pliny and Martial in ancient Roman times. Even though

A unique anisette can be sipped and bought at the historical Caffè Meletti in Piazza del Popolo, and the tender Ascolana olive, in brine, stuffed, or fried, can be tasted at Zè Migliori, a store with a special tasting section in front of the cathedral. *Taccole* and other vegetables can be bought at the Mastrosani farm in Montalto, and the nearby village of Campofilone is known for its pasta, particularly the famous *maccheroncini*, which can be bought at Spinosi. The Velenosi farm in Ascoli sells wine, as do the San Giovanni cellars in Offida.

Under the colonnade of Piazza del Popolo stands Caffè Meletti; opened in 1907 and recently restored, preserving its characteristic, elegant Art Deco style, a visit is obligatory to taste the anisette "with the fly"—with a coffee bean in the glass of liqueur. This was the beloved drink of the famous, including writer Ernest Hemingway, painter Renato Guttuso, muscician Pietro Mascagni, and operatic tenor Beniamino Gigli. Anisette liqueur (*anisetta*), with its distinctive anise flavor, is prepared with the fruit of the *Pimpinella anisum*, an herb very similar to star anise cultivated in the city's surroundings, which many people distill at home. In 1870 Silvio Meletti sold it in his little tobacco shop and it was in such demand that he decided to open the famous café in the neoclassical building in the Piazza del Popolo.

the extra virgin olive oil of the Marches is precious, only the smallest and bruised olives go to the presses, while the better, fatter olives are prepared *alla ascolana*. After being pitted by cutting the flesh in a spiral without breaking it, they are wrapped around a ball of savory stuffing of meat or sweet cream, rolled in breadcrumbs, and fried in oil. They are eaten warm as an appetizer or accompanying an aperitif.

Sangiovese and Montepulciano grapes that produce high-quality DOC wines are grown on the hills that descend from Ascoli to the seaside. Rosso Piceno, the most popular, is a full-bodied tannic wine with a hint of prunes and carob and a delightful scent of dried flowers and licorice. It is best drunk between the second and third year of ageing, though there is also a Superiore that is aged much longer, and it pairs well with bean or garbanzo soups, fresh stuffed pasta, sausage, main courses of meat, and surprisingly, with fish soups. Rosso Piceno Superiore is more mature and harmonious and is an excellent accompaniment to truffles, beef, game, and aged cheeses. Falerio dei Colli Ascolani is a fine white wine, with a pale straw-yellow color, scent of green apples and flowers, and a dry, smooth taste. Typically enjoyed when young as an aperitif, it is also a perfect match for fish, raw or steamed shellfish, vegetables, and soft cheeses. White and red DOC wines of note are produced on the hills of Offida. The red compliments the local food well and is excellent with *vincisgrass*, a special kind of lasagna pasta prepared with chicken giblets, stuffed pidgeon, or game. Offida Pecorino and Passerina are pleasantly acidic white wines (there is also a sparkling version) and they are coupled well with fish dishes and savory soups. A sweet, late-harvest *passito* wine and Vin Santo are also produced with these same white grapes and are best after a meal with aged cheeses and pastries.

left
Connoisseurs tasting
the Piceno wine.

below
Anisette "with the
fly," featuring the
omnipresent coffee
bean.

MACERATA

FAT PRINCES AND AMPHORAE OF WINE

IN THE HEART OF VALLE CAMERTE, PARALLEL TO THE COAST between Monte San Vicino and the Catria hills, the ancient Roman municipality of *Matilica* was settled atop a promontory dominating a bend in the Esino River. From this town's cellars comes a wine described by critic Mario Soldati, an expert in both wine and letters, as a "very refined rustic," referring to Verdicchio di Matelica, in its typical Etruscan amphora-shaped bottle—a shape now indicative of Verdicchio just as straw covered bottles distinguished Chianti. Verdicchio di Matelica is among Italy's great white wines, and all three versions in spumante, riserva and sweet passito are classified DOC, a rarity for wine produced from a single native vine. This unique wine has a strong personality, blond, fruity, slightly bitter flavor, and is best enjoyed within the first two years of age, though the special Riserva is aged twenty-four months. It pairs naturally well with fish, white meats, and many traditional dishes of the Macerata region, such as rabbit *in potacchio* with rosemary, roast pork with wild fennel, and even with salami and *stoccafisso* (dried cod). Verdicchio dei Castelli di Jesi, in still and spumante varieties, is a close relative, with a golden straw color, delicate and fresh flavor, bouquet of fruit and flowers, and pleasantly bitter aftertaste best savored young with fish and appetizers. Another high-quality native wine is the Vernaccia di Serrapetrona, a still red produced in dry and sweet varieties, the Marches only DOCG. The dry version is listed among the very important wines, whereas the sweet type is served with traditional desserts such as *pannociato* (a sweet bread cooked with spices, hazelnuts, and raisins), anise flavored biscuits, *torrone di Camerino* nougat, or with spicy cheeses. Up until the twentieth century it was offered on feast days with *sapa*, a syrup of white grape must. Another great wine that has yet to be more widely discovered is Colli Maceratesi, in both red and white types, also made from native vines. The white, like Ribona, is fresh, lively, and drunk young with shell fish, rice, soups, fish, and white meats, while the red and Riserva, somewhat less distinguished wines, go ideally with salami, pizza, cheese, and *vincisgrassi*, a very rich pasta casserole.

A bubbly version exists for many of these wines, and it is no surprise that there is a marked expertise in the production of *spumanti* in the Marches. Musician Gaspare Spontini used to drink it at his home in Maiolati at the beginning of the nineteenth century, a full fifty years before it began appearing in Piedmont, and by mid-century *spumanti* in the manner of "real champagne" were being produced in Fano and Jesi.

A classic bottle of Verdicchio dei Castelli di Jesi in the shape of an amphora.

facing page
The Abbey of San Claudio al Chienti is protagonist of Romanesque buildings around Macerata.

Vincisgrassi is a timbale of pasta similar to Emilian lasagna seasoned with a rich and spicy sauce of bacon, prosciutto, vegetables, chicken giblets, tomato, béchamel sauce, and pecorino and Parmesan cheeses. It was once an exclusive treat of the rich, the only who could afford it, and was called *salsa per princisgras* (sauce for fat princes) as described in the eighteenth century by Antonio Nebbia in his book *Il cuoco maceratese* (The Macerata Chef), probably referring to the obesity of the nobles who ate it. This name changed in 1799 when Austrian troops led by Prince Windisch Graetz invaded the Marches. The locals were so honored that the general liked their specialty that they decided to re-baptize it with his name, but because no one was able to pronounce "vindiscgraz" properly it was distorted into *vincisgrassi*.

Crisp, light Verdicchio wine can be bought in town at the Simoncini wine shop, or by going directly to the producers: Fazi Battaglia in Castelplanio, the most well-known producers of Verdicchio; the Tavignano farm in Cingoli; or Belisario, the cooperative cellars in Matelica, among others. Il Teatro restaurant is in a fifteenth-century palazzo in the center of Matelica, whose specialties are all regional dishes. The duchy of Camerino is also known for the *torrone* nougat made here since the seventeenth century, which can be bought today at Casa Franucci, or at La Marca along with many other typical products.

PESARO
AN INFINITE VARIETY OF *FUNGHI*

ALL OVER ITALY MUSHROOMS AND TRUFFLES ARE A REAL PASSION that inspires hundreds of hunters, rising at dawn from spring through fall, to scour woods and bushes to fill their baskets. In the Apennines around Pesaro many villages have made a very good living off of this natural treasure. Black and white truffles can be found almost everywhere and are collected year round in Borgopace, Cantiano, Casteldelci, Pennabili, Sant'Agata Feltria, and Sant'Angelo in Vado. Acqualagna can compete with Alba for its quality and quantity of white truffles; two thirds of all white truffles are collected here, and the most important wholesale mushroom market in Italy is also held here, featuring fresh produce, preserved mushrooms, and a multitude of mushroom-based creations. Depending on the season various kinds of mushrooms are found at Frontone and San Sisto and constitute the base of many local recipes. If the *porcino* (*Boletus* in its numerous varieties) is the king of mushrooms, then the *ovulo buono* (*Amanita caesarea*) is the emperor. It is one of the most sought-after, and it is so delicate and aromatic that it would be ruined by any kind of cooking. It is most often eaten with salad, and together with the *porcino* and white truffles is cut into thin slices and seasoned with a drizzle of extra virgin olive oil, salt, black pepper, and a drop of lemon juice. There are many other species of mushroom that are equally tasty even though they are less well known, and they fill shop windows and restaurant refrigerators of the entire area. The *parasole* (parasol, *Lepiota porcera*), also called the drumstick for its shape when still closed, is excellent raw in salad, grilled, or sautéed. The *piopparello* (*Pholiota aegerita*) is a delicate mushroom used in risotto, as a side dish, or preserved in spices and oil. The *prataioli bianchi* (*Psalliota campestris* and *Psalliota arvensis*), relatives of the classic champignon, are cultivated in grottoes and cellars, are much more savory and aromatic, and are eaten in salads or dried. The *orecchione* (*Pleurotus ostreatus*) is also cultivated on a wide scale, but those found in the autumnal woods beside the trunks of fallen trees are very notably better. They are fried, roasted in the oven with potatoes, and also eaten raw in salads. The *spugnole* (*Morchella deliciosa* and *Morchella conica*) have an excellent and distinctive aroma, and their curious hat is a beloved treat of gourmands, though one must be careful not to overindulge. The *finferli* (*Cantarellus cibarius*) are probably the most popular, with a delicate taste, an appetizingly strong perfume, and attractive look. They are ideal for risotto, with polenta, or as a side dish with meat they can be cooked with sweet onions and parsley.

The seventeenth-century fountain in Piazza del Popolo is fantastically decorated with seahorses and tritons.

facing page
A tempting basket of porcini mushrooms.

White truffles in autumn, and black truffles year round, can be bought at Le Trifole and Marini-Azzolini in Acqualagna. *Ciauscolo*, the pork specialty of Pesaro, is a soft pork salami, smoked and spiced, that is not cut with a knife, but spread like butter on bread, and can be bought at Bartera, in Orciano, or at the Baita, in Civitanova Marche. Bibi is the best place to buy wines, including the traditional Visner, a wine made of sour black cherries.

Bianchello del Metauro is a light, thirst-quenching wine that creates friendships and loves good company. It is a straw yellow color tending to green, transparent, with a light aroma of fresh fruit and spring flowers, pleasantly dry, and served within its first year with fish, raw shellfish, and other refined dishes. Colli Pesaresi Rosso is a light red color tending to violet, fruity yet dry, and best when drunk young with dishes with rich sauces, farmyard meats, and pecorino cheese freshly taken out of the caves and still humid. Colli Pesaresi Bianco is best enjoyed young as an aperitif or with anchovies, sardines, and other seafood appetizers. Vino di Visciola is a unique local wine, well worth trying, made from sour black wild cherries fermented with red wine and served with traditional desserts.

URBINO
THE MARKET'S BEST FOR THE DUCHESS

IN THE SECOND HALF OF THE FIFTEENTH CENTURY ARCHITECTS FRANCESCO DI GIORGIO MARTINI and Luciano Laurana built the Ducal Palace of Urbino for Federico da Montefeltro. It is an extraordinary complex that today holds one of the most prestigious art collections in Italy, and just outside the palace walls, under the elegant towers of the Ducal Gate, the market designed by Martini still stands. This large space was created to host the citizens' market, where farmers and shepherds sold the day's produce, and the first customer was certainly Beatrice d'Este, Duchess of Urbino and wife of Ludovico Sforza, the Duke of Urbino who was known as "the Moor." The Duchess, an enlightened noblewoman who promoted the arts and sciences, also appreciated fine cuisine. Local legend claims that she was an apprentice chef, even if the dishes associated with her name are more likely the result of the court's inventive French chefs. *Alla Beatrice* was the name given to the famous side dish of morel mushrooms, glazed carrots, and artichoke hearts, and she was also namesake of the *lumachelle all'urbinate,* snails with chicken liver, sausage, and Parmesan cheese. The duchess could count on having all the land's riches available, and the court received the best of everything, from vegetables to meat, and above all an excellent oil to perfume and delicately flavor every dish. Olive cultivation in the Marches has very old origins, as the excavation of oil containers from the eighth century BC testifies, and it was among the most prized oil. Venetian documents of 1263 refer to the duty levied on several ships that anchored at the Port of Ferrara on the Po River: twenty-five pounds of *marchigiano* oil were separated from the other oils to be taxed and resold at a higher price. *Frantoio* and *leccino* are the commonest cultivars, but mixed with some native varieties rediscovered in the past few decades they produce very different oils, with an infinite variety of nuances and aromas ranging from extremely delicate to spicy and almost bitter. Thanks to this rich variety an extremely high-quality "culture of oil" is developing, with a renewed interest in putting these special oils to the best use. Suggested combinations include: *plantone* from Mogliano to improve the taste of delicate seafood dishes and appetizers; *mignola* for dressing bruschetta, legumes, and grilled meat; *orbetana* for salads, tomato pizza, and cooked vegetables; and *coroncina* with legume soups, grilled meat, and vegetables.

The majestic Palazzo Ducale.

facing page
Harvesting ripe olives is done by hand to prevent them from bruising when they touch the ground.

Michelangelo Buonarroti was especially fond of *casciotta d'Urbino*, a springtime cheese he savored each April, at the seasonal height of its production. Made from sheep's milk and aged for only fifteen to thirty days, its youth ensures its sweet taste. It is best cut into squares and sprinkled with a little extra virgin olive oil and ground pepper, or enjoyed with figs, pears, or fresh, spring green fava beans. It is also used as filling in *tortelli* and ravioli, and the other pecorino cheeses of the region are often seasoned with marjoram, wild thyme, blackberry seeds, cloves, nutmeg, pepper, oil, and sometimes egg yolk. Alternatively, it is wrapped in chestnut leaves or herbs and preserved in oak barrels, and much like in Solgiano al Rubicone, Urbino also produces a pecorino aged in tufa caves called *Ambra di Talamello*.

The Fattorie Marchigiane di Montemaggiore, a farm in Metauro, produces and sell *caciotta* and other varieties of cheese, some flavored with truffles, as well as hosing tours of its farmstead. The Marches' best products can be tasted and bought at the historic Magia Ciarla wine shop, including wines and cheeses such as *caciotta* of Urbino and aged pecorino in walnut leaves. Villa Federici in nearby Serrungarina serves excellent dishes which superbly display the region's rich culinary tradition.

ROME

FROM THE ANCIENT ROMANS TO THE POPES

ROMANS' LOVE OF GOOD FOOD IS AN AFFAIR SPANNING SEVERAL MILLENIA. Ancient Roman banquets were sumptuous beyond all imagination, and in addition to the cuisine was entertainment to delight the soul. Nobles competed with one another, almost to the point of madness, to transform the table into a stage upon which to show off clever chefs and specialties imported from the most distant imperial colonies: prosciutto from Gaul, salmon from the Rhineland, tortoise from Arabia, hazelnut from Illyria, and wines from the Campi Flegrei near Vesuvius. The Latin historian Seneca wrote that Apicius, ancient Rome's most famous chef, fearing he might die of hunger, committed suicide when he realized that he had *only* ten million sestertius with which to prepare the banquets that had made his reputation. The dishes were probably more a show of expense and ostentation than a harmonious, hearty meal, when one considers the oft-repeated motto that "no one should guess what it is he really eats." Despite this, refined palates did exist—a point proven by the fact that culinary connoisseur Marcus Gavius Apicius was accused of distracting the youth because they preferred to pass time at symposia in his kitchen rather than attend lessons in rhetoric and science. He pioneered new recipes and approaches to cooking, feeding pigs with figs and grape must to make their liver tastier, and cooking snails in milk. The Popes later continued the pagans' good work, and save for a few exceptions, they were not distinguished for asceticism: Martin IV enjoyed eel marinated in Vernaccia wine; Boniface IX loved liver rissoles; Alexander VI had his meals prepared by his daughter Lucrezia Borgia; Julius III was fond of stuffed peacock; Paul IV sat at table for hours enjoying up to twenty dishes, and his successor Pius V had Bartlomeo Scappi, the most famous contemporary chef, in his service. His monumental *Opera dell'arte di cucinare* (The Art of Cooking) was published in Venice in 1570 and became the bible for noble kitchens across Europe.

Until the nineteenth century Rome was where the best food could be had at the best prices in all Italy. Famous recipes were invented in the Eternal City, and can be as simple as bruschetta or as elaborate as the timbale of Boniface VIII, as tasty as spring lamb (*alla cacciatora*), and as extravagant as *scottadito* (marinated meat stew), *saltimbocca* (browned veal scallops), and *puntarelle* (Catalonian chicory). However, whether one is dining at home or in any of Rome's hundreds of restaurants, the gold medal is invariably awarded to pasta: *spaghetti alla carbonara* (with egg and pancetta), *le penne alla puttanesca* (in a sauce of tomato, olive, and capers), and *spaghetti all'amatriciana* (imported from nearby Amatrice).

A Bernini angel on the bridge of the same name looks toward Castel Sant'Angelo.

facing page
Roman artichokes ready to be served *alla matticella*, with garlic, mint, and lemon.

The Colli Albani and Castelli Romani have been wine producing areas since the city's foundation, and are famous today thanks to the praise of famous ancient Romans. Most of this area's wines are white, enoyed young and fresh, and obtained from many varieties of Malvasia and Trebbiano vines. Frascati is probably the best known, has a straw yellow color, dry, delicate taste, and is the classic table wine savored in its first year with traditional Roman dishes. Velletri white, Zagarolo, and Montecompatri Colonna are also good whites. Colli Albani is typically served with appetizers, pizza, and bruschetta, while Marino pairs well with fish and dairy dishes, Colli Lanuvini with the local sausages and fish of Lazio. Almost all these wines are available in sweet, *spumante*, and *riserva* versions.

In the heart of Rome's historic center, a few steps from the Parliament, the Achilli wine shop provides an enormous assortment of wines, as well as local culinary specialties. In early evening as an aperitif they serve tasty little *spuntini*. The Buccone, a shop in another nearby historic building, has been selling wine since 1870. At Bomprezzi, a wine shop on Via Tuscolana, there is a fine selection of wines from the Lazio region at good prices. Pancrazio, a characteristic restaurant built over the ruins of the ancient theatre of Pompeii, serves traditional Roman cuisine, and other traditional Roman dishes and Jewish specialties are prepared at Giggetto al Portico d'Ottavia, near the theater of Marcello. Seasonal dishes and kosher products can also be enjoyed at the Il Sanpietrino restaurant, also in the ghetto.

A substantial Jewish community settled in Rome prior to the Christian era, and even constructed a synagogue in nearby Ostia. In the tenth century they settled near the Ponte Fabricio (a bridge to the Tiber island also called *pons iudaeorum* for its proximity to the Jewish quarter), expanding to the neighboring districts of Regola and Sant'Angelo. It was this expansion that induced Pope Paul IV to confine the group to a gated ghetto near the Theater of Marcellus, taking away their right to roam the city. The ghetto was officially abolished in 1870, but this area in the heart of the city's historic center remains home to over a hundred Jewish families who prepare their food as prescribed by their religion. Meat from non-ruminants, shellfish, pigs, rabbits, and hares are all considered impure. Animals brought to slaughter are butchered without suffering and completely bled before they are eaten. Several restaurants in the ghetto serve kosher food, with basic recipes modified into completely atypical specialties with Middle Eastern influences and savored with wine free of all additives and preservatives.

left
Outdoor dining with a view of the cloister of Palazzo Vitelleschi.

above
The classic Roman bruschetta is oven-toasted bread laced

with garlic, olive oil, and a little salt.

below
An abundant plate of penne *all'amatriciana*.

VITERBO
HIC EST VINUM BONUM

EST! EST!! EST!!! WINE OF MONTEFIASCONE IS PRODUCED WITH MALAVASIA and Trebbiano grapes grown in the volcanic earth surrounding Lake Bolsena. One of the most famous Italian wines, and one of the best white wines of Lazio, it owes its curious name to the story of Abbot Martino, who at the beginning of the twelfth century was hired by the German baron Giovanni Defuk (or Fugger) to travel before him on a voyage to Rome and indicate by writing *Hic est!* (it's here) at each inn where the wine was good. According to legend, Martino found a wine so good that he indicated it by writing *Est!* three times at Montefiascone, and that the baron drank so much of it that he died—his remains rest here in the church of San Flaviano. Est! Est!! Est!!!, a well-balanced white wine with a bright straw yellow color, fine aroma, and dry tending to sweet flavor, should be drunk very young, and is ideal with freshwater fish. It is produced in sweet and dry versions and as a *spumante*, and has a prime position at the annual *Fiera del Vino* wine festival in Montefiascone.

The characteristics of the earth and climate make Tuscia a particularly good area for high-quality vines, as can be seen from the centuries-old tradition. Many wines are sold with the DOC appellation Colli Etruschi Viterbesi, which is the most widespread, including a white, a nouveau red, a rosé, and some other local labels such as Grechetto, Moscatello, Rossetto, and Procanico. Vignanello is an equally rich vineyard area where a particularly good Greco Spumante is produced, and white, red, and rosé DOC wines are also produced on the hills surrounding Tarquinia. The most prestigious of all these wines is Aleatico di Gradoli, made exclusively from red Aleatico grapes grown on the slopes of the Volsini hills, producing a sweet muscat, garnet red with tones of violet, an aromatic scent, and the soft, velvety taste of fresh fruit. Reaching up to twelve percent alcohol and aged in bottles no more than four years, the best time to enjoy it is at two years, as an accompaniment to baked desserts. The stronger *liquoroso* type, on the other hand, is aged for a minimum of six months and often up to six years, reaching 17 to 18 percent alcohol with sweet, highly perfumed overtones, and is excellent served at the end of the meal or on its own throughout the day, though the best way to taste it is on the occasion of the *Pranzo del Purgatorio*, the Feast of Purgatory, traditionally held on Ash Wednesday in honor of all souls in Purgatory. Liquoroso Riserva is aged at least two years and is a classic wine of this region.

Palazzo dei Papi's crenelles viewed before a celestial background.

facing page
The wine cellar at La Torre.

The fish that live in the Tuscia lakes—Bolsena and Vico—are staples on the menu of many local restaurants. Most common is the *sbroscia*, a soup of fish from the lake that holds its own when compared with any saltwater fish soup. Tench is tender, tasty, and cooked *a porchetta*, stuffed with herbs and roasted on a spit with potatoes and wild fennel, or prepared as soup. Fillets of perch are prepared in many ways, most often roasted, and *Coregone*, very plentiful in lake Bolsena, are part of the salmon family, from which they take their taste and delicacy. They are cooked *alla bisentina*, as part of a mixed fried dish made with fillets of perch, slices of *lucci* (pike), and *lattarini* (tiny smelt). In his *Divine Comedy* Dante reminds us that the eel of Bolsena, the object of sinful gluttony that took Pope Boniface VIII to Hell, was the cause of perdition.

Est! Est!! Est!!! wine is produced and sold at the Falesco cellars in Montefiascone, and can also be tasted and bought at the Emporio Enogastronomico Meneghini in Viterbo, a small but well-stocked shop with many wines and other local products. This emporium is also home to the Provincial Olive Oil Producers of Viterbo. At Marta, on the shore of Lake Bolsena, the Gino restaurant serves delicious fish dishes. Hazelnuts flourish on the surrounding Cimini Mountains, and are used in a number of the sweetmeats and cakes of the area, such as the classic *tozzetti* biscuit. Higher up on the mountains high-quality chestnuts are gathered and sold, many destined for international markets. Locally they can be bought at the Giovannelli farm.

FARA SAN MARTINO
PASTA, FROM HOME COOKING TO HAUTE CUISINE

THE TRADITION OF PASTA IN ABRUZZO IS ALIVE AND WELL, whether it is homemade or commercially produced, and is not limited to classic spaghetti and macaroni, expanding to include new forms that are even the work of famous designers such as the industrial design firm Giugiaro. De Cecco's *Maccheroni alla chitarra* or *caratelle*, an egg-based spaghetti with a square cross-section named for the device used to make them, are typical of Abruzzese cuisine and are frequently served in restaurants. The *chitarra* (guitar) is a rectangular wooden frame across which very thin copper or steel wires are stretched just a few millimeters from each other, with a base to collect the cut pasta as well. The dough is laid in sheets over the device and pressed across the wires with a rolling pin. According to tradition the resulting pasta must be "thin as a hair, light as a feather, and perfumed like a flower." *Maccheroni al rintrocilo*, less famous but equally widespread, take their name from the carved rolling pin that is pressed into the dough to make oval strings of pasta about as thick as a pencil. *Maccheroni alla ceppa* are made by rolling little squares of pasta around a stick of wood (the *ceppa*), while *maccheroni alla molinara* are made of one single string of pasta worked by hand, a recipe that requires great ability. All are served with various sauces that are inevitably very flavorful, like the typical Abruzzese ragù made of veal, pork, sausage, cow's tongue, turkey, rabbit, bacon, chicken, lamb, goose, and chicken liver browned with fresh peppers, leek, onion, and garlic seasoned with juniper, marjoram, thyme, dried porcini mushrooms, and extra virgin olive oil.

Gentle hills at the foot of the Maiella area.

facing page Maccheroni, spaghetti, linguini, and *farfalle* are only some of the many shapes of pasta.

The best dried pasta in the region comes from Fara San Martino, in the foothills of Maiella Mountain, where two famous firms make wonderful pasta just a short distance from each other—Delverde and De Cecco. The quality of their pasta is due first to the spring of the Verde River, which rises out of the earth at a temperature of forty-six degrees Fahrenheit, and secondly to the durum wheat flour and the use of copper wire. The third factor is the slow drying at low temperatures, which can last for fifty to sixty hours, so that the surface of the pasta acquires an ideal roughness that allows it to cook well and perfectly absorb the sauce. Special pastas flavored with saffron, salmon, garlic, truffles, and many other, often unexpected, natural ingredients are also made. The De Cecco pasta company lists over one hundred sixty three types of pasta in its catalog, including those made of durum wheat, spelt flour, whole wheat, and other base doughs.

The *ventricina*, also called *vescica* or *miletta*, is the queen of Abruzzo's rich salami tradition. This extraordinary meat, which the King of Naples nicknamed "treasure of my Abruzzo" and poet Gabriele D'Annunzio lauded for the sensuality of its sweet, sharp taste, is a raw sausage in the shape of a sphere made from the noble parts of pigs raised in open pastures fed with cereals and legumes. The meat is cut with a knife, not minced, and seasoned with a hand-ground powder of sweet and spicy dried peppers, wild fennel, a little black peppercorn, and the only preservative allowed is salt. The bladder is stuffed with the meat, tied with string, covered with lard to preserve its softness, and hung to age in a dry, airy place for at least ninety days. It is served with fresh tomatoes and a classic red Montepulciano d'Abruzzo wine.

While the great pasta factories of Delverde and De Cecco produce excellent pastas, artisan pasta producer Cavalier Cocco makes unparalleled dry pasta with traditional methods and machines recovered from the ruins after the war. Many traditional shapes, such as *sagnarelli*, *taiarelli*, *rigatoni*, and egg based *farfalle* with saffron, can be bought here, and the fresh pasta made at La Sfoglia in Guardiagrele—where one can eat at the famous Villa Maiella restaurant—is also excellent. *Ventricina*, a soft salami, can be bought at the Fattorie del Tratturo in Scerni.

L'AQUILA

SPICES AND CHEESES OF THE HIGH PLAINS

THE GRAN SASSO D'ITALIA IS AN IMPOSING AND UNUSUAL LIMESTONE MOUNTAIN in the green backbone of the Apennines surrounded by high plains that slope toward the valley of L'Aquila, where an extraordinarily abundant variety of herbs grow. Campo Imperatore, a plain about eleven miles long at an altitude of almost six thousand feet, is the ultimate pasture, hosting thousands of well-fed sheep each summer. For centuries the shepherds of Castel del Monte, a village of medieval origin on the edge of the plains, have made *canestrato*, a pecorino cheese whose flavor varies according to where the sheep graze—Campo Imperatore in summer and Puglia in winter. *Canestrato* is a strong cheese with a definite personality, and a simple production because the shepherds had to follow the flocks and had little time to let the milk curdle and produce the cheese. It is aged between two months and a year, and is best enjoyed as the shepherds savored it: with a piece of *solina* bread made from a wheat flour cultivated on the central Apennines since ancient Roman times.

On the plains of Navelli, the best saffron in the world is produced thanks to a particular type of soil and the winds of the Maiella area. The stamens of the local crocus are larger and more aromatic that those in Iran and Spain and have won many international spice prizes. The *Crocus sativus*, the plant from whose flower saffron comes, is part of a distant culture and literature. Historically, saffron is one of the most precious spices in ancient gastronomy and medicine, and was used as a dye in painting and textiles. Saffron is literally worth its weight in gold; to gain a sense of its value one must only note that it was exchanged by the peasants who gathered it for an equal weight in gold coins, and in Florence in the Middle Ages one could more easily obtain a loan by offering two pounds of saffron as surety rather than one's own land or servants. This precious spice has roots in Asia, Tunisia, Spain, and the Mediterranean. Though there were strict Spanish laws banning its exportation, saffron was imported to Italy in about 1200 by a Dominican monk of the Santucci family, originally from Navelli. Crocus bulbs are planted at the end of summer and the flowers are gathered during the first light of October and November mornings. The stamens are removed, dried in a sieve over heated embers, and ground to obtain the famous fine yellow powder. Two hundred thousand flowers are required to make merely two pounds of saffron, worth approximately three to four thousand Euro, and each year just over twenty pounds of saffron powder are produced from the twenty-two cultivated acres surrounding Navelli.

The thirteenth-century Fontana delle 99 Cannelle has nearly one hundred spouts; each mask represents a lord of the nearby castles.

facing page
Crocus flower pistils are gathered for prized saffron.

Campotosto, a village on the western slopes of Gran Sasso, is the heart of a tradition and legend born on the banks of the eponymous reservoir, also the largest artificial lake in Europe. Mortadella of Campotosto is prepared with finely minced pork seasoned with salt, pepper, and several herbs. As it is packed a bar of lard is pressed through the middle, imparting flavor and preventing it from drying out too much during the ageing process. The little *mordatelle* are then tied in twos, hung on a beam to be smoked over a fire of oak and beech wood, and after fifteen days are transferred to the open air where they are exposed to the cold temperatures at 4,000 to 4,500 feet of altitude and the north wind, which ensures an excellent result. After three months spent absorbing this special atmosphere they are ready to be enjoyed.

Saffron and its derivatives can be bought from any local grocer, and from the producers like the Cooperative in Navelli, the farms of Papaoli in L'Aquila, and Peltuinum in Prata d'Ansidonia. *Canestrato* is produced at the cooperative of Campo Imperatore, and *mortadella* at the Mascionara Company in Campotosto. The lentils of Santo Stefano di Sessanio are well-known and can be bought from many of the farming companies, including Gabriella Costantini and Amalia Cardelli in L'Aquila.

Santo Stefano di Sessanio is an ancient village near Castel del Monte that has preserved the Renaissance architecture of its elegant palazzos—a vivid reminder that these lands were a fiefdom of the Medici rulers in Florence and witness to a flourishing economy in a mountainous area that otherwise appears harsh and lacking in resources. This well-being comes from the high-quality produce of the nearby fields, which are laboriously extracted from the rocky slopes of the Gran Sasso at an altitude of three to five thousand feet and are virtually free of insects and parasites. No chemicals are used, and each spring the fields become a jewel of innumerable wildflower colors. Since the eleventh century this is where, along with other vegetables and grains, prized tiny lentils have been cultivated. Grown in the same manner for countless ages, they are no more than a fraction of an inch in diameter, and are highly sought after. These miniscule *lenticchie* of Santo Stefano di Sessanio are tiny but contain a unique flavor and texture that shine in simple soups, many of which can be tasted in the village restaurants. Because of their porosity these lentils require no soaking prior to preparation, and are simply placed in a pot and covered with water. After adding a couple of garlic cloves, laurel, salt, and extra virgin olive oil, the lentils are boiled for about twenty minutes, after which the soup is poured into a bowl over a slice of slightly toasted bread and dressed with a drizzle of flavorful extra virgin olive oil from Ofena.

left
Lentil soup is typically served with fried or toasted bread.

below
Sheep have been grazing at Campo Imperatore in Gran Sasso for centuries.

PESCARA
D'ANNUNZIO DESSERT

THE DOME-SHAPED *PARROZZO* IS THE TYPICAL SWEETMEAT OF PESCARA. Prepared today with flour, butter, eggs, sugar, almonds, and bitter chocolate, it is the sweeter, more modern version of a similar bread that used to be made with corn flour. Writer Gabriele D'Annunzio, a native of Pescara, named it at the beginning of the twentieth century, possibly playing poetically with the words *pane rozzo* (rough bread), the name given it by local peasants to distinguish it from the refined white bread of the rich. *Parrozzo*'s true inventor, pastry chef Luigi d'Amico, substituted the yellow flour of corn with eggs, used chocolate to imitate oven-charred bits of crust, and added chopped almonds to the wheat flour in honor of regional tradition whereby sweetmeats are always almond- or walnut-based. D'Annunzio liked this sweet enough not only to name it, but he also dedicated a sonnet to it, a verse that still appears today on the trademarked packaging of the Parrozzo D'Annunziano. Several other handmade versions have other names—*Pan d'Aligi, Pan dell'orso, Pan ducale, Presentosa*—all of which share the same basic recipe. Amid *Parrozzo*'s class of sweets worth tasting are also the *neole* or *ferratelle*, wafers prepared according to tradition for important occasions such as weddings and baptisms. They are flavored with lemon peel or anise seeds and liqueur, and can be soft or crisp according to the type of dough and cooking; the soft version is rolled and filled with jam, cream, or chocolate, while the crisp type has filling layered between brittle wafers cooked in a special long-handled iron pan which was hand-forged and often decorated with the family crest or owner's initials. It's proper baking time was set by reciting an Ave Maria on one side, flipping the dough, and reciting a Pater Noster on the other. At Sant'Egidio alla Vibrata, a village bordering the nearby Marches, during Christmas festivities *Sassi d'Abruzzo*, irregularly-shaped sweets resembling dark pebbles, are prepared. First made to use up leftover almonds that were broken or somehow imperfect and therefore couldn't be used otherwise, these sweet stones are toasted and dipped in hot liquid sugar, cacao, chocolate, grated lemon peel, and cinnamon. Sometimes rum and cloves are also added before they are then cooled on a marble surface.

The canal port filled with fishing vessels and sporting boats.

facing page
The poet and author Gabriele D'Annunzio invented the name *Parrozzo* for his preferred dessert.

During his journey around Italy retold in the book *Bel Paese* (Beautiful Country), Abbot Antonio Stoppani refers to the fact that in the main and upper valley of the Pescara River the "wine is ambrosia, and oil is sweetness itself." Olive trees have been cultivated in this area since the fifth century BC and the delicately aromatic oil they produce was among the first to obtain the DOP recognition from the European Union. Unmistakable red Montepulciano and white Trebbiano are the region's wines par excellence, but aren't the only ones worth a taste. Moscatello is produced at Castiglione a Casàuria from a vine cultivated there since the seventeenth century and whose grapes are left to dry slightly on the vine, producing a dark straw color. This well-balanced dessert wine has the typical aroma of muscatel, is sweet with a bitter aftertaste, and can reach 15 percent alcohol, making it the perfect pairing for the region's sweets.

Luigi D'Amico, creator of the *Parrozzo D'Annunziano* dessert, produces it in smaller single portions called *Parrozzino*, and in a version without chocolate coating, called *l'Altro Parrozzo*. His shop, along with Caprice and other confectioners, is on Via Pepe, a street where many other delicacies of Abruzzese confectionary can be found. Moscatello and other local wines are produced by the Marrimiero cellars in Rosciano and Filomusi Guelfi in Tocco di Casuaria. The D'Alessandro wine shop, in the center of town, is a veritable boutique of Abruzzo's many delicious specialties.

SULMONA
THE ART OF DESSERT

THE CONFECTIONERS OF SULMONA ARE UNDENIABLY CREATIVE; D'Alessandro, who specializes in candied almond mosaics, was asked to decorate the table of the G7 meeting in Naples. He is famed for his spectacular desserts, including a candied almond caravel created to celebrate the five hundredth anniversary of America's discovery, now housed at the Columbus Foundation in New York, and an almost life-sized statue of a baseball player given in homage to Joe DiMaggio when he visited Italy.

It is well worth visiting Sulmona's Pelino Confectionary Museum to observe how the preparation of candied almonds became a specialty of the Peligna basin. The town's history predates the arrival of the Romans in the first century BC, and the well-preserved old town, with its fourteenth-century walls, attests to Sulmona's importance as a commercial center. The local confectionary tradition began in the fifteenth century, when Venetian traders brought their Middle Eastern imports in exchange for the rich produce of Abruzzo. Among the Venetians' novelties was a sugarcane syrup, and a local confectioner discovered that when the syrup was sufficiently heated it turned into a crystalline white paste with which almonds, hazelnuts, and orange peel could be coated. These treats were an immediate success and led to the infinite variety now produced to celebrate each and every special occasion. The colors, all achieved by natural means, are strictly coded: pink and blue for newborn babies, plain white for weddings, green for marriage engagements, silver and gold for twenty-fifth or fiftieth wedding anniversaries respectively, red for university graduation, and so on. Historically, these sweetmeats were produced in large cauldrons heated by wood or coal and shaken by hand to prevent the almonds from sticking together, a technique by which it took four days to achieve a layer of sugar compact enough to completely cover the almonds. The same approach is still used, although the exact method has been modernized in order to expedite the process. Sulmona is still home to five confectioners who produce these sweets using pure sugarcane syrup, without the addition of any starch, to coat blanched and unblanched almonds, hazelnuts, and pistachios. In addition to coating nuts, these candy shells also coat chocolate or liqueur centers and are presented in colorfully designed patterns.

The long medieval aqueduct built in 1256 by Manfredi, son of Frederick II.

facing page
All sorts of flowers for every occasion are handmade from colored confetti.

Lunch and dinner in Abruzzo are always followed by an *amaro* (bitter digestive), and the Casauria distillery still makes Centerba Toro using the recipe that Beniamino Toro perfected in 1817. This secret mixture of herbs from the surrounding Maiella area and Middle Eastern spices creates a liqueur that tastes slightly of mint, and with an alcohol content of 70 percent it is also incredibly strong. It is usually enjoyed after coffee and is sometimes poured over gelato or the local ricotta cheese for a unique dessert. A somewhat tamer, sweeter version with only 45 percent alcohol is also available. The same distillery produces Ratafiat, an elixir of Montepulciano wine and wild cherry juice, as well as Liquirizia (licorice-based liqueur), an excellent aid for digestion. Infusi dell'Eremo, a neighboring distillery, produces Ghentianè, an extraordinary cold infusion of gentian root and alcohol which is especially prized, as the wild yellow gentian grows almost exclusively in the high mountains of this region.

Among the many confectioners in the town, the history of the Fabbrica Confetti Panfilo Rapone can be traced back several centuries. These candy makers design artistic and original *bonbonnières*—boxes of assorted sweets. Pelino, another confectionary, was founded in 1783 and today produces fifty-four kinds of sweets, whose creation can be viewed in its annex containing a museum of the art and technology of confectionary. Cesaroni produces traditional homemade liqueurs, as well as the famous Centerbe della Maiella digestive, and the historic Casuaria distillery, located in Tocco di Casuaria, produces the Centerbe Toro.

TERAMO
SPECIALTIES OF THE SHEPHERDS

For thousands of years sheep have been raised and the land farmed in the mountains surrounding Teramo. The historic but today almost defunct ritual of the *transumanza* is still alive in this region; each May thousands of sheep gather in the high-altitude pastures, and each autumn they are herded to the foothills or migrate south all the way to Tavoliere delle Puglie, the plains of Puglia where a duty was paid before they were allowed to graze. Thus the local diet has always consisted chiefly of vegetables, cheeses, soups, and lamb served in infinite ways.

The most popular lamb recipe calls for cooking *al coppo*, in an earthenware bowl placed below the fires' embers, or *incaporchiato*, roasted and served with a side of potatoes. Innards are used to make tripe and *torcinelli*, giblets wrapped in bacon and lettuce. Large pieces of mutton are either roasted or stewed *alla cottora* and served with polenta, while the more tender pieces are sliced and grilled on skewers, making *arrosticini* so delicious that they are served throughout the day between meals.

In a tiny area west of the Gran Sasso mountain range the famous Farindola ewe's-milk cheese is produced. A secret method of production makes gives this cheese a unique character, and the rennet the farmers use is obtained from pork belly, a technique practically unknown anywhere else in the world and which imparts a special flavor and smell. It is sometimes aged for over a year, first in wooden cheese moulds and later in cupboards, and is periodically washed with extra virgin olive oil and vinegar, a process which turns the rind brown while keeping the core soft. The younger version is eaten after only three months, when it is considered perfectly ripe with a well-developed flavor. It is often savored at length in the mouth before swallowing because the distinctive flavor gradually expands. Farindola is regrettably hard to obtain, as only a very limited quantity is produced.

Vegetables enliven all first courses: *Scrippelle*, a type of crêpe, are either baked into a thin timbale with artichokes and scamorza cheese or served *m'busse*, in chicken broth sprinkled with pecorino cheese; *sparre*, lozenge-shaped homemade pasta, has a special mushroom and saffron sauce; and *pavoncelle*, butterfly-shaped pasta, come elegantly dressed in a vegetable sauce. Teramo's great pride, however, is a soup called the Seven Virtues. A delicacy requiring hours of preparation, it is served on May Day and is prepared with seven types of dried legumes, seven fresh vegetables, seven varieties of meat, and seven different leftover pastas which the good homemaker never wastes, hence the soup's name recognizes this wise, virtuous frugality.

The little church of Santa Maria delle Pietà, near Rocca Calascio, dominates the southern slope of the Gran Sasso.

facing page
A shepherd milks his sheep in a rudimentary pen before laboring to make savory cheeses.

Montepulciano d'Abruzzo is a smooth, well-structured, dark ruby red wine with slightly violet overtones and a cherry and licorice bouquet. Cerasuolo, another wine, is made of the same grapes left to ferment with their skins for ten to twelve hours. This is a cherry colored wine with a fruity nose whose delicately fresh flavor has a slight almond aftertaste. The first written reference to Montepulciano d'Abruzzo grapes dates from 1792 when they were cultivated in the Peligna Valley. These vines were introduced to the hills of Teramo in the early twentieth century, and in 2003 Montepulciano d'Abruzzo Colline Teramane was awarded the coveted DOCG quality rating. Its production is limited to only the best sun-drenched hillsides and it is aged in vats for at least two years, or three years for the Riserva variety.

Montepulciano d'Abruzzo wine can be bought at the Barone Cornacchia farm in Torano Nuovo, and for tastings the ideal place is the Enoteca Osteria Centrale in town, where traditional dishes of the region are served. The Locanda del Duca d'Atri, in the eponymous town, offers a broad selection of red Abruzzi wines, in addition to traditional products and dishes. The sweet *sassi* stone-shaped candies are made by the Galiffa di Sant'Egidio alla Vibrata confectioner.

Sunset over Capo Caccia, near Alghero, in Sardinia.

SOUTHERN *Italy and the* ISLANDS

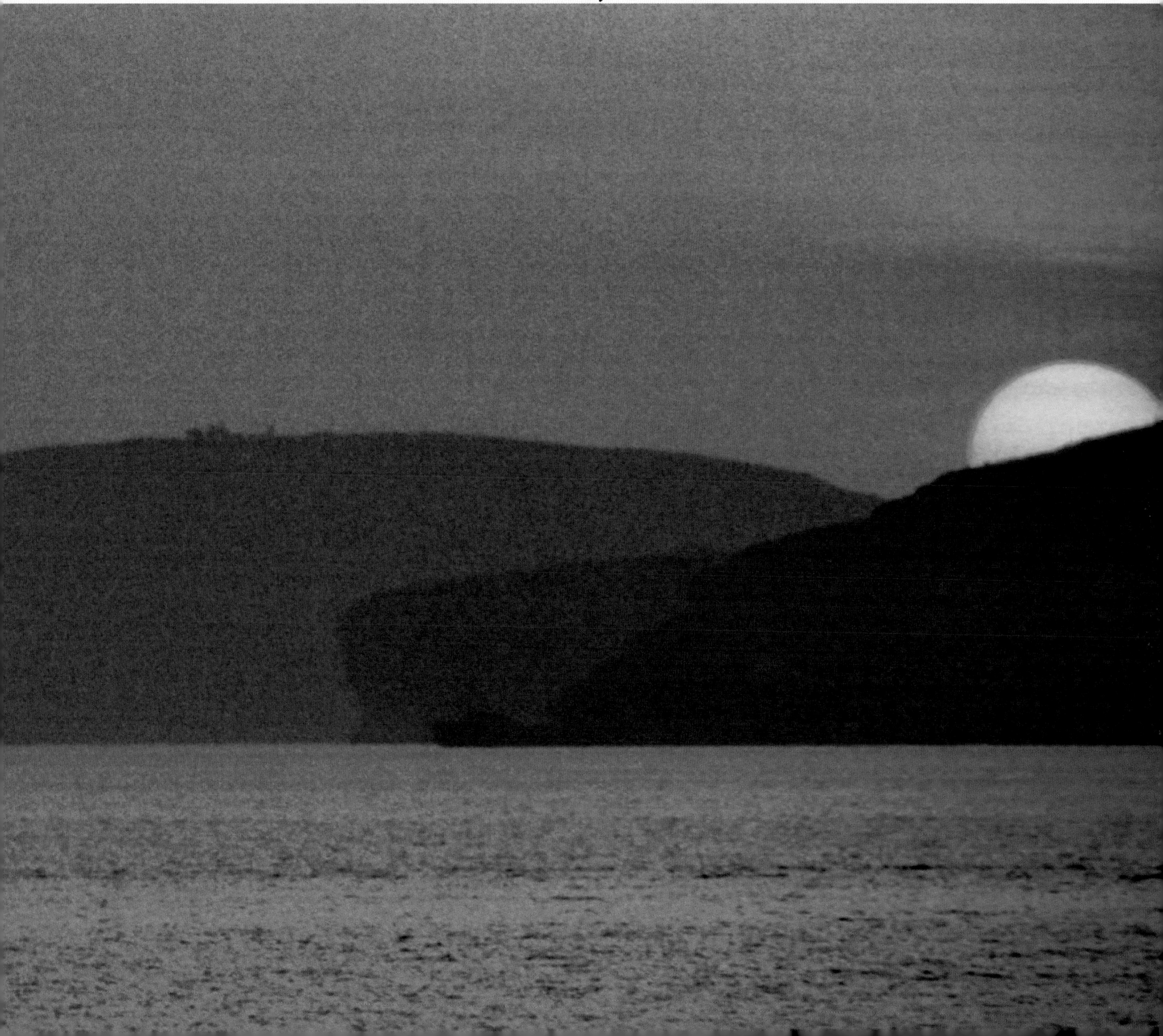

AVELLINO
THE NOBLE WINES OF IRPINIA

OFFICIAL "CITY OF WINE" AND CENTER OF A WELL-KNOWN ENOLOGICAL SCHOOL, Avellino is capital of a territory that in ancient times was inhabited by the proud Hirpini people, whose rule was enviously contested by the Etruscans, Samnites, and Romans. Local cuisine is based on a rich variety of vegetables, and the area boasts three great and historic DOCG wines. Avellino is off the beaten path of most tourists, but not even the many earthquakes that have tormented the area have managed to dull the landscape's beauty or cancel the traces of its glorious past. Remains of the ancient Roman *Abellinum*, medieval castles, and feudal palazzos in the area's numerous villages attest to this heritage. Agriculture and vineyard cultivation in particular are an inseparable part of Irpinian culture, and Taurasi was the first southern Italian wine granted DOCG recognition. One of the most famous red wines of Campania, Taurasi is produced in the Calore Valley sheltered within the protected natural reserve of the Picentini Mountains. *Vitis hellenica*, the vine introduced by ancient Greek settlers from which it is produced, today is called Aglianico, and its characteristics are due to the local climate and clay soil. Taurasi, which ages for three years in oak or chestnut barrels, is ruby red in color and acquires vermillion reflections as it ages. Deemed Vecchio (old) after three years, and Riserva after four, its bouquet is intense and persistent, aromatic and full-bodied. It is the ideal accompaniment to red meat, game, or hard and spicy aged cheeses, and is traditionally served with Neapolitan lasagna. Greco di Tufo is another fine wine celebrated by the writer Lucius Columella in his first-century book on vine cultivation. Grown in the Sabato River valley north of Avellino, this grape shares a Greek heritage with the *animea gemella*, brought to Italy from Thessaly. Considered an authentic nectar worthy of the gods on Mount Olympus, its color is straw yellow or golden, has a pleasant aroma and dry flavor, and is particularly well suited to fish dishes. Fiano di Avellino is an excellent white wine; light yellow in color, rich, with flowery aromas of peach and plum, a dry, well-balanced flavor, and a delicate aftertaste reminiscent of toasted hazelnuts. It is produced from the *vitis apiana*, named for the fact that the sweet grapes attract many bees, grown in a little-known area in the heart of Irpinia. Best served with fish and risotto, or as an aperitif, its characteristics lend themselves well to Fiano Spumante, a rare sparkling wine found in the best wine shops.

Lake Lacero, in the Picentini Mountains, is the only place one can ski with a view of the sea.

facing page
Bread, wine, and chestnuts help soften the onset of the first cold spells.

The incomparable chestnuts of the Montella are the stars of many culinary pleasures: they can be roasted in a traditional perforated pan; dried and made into flour with which *castagnaccio* or pasta (often tagliatelle and gnocchi) is prepared; used in jams, preserves, and cakes such as Mont Blanc, with marron glacé and whipped cream, or the *tronco di castagne*, a sweetmeat made of chestnuts, cacao, brandy, and cream. *Castagne del prete*, priest's chestnuts, are typical of the New Year holiday, and are made by placing the unshelled fruit in layers on wooden grates under which a fire of chestnut wood is kept lit for a fortnight. They are then toasted in ventilated ovens and rehydrated with a water-soaked cloth to prevent the shells from breaking. Once shelled, one can enjoy their smoky taste, which contrasts pleasantly with the sweet of the chestnut itself—a taste appreciated internationally, as half of Montella's chestnut production is exported to the United States and Canada each year.

The classic wines of Irpinia are sold in many farms and cantinas, including the Antica Hirpinia in Taurasi, the Feudi di San Gregorio in Sorbo Serpico, and Marsella in Campo di Maio. Hazelnuts are a special agricultural product of Irpinia, and nearly half of all hazelnuts cultivated here are destined for the national confectionary industry. Avella, a village near Avellino, has particularly sought after hazelnuts which are toasted in the oven and sold laced up like necklaces at the Antica Fattoria di Sant'Angelo all'Esca.

BENEVENTO
WITHCHES' LIQUEUR AND PAPAL NOUGAT

MEDIEVAL BENEVENTO WAS THE EPICENTER OF SATANIC RITES IN SOUTHERN ITALY, though today local reminders of the presence of witches is limited to a liqueur and a prestigious literary prize financed by an organization for Italian literature. One speculation is that the witches fled when the city began to prepare *Torrone del Papa*, a nougat prized by the nineteenth-century church's high prelates. *Torrone* and Strega liqueur are the two gastronomical specialties of Benevento, a city that also offers other, less exportable points of interest, including the ancient Roman Arch of Trajan, the Theater of Hadrian, and the Cathedral of Santa Sofia and the Duomo, both built during Lombard rule.

Strega liqueur, the famous drink of aromatic medicinal herbs, was first produced commercially in 1860 by Giuseppe Alberti when he rediscovered its recipe in an old Benedictine book of prescriptions. The Strega Literary Prize, created by his well-read grandson Guido in 1947, is still the most sought-after prize for contemporary authors. After a century and a half, the sixth generation now runs the business, and the headquarters are still in the nineteenth-century buildings in front of the railway station, where one smells the herbs and spices immediately upon arrival by train. As many as seventy aromatic herbs and medicinal substances are used to prepare the elixir, and its strictly natural preparation is a closely guarded secret—only two people within the company know it by heart. After distillation through steam-warmed filters, the liqueur is aged for six months in oak barrels before it is put into its classic transparent bottles, where it best shows off its golden color behind its original and uniquely ornate nineteenth-century label.

Torrone is a rather simple sweetmeat with a base of egg whites, honey, almonds, and hazelnuts. These few ingredients, however, require refined elaboration with constant attention, patience, and dedication. A similar nougat was made by the ancient Romans and sold in the streets by traveling vendors, and it became more widespread in the seventeenth century, when it was enriched with essences and liqueurs. During this period the first specialized varieties appeared, such as *Perfetto Amore*, a "perfect love" covered with chocolate, lemon, or coffee, and *Ingranito,* decorated with sugarcoated almonds and filled with crunchy "granite-like" sugar crystals. Under the Bourbon rule of the Kingdom of Naples hazelnut *Cupedia* became the traditional Christmas nougat. Today, classic white nougat with almonds, *Cupedia*, a soft variety with almonds, and many other tasty nougat specialties are produced in Benevento and await the honor of IGP distinction.

The Roman amphitheater is today host to summer productions.

facing page
Benevento's ancient nougat tradition lives in a place beyond time.

Benevento is an official "City of Wine"—certainly not because of its Strega liqueur, but because it takes first place in all of Campania for vineyard cultivation and can boast more than sixty types of wine, many of which are DOC and IGT. These wines are produced on the sun-drenched hillsides bordering the Calore River and in the vineyards of the Solopaca hills along the Telesina Valley, following a rich tradition dating back many centuries. The local white is crisp, excellent for the whole meal, and best enjoyed in its first or second year; the red has an intense and characteristic bouquet, a ruby color that softens with age, and a harmonious, velvety taste ideally savored within the first two years accompanying meat and lamb. The rosé, a delicate dry wine with a pale pink color, very perfumed and with a velvety taste, can be enjoyed as a refreshing glass between meals.

In addition to the famous Strega liqueur, the Alberti company produces sweetmeats and nougats that can be bought at their shop in Piazza Vittoria Colonna. Their *magie,* a type of *babà* with rum, are delicious. Wines and liqueurs are sold in town at Euroliquori and at the Cantina Sociale in Solopaca. Nougat is produced by almost every local confectioner, and is sold at the Fabbriche Riunite. Well worth a taste are the *Torroni Baci,* a paste of almonds and hazelnuts covered with chocolate, a specialty of the Vincenzo Borrillo pastry chefs in San Marco dei Cavoti, a village not far from Benevento where the nougat tradition includes a scrumptious crunchy variety.

CAPRI
A MAGICAL ISLAND

ONE NEEDS NO MORE THAN A SINGLE DAY TO FALL UNDER THE SPELL OF CAPRI and its scents, which change from dawn to dusk with a thousand different nuances. A single glass of Limoncello is enough proof that Capri is a magical island with a deep, hidden spirit that reveals itself only after long pilgrimages, after having "divested the tourist's garb," according to Chilean poet Pablo Neruda, who spent a long time in political exile here. The scent of oranges and lemons that billows out from under the funicular's terrace in spring is an unforgettable sensation preceding an extraordinary panorama. The same scent, with a slightly different undertone, permeates the air as one enjoys a pizza or a glass of wine from Monte Solaro under pergolas resplendent with lemons. Carthusian monks from Amalfi planted the first lemons on Capri after they had taken up residence at the monastery of San Giacomo in 1378, and it was probably the ancient Romans who had spread their goodness throughout southern Italy after discovering them from contact with the Arabs. For ages, however, Italian lemon trees were used merely as garden decoration, even if the Arabs had already discovered the precious quality of the essential oils from the flowers, fruit, and peel. It is also to the Arabs that we owe the invention of the distiller for obtaining its alcohol (*al-kuhul*) through the *alambicco* (*al-inbiq*), or filter. The resulting elixir (*al-iksir*), with the addition of herbs, was a vital element of the pharmacopoeia for centuries. Monks mixed the alcohol with aromatized syrups and began to produce *rosolio*, liqueurs, and bitters. Limoncello is one of these, and today a seafood lunch invariably concludes with a tiny cup of intense Neapolitan coffee and a glass of limoncello. It is also enjoyed in long drinks, poured over ice cream and fruit salads, used as a base for cream pastries, as filling for cordial chocolates, in *babà* pastries, and as a tangy center for various candies. Limoncello is a natural liqueur produced by soaking the rind of the *ovale di Sorrento* lemon, whose thick and wrinkled exterior is highly scented and rich in essential oils. This particular lemon is cultivated on Capri and the Sorrento peninsula with biological methods intended exclusively for this use. Preparation is simple, but requires forty days of infusion, and forty more to age before it can be tasted in full maturity. Limoncello liqueur has existed for centuries, but it was Donna Vincenza Canale who spread its use as a digestive throughout the island. In the early twentieth century, at the end each dinner in her Pensione Mariantonia in Anacapri, she served it to her famous guests, including the German industrialist Friedrich Alfred Krupp and Swedish writer Axel Munthe, as a "glass with a drop of sunshine in it."

The Faraglioni of Capri viewed from the gardens of the Villa of Augustus.

facing page
Only the best lemons create an excellent Limoncello.

Cetara, a fishing village on the Amalfi coast, specializes in making anchovies bottled with a bunch of oregano and steeped on the windowsill in the sun for an entire year. This process, called the *colatura* (pouring), requires extreme patience: work begins in May when the fattest anchovies are fished, cleaned, decapitated, and left for a day in a basin with saltwater to be completely drained of blood. They are then layered into barrels, salted with very dry sea salt, sealed shut with heavy stones, and put in cellars where they remain for eight months for proper ageing. In December the barrels are pierced and the liquid is collected (hence the name *colatura*), filtered, and bottled for flavoring pasta and boiled potatoes.

True Limoncello di Capri is produced by the company of the same name in Anacapri with Sorrento lemons grown by the Solagri cooperative using completely organic methods. In addition to this sunburst liqueur they also make a cream of limoncello called Liolà, limoncello chocolates, and limoncello babà. *Ciocconcello* is a chocolate cream with lemon, and sweets and a distillation of lemon called *Il Limen* are also made here. *Colatura di alici*, a prized liquid obtained from anchovies pressed under salt, can be bought at Nettuno in Cetara, which also preserves anchovies in salt and sells many other fish products.

CASERTA
NECTAR OF THE *TERRA DI LAVORO*

FALERNO WINE IS THE QUINTESSENCE OF THE *TERRA DI LAVORO*—the land of work, as the countryside around Caserta is called. Rather than referring to hard work, this indicates that the land is easy to work, generous in all seasons, rich in every kind of fruit and vegetable, and laced with vines that the Greeks brought in the first century BC when they landed in Campania, forcing the Etruscans to move north. Marcus Terentius Varro was a prolific Latin author of that period who wrote six hundred and twenty books, including *De re rustica*, a fundamental treatise on cultivation and farm animal breeding. He refers to Falerno as the best of all wines, created by Bacchus himself. Caesar toasted his battle triumphs with a glass of this nectar, and Cleopatra prepared her weapons of seduction with it. Falerno was also the first DOC wine, because for the first time in enological history a wine's territory of production—the Agro Falerno, at the foot of the Massico Mountains along the Via Appia—was specified. Fossils of a vine were unearthed here together with ancient Roman ceramic remains. For centuries ships left the *Porto Vinario* (wine port) at the mouth of the Garigliano River destined for ports all around the Mediterranean; an amphora of this wine was worth more than a slave, a fact that naturally resulted in it being the first wine broadly imitated.

Both the red and white Falerno of Massico are DOC wines today. Asprinio also has ancient roots, obtained from the only vine in Italy that is still cultivated *ad alberata*, as the Etruscans grew their vines, letting them intertwine with the branches of elms and poplars. A sharp wine with relatively low alcohol content, Asprinio does not last long, and used to be consumed by the farm workers who could drink as much as they wanted without getting drunk, though it has also recently gained some illustrious aficionados. It is a pleasant summer drink and is the ideal accompaniment to foods such as pizza margherita, with a simple but remarkably savory tomato sauce. Casavecchia is another local wine whose origins are more mysterious. It is a vine with red grapes about which nothing is known, except that its name comes from the fact that after the nineteenth-century epidemics of ioidium and phylloxera parasites, a large plant with a trunk twenty inches wide was found in perfect health beside the ruins of an old house at Pontelatone, where in ancient Roman times Trebuano, one of the most prized vines around Caserta, was produced. Perhaps it is the worthy heir of that ancient enological pedigree, harmoniously complete and well balanced, as befits a red of good breeding.

Fresh tomato, mozzarella, basil, and, naturally, olive oil make up the simple ingredients of the classic *caprese* salad.

facing page
The famed Fountain of Ceres in the palace garden of Caserta.

Buffalo mozzarella has been a local tradition since the third century, when the monks of San Lorenzo di Capua offered it to the canons who came in procession to the convent, and throughout Campania it has been produced intensively since the seventeenth century. This fresh cheese can should be eaten within a day or so, though it is also exported to Japan and the United States, where it arrives forty-eight hours later. It is named for the technique whereby the fresh cheese *mozzata* is delicately cut up into small pieces. After the buffalo milk is boiled its paste is sieved into a container where it is melted, then cooled, cut into pieces, and worked into its characteristic braided or ball-shaped form. After a few hours in salt and water it is ready to be savored, and is eaten fresh, seasoned with a drizzle of extra virgin olive oil. The cow's milk *fiordilatte* variety, which it resembles in form and texture but not taste, is better for cooking.

Le Bifore wine shop in the city center has a good selection of Campania wines and specializes in wines from native vines. A superb Falerno del Massico can be bought at the Moio cellars in Mondragone. Campania buffalo mozzarella and other cheeses of buffalo milk are available in Aversa at the dairy Andreozzi in Falciano del Massico, or at the Ater Consortium in Contursi Terme, who also produces *burrino*, ricotta, and *scamorza*.

GRAGNANO

SUNBATHED MACCHERONI AND SPAGHETTI

AT THE END OF THE NINETEENTH CENTURY GRAGNANO WAS THE CITY that produced the most maccheroni in all Italy. Cited as early as 1474 by Bartolomeo Sacchi, prefect of the Vatican Library, the region held this distinction well into the early twentieth century, when the pasta was still laid out to dry on rows of canes, and was removed to safety whenever a flock of sheep passed by. It is difficult to determine exactly what makes the pasta of Gragnano so good—perhaps the spring water from Monte Faito and the breezy microclimate ideal for drying the pasta. A dense concentration of artisan pasta makers still call Gragnano home, and there is evidence throughout the city and surroundings of this ancestral tradition, including the mills and shop signs of the old pasta producers along the main street.

Pasta has been made for thousands of years by many Mediterranean cultures. The ancient Romans learned how to prepare it from the Lucanians, who mixed flour with water and hung it out in large sheets called *lagana*, a predecessor of lasagna. It was then cut into large strips and cooked in the oven with a condiment that acted also as cooking liquid, just as some chefs make it today. Only in Medieval times did pasta achieve an important place at the table, and an infinite variety of shapes developed—wide and narrow, long and short, solid, stuffed, or hollow—and the practice of boiling it in water, broth, or even milk was established. The use of dry pasta also dates back to this period, as it allowed a lengthy preservation, easy transport, and thus commercialization on a grand scale. Many culinary historians attribute the invention of pasta to the Arabs, who created it as a means to transport food supplies during their wide desert travels, and later taught this technology to the Sicilians. Twelfth-century geographer Edrisi, who lived in Trabia, near Palermo, notes that a vast quantity of pasta was exported to many Muslim and Christian countries thanks to Genoese merchants, who were the first to spread the use of Sicilian pasta, and in turn later became producers of vermicelli and other types of dried pasta.

A view of the aerchaeological site at Pompeii.

facing page
Spring water, mills, durum wheat flour, and an ideal place to dry the pasta have secured Gragnano's fortune for centuries.

Gragnano Città della Pasta is an association of nine historic consortia who make over 160 pasta shapes, many of which are quite unusual. They are handcrafted and can be bought at the Storico Pastificio Garofalo or at the Antiche Tradizioni di Gragano. The La Verde Fattoria dairy in Moiano di Vico Equense produces a special sharp provolone cheese and a sweet version called *caciocantina*.

Provolone del Monaco—monk's cheese—has nothing to do with the classic provolone produced in the Po Valley. It is a round *caciocavallo*, a young cheese with a hard, smooth skin produced with raw cow's milk from cattle raised in sheds and fed with leaves and the strongly scented hay of the Lattari Mountains. Its name comes not from the fact that it used to be produced in a convent, but from the color of the rind, which is similar to the robes of Capuchin monks. After the tiring process of filtering, which often requires two people, it is drowned in brine and aged for at least 120 days, and often up to fifteen or eighteen months. It is sweet when fresh, and tasting it when just prepared is an experience not to be missed. It becomes sharp with age, acquiring a scent of hazelnuts, grass, and noble mould, and when mature it pairs best with a full-bodied red wine such as Aglianico or Montevetrano.

Pasta significantly changed the eating habits of Italians. It was historically cooked for a long time, not eaten al dente as it is today, and was served as a side dish to other food, most often meat. These habits still prevail in Northern Europe. The difficulty of gracefully managing pasta, in addition to its slipperiness and boiling-hot temperatures, led to the invention of the fork, a utensil used in Italy in the fourteenth century while in other European countries people still ate with their hands into the seventeenth century.

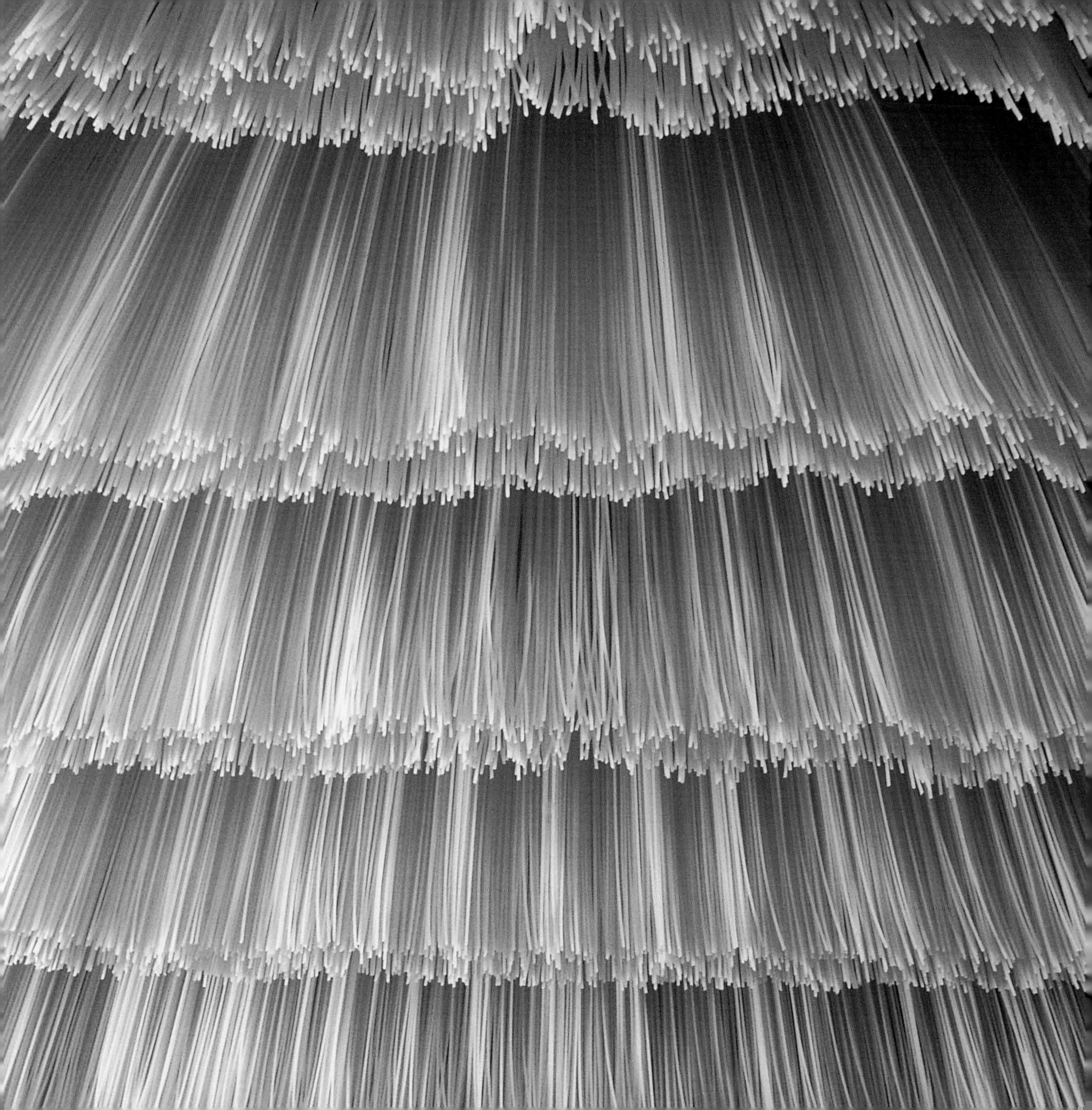

NAPLES
SWEET TREATS UNDER VESUVIAN SHADOWS

ACCORDING TO A NEAPOLITAN SAYING, NAPLES HAS THREE BEAUTIFUL THINGS: the sea, Vesuvius, and *sfogliatelle*. The *sfogliatella riccia*, a symbol of the seventeenth-century Rococo that made Naples a fashionable European capital, is a shell of thin layers of crisp pastry arranged with geometrical mastery and filled with a cream of semolina, ricotta, eggs, and candied fruit scented with orange blossom water, vanilla, and cinnamon. Nuns of the Monastery of the Cross are credited with the invention of this fanciful dessert, but inn owner Pasquale Pintauro later redesigned it to be held in the hand and enjoyed while strolling in the *passeggio*, a ritual city-wide promenade. This unparalleled dessert can be tasted fresh from the oven at the inn between Via Santa Brigida and Via Toledo, where Pintauro created it. The *pastiera* is the ultimate Neapolitan dessert, an Easter tradition since the fourteenth century and widely recognized symbol of spring. Local lore recounts that Maria Theresa of Austria, the wife of King Ferdinand known as "the queen who never smiles," tasted it at the insistence of her rather gluttonous attendant and liked it so much that she smiled. *Pastiera* is a base of short pastry that envelops a core of wheat grains, fresh ricotta, orange blossom water, cinnamon, candied fruits, and orange rind cooked on a copper baking sheet with a fairly high rim, and is served in this container because, even though it is only about three inches tall, it is extremely fragile. The popular nuptial *confarratio* was a similar dessert prepared by the ancient Romans to celebrate the return of spring, using ricotta mixed with wheat or spelt, but more recent Neapolitan tradition attributes its invention to the nuns in the convent of San Giorgio Armeno. Looking to create a dessert symbolizing Christ's resurrection, they mixed ricotta with grain, symbol of life ready to germinate, added eggs as a symbol of new life, and citron and spices that smell of spring flowers. Another traditional sweet, *babà al rum*, is associated with the eighteenth-century Bourbon regime, and is a mushroom-shaped dessert soaked in rum, filled with custard and cherries, decorated with whipped cream and strawberries, and accompanied with an egg cream enriched with marsala. The name comes from *baba* (grandmother) and is attributed to Polish King Stanislaus I, who took it to Paris where the Neapolitan court chefs then learned the recipe. It was a short step from aristocratic tables to public cafés, and it became so popular in Naples that a beloved, sweet person is still called a *babà*.

The dramatic entrance of the Maschio Angioino between two towers.

facing page
A mouth-watering display of Neapolitan pastries in the famous Café Gambrinus.

Tomatoes were brought to Europe from the Americas in the middle of the sixteenth century, but they were thought to be poisonous, and for over two centuries they were used only as ornamental plants in the garden. Only halfway through the eighteenth century did they find their way into the kitchen, and from then on their use spread exponentially, soon growing to support an industry of canning, bottling, and conservation so they could be used throughout the year. Today tomatoes are the preeminent vegetable of Italy, and the most famous type is undoubtedly San Marzano, cultivated on the lower slopes of Mount Vesuvius. This variety's firm and aromatic fruit is used to prepare sauces and preserves, and is reputed the absolute best for pasta sauce. Tins of peeled, diced, puréed, and concentrated San Marzano tomatoes are exported around the globe.

The Antica Pasticceria Carraturo has been in business since 1837, and is the ideal place to savor Neapolitan cakes. One of the most famous confectioners in the city is Scaturchio, founded at the beginning of the twentieth century in the heart of Naples, where you can find every type of warm *sfogliatella* fresh out of the oven. To sip a great coffee in the Neapolitan tradition, one must go to another historic establishment, the Antico Caffé Prencipe in Piazza Municipio. Many fine restaurants in Naples serve oven-fresh pizza, including Europeo and Poeta.

Pizza's uncertain origin dates back centuries, possibly to ancient Roman times, but the first records of true Neapolitan pizza, with tomatoes, anchovies, and capers, are rather recent, dating only from the mid-nineteenth century. In 1889 King Umberto I of Savoy, ruler of recently unified Italy, went to Naples with Queen Margherita, who asked to taste the famous pizza. Pizzaiolo Raffaele Esposito prepared a special pie with green basil, white mozzarella, and red tomato, to feature all the colors of the Italian flag, and called it pizza margherita in homage to the queen. Today pizza is known worldwide and protected by a certification that prescribes the base ingredients and their preparation in the minutest detail, even though it is made with increasingly diverse ingredients, including all imaginable cheese, fish, and vegetables. It is curious to note that this tasty flat bread, which could be bought at any Neapolitan street stand, became popular abroad long before it was popular in the rest of Italy beyond Naples. The first pizzeria outside Naples' walls opened in New York in 1905, and by the middle of the twentieth century it was popular in the cities of northern Europe, though in Milan it started to be eaten as a quick meal only in the 1960s.

below
Tomatoes, the base of many Mediterranean sauces.

left
Classic pizza margherita, with only tomato, mozzarella, and basil.

B A R I
LEGEND OF THE GODS' TREE

NO TREE IS DEARER TO THE GODS OR MORE WORTHY OF REPRESENTING nature's gifts and whims than the olive, whose trunk has been contorted and burdened with symbolism following nature's fancy. Symbol of fertility for Muslims, in Christianity the olive tree represents the life and peace God sent to Noah in the dove's beak after the Flood. Believed to come from Armenia, from Mount Ararat where the Ark came to rest, it more likely comes from an area between the Pamir Mountains of Tajikistan and Turkestan, and most certainly was familiar to the Sumerians and the Egyptians over two thousand years before Christ. It probably existed on the earth before humanity's arrival; when Adam died and was buried on Mount Tabor, a cedar, a cypress, and an olive tree grew from his remains, from the three seeds that the Angel had given to his son Seth. Zeus, the father of the Greek gods on Mount Olympus, rewarded Athena for having grown a tree that was so bountiful, and the statues of the deities on the Parthenon were rubbed with oil to help preserve them. Olympic games winners were crowned with olive wreaths, and the Spartans laid their dead on olive leaves. The tree spread over the Mediterranean five thousand years ago, conditioning the eating habits of all the region's populations. Ancient Romans set up an oil industry and held a stock exchange of sorts, the *arca olearia*, that controlled the flourishing commerce. The historian Pliny the Elder cites fifteen different varieties of oil available at market.

Wild olive trees were certainly present in the Murge Mountains around Bari, but the *Olea europaea sativa* was probably brought by the Phoenicians in the first millennium BC, and Achaean settlers planted them in the eighth century BC with techniques that they used in their homeland. Today the olive is an especially important source of income for Bari; oil from Puglia represents 40 percent of the national total, 20 percent of the European Community's total, and 12 percent of the world's olive oil production. Historically, olive oil was key for the local economy—Basilian monks arrived from the East in the thirteenth century, and taking advantage of the climate and soil they produced the first intensive cultivation. During the same period the first *masserie*, large farms, began to flourish (many of which have recently been turned into inns and hotels), and the port of Bari became a significant point for the export of oil sent all over the world. The quality of Bari's extra virgin olive oil is unequalled, and its prestige is slightly diminished only by the sheer quantity produced. Many producers are trying to combat this by guaranteeing the correct treatment of the plants and the harvesting of the olives at the right time in the most traditional way.

A glimpse of the Cathedral of San Sabino in the old city.

facing page
The grinding wheel of the olive press, as functional today as it was in Phoenician times.

There are many places that produce and sell excellent extra virgin olive oil: Cagno Abbrescia in Andria; Liso Nunzio, who also sells organic oil; oil from the first pressing at De Carlo in Bitritto, and Minervini in Molfetta, who produce one of the best extra virgin olive oils of Puglia. *Orecchiette* can be bought at the Ancora Fiore pasta producers, and the Centro Storico restaurant in nearby Locorotondo serves excellent *orecchiette*, with broccoli in the winter and tomato, basil, and *cacioricotta* cheese in the summer.

In and around Bari homemade pasta is created in the most diverse shapes, but always to insure that it will hold as much sauce as possible, as is the case with the *cicatadde* (known elsewhere as *accecati*) and the *strascinate*, little rectangles of pasta put through a special cutting machine that makes them rough on one side. The *recchietelle* (also called *orecchiette*, or little ears), symbol of Bari, are made from flour worked into warm, salted water and formed into serpentine finger-sized rolls. These are then cut into pieces a half inch long, pressed with the tip of the thumb to make a classic shell shape, folded back with a quick shake, and left to dry. *Orecchiette* cook in a few minutes in boiling salted water and are served with broccoli rabe tops, the quintessential vegetable of Puglia, cauliflower, or grated *ricotta marzolina*, an aged and slightly spicy cheese.

In Bari octopus is eaten *arricciato*, energetically beaten until it is soft and looks like a curled camellia blossom, and boiled for half an hour with onion, tomato, parsley, and hot pepper. This is the way the fishermen prepare it around the port, where there are strict rules governing its tenderizing, as in a challenge where the victor is already known. First the ink sac is delicately removed with one's teeth, carefully avoiding puncturing, as this part, called the malandra, rolled in flour and fried, is the most savory. The upper membrane is then removed, and the octopus is placed on a smooth stone and tenderized with a wooden stick. To truly complete the arricciata, the head must be held firmly and beaten at length rather violently on the rocks until the fibers have been completely destroyed. Finally, having washed it in seawater to remove any unpleasant liquids, the chef arrives at the last operation, which requires great patience and has a miraculous aspect to it. The tenderized octopus is put into a basket and rocked like a swing, so that the limp tentacles slowly begin to tremble as though alive, and then curl up until they look like curly hair, after which they are ready for cooking.

left
The sun sets behind
the roofs of the *trulli*.

below
Homemade
orecchiette.

205

FOGGIA
ITALY'S GRANARY

THE PLATEAU KNOWN AS THE TAVOLIERE DI PUGLIA is swept by a harsh and windy climate, and its soil is mineral-rich, but also chalky and porous, quickly losing any rain water that occasionally falls. This has been a land of oil and wine since the Phoenicians brought the first vines and the Greeks the first olive trees, but since ancient Roman times it has been known above all as the granary of Italy—the area that produces the most durum wheat. *Triticum durum*, with its heavy grains and paucity of starch, is by far the best for pasta and bread. Wheat has such a close relationship with the people of Puglia that it is not only milled, but also used directly in soups and sweetmeats. The oldest known recipe in which wheat appears is an inheritance of Cato the Censor, Roman consul of a plebian family, who taught the people how to polish grain in a mortar and use it to prepare polenta. For centuries local farmers have cooked *grano pestato*, a milled grain recipe in which the grain is pounded in great mortars to clear it of the husk, put in a basin to dry in the sun, washed, cooked in saltwater, drained, and served and seasoned with sliced onions sautéed with oil, salt, and pepper. In the wealthier households the seasoning was meat ragù, grated pecorino cheese, or sweet ricotta, and a more elaborate version of this recipe has been adopted by many restaurants in the region, which serve *grano pestato* seasoned with minced veal or pork, tomato, mixed vegetables, white wine, the local pecorino canestrato cheese, mixed herbs, and a variety of spices. An ancient soup, *lu farricèdde*, is still prepared on the Gargano peninsula, and differs from the *grano pestato* in that the grains of durum wheat are coarsely ground, mixed with the grains of soft wheat, soaked overnight, and then cooked and served with freshly sliced raw onion. In Foggia and its surroundings pasta is almost always homemade, but there are also several industrial pasta factories, many of which use traditional methods, running the pasta through bronze drawplates to give it a rough texture, and drying it slowly at a low temperature so as not to destroy the gluten. As soon as it is cooked the pasta gives off the scent of fields of grain, and the sauce that it has captured leaves a lasting taste of the wheat grain's core. The homemade bread of Foggia is also known for its high quality, and comes in many shapes, big and small; its taste is always delicate, whether it is sweet or salted, and though bread made from durum is not completely white, it keeps longer and better, and does not quickly harden as other breads do. The bread of Altamura is famous for its crisp crust and compact, porous center.

The road to San Severo is lined with chapels that lead to the Baroque Chiesa delle Croci, or del Calvario.

facing page
Wheat grains the color of gold.

San Ferdinando is one of the world's most important centers for the production of artichokes, known as *violetti di San Ferdinando*, Saint Ferdinand's violets. The ancient Romans called this prized vegetable *Cynara*, but it was Catherine de' Medici's gardeners who transformed the hard and spiny *Cynara cardunculus* into a tender and tasty plant now savored in many different cultivars. It can be eaten raw in salad or cooked in many ways: in a pan with garlic and oil, in the oven with olives and mushrooms, fried in oil, or stuffed *alla romana*. A real ceremony is to enjoy it *pinzimonio*, dipping it in oil, vinegar, salt, pepper, and spices. Being careful not to get pricked, take each leaf and dip it into the *pinzimonio*, tearing the tender part away with your teeth, until you reach the heart of the artichoke, which, after removing the inedible beard of surrounding fibers, is the most delicate part of the vegetable, deliciously dipped in the *pinzimonio* and recovered with a fork.

The most famous bread in Puglia is baked in Altamura, prepared with the hard wheat of the Murgia area and sold by Nunzio Ninivaggi, who also shapes it into strange forms such as crisscrossed braids or in the form of a priest's hat. The Pr.Ali.Na— Production of Natural Foods, with the curious abbreviation read like "praline"—is located in Melpignano, and transforms fruit and vegetables into preserves prized internationally as far and wide as Japan, the United States, and Australia, and are also found in many shops throughout the region. Local fruit preserves, as well as classic sauces of basil, olives, or hot pepper *arrabbiata*, are delicious, as are the typical southern sauces with artichokes, eggplant, peppers, and creams and pâtés to spread on toasted bread.

L E C C E
GRAPES FOR WINING AND DINING

THE ANCIENT ROMANS TRAVELED AROUND THE PROVINCES OF THE EMPIRE, and upon reaching the Salento, the heel of the peninsula, they would get drunk on *merum*. Merum was their true wine, and quite different from the *vinum* of the hills around Rome. They also enjoyed table grapes, of which many excellent qualities are still cultivated today and sold in over half the markets of Europe. For many years the wine of Lecce had a poor reputation among consumers, and was perceived as too strong and rough to drink socially, but northern wine experts and producers knew better—in particular the French, who in the nineteenth century had bought it to strengthen their own fairly weak wines. Today the Salento exports its grapes and wine to northern vintners who make vermouth and must used instead of beet sugar to raise the alcohol content of weaker wines. In recent decades there has been a great increase in quality, since almost every town now has its own DOC wines, including some of the most prized: Rosato del Salento; Salice Salentino, the oldest DOC in Puglia; and the Cacc'e mitte di Lucera, which roughly translates as "the more you drink, the more you like it."

A Salentino custom still practiced is the preparation of cooked must, a sweet syrup that comes from the fresh must of wine heated to reduce it to half its quantity. The ancient Romans mixed this syrup with snow for sorbets, and in the Middle Ages it was left to rest hermetically sealed for a month, after which it was employed in the preparation of sweets or mustard, whose name is a derivation of *mosto cotto*, or cooked must. Its preparation calls for grapes passed through a fine sieve into a copper pot to be boiled until a froth gradually forms that is then skimmed off. When the liquid has been reduced to less than half its original volume, the syrup is ready to be poured into tins or bottles and hermetically sealed. According to ancient belief, no woman who does not belong to the family may be present during preparation, as the must will not amalgamate properly, causing the sugars to sink to the bottom and the liquid to remain on top. At one time in Puglia cooked must was also made with ripe figs collected in the last half of August, cooked in a wood-burning oven for several hours until they became a soft paste, and then put it into cloth sacks that were hung in a well-ventilated room for twenty-four hours to drain the excess liquid. The paste was then put into pans and cooked again over a low flame for a few more hours until it became a dense liquid kept in sealed bottles.

The seventeenth-century Palazzo Vescovile.

facing page
The Regina table grape, the queen of Italian *uve*.

Many full-bodied wines of Lecce can be bought at the Giardino del Re and tasted with salami and cheese at Di Vino Bicchiere. Cheeses and other regional products are available at Sapori del Salento in nearby Tricase, and Calogiuri in Lizzanello has been producing *vino cotto*, a syrup of sweet grapes from fresh must, from a traditional recipe since 1825 without preservatives, additives, alcohol, or sugar and aged four years in oak barrels. In addition to traditional *vino cotto*, Calogiuri also produces liqueurs of lemon, figs, carob, and raspberry.

Canestrato, Puglia's most famous cheese, is named after the cane basket that gives it its shape. It is made from ewe's milk left to mature for several months until it becomes a hard, friable, sharp paste ideal for grating. Burrata, on the other hand, is a soft rolled sack filled with a spongy, creamy cheese invented by chance in the 1930s in Andria and now made across the region, though it differs from the similarly named burrino, which is a type of provolone with a heart of butter. Fortigna is a strong ricotta excellent for spreading on bread, and also used to season soups and pasta. Caprino, the archetypal cheese of Lecce, is produced in little round forms and eaten either fresh or aged, and ricotta marzotica is a light, fresh cheese covered with wild herbs.

TARANTO
TWO SEAS FOR A SINGLE PORT

A DEEP INLET IN THE AEGEAN SEA, CLEANLY DIVIDED INTO TWO ADJACENT BAYS, forms the *Mar Piccolo* (Small Sea) and *Mar Grande* (Grand Sea), which since ancient times have marked the destiny of Taranto as an ideal refuge for mercantile ships and as a key fishing port. The fish that reach the city market each day are so fresh they can be eaten raw, which is what was done for ages before the Japanese exported sushi and sashimi to the West. The fish should also be young, and sometimes even newborn, better for the unique strength of their flavor. Passing through the market one hears buyers at the stalls request tiny mullet, little prawns, little cuttlefish, little squid—everything diminutive, cute enough to inspire tenderness, not to mention a healthy appetite. True good fortune is manifested in any fisherman who cries "*alisce, alisce*" offering tiny anchovies fresh from the nets, providing a rare opportunity to really taste the flavor of the sea by savoring them raw and whole, complete with heads, tails, and bones. The same can be said for the sea urchins sold on the street in March and April, whose eggs are considered the best in the world, excellent as a sauce with spaghetti, but also simply with a piece of bread. Other traditional ways to prepare fish and mollusks worth tasting are endless: clams *arraganate*, with the upper valve removed and put in the oven with croutons, various herbs, tomato, and garlic; mullet in a paper carton with raisins, pine nuts, and aromatic herbs; mullet *a la crudele*, placed on the grill while still alive, or *a la tiella*, with rice, potatoes, clams, fresh tomatoes, parsley, garlic, bread crumbs, and grated pecorino cheese; anchovies *allo scapese*, fried and then marinated in vinegar and saffron, were prized by Frederick II. Finally, to taste them all together, there is the fish soup, which includes scorpion fish, gurnard, ray, sole, conger eel, crab, lobster, and shrimp. A rare sausage, *il tarantello*, is made from minced tuna seasoned with spices.

One of the greatest breeding areas in Italy for mollusks is Taranto's Mar Piccolo, considered one of Europe's best because the seabed teems with *citri*—underwater springs of freshwater—which provide the clams and oysters with a habitat that makes their flesh sublime. The largest *citro*, whose vortex is visible even on the sea's surface, springs from a depth of sixty meters and has been named *annello di San Cataldo* in honor of the city's patron saint, because legend has it that Bishop Cataldo threw his ring here to placate the stormy sea and avoid disaster. Taranto's clams, which are light yellow if male and brick red if female, are so good that it seems they are lost in local recipes—which serve them stuffed, with sauce, gratin, or with artichokes in a torte—and even simply looking at them one succumbs to the desire to don a metal glove, open them with a knife, and eat them raw with a fresh drop of lemon.

San Cataldo, patron saint of the city.

facing page
shellfish, including muscles, cockles, sea snails, and squid, among many others.

Manduria is an ancient Messapian city at the center of the Salento peninsula. It was protected by three circles of megalithic walls that have recently been excavated, and is the heart of an unequalled red wine land: the strong primitivo, named not because it is rough but because of the speed with which the grapes mature, was probably imported from Dalmatia centuries ago, and is similar to the Hungarian Zinfandel. This DOC wine has a pure, intense color, characteristic bouquet, can be dry or slightly sweet, and is excellent served with substantial first courses, meat, and aged cheeses. Primitivo di Manduria is also produced in naturally sweet and fortified versions, which can be enjoyed between meals or with dessert.

The Buongustaio boutique carries the typical products of Lucania, including some of the best goat cheeses, *caciocavallo podolico* cheese, dried cherry tomatoes, and eggplant with herbs. The Spiga d'Oro sells fresh pasta of all shapes, *cavatelli, sagne incannulate, fusili,* and *orecchiette* are among the most popular. The Casino del Diavolo is a local restaurant that specializes in homemade pasta dishes, particularly *maccheroni ai ferri* with fried bread. Matinelle, an inn on the provincial road between Matera and Gravina, is known for its fresh pasta dishes. A typical first course is *cavatelli a uno e tre dita*, a version of gnocchi pressed with one or three fingers, with different sauces according to the seasons. A superlative Canestrata of Moliterno wine is sold at Viola in Gorgoglione.

MATERA
WHIMSICAL PASTA

MATERA'S CUISINE IS SIMPLE YET IMAGINATIVE, exalting decisive flavors amid archaic surroundings that render each meal unmistakable, and homemade pasta is the quintessence of this unique gastronomical tradition. Dozens of different types are made with durum wheat flour and water, produced with creativity and possessing picturesque names. *Cavatelli*, small pieces of pasta rubbed between the thumbs, are one of the oldest and most common shapes of pasta in southern Italy, but here there are many variants—*capunti, strascinari, rascatelli* (called *raskatelle* in *Arbereshe* dialect, the language of the Albanese minority that lives in this region). Special instruments found nowhere else are used to make pasta, such as the *maccarunara* used to make maccheroni, or the *cavarola,* a small wooden cutting board used by shepherds on which pasta is rolled into *strascinati.* Many pasta forms are made with the *ferro* (iron), a square wire mesh; *ferretti* are made by rolling pasta dough around a tube until it forms spaghetti with a central hole much like a straw. *Minnicchi* are shorter and wider, made with the *ferro,* while a wooden stick or cane is used to make twirled *fusilli.* Where equipment is lacking handmade pasta becomes inimitable, like the *tria,* twenty- to thirty-inch long strings of pasta formed by making a hole in a ball of dough, widening it into a doughnut shape with swift circular movements until it forms a sort of long, thin rope, which is then wrapped like a ball of yarn, making sure that the strings do not break and do not stick together.

The oldest pasta of this region, formerly called Lucania, is *lagana*, which was enjoyed by the ancient Greeks and Romans, and is simply a layer of pasta cut into strips and seasoned with meat sauce or the more traditional sauce of garbanzo beans and tomato. Pasta *a mischiglio* is also of ancient origin, and is made with semolina flour and garbanzo beans, or barley and fava beans, and seasoned with bits of *cacioricotta* cheese and hot red peppers, or with fried bread flavored with chili pepper or horseradish. *Scorze d'amell,* "almond shell" pasta, is typical of Matera, and was historically prepared only on holidays. It reproduces the shape, roughness, and curled edges of almonds in their shells, which makes them ideal to hold the meat ragù sauce of lamb or kid. *Calzoncini materani* are unique ravioli of egg pasta with a filling of ricotta, sugar, cinnamon, and nutmeg seasoned with lamb ragù.

The shape of pasta is always a surprise.

facing page
Matera's Duomo rises on the spur of Sasso Barisano.

Lucania produces ewe and goat milk cheeses in abundance, and the most famous is canestrato, which has been produced since the Middle Ages at Moliterno, a town whose name comes from *mulcternum,* "the milking place." It is a hard cheese made from ewe and goat milk aged for eight months, resulting in a spicy and aromatic paste. Casieddo, another tradition in Moliterno, is a round goat cheese wrapped in fresh, plaited ferns, with the taste of mint leaves that flavor the milk before rennet is added. At the foot of the Lucanian Dolomites a cheese called *dei zaccuni* is made, named after the stubbly grass burned by the sun and eaten by the goats in the summer. This soft and savory cheese is excellent when warmed on the grill or breaded and fried. Local ricottas are also superior either fresh or aged in clay containers, and often flavored with hot chili pepper.

All the quintessential products of the Lucania region, including its incomparable goat cheeses, *caciocavallo* cheese, sun dried tomatoes, and eggplant with herbs, are available from the Buongustaio culinary shop. The Spiga D'Oro store sells fresh pasta of various kinds, including *cavatelli, sagne incannulate, fusili,* and *orecchiette.* The Casino del Diavolo restaurant specializes in first courses of pasta, and their masterpiece is grilled maccheroni with fried bread. The inn at the Matinelle farm, on the regional highway between Matera and Gravina, is famed for its homemade pasta, and their most beloved dish is *cavatelli* dressed with fresh sauces that change according to season.

POTENZA
THE LAND OF THE LUCANICA

IT IS SAID THAT THE SAUSAGE, OR *LUCANICA*, WAS BORN IN LUCANIA, whose name comes from the region that is also referred to by the Latin historian Marcus Terentius Varro in the first century BC. It was a stuffing of pork that had been prepared by the ancient peoples of the Lucani and today is made from choice lean meats of filet or thigh of pork seasoned with various herbs such as chili peppers, peppercorns, and fennel.

The ancient Romans knew them and appreciated them as part of the centurions' ration. They marched up the Basento River, which delineates the region as though it was its spine, and built the city of *Potentia* upstream. All around are lonely lands that live in contrasts, arid and serene at the same time, with pastures and forests, inhabited by hospitable and generous country folk. The name Lucania is derived from *lucus*, meaning wood or forest.

Pietrapertosa is a village clinging to the sandstone of the Dolomites of Lucania. The crest of the town bears an inscription addressed to their guests by the Saracens who founded the town around the year 1000: *Ahalan wa sahlan,* "You came among our people and your life is safe." The Val d'Agri lies at the foot of the Aliano and the aridity of the badlands on which it is built inspired Carlo Levi, the anti-Fascist author of *Christ Stopped At Eboli*. However, luxuriant forests, orchards, fields of vegetables and spices are spread out below.

Strong, genuine tastes—the *soppressata* and the *lucanica* sausages.

facing page
Olive and fruit trees with the Pollini Mountains in the background.

Tramutola, a butcher in the heart of town, produces sausages spiced with fennel, *soppressata*, *capicollo*, and spicy bacon. Lucana Salumi in nearby Piperno is particularly known for its sausage and is in the center of the Lucanica IGP area. The Perbacco wine shop in Lagonegro offers nearly all the wines of Basilicata and is considered one of the best regional wine stores. A renowned Aglianico wine is available in Rionero in Vulture from the Cantine del Notaio and the D'Angelo cellars.

To the south rises the mass of the Pollino, protected by one of the most intriguing natural parks in Italy. Northward is the Vulture, a mountain that remained unknown until it was discovered that the vines on the hillsides produced such high-quality wines that they are famous around the world. Pig farming has been the main activity in Potenza for centuries, although not on a large scale. The animals are fed with natural products such as maize, acorns, and broad beans. Apart from the *lucanica*, there are other pork specialties that should be sampled. The *pezzenta*, typical of the Alto Vulture, is prepared with the less noble parts of the animal and is abundantly spiced with chili peppers and fennel seeds. The *capicollo* is prepared from the part between the shoulder and the neck and seasoned with finely chopped chili peppers, salt, and pepper. The *vecchiareddra*, typical of the area of Pollino, is a sausage that is eaten cooked. The *ventresca* from Rionero is seasoned with chili peppers and garlic. The *soppressata* is prepared with the filet of the purebred black pigs reared in Lagonero. The rounded *vescica*, is probably the most typical of the sausages of Lucania. This is sausage and *soppressata* drowned in lard and stuffed into a pig's bladder. The prosciutto and the sausage of Bella-Muro are produced in limited quantities.

Imposing and isolated, Monte Vulture (from the Latin *vultur*, meaning predatory) is keeper of an ancient patrimony associated with Frederick II of Swabia, the most illuminated sovereign of the Middle Ages. It gave birth to Aglianica, one of the best Italian red wines (DOC since 1971). The Enotri planted it 2,500 years ago in the first *ellenico* vineyards. The name was twisted to *aglianico* during the Spanish Aragonese domination in the fifteenth century. The volcanic soil of the Vulture made it unique. Today it is produced on the hills of Melfi and is an ideal companion to roasts and game. It is aged in oak barrels and matured for at least two years, after which it displays a ruby red color with orange reflections and is characterized by an intense bouquet and an aroma of berries.

215

COSENZA
HEAVENLY HELLFIRE

HOT CHILI PEPPER IS THE WONDERFULLY DIABOLICAL SOUL OF CALABRIAN CUISINE, a direct line to the underworld, and called locally *pipi infernali* (infernal pepper) and the olive oil in which it is soaked is called *diavolicchio* (devilish). These names, rather than cause for guilt, are instead a reason to boast. The Italian Academy of Chili Pepper, headquartered in Diamante, a town near Cosenza, promoted a festival of "Three Hot Days" in New York in the spring of 2004, with conferences, exhibitions, tastings, and gastronomy competitions at the Italian Culinary Institute on Fifth Avenue, all intensely infused with chili pepper.

Chili peppers come in various types—long and horn-shaped, which the poet Gabriele D'Annunzio called "mad, fire-red devil's teeth," or small and round, red or green, mild or hot. The early-twentieth-century Futurists, led by writer Filippo Tommaso Marinetti, ate them raw with bare hands. When fried with the seeds removed they make a savory accompaniment to an aperitif, but they are mostly used in the kitchen after they have been dried in the sun and tied in long necklaces. Crushed by mortar and pestle, hot pepper is used everywhere to perk up otherwise plain food and add flavor to pork sausages, sauces for pasta, and meat gravy—it is even used to give an intriguing nip to dark chocolate. As child of necessity in a poor farming civilization, the chili pepper was used for centuries to mask the taste of unpalatable dishes of meat and to preserve food. Today, however, great chefs have been converted to its use, albeit with care, and they prepare refined dishes like oysters gratin with pecorino cheese and chili pepper, swordfish roe with eggplant purée and chili pepper, spaghetti with filet of sea bass and Calabrian "little devils," white chocolate mousse and chili pepper, and innumerable other delicacies.

The origins of the Capsicum plant, as befits an infernal being, are partly shrouded in mystery. Some claim it comes from the Orient, and in the Republic of Venice a red powder made from it was sold as "Indian pepper." Others say that Christopher Columbus brought it to Europe after discovering it on the island of Hispaniola (Cuba) and describing it as "a spice that burns, much more so than our pepper, and is here considered a panacea for many ailments." It is hard to say which theory is correct, because the same species of chili pepper grown in the Mediterranean are also found in Mexico and in India. The best example of these uncertain origins is that the scientific name of the habañero chili, thought to be the hottest pepper in the world and popular throughout the Caribbean and Yucatan, is *chinense*—"from China."

A pathway in the medieval quarter of the Castello Svevo.

facing page
Tied up with string, chili peppers are hung out to dry.

The licorice tree (*Glycyrrhiza glabra*) is typical of the Mediterranean scrub and has been cultivated for centuries for its healing properties. Calabria, one of the prime producers in the world, boasts the highest quality licorice root, recognized even by the *Encyclopaedia Britannica*. Its roots are minced to obtain a concentrate of black syrup that solidifies and is cut into slices or blocks. Soft licorice sticks and sweetmeats are obtained by adding gum arabic, and it is made into all sorts of confectionary delicacies, nougat, and liqueurs, and is often accompanied by mint, anise, orange, and violet essences. There are many producers around Cosenza; the most famous is Rossano Calabro, on the fertile slopes of the Sila Greca area, and the nearby Amarelli Company, founded in 1731, has a worthwhile licorice museum documenting its history.

The foods that best represent this region can be bought at I Magnifici del Mezzogiorno, where one can find all the many varieties of chili pepper: powdered, whole, creamed, stuffed, in syrup, and in preserves. Natura Med carries licorice, but the best place for anyone who loves this marvelous root is at Rossano Scalo at the historic Amarelli factory, which has been producing it since 1731 and where one can visit the unique licorice museum. Amarelli was awarded the Guggenheim Prize for entrepreneurship and culture in 2001, granting it an international importance. The Dottato variety of figs, particular to this area, are produced by Garritano in Cosenza and by the Marano brothers in Amantea.

Calabria's sweetmeats have been influenced by the Near East, and are extremely rich in sugar, honey, and candied fruits. A specialty in Cosenza is *bucconotti*, a small bun filled with candied jam or chocolate and minced almonds dusted with powdered sugar and eaten cold. *Chinuliddri* are typical Christmas sweets, shaped in a half moon filled with raisins, melted chocolate, minced almonds, cooked grape must, and cinnamon. *Cabbaita* or *cumpitti* is a soft nougat that resembles Turkish sweetmeats made with sugar and sesame. Spiral-shaped *scalille* are fried in oil and glazed with sugar or coated with chocolate. Rich iced nougat, shaped like a long cylinder, is sweet and colorful, made with marzipan and melted sugar full of cubes of candied fruit and covered with chocolate. The most noteworthy and characteristic sweetmeats of Cosenza are stuffed dried figs, and the *Dottato di Cosenza* fig is the best of the seven hundred varieties of figs in existence. After being sun dried for two weeks it is used in many ways, either alone or filled with various ingredients; the most typical version, which dates back to ancient Roman times, is sliced in half, leaving the peduncle, and filled with nuts, lemon, and orange rind. They are then set four by four in the shape of a cross, pressed, placed in the oven, and sprinkled with sugar, powdered cinnamon, and orange. Other versions are filled with minced hazelnuts, peanuts, toasted almonds, and bitter chocolate, or glazed with chocolate, molasses, or flavored with a myrtle berry liqueur. In the town of Guardia Piemontese, on the Tyrrhenian coast, boiled dried figs are shaped into balls, wrapped in orange leaves, and roasted into an unforgettable delicacy.

above
Delectably strong bits of licorice.

below
Branches of the licorice plant can be crushed to make licorice, or it can be nibbled whole to pass the time.

right
Figs laid out to dry in the sun.

SCYLLA
AND CHARYBDIS
RITES OF THE SWORDFISH

SCYLLA IS THE ONLY COASTAL VILLAGE ON THE TYRRHENIAN SEA toward the tip of the Italian boot to have refused the invasion of tourism. The main, centuries-old activity still alive today is the annual fishing of swordfish as they swim up the Strait of Messina from April to October. The old *luntre*, special high-masted rowboats, are no longer used, and the last specimen of this type of boat is preserved in the fortress over-looking the village. A sailor would perch atop the mast, often as high as thirty or forty feet above the deck, and look out for the fish. Once captured the fish were hung from the mast. Today's harpoon throwers stand on more modern gangplanks, but the ritual remains what it has been for centuries—including the cruel custom of killing the female first, knowing that in mating season the male will not resign at the loss of its companion, and is therefore easily captured. "Lu pisce spada," a haunting song of love and death by Domenico Modugno, poet-ically immortalized this dramatic relationship in the 1950s.

Scylla, on the tip of Calabria, is almost pushed into the sea by the Aspromonte promontory. This calm and charming fishing village's houses seem to emerge magically from the rocks, its narrow streets lead directly down to the sea, and lanes are often washed by stormy seas dur-ing bad weather. The name Scylla is inappropriate, considering that it derives from the Greek *skilax*, meaning bitch, and refers to the mythical monster with twelve deformed legs, six heads at the end of six long necks, and three rows of teeth, "pregnant with black and mortal poison," that lurked underwater and has entered, along with Ulysses, into the collective imagination thanks to Homer's epic poem. On the neighboring Sicilian shore, close enough to almost touch, stands Charybdis. For sailors he was yet another mythical monster who continuously swallowed and spewed the waters of the strait, caus-ing terrifying, ship-sinking whirlpools and strong, unpredictable currents. Unforgotten through the ages, today these legends live on, rendering this part of the Mediterranean even more seductive.

Swordfish steaks cooked in *agghiotta*, a special skillet, are a local delicacy covered with soft bread, toma-to sauce, potatoes, celery, capers, olives, onions, and occa-sionally pine nuts and raisins. *Alla bagnarese*, marinated in oil, lemon, parsley, oregano, and capers, is another specialty. If one is lucky enough to taste a freshly caught swordfish, it is best savored raw, finely sliced into a light *carpaccio*, or simply scorched for only an instant on the grill and seasoned with *salmoriglio*—oil, lemon, parsley, and oregano mixed with a drop of seawater.

Filets of freshly caught swordfish.

facing page
The Ruffo Castle on Scylla's promontory overlooks the sea separating it from Sicily.

Swordfish, and all the other fish that the market offers daily, can be tasted at the archetypal La Pescatora restaurant on the beach at Scylla, or at Glauco in nearby Chianalea, while enjoying the splendid view of the sea. The Grotta Azzurra seaside restaurant in Scylla also serves a candlelight dinner on boats that sail along the coast. The Bouteillerie and the Wine Shop in Reggio Calabria have a good selection of regional wines.

Calabria has produced unique wines since time immemorial, and in large quantities, if local historians are credible when they recount that seaside port cellars received wine from the hillside vineyards by means of an underground network of canals—called *enodotti*, or oenoducts—crossing the Sibari plain, and that vines were classified as trees, with such large trunks that statues and columns could be carved from them, like those unearthed in the temple of Juno at Metaponto, an ancient city on the coast of Basilicata along the Ionian Sea. According to the Tablets of Heraclea, written in the third century BC, vineyards cost six times more than an equivalent field of wheat. Seven hundred *palmenti*, sculpted stone vases for use in wine making, were found near Bruzzano, where a garden of ancient vineyards is being prepared, and will include two hundred ancient native vines, many of which were found in the surrounding woods and uncultivated fields.

TROPEA
AN ONION PANACEA

KNOWN AS THE "PEARL OF THE TYRRHENIAN SEA," TROPEA reigns high on a cliff surrounded by a fertile plain with excellent soil and a mild climate—even in winter. The red onion of Tropea has been cultivated here for millennia and is prized for its sweet, delicate taste, high mineral salt content, and the blessing that one's eyes never sting or water when it is sliced. The many positive properties of onions were beneficial even to the ancient Egyptians, who used it as a cure for snake wounds and insect bites. Ancient Roman doctors prescribed it in diets to maintain a healthy skin color and sound physical condition. Recent research has confirmed its diuretic properties and that it aids in the prevention of obesity, heart attack, other heart diseases, and helps purify veins and arteries. Historically, peasants used it to forecast the weather; they would remove twelve layers from the onion, spread salt over them, and by interpreting the degree of condensation that rose to the surface they could predict the following day's weather. Phoenicians brought the onion to the western Mediterranean a few centuries before the birth of Christ, and Greeks planted it in southern Italy, but only in the plains around Tropea did it acquire certain characteristics. People have tried to plant these special onions elsewhere but inevitably get unexpectedly different results. By the seventeenth century the fame of Tropea's onions had reached France and England, and in succeeding centuries local annals refer to the onion crops as the only important harvest that promoted commerce and produced wealth in the entire region. Its delicate fragrance makes it excellent for eating raw in salads, and it is also good cooked in the oven, in soups, fried, in preserves and jams, and served with strong cheese or meat dishes.

Curiously, local eggplant has never received the flatteries that the onion has. Originally from India and China, eggplant was brought to Italy by the Arabs at the end of the sixteenth century and found favorable growth conditions in Calabria's warm, dry climate whose silicate-rich, low-limestone soil imparted a sweet taste. This hearty plant received little culinary recognition until the second half of the nineteenth century, and was particularly ignored in northern Italy because it was believed to cause mental disturbances. In spiced oil or cooked with tomato and mint, eggplant is above all savored *alla parmigiana*. The name would lead one to believe that this dish originated in Parma, but it only refers to the use of Parmesan cheese, and the people of Calabria pride themselves for having created this famous recipe.

Oranges, mandarins, clementines, and bergamot are cultivated in the plains surrounding Tropea for their essences and are used in perfumery, pastries, marmalade, and other local specialties. The Costa dei Cedri, or Citron Coast, extends to the north and is full of these scrupulous trees that call for a particular soil and climate in order to thrive. The citron is the fruit of the Jewish *Festa delle Capanne* and is also used in perfumes and sweetmeats, while the thick rind is often candied and used in cake fillings or in refined praline chocolates. Citrus liqueurs are a popular tradition of this region, and are made from rinds steeped in alcohol for two to three weeks to absorb the essential oils. After the rinds are removed, the fruit-infused alcohol is mixed with a syrup of water and sugar, filtered, and left to rest and improve in flavor for another two or three weeks before it is enjoyed after a good meal.

facing page
A rope of red Tropea onions.

below
The Gothic church of Santa Maria dell'Isola, clinging to a precipitous seaside cliff, is the symbol of Tropea.

Highly scented
bergamot, a major
essence used in
pharmaceutics and
perfumery, also
lends its aroma to
sweetmeats and
liqueurs. *Bergamotta*
is a dome-shaped
pastry symbolic of
Reggio. Refined
bergamot-infused
liqueur is made by
La Spina Santa
agricultural group in
Bova Marina, and a
wonderful
bergamot-flavored
torte is the specialty
of the Pasticceria
Mimosa, also in
Reggio. Riviera dei
Cedri, a renowned
liqueur made with
an infusion of cedar,
can be purchased at
the Fabbrica Liquori
in nearby Santa
Maria del Cedro.
The agricultural
produce available
from Delizie Vaticani
includes the sweet
onion of Tropea,
which is also a key
ingredient of
delicious soups,
spicy pâtés, a
unique dish of finely
sliced onion with
raisins, an onion
marmalade, and the
bomba vaticana—a
hot sauce of onions
and chili peppers.

AGRIGENTO
SCENTS OF THE SEA MEET
FLAVORS OF THE FIELDS

FACING THE SICILIAN CHANNEL AT THE CENTER OF SOUTHERN SICILY, Agrigento combines the flavors of the sea with those of the land, and is as proud of its maccheroni with tomato and eggplant sauce as it is of its spaghetti with octopus ink, grouper soup, and pasta *'ncaciata*, covered with pecorino cheese and browned in the oven. On the hills behind the Valley of the Temples sheep graze freely, feeding on aromatic herbs, and cheese from their milk is prepared using ancient wooden and cane instruments and aged in natural caves. Classic Sicilian pecorino is the oldest cheese on the island, and Latin historian Pliny the Elder cites it in his *Naturalis historia*, indicating Agrigento as home of the best, and owes its excellence to the fact that in thousands of years it has not changed. When it is fresh and still unsalted it is sweet and aromatic, after which it undergoes two successive applications of salt. Following at least three months of ageing it becomes the real pecorino siciliano, a compact cheese with tiny holes, perfumed and tasty, excellent served in slices or grated. It is also produced in a version with little grains of black pepper that give it a strong, spicy taste, and it is traditionally accompanied by a red Nero d'Avola or Cerasuolo di Vittoria wine.

The Greek Temple of Concord, emblem of the Valley of the Temples.

facing page
Pecorino, *provola*, and *burrino* cheeses displayed in a Sicilian market.

Sicily is a large triangular island (hence its other name, *Trinacria*) surrounded by seas rich with many varieties of fish. Swordfish is caught in the Strait of Messina, and as far south as the Ionian Sea there are great schools of grouper, bream, and mackerel. On the northern coast along the Tyrrhenian Sea, striped sea bream, cuttlefish, squid, and crustaceans can be found. The Sicilian Channel meets the southern coast at the most active fishing port of Sicily, Mazara del Vallo, where everything from tuna to anchovies can be fished. Naturally, fish is almost omnipresent in the island's meals, cooked in many ways, served on its own, or with pasta. The recipes leave much to the imagination of the chef, but every one of them enhances the taste of each kind of fish. Accordingly, bream is grilled, dentex is roasted on a bed of onions and broth so that the flesh stays tender, anchovies are placed in a pan with slices of lemon and olives and drizzled with the juice of oranges, hake is flavored with filets of anchovy, and sardines are eaten *a beccafico*, one of the classic dishes of the island—placed in a pan, covered with breadcrumbs and fillets of anchovies melted in hot oil, raisins, and cinnamon, all drizzled with a dash of fresh orange juice.

Wild strawberry (*Fragaria vesca*) is a perennial that grows in the woods on hillsides and mountains. It is tasty, highly scented, and rich in vitamins and minerals, and is eaten either on its own, with sugar and lemon, doused in balsamic vinegar, or in jams, risotto, gelato, and cakes. Throughout Sicily strawberries grow wild on the Madonie Mountains and on the volcanic slopes of Mount Etna. Vast cultivated strawberry fields can be found around Ribera and Sciacca, west of Agrigento, where the climate, rich soil, and underground freshwater springs encourage successful crops. Wild strawberries were brought to Ribera by Sicilian soldiers on their way home from World War I after fighting in Friuli. Cultivation took hold in the 1950s, along with orange groves, and today it covers several thousand acres despite competition with another, more commercially diffuse strawberry cultivar grown in greenhouses.

The Trattoria dei Templi offers a menu that starts with the sea and progresses to the land, combining the distinctive local flavors of surf and turf. Traditional cuisine, including a Gattopardo menu available upon reservation, is offered by the Dèhor restaurant in the Baglio della Luna hotel, located in a watchtower in the countryside with a beautiful view of the Valley of the Temples. Pecorino cheese can be bought at Casa del Formaggio in Santo Stefano Quisquina, and Ribera strawberries are found in all vegetable shops and at local growers, such as Pietro Cibella. Paolo Ganduscio cultivates highly scented seedless oranges also typical of Ribera, and enjoyed as dessert or as an accompaniment to prosciutto or shellfish.

CASTELBUONO
MANNA OF THE MADONIE

SLIGHTLY INLAND ALONG THE TYRRHENIAN COAST OF SICILY STRETCHES THE MADONIE MOUNTAIN range, a botanical paradise in which 2,600 plant species have been identified, 150 of which are native to the region. This region is home to a process unknown to the rest of the world—manna, a product many people consider a figment of the imagination or mere biblical legend, is actually a natural substance obtained by drying the lymph of certain species of ash tree (*Fraxinus ornus* and *Fraxinus angustifolia*). Whitish in color, light and spongy, with a sweet taste, this treasured powder used to be called "heavenly perspiration," "honey dew," and "tears of the stars." Mentioned in the Koran, it also features in the Bible, where it rains manna for forty days until the chosen people finally arrive in Canaan. The Latin historian Pliny the Elder tells that during the hottest days the branches of the trees were laden with a "dewlike honey" that fell from the sky and upon the people below. In ancient times it was used as a sweetener, and its therapeutic properties were widely employed by the famous pharmaceutical school of Salerno. Manna is used today to sweeten products for diabetics, but is also employed in the cosmetics industry and in the medical industry for its health-giving properties, which aid the liver's metabolism and detoxification. Despite these uses, an aura of mystery still surrounds it; 10 percent of its components remain chemically undetermined, and there are neither theories nor explanations regarding its formation.

The Castello di Ventimiglia, a massive cubic construction around which the village of Castelbuono rose in the fourteenth century.

facing page
Manna, the biblical sweetener, drips from the trees.

Cultivation of manna-bearing ash trees dates to the Arab rule of Sicily in the tenth century, and the first document to mention it was signed by the bishop of Messina in 1080. In 1700 Sicily was the Mediterranean's major producer, and in the 1920s more than one thousand tons of Sicilian manna were exported annually to South America. In the first years of the twentieth century there were more than four-hundred thousand acres of cultivated ash trees in the Madonie, but more recently the market for manna has been supplanted by the ever-multiplying sweeteners produced by sugar factories.

The lymph produced by the trees is gathered by making an incision in the bark. This is done in July, when the trees are fertile, and continues until mid-September. A blue-white, bitter liquid called *lagrima*, or tears, is secreted from the incision. As it solidifies in the heat it sweetens, forming stalactites which are gathered with an instrument called a *rasula*, a special type of rake. The manna is laid out to dry in the shade for about a day, followed by a week in the sun. The most prized manna comes from Pollina, where it is called *cannolo*.

Provola of the Madonie has the typical shape of a fat flask with a short neck, and the first reference to this cheese appears in the sixteenth century in the price-controlling ledgers that regulated its sale to the public. Provola is made from raw cow's milk and is aged for ten to fifteen days during which it acquires a thin, smooth crust that is straw yellow in color. The inner cream is tender and elastic, with a delicate taste, and can be enjoyed on bread made from local durum wheat cooked in wood-burning ovens accompanied by a light, dry red wine, such as the local Inzolia. There is a slightly smoked version of the provola, and if the cheese is aged for several months it becomes tastier and a bit spicy, and is better paired with full-bodied red wines such as Nero d'Avola, also produced locally.

Typical provola of the Madonie is available in town at Filippo Abbate, and pure manna of the best quality can be bought at Giulio Gelardi, who is also responsible for the producers' consortium in Pollina. Manna graces many sweetmeats made at the Fiasconaro bakery in Castelbuono, and the Vecchio Palmento and Nangalarruni restaurants serve the traditional cuisine of the Madonie.

CATANIA
OPULENT CUISINE AND OPERATIC PASTA

CATANIA'S CUISINE CHALLENGES UNTAMED APPETITES, made not only to satisfy the city's nobility, but also prelates closed in convents and aristocrats with an insatiable desire for sumptuous food. This curious combination is attributed to the *maggiorasco* law, an ordinance that gave the firstborn the entire inheritance of his family and forced all younger children to take religious vows and adopt an ecclesiastical life. Though they

Violet and voluptuos Sicilian eggplant is the key ingredient of many complex dishes.

facing page
A charming view with cupolas and rooftops.

donned religious robes, the others had no intention of living a monastic life that differed in any way from life in their former palazzo, so they entrusted each meal to *monsù* educated in noble French kitchens. The monastery of San Nicolò l'Arena is in the heart of historic Catania and today houses the University, but it was once among the most powerful Benedictine abbeys in the world, second only to the one in Cismeros, Portugal. In the book *I Vicerè* by Federico de Roberto, eight cooks and a battalion of helpers worked in the kitchens of the convent. The stoves were always lit, topped by huge pots so large they could contain an entire haunch of veal, and the grills were large enough to roast an entire swordfish, complete with tail and sword. An entire form of cheese weighing over twenty pounds was grated each day to season the pasta, and enough lard was consumed daily to feed a rich family for a month. The kitchen of San Nicolò became legendary across the city, and no chef could match the convent's short pastry timbales, its melon-sized rice croquettes, the crisp honey *crespelle*, sweet spumoni, or its soft and perfumed cassata. In *The Leopard*, the classic epic by Giuseppe Tomasi di Lampedusa, the Prince of Salinas would have a timbale of maccheroni served at his nearby summer residence at Donnafugata, leaving his guests spellbound by this edible work of art and dispelling their fear of being served the clear and insipid *consommé* that was fashionable at the time. The first course of pasta is the keystone of all Sicilian meals, and every province has its own representative recipe: in Agrigento, homemade maccheroni with tomato and eggplant; in Messina, *sedanini*, a curved maccheroni with cubes of swordfish; in Palermo, *bucatini* with fresh sardines and raisins; in Ragusa, rigatoni with fava bean cream; in Syracuse, finely fried capellini seasoned with honey and fresh orange juice, one of the oldest recipes of the island; in Trapani, spaghetti with lobster. In Catania, in homage to Vincenzo Bellini's opera *La Norma, maccheroni alla Norma* were invented, a symphonic dish of pasta richly seasoned with tomatoes, fried eggplant, salted ricotta, pecorino cheese, garlic, pepper, sugar, extra virgin olive oil, and basil.

The turbulent lava slopes of Etna have provided an excellent vineyard habitat for centuries, and today both red and white DOC wines of the highest quality are produced. The white comes chiefly from the local Catania white grapes with the addition of other less aromatic grapes, and has a straw yellow color with gold reflections, a delicate perfume, and dry, well-balanced flavor best brought out when young and enjoyed with appetizers and fish dishes. The red comes from nearly black *nerello* grapes, producing a ruby red tone that turns garnet with age, and has a decisive taste best in its fourth or fifth year with meat and cheese. The *nerello* grape also produces a rosé with an intense bouquet, ideally savored within two years accompanied by the unmistakable Sicilian couscous.

Two of the best restaurants in Catania—La Siciliana and the Osteria Tre Bicchieri—have a section dedicated to local wine where a quick, light meal can also be enjoyed. The Enoteca Regionale di Sicilia wine shop in the city center offers a good selection of regional wines, and the Benanti cellars in Viagrande produce fine Etna Rosso and Bianco DOC wines.

Sicilian *granita* is a type of sherbet inherited from the Arabs, who collected snow from Etna, mixed it with honey and fruit juice, and ate it with bread, a legacy which explains the typical Sicilian habit of eating their *granita* and gelato with a brioche. Almond milk is another Arab specialty, a delicious, thirst-quenching drink prepared with creamy crushed almonds. Almonds are the key ingredient of many sweetmeats, especially Sicilian marzipan, which is also said to have been introduced by the Arabs. The most sought after are the pointed almonds of Avola, with their elongated oval form and an intensely sweet, aromatic flavor. Almonds are used in innumerable ways around Catania—eaten raw or toasted, as filling and decoration in sweetmeats, and even add a special taste to the most imaginative recipes. By grinding them finely and adding only sugar and a drop of water, a creamy spread is obtained for the preparation of many recipes, including cakes, tarts, and mousses. When mixed with wheat starch this spread becomes the delicate *biancomangiare*, a rich ring of raw almond paste, chocolate, pistachios, pine nuts, and sugar. Another version with a slightly stronger taste is made with roasted almonds.

left
The Fountain of the Rape of Proserpine in Piazza Giovanni XXIII.

below
The blood orange of Sicily named for the ancient fortune-telling cards—*tarocco* (tarot).

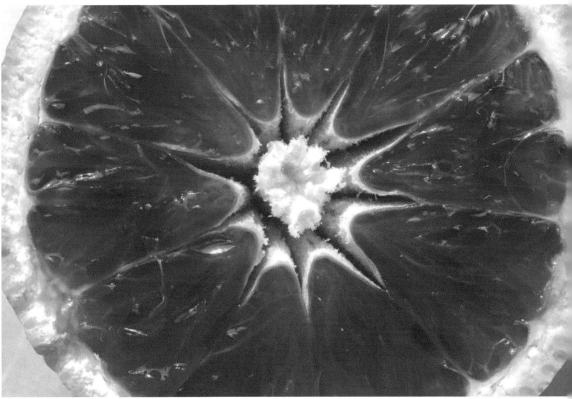

FAVIGNANA
THE LAST TONNARA

THE OFFSHORE CURRENTS IN THE SICILIAN CHANNEL BETWEEN TRAPANI and the Egadi Islands make the sea home to hundreds of fish species, and tuna is particularly plentiful here. These large fish arrive from Northern Europe in vast schools to spawn in the warm waters of the Mediterranean. Favignana, the largest island of the archipelago east of neighboring Levanzo and Marettimo, is the final resting place of the last

Tuna carpaccio with lemon.

facing page
Marine traffic in the port of Favignana.

tonnara—a plant where tuna was processed after being brought in from vast, elaborate fishing nets set out like a maze in the sea to confuse and consequently capture the tuna. Until just a few decades ago there were hundreds of *tonnare* lining the Sicilian coast to process the high-quality fish prized in both domestic and foreign markets. The best fish now fetch a high price in Japanese markets for sushi. The specialized traps are a complex system of nets that force the fish to follow a path spiraling into the final "chamber of death," in which they are caught and killed in the *mattanza*, an archaic, cruel spectacle that dyes the surrounding sea with blood. This ancient ritual has nearly died out after trying to compete with the newer technology of foreign fishing boats equipped with radar, but continues to be an important anchor in the cultural identity of the island, as it was once a holiday for the entire village and punctually marked the seasons. In the morning, immediately after Mass, the boats are blessed, and the fishermen take them to sea with the *rizza*, the system of nets anchored on the seabed with heavy stones, with which they build a series of chambers from which, once inside, the tuna cannot escape. At dawn, when the nets are full, the *rais* (the head fisherman) gives the order for the *mattanza* (killing) to begin. The fishermen begin to pull the nets ever tighter, forcing the fish into the final chamber, where the real *mattanza* begins, and the *rais* dictates which of the now thrashing fish are harpooned and pulled on board. After the boats are filled they return to shore, where the fish are weighed and immediately worked, as tuna spoils quickly and requires swift processing.

Rosolio liqueur is a relic of baroque salons with heavy brocade curtains and lively ladies sipping it in finely decorated crystal glasses. Today its fame is more modest, and it is used mainly in cocktails or as a digestive accompanying traditional Sicilian desserts of almond and pistachio. It is, however, gaining popularity with a younger crowd that has recently come to appreciate its refined taste and delicate perfume. A few Sicilians still produce it with care, closely following the ancient traditions and employing genuine products: natural rose petal infusions in pure alcohol absolutely free of preservatives and colorants. Rosolio is also made with overtones of peach, wild strawberry, laurel, prickly pear, basil, lemon, honey, and green mandarin orange, all best enjoyed ice cold.

Tuna can be eaten in many ways. It is excellent in oil or brine and is delectable eaten raw in thinly sliced *carpaccio* lightly drizzled with oil and fresh lemon, or in hearty steaks cooked on a grill with olives and capers. Parts of tuna are used for local delicacies: *bottarga* is prepared with the roe-filled ovary sacs, pressed, and dried in the sun for later use in sauce, eaten raw, or steamed and cut into thin, seasoned slices; *ventresca*, the fattest ventral part of the tuna, is cut into strips, salted, and pressed; *occhi rassi*, from the eye area, is kept barreled in salt and seasoned with pepper and wild fennel.

The Florio Tonnara prepares the *tonno di corsa* in Favignana, separating the flesh of the various parts of the fish and giving them special names. *Mascolino* comes from the back and the upper part of the belly, *ventresca* is the soft, fatty part of the belly, *tarantello* lies between the *mascolino* and the *ventresca*, and *bodano* is the flesh nearest the spine. The Conservittica Sammartano is a producer specialized in the preparation of tuna derivatives, including *bottarga*, *mosciame* (dried dolphin), and tuna heart. Rosolio liqueurs of many varieties are produced at the Tuccari pharmacy.

AEOLIAN ISLANDS
AN ARCHIPELAGO
IN A SEA OF MALVASIA

THE VOLCANIC AEOLIAN ISLANDS SCATTERED OFF THE NORTHERN COAST of Sicily produce a fortified Malvasia wine unequaled anywhere else. The Seven Sisters, as these islands are called, look as though they have been randomly tossed into the Tyrrhenian Sea, but their formation follows a line of volcanic craters that appeared in logical succession beginning two millennia ago. Alicudi, firstborn of the islands, has exhausted its powers of eruption, but Stromboli and Vulcano, the youngest two, are still very active and foretell the possibility of future additions to the family. The Aeolian Islands preserve traces of an ancient civilization dating back to the fourth century BC, have a wild, almost savage appearance, and are inhabited by people torn between ties to ancient tradition and a desire for the sweet life. The landscape alternates between age-old stone walls covered with capers and rows of low vines. Salina is the greenest island, with a permanent cap of clouds surrounding the highest point of the archipelago. Monte Fossa delle Felci, reaching over three thousand feet above sea level, and nearby Monte Porri give the island its ancient name *Didyme*, or twins. Malfa lies at the foot of the two volcanoes, and from its port a fleet of one hundred ships first sailed off into the world laden with barrels of a sweet, aromatic, gold-colored wine. Today a mere two hundred and fifty bottles of this fine wine is produced, reaching many of the important wine shops and restaurants of Europe and the United States. Though local legend claims the Aeolian vines are as old as the islands themselves, it is more likely they were planted by monks who settled here in the Middle Ages and who produced *zebibbi*—late-harvest wines made from dried grapes highly valued and in great demand.

The crystalline waters of Panarea, the most beautiful of the Aeolian Islands, with its alternating volcanic cliffs and thick Mediterranean scrub.

facing page
A bag of capers from Salina, where the plant is an integral part of the landscape.

Malvasia delle Lipari received DOC recognition in 1973 and is produced in three versions; normal, naturally sweet *passito*, and dessert liqueur. The normal type, typically aged in bottles for at least a year, has a bouquet of broom and privet, is sweetly aromatic with hints of wisteria and wild berries, and is an ideal drink between meals or with small cakes. When the same grape is dried it produces naturally sweet Malvasia, an elegant late-harvest wine with a minimum of 18 percent alcohol, intense amber color, and bouquet of eucalyptus, honey, apricot, and Mediterranean wildflowers. It is refined for at least six months, and can age up to four years, resulting in a superb vintage wine. Malvasia liqueur is the same wine with a higher alcohol content, around 20 percent, and is at its best after five or six years of ageing. It should be savored with almond sweets, sharp cheeses, and fine blue cheese.

Capers are sold at all local groceries and can also be bought directly from producers, such as the Caravaglio or De Lorenzo farms in Salina. A superior Malvasia wine of Lipari is produced in Vulcano by the Stevenson cellars, who also have a good selection of wines for tasting accompanied by the rare *ricottine* of the islands. Stevenson was a rich Welshman who bought a large part of the island in 1850 for its sulfur. Both natural and *passito* Malvasia can also be bought in Messina from the Colosi cellars, who have their own vineyards.

Tondina and Nocellara capers are cultivated on the island of Salina, producing almost a thousand tons of firm and heavy capers annually. The buds are collected from May to August and set out to dry in the shade on sheets of jute to prevent them from flowering. They are then salted in the *tinedde*, wooden containers made of old barrels cut in half. Each layer of capers is covered with a layer of coarse sea salt, they are periodically poured from one barrel to another to prevent fermentation, and after a month they are ready to eat. The beautiful white flower is called Orchid of the Aeolian Islands, and if left on the branch it withers and turns into *cucuncio*, a berry in the shape of a little gherkin that is collected and preserved in salt for later use.

234

MARSALA
ADMIRAL NELSON'S VICTORY WINE

PRODUCED IN THE EPONYMOUS CITY ON THE WESTERN TIP OF SICILY, Marsala is a fortified wine that provides a poetic open or close to every great meal. British Admiral Horatio Nelson discovered this beloved drink when passing through the port city in 1800, and he ordered five hundred barrels for his fleet stationed at Malta. John Woodhouse, who produced the wine for him, dedicated the Marsala Victory Wine to Nelson in 1805 when he defeated the Franco-Spanish fleet at Trafalgar.

Marsala's precise date of birth is unknown, but the history that has made it famous around the globe is well documented. In 1779 the young Englishman John Woodhouse was en route to Mazara del Vallo, on Sicily's southern coast, but he was surprised by a storm and took shelter in the port of Marsala, known locally as *Marsch-allà*, from the Arabic for "port of god." For consolation during such misadventure he went from tavern to tavern drinking the local wine, and eventually he realized he had in hand a great fortified wine that could easily compete with the Spanish and Portuguese Madeira and sherry wines that were so expensive back in England.

He began production, and after three years shipped the first bottles home. They were such a great success that he had to organize a regular ship service between Marsala and Liverpool, an idea previously unthinkable. In 1806, Benjamin Ingham, another young and enterprising Englishman with a nose for business, also arrived in Marsala. In 1821 he set up a business not far from John Woodhouse, becoming popular with the peasants by giving them good advice on how to increase their harvests and improve the quality of grapes, and his ten commandments of wine growing are still followed by locals. In 1834, Sicilian businessman Vincenzo Florio took the reins by buying all the land between the two English vineyards, and with a label starring a drinking lion he launched the fortune of Marsala Florio, one of the best sellers today. There are various types of Marsala, named for the color of the grapes it comes from. Some take on the color of setting sun and have a full-bodied, satisfying taste that varies according to the sugar content and the duration of barrel ageing. Marsala Oro comes from white grapes and is golden colored. Ambra, from the same white grapes but with a small percentage of cooked must added, is amber colored. Rubino is made with red grapes and the color is an intense ruby red. All three can be sweet, semi-sweet, or dry, and depending on the period of ageing in barrels, which ranges from two to over ten years, they are labeled Fine, Superiore, or Riserva.

Once the Baroque Church of Purgatorio, this is now the Auditorium of Santa Cecilia.

facing page
Marsala Florio—the most famous but not the only marsala wine—is known all over the world.

Marsala is the archetypal dessert wine and can be tasted and bought at the Alhoa bakery in the center of town. Here one can also sip a cup of coffee or have a brioche with sherbet or gelato, a typically Sicilian custom inherited from the Arabs, who would collect snow from Etna and mix it with honey or citrus juices and eat it with bread. The best and most famous Marsala come from the Florio cellars; also worth noting are the Rallo and Buffa cellars.

Opuntia is a prickly pear cactus with large, spiky leaves resembling elephant ears, and can be found all over Southern Italy under the name of *fico d'India* (Indian figs), even though it was imported from Central America. It was once used to delineate territorial boundaries and for a red dye extracted from the cochineals that infested the plant, but its sweet and fleshy fruit has long been prized, leading to its widespread cultivation. Of the many varieties, the most widespread is *sulfarina*, *sanguigna* has small, tasty, carmine red fruit, and the greenish fruit of the *muscaredda* is eaten well chilled. A special variety with yellow flesh is found across western Sicily, and is peeled, sliced, and eaten sprinkled with Marsala or in fruit salads.

MODICA
AZTEC CHOCOLATE

MODICA, AN ANCIENT TOWN FOUNDED BY SICULAN TRIBES IN SOUTHEASTERN SICILY, is known as the City of One Hundred Churches, a Baroque jewel recognized by UNESCO as a world heritage site. Its fame is owed not only to the many churches but also to its unequalled chocolate, prepared in dozens of artisan workshops according to recipes inherited from the Aztecs, the first people to use cacao beans in sumptuous

A detail of the Church of San Giorgio, a monumental example of Sicilian Baroque.

facing page
Modica has become a veritable "chocolate district."

sweets. Montezuma II, sixteenth-century Emperor of the Aztecs, had a daily drink prepared made from cacao beans hand-ground on a curved stone mixed with cooked maize flour and dissolved in water flavored with vanilla, cinnamon, and chili pepper. This potion was probably not sweet, as it was called *xoxoàtl* (bitter drink), but it imparted spiritual serenity and physical vigor. With the same mixture of maize and cacao the Aztecs also prepared a solid chocolate, shaping it into little cigars, though another legend gives credit to friar Bernardino da Sahagùn for being the first to innovate this readily transportable shape and introduce it to the rest of the world. Whichever way it happened, it is certain that conquistador Hernán Cortés was graciously received as a divinity by Montezuma, a gesture that would cost the emperor his life. Cortés took over the Aztec kingdom and in 1519 brought cacao beans and many recipes for their preparation to Europe. Cacao arrived in Modica during the Spanish domination of Siciliy, which lasted seven centuries, and up until the twentieth century *ciucculaturu* chocolate vendors traveled the city from house to house preparing chocolate on the spot in the Aztec manner, crushing the cacao seeds with a curved stone and turning them into a drink. This *dolce degli dei* (sweet of the gods) is still prepared following original recipes, resulting in the traditional *cioccolato con i cristalli*, a uniquely flavored crystallized chocolate. The *cioccolato con i cristalli* of Modica is a dark chocolate prepared with cacao from the Ivory Coast, granulated sugar, and various spices. The legendary lover Giacomo Casanova would eat it with cinnamon, vanilla, and chili pepper as an aphrodisiac before his amorous appointments. The sugar does not dissolve, thus the crystals remain intact and all the cacao's aromas are preserved. To fully appreciate this chocolate, it should be slowly melted in one's mouth, dissolving the sugar first and leaving the unmistakably rich taste of cacao lingering on the tongue. It is often served with a sweet Marsala dessert wine made from dried grapes.

In 1607 Vittoria Colonna, Countess of Modica, founded a city (named Vittoria after herself) at the foot of the Hyblaean Mountains with the goal of maximizing the great agricultural potential that has since earned the area the name "greenhouse of the choicest young produce." Frappato vines flourish here, and produce a dry, pleasant wine often used as a base for the more famous and sought after Cerasuolo di Vittoria, a mixture of Frappato, large black Calabrese grapes, and Nerello Mascalese grapes. Cerasuolo is a cherry red wine, with a delicate bouquet, fruity, warm, dry, well-balanced taste which undergoes a moderate ageing of two to three years. Known for its strength, it reaches a minimum of 13 percent alcohol and has a long life in bottles, but reaches its best in the first five or six years, and is ideally served with lamb.

Modica is an official "City of Flavors," and chocolate is available at every confectioner in town. The Antica Dolceria Bonajuto, founded at the end of the nineteenth century, Rizza, and the Caffè dell'Arte are all found on Corso Umberto and sell some of the most delicious specialties. For a polar opposite in taste, try Ragusa cheese; made from free-range Modica cows in the pastures of the Hyblaean Mountains; it can be bought at the Casa del Formaggio in Modica. Cerasuolo di Vittorio wine can be tasted at the Valle dell'Acate cellars.

239

N O T O
LAND OF ALMONDS

TOGETHER WITH CITRUS FRUIT, THE ALMOND IS AMONG THE MOST quintessential plants of the Sicilian agricultural panorama. In winter months the countryside around Noto is characterized by an explosion of white flowers that leave as enchanting an impression as the sumptuous Baroque architecture of the city's historic center. In summer months groups of gatherers shake the branches with long sticks to make the almonds fall onto sheets spread below the trees. Once collected they are put through a roller that separates the husks from the nuts, are spread in the farmyard to dry, and sent to vegetable markets and confectioners' shops across the region. Many varieties are cultivated on the hills surrounding Noto; *pizzuta d'Avola*, with evenly shaped nuts and an aromatic scent, is the best and most sought after; *romana* is pinkish white, with a more intense taste, and a thick, hard husk that keeps in the oils and aromas, but is also less popular in the market because of its irregular shape. Despite this slight yet superficial defect, this type is best for the preparation of almond paste, the *pasta reale* (royal paste) which has inspired an infinite number of recipes in the refined, graceful Sicilian confectionary tradition. Its oyster-white color, delicate floral scent, and exquisite taste are all reminders of the Near East, where it was first prepared. Noto's traditional almond paste comes from the *romana* almond, peeled and finely minced while still raw; Central European marzipan is made differently. According to an oral tradition handed down through the generations, only a little sugar is added and some water to make it soft—absolutely no seasoning whatsoever. Another version, made with *brustolite* almonds toasted at low temperatures and minced along with the skin that covers the almond's core, has a much more decisive taste from the aroma imparted during toasting.

Latte di mandorla, a refreshing almond milk drink, is prepared all over Sicily with diluted *pasta reale*, creating an extremely popular thirst-quenching beverage. *Biancomangiare* is an almond-based dessert served on lemon leaves, imbuing each spoonful with the fragrance of the essential citrus oils. Many other special sweets are prepared in Noto with almond paste: sweets shaped like miniature fruits and vegetables are topped with crystallized sugar and sold in jars; shells filled with citron marmalade; *mustazzoli*, a honey paste in serpentine form filled with minced almonds and orange honey; and *cassata*—the ultimate Baroque dessert—is a cake of *pasta reale* with pistachios and sweet sheep's milk ricotta between two layers of sponge cake lightly glazed with sugar.

Palazzo Ducezio is a curious eighteenth-century building in a predominantly Baroque city.

facing page
The superb quality of Noto almonds is unrivalled.

About a dozen almond growers of Noto are part of the local consortium, and to purchase their prized almonds one should go to Giuseppe Carbone at the consortium's headquarters in town. Almond cream and sweetmeats prepared with it can be tasted at the Caffè Sicilia in Noto's historic center, where one of their specialties is the *biancomangiare*, or at the Caffè del Ponte in nearby Syracuse.

Noto is an official "City of Wine," and an ideal local dessert wine is the Moscato di Noto, produced in natural, *spumante*, and sweetly fortified liqueur versions. Moscato is a sweet wine with an intense gold color and characteristic aroma of the local Muscat grape, best served young and well-chilled at the end of a meal. The *spumante* version comes from the same Muscat grapes, and is clear and brilliant, sweet and aromatic, and also served chilled at the end of the meal within two years of age. The fortified liqueur is made from the natural grape with alcohol added, and is a dark, intense yellow color with a delicate and fragrant bouquet and a sweet, pleasant, velvety taste. It contains a minimum of 22 percent alcohol, is aged for a period from six months to over ten years, resulting in a superbly nuanced wine at almost any age.

PALERMO
MARTORANA FRUITS

PIAZZA BELLINI, HEART OF PALERMO SINCE THE MIDDLE AGES, acts as stage and front yard of Santa Maria dell'Ammiraglio, the Norman church built in 1143 by Giorgio d'Antiochia, Admiral to King Roger II. In 1194 Eloisa Martorana founded a Benedictine monastery in an annex of the church, but this complex is famous neither for its almost thousand-year history, nor for its artistic worth. Its fame is guaranteed instead thanks to the convent's nuns, who prepared sweets of unequalled quality adapting recipes inherited from the Arabs. Cassata, a sponge cake soaked in maraschino liqueur and filled with fresh ricotta, sugar, candied fruit, dark chocolate, and pistachios, all glazed with sugar and egg white decorated with candied fruit, is the archetypal Sicilian dessert. Another unmistakable delicacy is the vividly colored marzipan one sees all around this island, shaped like every type of fruit and vegetable imaginable. Born in the convent of Martorana, this special marzipan has become the emblem of Sicily's sweetmeat traditions. Made with almonds crushed in a mortar and pestle mixed with sugar, orange flower water, and vanilla, marzipan is named after a type of vase from the Indian city of Marthaban; the Arabs stored their almond sweets in these vases, and the name traveled with them when they brought the recipe to Italy. Once the Arabs left the tradition was kept alive in the monasteries, and the nuns of Martorana gave saint-shaped sweetmeats colored with pigments from roses, saffron, and pistachio to the king and his court. This contributed greatly to marzipan's fame, and also explains why the creamed almonds used to make it were called "royal paste." The secrets of marzipan preparation eventually leaked out of the convents, but the nuns continued making it from morning to night, neglecting their religious duties. In 1575, the Synod of the Diocese of Mazara del Vallo tried to forbid this "devoted production" at least during Holy Week, but this had few positive results—unless one considers that it effectively encouraged the nuns to create new shapes, such as the Easter Lamb, made of "royal paste" filled with citron marmalade. This is one of the classic sweets of Sicilian Easter celebrations, and is presented on a tray surrounded by fruit made of marzipan. Over time each religious festivity came to have its own figure: lambs at Christmas, donkeys for the feast of Saint Anthony, and pigs for Saint Sebastian, while Palermo's secular confectioners indulged in less canonical characters, such as the *minni di Virgini* (breast of the Virgin), figures of the Madonna decorated with halved cherries.

A glimpse of the Cathedral of Palermo.

facing page
A basket of ripe oranges ready to enjoy.

The hills delimiting the Conca d'Oro, the "golden shell" basin surrounding Palermo, are cultivated with vines that produce some excellent DOC wines, sold with the label of the vineyards they come from: Ansonica, Catarrato, Grecanico, Grillo, Nerello Mascalese, Nero d'Avola, Perricone, and others. The ancient village of Monreale, clinging to a prominent hill overlooking the wide gulf, gives its name to the quintessential DOC wine, made in white, late-harvest white, red, and rosé varieties. Contessa Entellina whites, reds, and rosés are produced in the same district of Palermo, and Contea di Sclafani DOC is known above all for a white wine produced in several versions—including dry, sweet, late harvest, and *spumante*—and a nouvelle red wine enjoyed each autumn.

Cappello, hidden away near the cathedral, and the historic Mazzara are two of the best confectioners in town. For sweets in nearby Mondello-Valdesi one should go to Scimone. Almond paste is available at I Peccatucci di Mamma Andrea, and the entire array of Sicilian wine is represented at the Picone wine shop, with more than 4,500 labels. Particular attention is paid to the small producers, and the wines can be tasted with salami and cheese. Olive oil and other products typical of the region are also of a high quality in most of Palermo's shops.

Tarocco, Moro, and Sanguinello compose an inimitable triumvirate of strictly Sicilian oranges with bright red flesh and sweet-tart juice rich in vitamins and minerals. They are consumed as a natural prevention against colds, cellular ageing, and tumors, not to mention for sheer pleasure. Sicily produces 70 percent of the oranges and 90 percent of the lemons—fruits that are closely tied to the land—in Italy; even the same varieties cultivated elsewhere have a different color and less characteristic flavor and scent. In addition to eating orange slices or drinking its freshly-squeezed juice, blood oranges are frequently served in salads with onions and walnuts, seasoned with extra virgin olive oil, lemon juice, fennel seeds, and parsley. Though this may at first seem an unusual contrast, it is a union of wonderfully fresh tastes, and is part of the beautiful Sicilian tradition of inventing surprisingly sumptuous dishes with the most unexpected flavor

combinations. Blood oranges are also used in risotto with butter, minced orange rind, shrimp, orange juice, and black pepper. Likely brought west from China or India, where they have been known since the eighth century BC, the Arabs introduced this heavenly fruit to Sicily in the eleventh century, building great irrigation networks to aid their cultivation. Describing the lemons of Palermo's gardens, the Arab poet Ibn Zaffir wrote, "The trees have leaves of fire and their feet in water." Five centuries later the monks intensified citrus farming in the Conca d'Oro, making the most of a terrain particularly propitious for this kind of plantation. Mandarin oranges, originally from the island of Samoa, and grapefruit originally from eastern India, have been cultivated here as well since the nineteenth century.

above
Fabulously false strawberries, apricots, and mandarin oranges— these marzipan are modeled and shaped to look real.

right
The famous market of Vucciria is colorful, tasty, and endlessly tempting.

244

TRAPANI
MOTHER NATURE'S SALT FACTORY

THE WESTERN COAST OF SICILY BETWEEN TRAPANI AND MARSALA IS A MOSAIC of pastel-colored, mirroring pools of seawater punctuated by windmills. This peculiar scenery is the result of work begun thousands of years ago by the Phoenicians, and first documented by the Arab geographer Edrisi in 1154. The landscape of these salt flats, which provided a source of wealth when salt was the primary food preservative, were also a theater of war during numerous territorial battles. Frederick of Swabia, King of Sicily in the fourteenth century, decreed a state monopoly on all salt, a verdict that remained in effect throughout Italy until a few years ago. Today the natural reserves of Trapani, Paceco, and the Isole dello Stagnone (the islands dotting the lagoon south of Trapani) are protected areas that hold an irresistible fascination for thousands of tourists. Though some of the land appears artificially expanded toward the open sea, it is perfectly integrated into nature and sustains a commercial activity using only the harmless, waste-free, very effective forces of wind and sun. The salt marshes harmonize and improve the natural landscape of this coast, exemplified by marine lagoons of warm, shallow water. This coast is entirely subject to geological submersion and uplift that in the past has caused the seabed to vacillate, at periods in history connecting the Sicilian mainland with the Egadi Islands several miles to the west, and later submerging the low-lying lagoon islands under thirty feet of water. The lagoon of the Stagnone perfectly reveals the varying sea levels over time, and a Phoenician stone road to the settlement of Motia, on the island of San Pantaleo, can be seen today about four feet below the surface.

The sea salt of Trapani contains more magnesium, more potassium, and less chloride than most kitchen salts, and therefore tastes saltier. It is collected by hand in the summer, when strong sunshine, little rain, and wind expedites evaporation and propels the windmills. During winter, when the water is cleaner, the salt is collected in great basins beside the open sea. Fish, including sea bass, bream, and grey mullet are bred here, and these basins also provide a resting place for migrating birds including herons, flamingos, and storks. Historically, the water was circulated through the salt marshes by Archimedean screws run with the force of the windmills, but today pumps transfer the water into ever smaller and shallower basins, allowing constant evaporation and increasing the concentration of salt. The final set of basins, called *caure*, are square pools where the water evaporates completely and the salt is collected into great white mounds that shine like ice. Covered with terracotta tiles, the resulting salt is crumbled into small granules and further dried to remove excess humidity.

An aerial view of the city spread out on three sides toward the sea, with the salt flats in the background.

facing page
Salt and windmills.

The Sicilian Canal, which separates the Sicily from the northern coast of Africa, is home to the highest quality fresh fish, the main protagonists of Trapani's cuisine. Spaghetti with lobster, *sarde a beccafico* (pasta with sardines), fish soup, or simply fish and crustaceans cooked over an open fire and drizzled with olive oil and seasoned by garlic and parsley are choice dishes worth tasting. In the northern quarters of the city *cuscusu*, a dish of Arab origin prepared much like Tunisian couscous, is the specialty. A food festival based on couscous—a type of pasta made from bran flour that is worked into tiny balls and dried in the sun—is held in San Vito lo Capo and served steamed in special containers with a delectable mixture of local fish and crustaceans.

The unrefined sea salt of Trapani, for which there is also a kosher certification, is collected by hand along the salt flats of Attore and Infersa and refined in the perfectly functioning ancient mills. Sosalt, a local company that employs modern techniques for salt collection and production, uses the technology in such a way as to completely preserve salt's nutritional properties. Sosalt also produces the natural sea salt of Mozia, which is more soluble, richer in trace minerals, and is particularly good for achieving a well-balanced diet. *Cuscusu* and other Tunisian specialties are served at the Tha'am restaurant in San Vito Lo Capo, where a couscous festival is held each year, and the local fish *cuscusu* is available at the beachside Delfino restaurant.

CAGLIARI
SACRED BREAD

DURING PERIODIC INVASIONS AND TERRITORIAL WARS THROUGHOUT HISTORY Cagliari has lost much of its artistic and architectural beauty, but its rebellious spirit and love for tradition have only been reinforced, and together with its singular landscape these characteristics make Sardinia a unique "continent" unto itself. Mascot of the island's tradition is most certainly its bread, cornerstone of every meal, and the Sardinian people rightly defend the quality of their flour and methods of preparation, leavening, and baking. Bread here is truly sacred; before putting a loaf into the oven the sign of the Cross is etched into it, and it is never be wasted, nor should it ever be placed on the table upside-down. Sardinian dough is kneaded as though it were modeling clay for everlasting sculptures given as gifts on special occasions or to the sick as an amulet for quick recovery. In many villages on Palm Sunday *pane de pramma* is prepared in the shape of a palm, and for Lent *su Lazareddu* is a tradition, shaped as an effigy of Lazarus wrapped in bandages. A shepherd-shaped loaf is hung in stalls where sheep are kept overnight, girls are given dolls of bread, and boys are given bread in the shape of bicycles—reminders of a time when families could not afford to buy gifts for their children. *Coccu*, a doughnut-shaped loaf made with bran and anise, or *coccu illa zidda*, a flat bread cooked under ashes, are for engagement celebrations, and there are many forms of wedding bread, sculpted and polished to look like shining ceramic: garlands of roses, doves, and young hens, a symbol of fertility and prosperity. The most famous Sardinian bread, so popular it is now made even on the mainland, is *carasau*, called *carta da musica* because it looks like the parchment on which music scores were written. These large, round, thin sheets of crisp wafer are golden in color and resplendent with the taste scent of hearty granaries. It is the typical food of the shepherds, who still use it because it does not easily become soggy or stale and therefore can be kept for a long time. Baked twice in the oven, the first cooking makes the sheet swell into a ball that is then carefully cut in half to prevent breakage; the two halves are then put back into the oven for a second baking. It is excellent with a few drops of extra virgin olive oil (*guttiau*) with a dusting of salt and rosemary, and is also used to make *su pane frattau*, a soup made with *carasau* layered into the plate and soaked with sheep broth or mixed meats and covered with tomato sauce, grated pecorino cheese, and a poached egg.

The Gothic Catalan sanctuary of the Madonna di Bonaria.

facing page
Unleavened *carasau* bread.

The hills and plains around Cagliari produce great wines. Nasco is a white wine with a golden color and a woodsy bouquet that is a fine accompaniment to sweet desserts or blue cheeses. Girò is a sweet and velvety ruby red wine best when matured for over ten years and ideal at the end of a meal with aged ewe's milk cheeses, fruit tarts, and almond sweetmeats. Moscato Dorato has an intense bouquet of honey, and is best at the end of a meal with dessert. Nuragus is characterized by beautiful greenish reflections, a slight perfume of raw apples and acacia, and is a dry, light wine best with lean appetizers, light first courses, mollusks, and crustaceans. Ruby red Monica is usually enjoyed at the end of the meal with pecorino cheese and dry almond-based desserts, and Carignano del Sulcis is another intense ruby red with a bouquet of wild berries that best complements meat dishes in hearty sauces or stews.

The largest selection of wine in the Cagliari is found at the Antica Enoteca Cagliaritana, but for a more scrupulously selected set of wines and other island products it is advisable to turn to Gianni Bonu. *Carta da musica* bread is available at the Tavola degli Antichi, and nearby Sulcis is the largest producer of saffron in Italy; thousands of acres of crocus are cultivated for this golden treasure, the majority of which are around San Gavino Monreale. The powder's color is so intense that it is used to dye cotton fabrics, particularly the head scarves worn by women during the Festival of Saint John each June, and saffron can be bought at the Su Zafferanu Cooperative in San Giovanni.

NUORO
FIORE SARDO

THE OLDEST CHEESE OF SARDINIA, FIORE SARDO (SARDINIAN FLOWER), is produced with raw ewe's milk shaped in a chestnut wood mould, on the bottom of which a flower and the producer's initials are carved. In 59 BC the Latin historian Diodorus Siculus wrote that Fiore Sardo was eaten by shepherds taking refuge from marauding invaders deep in the mountains, and the first description of this cheese's preparation dates from the same period. Wild artichoke or fig juice was used as rennet; the milk and rennet were placed on cane mats above a hole, and a fire was lit beneath it to smoke the fresh cheese. In the nineteenth century there was a high demand in the markets of Livorno and Naples, and in Genoa it was used for pesto. Today the methods of production have remained much the same: after soaking in brine it is lightly smoked, aged in airy cellars, and occasionally rubbed with olive oil to prevent drying or mould formation on the exterior. All this results in a hard cheese, straw yellow in color, slightly piquant, an excellent table cheese when fresh, and ideal for grating onto pasta when aged.

Sardinian pecorino cheeses at various stages of aeging.

facing page
The countryside at the foot of the Gennargentu.

Sheep farming is an old tradition in Sardinia, as is apparent from a recently excavated statue of a shepherd and ram dating back to the first century BC, and pecorino romano cheese shares these ancient origins. The practice of shepherding was documented in the Lazio countryside around the first century AD, and is described in *De re rustica* by the ancient Roman agronomist Lucius Columella, who wrote that it was a key ration for the Roman troops. Surprisingly, the first pecorino romano production in Sardinia dates only to the nineteenth century, though sheep farming was already widespread, and master cheesemakers moved to the island creating the tradition which now surrounds it throughout Sardinia. Pecorino can be served sliced as a fine table cheese or grated into pasta dishes, and is the main protagonist of the typical *cacio e pepe*, a first course of pasta, pecorino, and black pepper.

Sardinia may be the home of pecorino, but it is also known for an excellent cow's milk cheese called *casizolu*, produced in Montiferru. Prepared by local women who knead the boiling curds by hand, the first mention of this cheese dates to 1279 and was found in a document stating that the Church of San Pietro di Scano in Montiferru paid a tribute to the San Michele Church in Pisa not only with coins, but also with cheese, including the local caciocavallo. *Casizolu* production is limited because it comes from the milk of sardo-modicane cows, a working breed fed exclusively at pasture, therefore producing much less milk than their stable and farmyard counterparts.

The Cannonau vine dates back to the fourteenth century and was presumably brought to Sardinia by the Spanish during their rule of the island. A full-bodied, well structured, ruby red wine with a rich bouquet of flowers and fruit, Cannonau is dry and pleasantly bitter. It ages well between two and six years, and is best served with spicy red meat, game, and aged cheeses. Oliena, another local wine, earned the praises of poet Gabriele D'Annunzio, who called it Nepente, a drink the Greeks believed produced dreams and visions. Monica grapes, another vine of Spanish origin, were introduced by the Camaldolese Monks in the eleventh century, and make an excellent, clear, ruby red wine that takes on a cherry color with age, has an intense bouquet, and a flavor that varies between dry and sweet, always leaving a distinct aftertaste.

Cheeses, particularly the distinct Fiore Sardo, can be bought at the Rubanu farm in Orgosolo and the Pastori Cooperative in Dorgali. The Spirito di Vino wine shop in Nuoro offers more than 300 labels of Sardinian wine, and the Cooperativa Vitivinicola in Jerzu produces an excellent Cannonau wine. The Su Gologone restaurant serves delicious regional dishes and is affiliated with a charming hotel, furnished in typical Sardinian style, in the heart of Barbagia, beside the springs of the Gologone.

Sardinian shepherds often spent long months in the mountains without a well-equipped kitchen, nor could they afford to put much on the table. For weddings, important holidays, and special occasions they cooked *suppa cuatta*, a broth with sliced homemade bread and fresh cheese cooked in the oven until it forms a delicious golden crust. In the instant it was served at table it was seasoned with various ingredients, often including raisins, leftover lard, fresh fava beans, dried black olives, extra virgin olive oil, and a dash of black pepper. Typically, however, shepherds mainly ate meat, either grilled or roasted on a spit. One cannot leave Sardinia without having tasted the *porcheddu a carraxiu*, piglet cooked in a hole dug in the ground and covered with embers from the surrounding Mediterranean shrubs, or grilled baby goat browned on a spit by the fire. The *carraxiu* of Villagrande exceeds all imagination; the custom is to stuff one animal with another, such as turkey with chicken. In Villagrande a young bull is stuffed with a goat, which in turn contains a piglet stuffed with a hare, which contains a guinea fowl that already has a small bird in its stomach. Given this opulent grandiosity, it is only understandable that before this *carraxiu* is cooked the master village cobbler is called in to sew up the stomach of the young bull.

above
A flock of hungry sheep in the shadow of a nuragh.

inset
Hard-working, hungry shepherds patiently grill their meat.

ORISTANO
DELICACIES OF AN INLAND SEA

SEVERAL VAST LAGOONS LACED ALONG SARDINIA'S WESTERN COAST are spread like a crown around the gulf of Oristano and the Sinis peninsula. From the Phoenicians founders of Tharros to the subsequent populations in the surrounding Arborea, locals have used the large pools for centuries to breed fish. The sea of Sardinia is the most beautiful of the whole Mediterranean, and has admirers throughout the world. Sardinians themselves, however, have never had an ideal relationship with it, and were repeatedly forced to withdraw inland every time a sail appeared on the horizon, whether it was a friend or foe, a Phoenician or a Saracen. They certainly did venture out to sea, and continue to do so, to fish tuna and lobster, but are decidedly not a seafaring people, having always preferred to work the land and obtain fish, when possible, from the inland lagoons. In 1580 the historian Fra described the lagoons of Oristano as "full of fish," describing eels, bass, bream, crab, and mullet in particular as thriving in great abundance. Sardinians still refer to mullet (*Mugil cephalus*) as *su pisc*, the ultimate fish, used to prepare *magheddu* and *merca*, curious specialties found only around the pools of Cabras. *Magheddu*, also called *su pisci affunau*, is mullet that has been salted, dried, smoked, and

Abbasanta, a stele fragment from the tomb of the Giganti Su Pranu, datable to the early Bronze Age.

facing page
A selection of simple recipes based on *bottarga*.

seasoned with oil, vinegar, and parsley. *Merca* (*merk* in Punic means salty food) is mullet boiled in salt water, wrapped in tufts of *silicornia*, an aromatic lakeside herb, and tied firmly until it is served. *Bottarga* can be made from either bred or wild fish, and uses sun-dried mullet roe. The entire ovary sac is extracted, spread on a wooden surface, covered with sea salt, pressed, left for twenty-four hours, collected, and the excess salt is removed and it is hung in the sun to age. Sardinian *bottarga* is an expensive rarity because it is produced in limited quantities and has to compete in the market with the more economical frozen roe of other Mediterranean countries, which is often from tuna fish and therefore has a less nuanced flavor. *Bottarga* is cut into thin slices and drizzled with a little olive oil eaten as an appetizer, or it can be used in pasta sauces, and instead of grating it directly onto the plate, it imparts more flavor if cut into thin slices and soaked in olive oil for about ten minutes.

Vernaccia di Oristano, flag-bearer of Sardinian wines, was the island's first to receive the DOC classification. Often compared with wines like Jerez, its peculiarity is due to ageing in chestnut or oak barrels, inside which a veil called *flor* forms, imbuing it with a unique aroma. Vernaccia, with its golden color, scent of almonds, bittersweet hint of fruit, and benefits for both one's digestion and soul, should be judged with all the senses. Local lore credits the Phoenicians of Tharros for improving upon the vine's natural characteristics, and the Romans later baptized it *vernacola*, meaning local vine. Its cultivation was of such importance that the Carta de Logu, a series of laws passed by Eleonora d'Arborea at the end of the fourteenth century, decreed that anyone who dug up a vine or set fire to the vineyards would have his right hand cut off. Vernaccia is the perfect accompaniment to Sardinian *bottarga* and smoked fish fresh from the lagoons.

Grey mullet *bottarga* can be bought from the Manca brothers, who are part of the Fishermen's Cooperative of Cabras, or from the Tradizioni Nostrane shop, also in Cabras. Vernaccia wine is sold at the Cantina Sociale della Vernaccia Cooperative. Myrtle is the symbol of Sardinia, and from its berries unique jams and liqueurs are produced. The Tremontis distillery in Paulilatino produces the typical liqueur of myrtle called *mirto*, which is difficult to find outside of Sardinia. Salvatore Troncia, in Masullas, uses it to flavor nougat, giving it an absolutely singular, delicate taste.

ADDRESSES

agrigento (sicily)

Informazioni Turistiche
Via C. Battisti, 15
92100 Agrigento (AG)
phone +39 0922 20454, fax +39 0922 20246
aastagrigento@oasi.net

Hotel Della Valle
Via U. La Malfa, 3
92100 Agrigento (AG)
phone +39 0922 26966
jollyvalle@asinform.it

Hotel Dioscuri Bay Palace
Località San Leone, Lungomare Falcone
e Borsellino, 1
92100 Agrigento (AG)
phone +39 0922 406111
dioscuri@framon-hotels.com

Hotel Villa Athena
Passeggiata Archeologica, 33
92100 Agrigento (AG)
phone +39 0922 596288

Ristorante Leon d'Oro
Località San Leone, Viale Emporium, 102
92100 Agrigento (AG)
phone +39 0922 414400
closed: Monday

Trattoria dei Templi
Via Panoramica dei Templi, 15
92100 Agrigento (AG)
phone +39 0922 403110
closed: Thursday (except July and August)

Ristorante Il Dèhor
Contrada Maddalusa S.S. 640
92100 Agrigento (AG)
phone +39 0922.511335
info@bagliodellaluna.com
www.bagliodellaluna.com
closed: Monday for lunch

Consorzio tutela pecorino siciliano
Via Roma, 37
92022 Cammarata (AG)
phone +39 091 8214151

La Casa del Formaggio
Via Maranzano, 11
92020 Santo Stefano Quisquina (AG)
phone +39 0922 982035

Pietro Cibella
Via Canale, 30
92016 Ribera (AG)
phone +39 0925 63483

Paolo Ganduscio
Via Ospedale Cortile, C 6
92016 Ribera (AG)
+39 0925 62610

alba (piedmont)

Consorzio Turistico Langhe Monferrato Roero
Piazza Medford, 3
12051 Alba (CN)
phone +39 0173 35833, fax +39 0173 363878
info@langheroero.it
www.langheroero.it

Ristorante Trattoria del Castello
Via Castello, 5
12060 Grinzane Cavour (CN)
phone +39 0173 262172

Hotel I Castelli
Corso Torino, 14
12051 Alba (CN)
phone +39 0173 361978
info@hotel-icastelli.com

Hotel Savona
Via Roma, 1 (Piazza Savona, 2)
12051 Alba (CN)
phone +39 0173 440440
info@hotelsavona.com

Ristorante Daniel's al Pesco Fiorito
Corso Canale, 28
12051 Alba (CN)
phone +39 0173 441977
closed: Sunday (never in Fall)

Ristorante Il Vicoletto
Via Bertero, 6
12051 Alba (CN)
phone +39 0173 363196
closed: Monday

Osteria dell'Arco
Piazza Savona, 5
12051 Alba (CN)
phone +39 0173 363974
closed: Sunday and Monday

Enoteca Fracchia & Berchiella
Via Vernazza 9
12051 Alba (CN)
phone +39 0173 440508

I Piaceri del Gusto
Via Vittorio Emanuele II, 23
12051 Alba (CN)
phone +39 0173 440166

Polleria Ratti
Via Vittorio Emanuele II, 18
12051 Alba (CN)
phone +39 0173 440540

Antica Dispensa Bricco Bastia
Via Bava Beccaris, 3
12051 Alba (CN)
phone +39 0173 787120
www.anticadispensa.it

ancona (marche)

Azienda di Promozione Turistica Regionale
Via Thaon de Revel, 4
phone +39 071 3589902, fax +39 071 801454
60100 Ancona (AN)
aptrr@regione.marche.it
servizio.turismo@regione.marche.it
www.le-marche.com/italia/marche

Stazione Marittima
phone +39 071 201183
iat.ancona@regione.marche.it

Hotel Ristorante Il Fortino Napoleonico
Località Portonovo, Via Poggio, 166
60100 Ancona (AN)
phone +39 071 801450
fortino@fastnet.it

Hotel Emilia
Via Collina di Portonovo, 149/a
60100 Ancona (AN)
phone +39 071 801145
info@hotelemilia.com

Ristorante Al Rosso Agontano
Via Marconi, 3
60100 Ancona (AN)
phone +39 071 2075279
closed: Sunday

Ristorante Il laghetto
Località Portonovo, Via Poggio
60100 Ancona (AN)
phone +39 071 801183
closed: Monday (except in the summer)

Osteria Teatro Strabacco
Via Oberdan, 2
60100 Ancona (AN)
phone +39 071 54213
closed: Monday

Trattoria Carloni
Località Torrette, Via Flaminia, 247
60100 Ancona (AN)
phone +39 071 888239
closed: Monday

Ristorante Boccon Divino
Via Matteotti, 13
60100 Ancona (AN)
phone +39 071 57269
closed: Monday and Tuesday for lunch

Ristorante Da Emilia
Nella baia
60020 Portonovo (AN)
phone +39 071 801109
daemilia@tin.it
closed: Monday (except in August)

Salumeria Ittica Anikò
Piazza Saffi, 10
60019 Senigallia (AN)
phone +39 071 7931228
info@madonninadelpescatore.it
www.suscibar.it

Mimotti
Via delle Grazie, 42
60100 Ancona (AN)
phone +39 071 2802359

Fattoria Le Terrazze
Via Musone, 4
60026 Numana (AN)
phone +39 071 7390352
info@fattorialeterrazze.it
www.fattorialeterrazze.it

aosta (valle d'aosta)

Azienda di Informazione e Accoglienza Turistica (AIAT)
Piazza Chanoux, 45
11100 Aosta (AO)
phone +39 0165 33352, fax +39 0165 40532

Piazza Arco d'Augusto
phone/fax +39 0165 235343
aptaosta@aostashop.com
www.aostashop.com/apt.htm

Hotel Europe
Piazza Narbonne, 8
11100 Aosta (AO)
phone +39 0165 236363
hoteleurope@ethotels.com
www.ethotels.com/hoteleurope.html

Hotel Holiday Inn Aosta
Corso Battaglione Aosta, 30
11100 Aosta (AO)
phone +39 0165 236356
hotelholidayinn@ethotels.com
www.ethotels.com

Hotel Villa Novecento
11013 Courmayeur (AO)
Viale Monte Bianco, 64
phone +39 0165 843000
villa-novecento@romantikhotels.com
www.romantikhotels.com/courmayeur

Ristorante Le Foyer
Corso Ivrea, 146
11100 Aosta (AO)
phone +39 0165 32136
closed: Monday night and Tuesday

Ristorante Vecchio Ristoro
Via Tourneuve, 4
11100 Aosta (AO)
phone +39 0165 33238
closed: never

Cooperativa Jambon de Bosses
Località Saint Leonard, 10
11100 Saint Rhèmy-en-Bosses (AO)
phone +39 0165 780821
info@jambondebosses.it,
www.jambondebosses.it

Bottega degli Antichi Sapori
Via Porta Pretoria 63
11100 Aosta (AO)
phone +39 0165 239666

Maison de la Fontine
Via Monsignor de Sales, 14
11100 Aosta (AO)
phone +39 0165 235651

Salumificio Bertolin
Località Champagnolaz, 10
phone +39 0125 9661444/966127
11020 Arnad (AO)
info@bertolin.com
www.bertolin.com

Enoteca La Cave
Via Challand 34
11100 Aosta (AO)
phone +39 0165 41123

Istitut Agricole Regional
Regione La Rochère 1/a
11100 Aosta (AO)
phone +39 0165 215811
iar@iaraosta.it
www.iaraosta.it

Cooperativa Co-Enfer
Via C. Gex, 65
11011 Arvier (AO)
phone +39 0165 99238

Cave du Vin Blanc de Morgex e de La Salle
Località Chemin des Iles, 19
11017 Morgex (AO)
phone +39 0165 800331
caveduvinblanc@hotmail.com

arezzo (tuscany)

Azienda di Promozione Turistica (APT)
Piazza Risorgimento, 116
52100 Arezzo (AR)
phone +39 0575 23952, fax +39 0575 28042

Piazza della Repubblica, 28
phone +39 0575 377678, fax +39 0575 20839
info@arezzo.turismo.toscana.it
www.turismo.toscana.it

Ristorante Il Falconiere
Località San Martino, 370
52044 Cortona (AR)
phone +39 0575 612679
info@ilfalconiere.com
closed: Monday and Tuesday for lunch (except from March to October)

Hotel Cavaliere Palace
Via Madonna del Prato, 83
52100 Arezzo (AR)
phone +39 0575 26836
info@cvavalierehotels.com

Hotel Val di Colle
Località Bagnoro
52100 Arezzo (AR)
phone +39 0575 365167
valdicolle@tin.it

Ristorante Buca di San Francesco
Via San Francesco, 1
52100 Arezzo (AR)
phone +39 0575 23271
closed: Monday night and Tuesday

Agriturismo Fattoria Montelucci
Località Montelucci, 8
52020 Pergine Valdarno (AR)
phone +39 0575 896525
info.montelucci@.it
www.montelucci.it
closed: Monday and Tuesday

Trattoria La Capannaccia
Località Campriano, 51/c
phone +39 0575 361759
52100 Arezzo (AR)
closed: Sunday night and Monday

Trattoria Il Saraceno
Via Mazzini, 6/a
52100 Arezzo (AR)
phone +39 0575 27644
info@ilsaraceno.com
closed: Wednesday

Luigi Romani
Località Palazzo del Pero, 96
52100 Arezzo (AR)
phone +39 0575 369195

Eugenia Bellucci
Località Rofelle, 33
52032 Badia Tebalda (AR)
phone +39 0575 714064

Macelleria-Gastronomia Aligi Barelli
Via della Chimera, 22
52100 Arezzo (AR)
phone +39 0575 357754

ascoli piceno (marche)

Ufficio di Informazione e Accoglienza Turistica (IAT)
Palazzo dei Capitani, Piazza del Popolo
63100 Ascoli Piceno (AP)
phone +39 0736 253045, fax +39 0736 252391
iat.ascolipiceno@regione.marche.it

Hotel Villa Seghetti Panichi
Via San Pancrazio, 1
63031 Castel di Lama (AP)
phone +39 0736 812552
info@seghettipanichi.it www.seghettipanichi.it

Hotel Pennile
Via G. Spalvieri
63100 Ascoli Piceno (AP)
phone +39 0736 41645
hotelpennile@tin.it

Ristorante Castel di Luco
Località Castel di Luco
63040 Acquasanta Terme (AP)
phone +39 0736 802319
luco@abitarelastoria.it
closed: Monday

Ristorante Gallo d'Oro
Corso Vittorio Emanuele, 13
63100 Ascoli Piceno (AP)
phone +39 0736 253520
closed: Sunday

Caffè Meletti
Piazza del Popolo
63100 Ascoli Piceno (AP)
phone +39 0736 259626

Gastronomia Zè Migliori
Piazza Arrigo, 2
63100 Ascoli Piceno (AP)
phone +39 0736 250042

Spinosi
Via XXV Aprile, 23
63010 Campofilone (AP)
phone +39 0734 932196
spinosi@tin.it
www.spinosi.com

Velenosi Ercole
Via dei Biancospini, 11
63100 Ascoli Piceno (AP)
phone +39 0736 341218
www.velenosi.com

San Giovanni
Contrada Ciafone, 41
63035 Offida (AP)
phone +39 0736 889032
www.vinisangiovanni.it

Consorzio tutela vini piceni
Località Centobuchi, 81ma strada, 19
63030 Monteprandone (AP)
phone +39 0735 588639

Vinea
Via G. Garibaldi, 75
63035 Offida (AP)
phone +39 0736 880005
vinea@libero.it

Azienda Agricola Mastrosani
Via Montecalvario, 5
63034 Montalto delle Marche (AP)
phone +39 0736 828397

asti (piedmont)

Agenzia Turistica Locale (ATL)
Via Grandi, 5
14100 Asti (AT)
phone +39 0141 353034, fax +39 0141 410372

Piazza Alfieri, 29
phone +39 0141 530357, fax +39 0141 538200

Hotel Reale
Piazza Alfieri, 6
14100 Asti (AT)
phone +39 0141 530240
www.hotel-reale.com

Hotel Salera
Via Monsignor Marello, 19
14100 Asti (AT)
phone +39 0141 410169
salera@tin.it

Ristorante Gener Neuv
Lungo Tanaro dei Pescatori, 4
14100 Asti (AT)
phone +39 0141 557270
www.generneuv.it
closed: Sunday night and Monday

Ristorante La Grotta
Corso Torino, 366
14100 Asti (AT)
phone +39 0141 214168
closed: Monday night and Tuesday

Pasticceria Daniella
Via Brofferio, 159
14100 Asti (AT)
phone +39 0141 355650

Pasticceria Giordanino
Corso Alfieri, 254
14100 Asti (AT)
phone +39 0141 593802

Gastronomia San Secondo
Corso Dante, 6
14100 Asti (AT)
phone +39 0141 592416

Al Beato Bevitore
Via Bonzanigo, 12
14100 Asti (AT)
phone +39 0141 437083

Cantina Sociale di Mombaruzzo
Via Stazione, 15
14046 Mombaruzzo (AT)
phone +39 0141 77019
mombaruzzo@vignaioli.it
www.mombaruzzo.com

Cantina Sociale Vinchio-Vaglio Serra
Regione S. Pancrazio, 1

14040 Vinchio (AT)
phone +39 0141 950903
info@vinchio.com
www.vinchio.com

avellino (campania)

Informazioni Turistiche
Piazza Libertà, 50
54277 Avellino (AV)
phone +39 0825 74732, fax +39 0825 74757
info@eptavellino.it

Hotel de la Ville
Via Palatucci, 20
83100 Avellino (AV)
phone +39 0825 780911
info@hdv.av.it

Viva Hotel
Via Circumvallazione, 121-123
83100 Avellino (AV)
phone +39 0825 25922
vivahotel@virgilio.it

Ristorante La Maschera
Rampa San Modestino, 1
83100 Avellino (AV)
phone +39 0825 37603
ristorantelamaschera@virgilio.it
closed: Sunday night and Monday

Antica Trattoria Martella
Via Chiesa Conservatorio, 10
83100 Avellino (AV)
phone +39 0825 31117
info@ristorantemartella.it
closed: Sunday night and Monday

Antica Hirpinia
Contrada Lenze, 10
83030 Taurasi (AV)
phone +39 0827 74730

Feudi di San Gregorio
Località Cerza Grossa
83050 Sorbo Serpico (AV)
phone +39 0825 986611

Marsella
Località Campo di Maio, Via Piano d'Ardine
83010 Summonte (AV)
phone +39 0825 626555

L'Antica Fattoria
Via Pergolo
83050 Sant'Angelo all'Esca (AV)
phone +39 0872 78121

bari (puglia)

Azienda di Promozione Turistica (APT)
Piazza Moro, 33/a
70122 Bari (BA)
phone +39 080 5242361, fax +39 080 5242329
aptbari@pugliaturismo.com
www.pugliaturismo.com

Hotel Palace
Via Lombardi, 13
70100 Bari (BA)
phone +39 080 5216551
info@palacehotelbari.it

Hotel Sheraton Nicolaus
Via Cardinale A. Ciasca, 27
70124 Bari (BA)
phone +39 080 5682111
info@sheratonicolausbari.com

Ristorante Alberosole
Corso Vittorio Emanuele II, 13
70100 Bari (BA)
phone +39 080 5235446
closed: Monday

Ristorante La Pignata
Corso Vittorio Emanuele, 173
70122 Bari (BA)
phone +39 080 5232481
ristorante.lapignata@infinito.it
closed: Monday

Ristorante Centro Storico
Via Eroi di Dogali, 6
70010 Locorotondo (BA)
phone +39 080 4315473
info@ilcentrostorico.biz
closed: Wednesday

Agricole di Cagno Abbrescia
Piazza Massari, 6
70100 Bari (BA)
phone +39 080 5214195

Liso Nunzio
Via Poli, 62
70031 Andria (BA)
phone +39 088 3541242
www.aziendaagricolalisonunzio.it

Frantoio Oleario De Carlo
Via 24 maggio, 54
70020 Bitritto (BA)
phone +39 080 630767

Gregorio Minervini
Via Cifariello, 17
70056 Molfetta (BA)
phone +39 080 3974369
marcinase@marcinase.it
www.marcinase.it

Pastificio Ancora Fiore
Via Re David Giuseppe, 67/b
70100 Bari (BA)
phone +39 080 5423290

bassano del grappa (veneto)

Informazioni Turistiche
Largo Corona d'Italia, 35
36061 Bassano del Grappa (VI)
phone +39 0424 524351
fax +39 0424 525301

Bonotto Hotel Belvedere
Piazzale G. Giardino, 14
36061 Bassano del Grappa (VI)
phone +39 0424 529845
belvederehotel@bonotto.it

Hotel Ristorante Villa Ca' Sette
Via Cunizza da Romano, 4
36061 Bassano del Grappa (VI)
phone +39 0424 383350
info@ca-sette.it
www.ca-sette.it
closed: Sunday night and Monday

Ristorante Hotel Al Camin
Via Valsugana, 64
36022 Cassola (VI)
phone +39 0424 566134
info@hotelalcamin.com
closed: August 7–21

Ristorante Al Ponte
Via Volpato, 60
36061 Bassano del Grappa (VI)
phone +39 0424 219274
info@alpontedibassano.com
closed: Monday and Tuesday for lunch

Grapperia Nardini Bortolo
Ponte Vecchio, 2
36061 Bassano del Grappa (VI)
phone +39 0424 227741

Poli-Museo della grappa
Via Gamba, 6
36061 Bassano del Grappa (VI)
phone +39 0424 524426

belluno (veneto)

Ufficio di Informazione e di Accoglienza Turistica (IAT)
Piazza Duomo, 2
32100 Belluno (BL)
phone +39 0437 940083, fax +39 0437 958716
belluno@infodolomiti.it

Hotel Villa Carpenada
Via Mier, 158
32100 Belluno (BL)
phone +39 0437 948343

Hotel Valgranda
Via Pecol 11
32010 Zoldo Alto (BL)
phone +39 0437 789151
valgranda@dolomiti.it,
www.dolomiti.it/valgranda

Ristorante Al Borgo
Via Anconetta, 8
32100 Belluno (BL)
phone +39 0437 926755
info@alborgo.to www.alborgo.to
closed: Monday night and Tuesday

Trattoria da Ninetta
Località Mezzocanale
32012 Forno di Zoldo (BL)
+39 0437 78240
closed: Wednesday

Pasticceria Al Soler
Località Pecol
32010 Zoldo Alto (BL)
phone +39 0437 789114

Bar Gelateria Centrale
Piazza A. Santin, 4
32012 Forno di Zoldo (BL)
phone +39 0437 78130

Gelateria Pelmo
Località Dont
32012 Forno di Zoldo (BL)
phone +39 0437 78238

Macelleria Dal Mas
Località Pecol
32010 Zoldo Alto (BL)
phone +39 0437 788795

Agriturismo Al Fagiolo d'Oro
Via Monsignor Slongo 49
32033 Lamon (BL)
phone +39 0439 9136

benevento (campania)

Informazioni Turistiche
Piazza Roma, 11
82100 Benevento (BN)
phone +39 0824 319938, fax +39 0824 312309
ept.bn@tin.it

Grand Hotel Italiano
Viale Principe di Napoli, 137
82100 Benevento (BN)
phone +39 0824 24111
italianoghotel@tin.it

Hotel Villa Traiano
Viale dei Rettori, 9
82100 Benevento (BN)
phone +39 0824 326241
info@hotelvillatraiano.it

Ristorante Pascalucci
Strada Provinciale per San Giorgio
del Sannio, Via Iannassi
82010 San Nicola Manfredi (BN)
phone +39 0824 778400
pascalucci@libero.it
closed: Monday

Trattoria Nunzia
Via Annunziata, 152
82100 Benevento (BN)
phone +39 0824 20431
closed: Sunday

Dolciaria Borrillo Antichi Sapori
Piazza Risorgimento, 5
82029 San Marco dei Cavoti (BN)
phone +39 0824 984767

Fabbriche Riunite Torrone di Benevento
Viale Principe di Napoli, 123
82100 Benevento (BN)
phone +39 0824 21624
info@frtb.it
www.frtb.it

Strega Alberti di Benevento
Piazza V. Colonna, 8
82100 Benevento (BN)
phone +39 0824 542928
www.strega.it

Euroliquori Orrera
Corso Garibaldi, 97
82100 Benevento (BN)
phone +39 0824 25158
euroliquori@libero.it

Cantina Sociale Solopaca
Via Bebiana, 44
82036 Solopaca (BN)
phone +39 0824 977921
www.cantinasolopaca.it

bergamo (lombardy)

Informazioni Turistiche
Viale Vittorio Emanuele II, 20
24121 Bergamo (BG)
phone +39 035 210204, fax +39 035 230184
aptbg@apt.bergamo.it
www.apt.bergamo.it

Hotel Excelsior San Marco
Piazza della Repubblica, 6
24122 Bergamo (BG)
phone +39 035 366111/366159
info@hotelsanmarco.com

Starhotel Cristallo Palace
Via B. Ambiveri, 35
24100 Bergamo (BG)
phone +39 035 311211
reservations@starhotels.it

Ristorante Da Vittorio
Viale Papa Giovanni XXIII, 21
24121 Bergamo (BG)
phone +39 035 213266
info@davittorio.com
www.davittorio.com
closed: Wednesday

Ristorante Lio Pellegrini
Via San Tomaso, 47
241210 Bergamo (BG)
phone +39 035 247813
info@liopellegrini.it
www.liopellegrini.it
closed: Tuesday for lunch and Monday

Taverna Colleoni e Dell'Angelo
Località Città Alta, Piazza Vecchia, 7
24129 Bergamo (BG)
phone +39 035 232596
colleonidellangelo@uninetcom.it
www.colleonidellangelo.com
closed: Monday

Cantine Medolago Albani
Via Redona, 12
24069 Trescore Balneario (BG)
phone +39 035 942022

Enoteca del Borgo
Via Santa Caterina, 46
24100 Bergamo (BG)
phone +39 035 239726

Ol Formager
Piazzale Oberdan, 2
24100 Bergamo (BG)
phone +39 035 239237

La Cantina Chel del Formai
Via Ghislanzoni, 3
24100 Bergamo (BG)
phone +39 035 237146
www.lacantinacompagnoni.it

Vineria Cozzi
Via Colleoni, 22
24100 Bergamo (BG)
phone +39 035 238836
www.vineriacozzi.it

Pasticceria Jean Paul
Via Moroni, 361
24100 Bergamo (BG)
phone +39 035 251337

Informazioni Turistiche
Piazza Maggiore, 1
40121 Bologna (BO)
phone +39 051 246541, fax +39 051 251947
touristoffice@comune.bologna.it

Grand Hotel Baglioni
Via dell'Indipendenza, 8
40121 Bologna (BO)
phone +39 051 225445
ghb.bologna@baglionihotels.com
www.baglionihotels.com/hotels_bologna.htm

Hotel Internazionale
Via dell'Indipendenza, 60
40121 Bologna (BO)
phone +39 051 245544
internazionale.res@monrifhotels.it

Hotel Dei Commercianti
Via de' Pignattari, 11
40124 Bologna (BO)
phone +39 051 7457511
commercianti@inbo.it
www.bolognarhotels.it

Trattoria Battibecco
Via Battibecco, 4
40123 Bologna (BO)
phone +39 051 223298
closed: Saturday for lunch, Sunday and holidays

Ristorante Diana
Via dell'Indipendenza, 24
40121 Bologna (BO)
phone +39 051 231302
diana@softer.it
closed: Monday

Ristorante Biagi
Via Della Grada, 6
40122 Bologna (BO)
phone +39 051 553025
ristorantebiagi@hotmail.com
closed: Tuesday

Enoteca Italiana
Via Marsala, 2/b
40122 Bologna (BO)
phone +39 051 235989
www.enotecaitaliana.it

Paolo Atti & Figli
Via Caprarie, 7
40122 Bologna (BO)
phone +39 051 220425
info@paoloatti.com

Dolce Sana
Via E. Nani, 11
40122 Bologna (BO)
phone +39 051 402156

Come una volta
Via della Crocetta, 15
40122 Bologna (BO)
phone +39 051 6142378

Villa Zarri
Via Ronco, 1
40013 Castel Maggiore (BO)
phone +39 051 700604
info@villazarri.com
www.villazarri.com

Antica salsamenteria Tamburini
Via Caprarie, 1
40122 Bologna (BO)
phone +39 051 234726
tambinfo@tin.it
www.tamburini.bo.it

Informazioni Turistiche
Via Stazione, 9
39042 Bressanone (BZ)
phone +39 0472 836401, fax +39 0472 836067
info@brixen.org
www.brixen.org

Hotel Ristorante Elephant
Via Rio Bianco, 4
39042 Bressanone (BZ)
phone +39 0472 832750
info@hotelelephant.com
www.hotelelephant.com

Hotel Lodenwirt
Via Pusteria, 1
39030 Vandòies (BZ)
phone +39 0472 867000
info@lodenwirt.it
www.lodenwirt.it

Hotel Dominik
Via Terzo di Sotto, 13
39042 Bressanone (BZ)
phone +39 0472 830144
info@hoteldominik.com
www.hoteldominik.com

Hotel Grüner Baum
Via Stufles, 11
39042 Bressanone (BZ)
phone +39 0472 274100
info@gruenerbaum.it

Ristorante Fink
Via Portici Minori, 4
39042 Bressanone (BZ)
phone +39 0472 834883
closed: Tuesday night (except in July and August)

Ristorante Sunnegg
Via Vigneti, 67
39042 Bressanone (BZ)
phone +39 0472 834760
gasthof.sunnegg@rolmail.net
closed: Wednesday and Thursday for lunch

Vinus-Peter's Weinbistro
Via Mercato Vecchio, 6
39042 Bressanone (BZ)
phone +39 0472 2831583

Cantina dell'Abbazia di Novacella
Via Abbazia, 1
39040 Varna (BZ)
phone +39 0472 836189
www.kloster-neustift.it

Shanung
Via Plose, 14
39042 Bressanone (BZ)
phone +39 0472 837748

Karl Zerzer
Via Generale Verdross, 23
39024 Malles Venosta (BZ)
phone +39 0473 831141

Informazioni Turistiche
Piazza Matteotti, 9
09100 Cagliari (CA)
phone +39 070 669255
aast.info@tiscalinet.it

Piazza Defennu, 9
phone +39 070 604241
enturismoca@tiscalinet.it

Hotel Regina Margherita
Viale Regina Margherita, 44
09124 Cagliari (CA)
phone +39 070 670342
htirm@hotelreginamargherita.com

Hotel Caesar's
Via Darwin, 2/4
09126 Cagliari (CA)
phone +39 070 340750
info@caesarshophoneit

Ristorante Dal Corsaro
Viale Regina Margherita, 28
09124 Cagliari (CA)
phone +39 070 664318
dalcorsaro@tiscali.it
www.dalcorsaro.com
closed: Sunday (except in August)

Ristorante S'Apposentu
Via Sant'Alenixedda, Teatro Lirico
09124 Cagliari (CA)
phone +39 070 4082315
info@sapposentu.it
www.sapposentu.it
closed: Sunday and Monday

Trattoria Da Lillicu
Via Sardegna, 78
09100 Cagliari (CA)
phone +39 070 652970
closed: Sunday

Antica Enoteca Cagliaritana
Scalette Santa Chiara, 21
09100 Cagliari (CA)
phone +39 070 669886

Bonu
Viale Diaz, 162
09100 Cagliari (CA)
phone +39 070 492167

La Tavola degli Antichi
Via Barone Rossi, 2b
09100 Cagliari (CA)
phone +39 070 655482
info@latavoladegliantichi.com
www.latavoladegliantichi.com

Cooperativa Su Zaferanu
Via Sauro, 12
09037 San Gavino Monreale (CA)
phone +39 070 9339207

**Azienda Autonoma di Soggiorno
e Turismo (AAST)**
Piazza Umberto I, 19
80073 Capri (NA)
phone +39 081 8370686, fax +39 081 8370918
touristoffice@capri.it

Via Orlandi, 19/a
80071 Anacapri (NA)
phone +39 081 8371524

Grand Hotel Quisisana
Via Camerelle, 2
80073 Capri (NA)
phone +39 081 8370788
info@quisi.com

Capri Palace Hotel
Via Capodimonte, 2b
80071 Anacapri (NA)
phone +39 081 9780111
info@capri-palace.com

Hotel Scalinatella
Via Tragara, 8
80073 Capri (NA)
phone +39 081 8370633
info@scalinatella.com

Ristorante La Colombaia
Via Camerelle, 2
80073 Capri (NA)
phone +39 081 8370788
info@quisi.com
www.quisi.com
open only at night

Ristorante La Capannina
Via Le Botteghe, 12 bis/14
80073 Capri (NA)
phone +39 081 8370732
capannina@capri.it
closed: Wednesday (open May and September)

Limoncello di Capri
Via Capodimonte, 27
80071 Anacapri (NA)
phone +39 0818 372927

Nettuno
Via Umberto I, 64
84010 Cetara (SA)
phone +39 0892 61147

Informazioni Turistiche
Piazza delle Carceri, 15
59100 Prato (PO)
phone +39 0574 24112
apt@prato.turismo.toscana.it

Hotel Paggeria Medicea
Viale Papa Giovanni XXIII
59015 Carmignano (PO)
phone +39 055 875141
hotel@artiminio.com

Hotel Giardino
Via Magnolfi, 4
59100 Prato (PO)
phone +39 0574 606588
info@giardinohophonecom

Ristorante Da Delfina
Località Artiminio, Via della Chiesa, 1
59015 Carmignano (PO)
phone +39 055 8718074
posta@dadelfina.it
closed: Sunday night and Monday

Su pé i Canto
Piazza Matteotti, 25
59015 Carmignano (PO)
phone +39 0558 712490

Biscottificio Mattei
Via Ricasoli, 20
59100 Prato (PO)
phone +39 0574 25756

caserta (campania)

Ente Provinciale per il Turismo (EPT)
Corso Trieste, 39
81100 Caserta (CE)
phone +39 0823 321137
enturismo.caserta@virgilio.it

Hotel Amadeus
Via Verdi, 72
81100 Caserta (CE)
phone +39 0823 352663
hotelamadeus@libero.it

Hotel Belvedere
Località Vaccheria, San Leucio, Via Nazionale
Sannitica, 87 (km 31)
81100 Caserta (CE)
phone +39 0823 304925

Ristorante Le Colonne
Via Nazionale Appia, 7/13
81100 Caserta (CE)
phone +39 0823 467494
info@lecolonnemarziale.it
www.lecolonnemarziale.it
closed: Tuesday and at night

Ristorante La Cucinotta
Via Pollio, 14
81100 Caserta (CE)
phone +39 0823 442807
www.lacucinotta.com
closed: Sunday night and Monday

Le Bifore
Piazza G. Matteotti, 26
81100 Caserta (CE)
phone +39 0823 220000

Moio Michele
Via Margherita, 6
81034 Mondragone (CE)
phone +39 0823 978017
www.moio.it

Andreozzi Nicola
Via Roma, 116
81031 Aversa (CE)
phone +39 0818 901898

Consorzio Ater
S.S. 91, Località Greci
84024 Contursi Terme (SA)
phone +39 0828 991079
www.consorzioater.it

castelbuono (sicily)

Informazioni Turistiche
Corso Ruggero, 77
90015 Cefalù (PA)
phone +39 0921 421050
info@cefalù-tour.pa.it

Hotel Riva del Sole
Lungomare Colombo, 25
90015 Cefalù (PA)
phone +39 0921 421230
lidia@rivadelsole.com

Ristorante Vecchio Palmento
Via Failla, 4
90013 Castelbuono (PA)
phone +39 0921 672099

Trattoria Nangalarruni
Via delle Confraternite, 5
90013 Castelbuono (PA)
phone +39 0921 671428
nangalarruni@libero.it
www.ristorantenangalarruni.it
closed: Wednesday

Abbate Filippo
Contrada Portella del Pero
90013 Castelbuono (PA)
phone +39 0921 671576

Giulio Gelardi
Via dei Caduti, 29
90010 Pollina (PA)
phone +39 0921 425206

Extra Bar Fiasconaro
Piazza Margherita, 9
90013 Castelbuono (PA)
phone +39 0921 671231
www.fiasconaro.com

catania (sicily)

Informazioni Turistiche
Via Cimarosa, 10
95124 Catania (CT)
phone +39 095 7306233, fax +39 095 7306233
apt@apt.catania.it
www.apt.catania.it

Excelsior Grand Hotel
Piazza Verga, 39
95129 Catania (CT)
phone +39 095 7476111
excelsior-catania@thi.it

Hotel Villa del Bosco
Via del Bosco, 62
95125 Catania (CT)
phone +39 095 7335100
info@hotelvilladelbosco.it

Ristorante Il Carato
Via Vittorio Emanuele II, 81
95131 Catania (CT)
phone +39 095 7159247
info@ilcarato.it
www.ilcarato.it
closed: Sunday and for lunch

Ristorante Il Dèhor
Contrada Maddalusa S.S. 640
92100 Agrigento (AG)

phone +39 0922 511335
info@bagliodellaluna.com
www.bagliodellaluna.com
closed: Monday for lunch

Osteria i Tre Bicchieri
Via San Giuseppe al Duomo, 31
95124 Catania (CT)
phone +39 095 7153540
info@osteriaitrebicchieri.it
www.osteriaitrebicchieri.it
closed: Monday for lunch and Sunday

Ristorante La Siciliana
Viale Marco Polo, 52/a
95126 Catania (CT)
phone +39 095 376400
lasiciliana@tiscalinet.it
closed: Monday and holidays at night

Enoteca regionale di Sicilia
Viale Africa, 31
95100 Catania (CT)
phone +39 095 7462210

Benanti
Via Garibaldi, 475
95029 Viagrande (CT)
phone +39 0957 893438
www.vinicolabenanti.it

Farmacia Tuccari
Via Etnea, 203
95010 Nunziata di Mascali (CT)
phone +39 095 969046
info@farmaciatuccari.it
www.farmaciatuccari.it

chiavenna (lombardy)

Informazioni Turistiche
Corso Vittorio Emanuele II, 2
23022 Chiavenna (SO)
phone +39 0343 36384, fax +39 0343 31112
aptchiavenna@provincia.so.it

Albergo Ristorante della Posta
Via Dogana, 8
23020 Montespluga (SO)
phone +39 0343 54234
salafaustoenoteca@tiscalinet.it
closed: never

Hotel Aurora
Località Campedello Est
Via Rezia, 73
23022 Chiavenna (SO)
phone +39 0343 32708
info@albergoaurora.it
www.albergoaurora.it

Hotel Crimea
Viale Pratogiano, 16
23022 Chiavenna (SO)
phone +39 0343 34343
crimea@clavis.it

Ristorante Al Cenacolo
Via Pedretti, 16
23022 Chiavenna (SO)
phone +39 0343 32123
closed: Tuesday night and Wednesday

Ristorante Passerini
Via Dolzino, 128
23022 Chiavenna (SO)
phone +39 0343 36166
info@ristorantepasserini.com
www.passerini.com
closed: Monday

Enoteca Marino
Via Dolzino, 64
23022 Chiavenna (SO)
phone +39 0343 32720
www.enomar.it

Macelleria Tognoni
Va Maloggia, 70
23022 Chiavenna (SO)
phone +39 0343 32314

Casa della Carne
Via S. Giovanni, 155
23020 Lanzada (SO)
phone +39 0342 453278
www.casadellacarne.com

La Casa del Formaggio
Via Dolzino, 83
23022 Chiavenna (SO)
phone +39 0343 32535

Ciapponi
Piazza 3 Novembre, 23
23017 Morbegno (SO)
phone +39 0342 610223

chioggia (veneto)

**Ufficio di Informazione e di Accoglienza
Turistica (IAT)**
Lungomare Adriatico, 101
30019 Sottomarina (VE)
phone +39 041 401068, fax +39 041 5540855
*apt-07@mail.regione.veneto.it www.chioggia-
apt.net*

Piazza Marconi
phone +39 041 550911, fax +39 041 5509581

Hotel Grande Italia
Rione Sant'Andrea, 597
30015 Chioggia (VE)
phone +39 041 400515
hgi@hotelgrandeitalia.com
www.hotelgrandeitalia.com

Hotel Bristol
Lungomare Adriatico, 46
30019 Sottomarina (VE)
phone +39 041 5540389
info@hotelbristol.net

Hotel Tegnue
Lungomare Adriatico, 48
30019 Sottomarina (VE)
phone +39 041 491700
info@hotelletegnue.it

Ristorante Al Centro di Marco e Melania
Piazza Baldini e Mantovan
30010 Cavanella d'Adige (VE)
phone +39 041 497501
closed: Monday

Ristorante Da Franco
Località Sant'Anna, S.S. Romea, 430
30015 Chioggia (VE)
phone +39 041 4950301
closed: Monday

Ristorante El Gato
Campo Sant'Andrea, 653
30015 Chioggia (VE)
phone +39 041 401806

Ristorante La Taverna
Via Cavalotti, 348
30015 Chioggia (VE)
phone +39 041 400265
closed: Monday

Ristorante Garibaldi
Via San Marco, 1924
30019 Sottomarina (VE)
phone +39 041 5540042
closed: Monday (from December to May also Sunday night)

Coopesca
Calle Sant'Andrea, 292
30015 Chioggia (VE)
phone +39 041 400220

cinque terre (liguria)

Informazioni Turistiche
Piazza Bastreri, 7
19025 Portovenere (SP)
phone +39 0187 790691, fax +39 0187 790215
www.aptcinqueterre.sp.it

Grand Hotel Portovenere
Via Garibaldi, 5
19025 Portovenere (SP)
phone +39 0187 792610
ghp@village.it

Hotel Belvedere
Via Garibaldi, 26
19025 Portovenere (SP)
phone +39 0187 790608
www.belvedereportovenere.it

Antica Osteria del Carugio
Via Cappellini, 66
19025 Portovenere (SP)
phone +39 0187 790617
www.anticaosteria.cjb.net
closed: Thursday

Hotel Cinque Terre
Via IV Novembre, 21
19016 Monterosso a Mare (SP)
phone +39 0187 817543
info@hotel5terre.com

Ristorante Miky
Via Fegina, 104
19016 Monterosso al Mare (SP)
phone +39 0187 817608
miky@ristorantemiky.it
closed: Tuesday (except in August)

Hotel Due Gemelli
Località Campi Est
Via Litoranea, 1
19017 Riomaggiore (SP)
phone +39 0187 920678
duegemelli@tin.it

Locanda Ca' dei Duxi
Via Colombo, 36
19017 Riomaggiore (SP)
phone +39 0187 920036
www.duxi.it

Ristorante Cappun Magru in casa di Marin
Località Groppo Via Volastra, 19
19017 Riomaggiore (SP)
phone +39 0187 920563
closed: Monday and Tuesday; for lunch except on Sunday

Locanda Gianni Franzi
Piazza Marconi, 1 - Via San Giovanni Battista, 41-47
19018 Vernazza (SP)
phone +39 0187 812228

Ristorante Gambero Rosso
Piazza Marconi, 7
19018 Vernazza (SP)
phone +39 0187 812265
closed: Monday (never in August)

Buranco
Via Buranco, 72
19016 Monterosso al Mare (SP)
phone +39 0187 817677
www.buranco.info

Pasini Molinari
Via Salita Castello, 137
19016 Monterosso al Mare (SP)
phone +39 0187 920136

Cooperativa Agricoltura di Riomaggiore
Località Groppo
19017 Riomaggiore (SP)
phone +39 0187 920435
www.cantinacinqueterre.com

Enoteca Franco Baroni
Via Cavour, 18
19032 Lerici (SP)
phone +39 0187 966301

Cooperativa Acquacoltura Punta Mesco-Cinque Terre
Via Guaini, 17/l
19015 Levanto (SP)
phone +335 7054676
www.puntamesco-5terre.com

Gastronomia Cerone Fragolina
Via Vittorio Veneto, 24
19100 La Spezia (SP)
phone +39 0187 732933

Cooperativa Agricoltori Vallata di Levanto
Via d. Ghiare, 20
19015 Levanto (SP)
phone +39 0187 800867

colonnata (tuscany)

Azienda di Promozione Turistica (APT)
Lungomare Vespucci, 24
57037 Marina di Massa (MS)
phone +39 0585 240063, fax +39 0585 869015
info@aptmassacarrara.it www.turismo.toscana.it

Hotel Carrara
Via E. Petacchi, 21
54031 Avenza (MS)
phone +39 0585 857616
info@hotelcarrara.it

Hotel Cavalieri del Mare
Via Verdi, 23
54039 Ronchi (MS)
phone +39 0585 868010
info@cavalieridelmare.com

Hotel Mediterraneo
Località Marina di Carrara, Via Genova, 2/h
phone +39 0585 785222

Ristorante Ninan
Via L. Bartolini, 3
54033 Carrara (MS)
phone +39 0585 74741
ninan@tiscalinet.it
closed: Sunday

Ristorante Venanzio
Piazza Palestro, 3
54030 Colonnata (MS)
phone +39 0585 758062
closed: never

Larderia La Conca
Via del Giardino, 6
54030 Colonnata (MS)
phone +39 0585 758066

Mario Guadagni
Via Fossacava, 27
54030 Colonnata (MS)
phone +39 0585 768080

Cooperativa Giogallo
Via Succisa Villa Vecchia, 19
54027 Pontremoli (MS)
phone +39 0187 874103

Cooperativa agricola Il Bosco
Località Santa Giustina
54027 Pontremoli (MS)
phone +39 0187 833628

comacchio (emilia–romagna)

Informazioni Turistiche
Piazza Folegatti, 28
44022 Comacchio (FE)
phone +39 0533 310161
iat@comune.comacchio.fe.it

Hotel Logonovo
Viale delle Querce, 109
44024 Lido degli Estensi (FE)
phone +39 0533 327520
logonovo@libero.it

Hotel Caravel
Località Lido di Spina, Viale Leonardo, 56
44024 Lido degli Estensi (FE)
phone +39 0533 330106
hotelcaravel@tin.it

Ristorante Aroldo
Località Lido di Spina, Viale delle Acacie, 26
44024 Lido degli Estensi (FE)
phone +39 0533 330948
belsandro@libero.it
closed: Tuesday (except from 5/15 to 9/15)

Ristorante La Barcaccia
Piazza XX Settembre, 41
44022 Comacchio (FE)
phone +39 0533 314080
trattoriabarcaccia@libero.it
closed: Monday

Pensione Al Ponticello
Via Cavour, 39
44022 Comacchio (FE)
phone +39 0533 314080
resca@libero.it

La Bottega di Fantinoli Anna & C.
Via Pescheria, 3
44022 Comacchio (FE)
phone +39 0533 313040

Pescheria Trepponti
Via Trepponti, 34
44022 Comacchio (FE)
phone +39 0533 381727

Manifattura dei Marinati
Via Mazzini, 200
44022 Comacchio (FE)
phone +39 0533 81159

Vino e...
Via O. Malagodi, 8
44042 Cento (FE)
phone +39 051 902663

cosenza (calabria)

Azienda di Promozione Turistica (APT)
Corso Mazzini, 92
87100 Cosenza (CS)
phone +39 0984 27485
aptcosenza@virgilio.it

Holiday Inn Cosenza
Via Panebianco
87100 Cosenza (CS)
phone +39 0984 31109
holidayinn.cs@virgilio.it

Hotel Centrale
Via del Tigrai, 3
87100 Cosenza (CS)
phone +39 0984 75750
hotelcentrale@tin.it

Ristorante L'Arco Vecchio
Piazza Archi di Ciaccio, 21
87100 Cosenza (CS)
phone +39 0984 72564
closed: Sunday

Ristorante L'Antica Osteria dell'Arenella
Piazza Arenella, 9
87100 Cosenza (CS)
phone +39 0984 76573
closed: Sunday and for lunch

Accademia Italiana del peperoncino
Via Gullo. 1
87023 Diamante (CS)
phone +39 0985 81130
accademia@peperoncino.org
www.peperoncino.org

I Magnifici del Mezzogiorno
Via degli Scavi, 55, Contrada San Bartolo
87020 Santa Maria del Cedro (CS)
phone +39 0985 5303

Nature Med
Corso Italia, 79
87100 Cosenza (CS)
phone +39 0984 393609

Fabbrica di Liquirizia Amarelli
Contrada Amarelli
87067 Rossano Scalo (CS)
phone +39 0983 511219
www.amarelli.it

Garritano 1908
Corso Vittorio Emanuele, 11
87100 Cosenza (CS)
phone +39 0984 71393
garritanofichi@tiscali.it

Fratelli Marano
Via Garibaldi, 9
87032 Amantea (CS)
phone +39 0982 41277
www.fichimarano.it

cremona (lombardy)

Azienda di Promozione Turistica (APT)
Piazza del Comune, 5
26100 Cremona (CR)
phone +39 0372 23233, fax +39 0372 534080
info@aptcremona.it
www.cremonaturismo.com

Delle Arti Design Hotel
Via Bonomelli, 8
26100 Cremona (CR)
phone +39 0372 23131
info@dellearti.com
www.dellearti.com

Hotel Impero
Piazza della Pace, 21
26100 Cremona (CR)
phone +39 0372 413013

Agriturismo Lo Stagno
Via Cascina Gerre del Pesce
26049 Stagno Lombardo (CR)
phone +39 0372 57055/2495603
info@lostagno.it
www.lostagno.it
closed: mai

Ristorante Al Caminetto
Via Umberto I, 26
26047 Scandolara Ripa d'Oglio (CR)
phone +39 0372 89589
www.ristorantealcaminetto.com
closed: never

Ristorante Il Violino
Via Sicardo, 3
26100 Cremona (CR)
phone +39 0372 461010
www.ilviolino.it
closed: Monday night and Tuesday

Enoteca Catullo
Via Santa Maria in Betlem, 28
26100 Cremona (CR)
phone +39 0372 32077

Enoteca Cremona
Via Ghisleri, 21
26100 Cremona (CR)
phone +39 0372 451771
divini@libero.it
www.enotecacremona.it

Latteria Soresina
Via dei Mille, 11
26015 Soresina (CR)
phone +39 0374 349111
info@soresina.it
www.latteriasoresina.it

Mazzini Gianfranco
Corso 20 Settembre, 49
26100 Cremona (CR)
phone +39 0372 21321

Pasticceria Lanfranchi
Via Solferino, 30
26100 Cremona (CR)
phone +39 0372 28743

Mostarda Luccini
Via Carducci, 1/a
26030 Cicognolo (CR)
phone +39 0372 830624
mostardaluccini@libero.it
www.mostardaluccini.it

cuneo (piedmont)

Informazioni Turistiche
Via Roma, 28 (Municipio)
12100 Cuneo (CN)
phone/fax +39 0171 693258
atl@cuneotourism.com
www.cuneotourism.com

Albergo Real Castello
Via Umberto, I 9
12060 Verduno (CN)
phone +39 0172 470125
castellodiverduno@castellodiverduno.com
www.castellodiverduno.com

Palazzo Lovera Hotel
Via Roma, 37
12100 Cuneo (CN)
phone +39 0171 690420
info@palazzolovera.com

Hotel Principe
Piazza D. Galimberti, 5
12100 Cuneo (CN)
phone +39 0171 693355
info@hotel-principe.it
www.hotel-principe.it

Ristorante Antiche Contrade
Via Savigliano, 12
12100 Cuneo (CN)
phone +39 0171 690429
info@antichecontrade.com
www.antichecontrade.it
closed: Thursday

Ristorante San Michele
Contrada Mondovì, 2
12100 Cuneo (CN)
phone +39 0171 681962
closed: Monday

Non Solo Toma
Via M. d'Azeglio, 1
12100 Cuneo (CN)
phone +39 0171 67142

Occelli Agrinatura
Regione Scarrone, 2
12060 Farigliano (CN)
phone +39 0173 746411
info@occelli.it
www.occelli.it

Pasticceria Arione
Piazza Galimberti, 14
12100 Cuneo (CN)
phone +39 0171 692539

Liquor Center
Corso Nizza, 86
12100 Cuneo (CN)
phone +39 0171 698260

Dispensa e Cantina Griva
Via Vittorio Emanuele II, 43
+39 0173 721345
12063 Dogliani (CN)

Antica Pasticceria Galletti
Via Giolitti, 41
12025 Dronero (CN)
phone +39 0171 918157

domodossola (lombardy)

Informazioni Turistiche
Stazione FS, Piazza Matteotti
28845 Domodossola (VCO)
phone +39 0324 248265
infossola@distrettolaghi.it

Hotel Ristorante Piemonte da Sciolla
Piazza Convenzione, 4
28845 Domodossola (VCO)
phone +39 0324 242633
rist.sciolla@libero.it
www.ristorantedasciolla.it
closed: Wednesday

Hotel Eurossola
Piazza Matteotti, 36
28845 Domodossola (VCO)
phone +39 0324 481326
info@eurossola.com

Ristorante Biglia
Vicolo dell'Oro, 22
28845 Domodossola (VCO)
phone +39 0324 248534
ristorantebiglia@libero.it
closed: Sunday night and Monday

Le Colonne
Piazzale Diaz, 3
28038 Santa Maria Maggiore (VCO)
phone +39 0324 94893

Enoteca Bava
Piazza 27-28 maggio, 8
28052 Cannobio (VCO)
phone +39 0323 71247

D.O.R Delizia dell'Ossola Rurale
Piazza della Chiesa, 10
28037 Domodossola (VB)
phone +39 0324 242928

Panificio Conti
Via Bonardi, 24
28030 Coimo di Druogno (VCO)
phone +39 0324 93027

Macelleria Crosetti
Via Roma, 16
28036 Crodo (VCO)
phone +39 0324 61001
Frazione Valdo 7
28030 Formazza (VCO)
phone +39 0324 463035

eolie islands (sicily)

Informazioni Turistiche
Corso Vittorio Emanuele, 202-204-231
98055 Lipari (ME)
phone +39 090 9880095, fax +39 090 9811190
aasteolie@netnet.it, infoaast@netnet.it
www.netnet.it/aasteolie

Hotel Ericusa
Località Berciato, Via Regina Elena
98050 Alicudi (ME)
phone +39 090 9889902

Hotel Villa Meligunis
Via Marte, 7
98055 Lipari (ME)
phone +39 090 9812426
info@villameligunis.it
www.villameligunis.it

Hotel Quartara
Via San Pietro, 15
98050 Panarea (ME)
phone +39 090 983027
info@quartarahophonecom

Ristorante Da Modesta
Via San Pietro
98050 Panarea (ME)
phone +39 090 983306
closed: 10/1-4/27

Hotel Bellavista
Località Santa Marina Salina,
Via Risorgimento, 242
98050 Leni-Isola di Salina (ME)
phone +39 090 9843009

Hotel Signum
Via Scalo, 15
98050 Malfa-Isola di Salina (ME)
phone +39 090 9844375
salina@hotelsignum.it

La Sirenetta Park Hotel
Località Ficogrande, Via Marina, 33
98050 Stromboli (ME)
phone +39 090 986025
info@lasirenetta.it

Hotel Les Sables Noir
Località Porto di Ponente
98050 Vulcano (ME)
phone +39 090 9850
reservation.lsn@framonhotels.it

Ristorante E Pulera
Via Isabella Conti Vainicher
98055 Lipari (ME)
phone +39 090 9811158
filippino@filippino.it

Ristorante Da Franco
Via Belvedere, 8
98050 Santa Marina di Salina (ME)
phone +39 090 9843287
info@ristorantedafranco.com
closed: December 1–20

Ristorante Porto Bello
Via Bianchi, 1
98050 Santa Marina di Salina (ME)
phone +39 090 9843125
teonadari@hotmail.com
closed: November 11–March 13

Ristorante Punta Lena
Località Ficogrande, Via Marina
98050 Stromboli (ME)
phone +39 090 986204
closed: November 1–April 1

Trattoria A' Tana
Via Porto
98050 Filicudi (ME)
phone +39 090 9889089

Azienda Agricola Caravaglio
Via Nazionale, 33
98050 Malfa-Isola di Salina (ME)
phone +39 090 9843420
caravaglio@virgilio.it

Giuseppe Di Lorenzo
Località Pollara, Via Leni, 10
98050 Malfa-Isola di Salina (ME)
phone +39 090 9843951

Cantine Stevenson
Via Porto Levante
98050 Vulcano (ME)
phone +39 090 9853247
www.netnet.it/conti

Colosi
Via Militare Ritiro, 23
98100 Messina
phone +39 090 53852
www.cantinecolosi.com

erbusco (lombardy)

Informazioni Turistiche
Corso Zanardelli, 34
25100 Brescia (BS)
phone +39 030 43418, fax +39 030 293284
www.bresciaholiday.com

Hotel L'Albereta
Via Vittorio Emanuele II, 23
25030 Erbusco (BS)
phone +39 030 7760550
info@albereta.it
www.albereta.it

Ristorante Gualtiero Marchesi
Via Vittorio Emanuele II, 11
25030 Erbusco (BS)
phone +39 030 7760562
ristorante@marchesi.it
www.marchesi.it
closed: Sunday night and Monday

Ristorante La Mongolfiera dei Sodi
Via Cavour, 7
25030 Erbusco (BS)
phone +39 030 7268303
vorreisapere@mongolfiera.it
www.mongolfiera.it
closed: Thursday

Ristorante Punta da Dino
Via Punta, 39
25049 Clusane (BS)
phone +39 030 989037
closed: Wednesday (open June to August)

Ristorante Al Castello
Via Mirolte, 33
25049 Iseo (BS)
phone +39 030 981285
closed: Tuesday and for lunch (except holidays)

Le Cantine di Franciacorta
Via Iseo, 56
25030 Erbusco (BS)
phone +39 030 775116
www.franciacorta.org

Bellavista
Via Bellavista, 5
25030 Erbusco (BS)
phone +39 030 7762000

Cà del Bosco
Via Case Sparse, 20
25030 Erbusco (BS)
phone +39 030 7766111
cadelbosco@cadelbosco.com

Cavalleri Gian Paolo e Giovanni
Via Provinciale, 96
25030 Erbusco (BS)
phone +39 030 7760217
www.cavalleri.it

fara san martino (abruzzo)

Informazioni Turistiche
Piazza del Plebiscito, 51
66034 Lanciano (CH)
phone +39 0872 717810
iat.lanciano@abruzzoturismo.it

Hotel Excelsior
Viale della Rimembranza, 19
66034 Lanciano (CH)
phone +39 0872 713013
reception@hotelexcelsiorlanciano.it

Ristorante Corona di Ferro
Corso Roma, 28
66034 Lanciano (CH)
phone +39 0872 713029
closed: Sunday night and Monday for lunch

Ristorante Villa Maiella
Via Sette Dolori, 30
66016 Guardiagrele (CH)
phone +39 0871 809362
info@villamaiella.it
www.villamaiella.it
closed: Sunday night and Monday

Pastificio Artigiano cav. Giuseppe Cocco
Zona artigianale, 15
66015 Fara San Martino (CH)
phone +39 0872 984121
info@pastacocco.com
www.pastacocco.com

La Sfoglia
Vicolo Baronessa, 3
66016 Guardiagrele (CH)
phone +39 0871 800664

Fattorie del Tratturo
Contrada Ragna, 59
66020 Scerni (CH)
phone +39 0873 914173

favignana (sicily)

Informazioni Turistiche
Piazza Saturno
91100 Trapani (TP)
phone +39 0923 29000
apttp@maill.cinet.it

Hotel Ristorante Aegusa
Via Garibaldi, 11/17
91023 Favignana (TP)
phone +39 0923.922430
info@aegusahophoneit

Conservittica Sammartano
91023 Favignana (TP)
phone +39 0923 921054
conservittica@virgilio.it
www.egadi.com/favoniocsf

Tonno Florio
91023 Favignana (TP)
florio_tonnare@tin.it
www.tonno-florio.it

ferrara (emilia–romagna)

Ufficio di Informazione e di Accoglienza Turistica (IAT)
Castello Estense
44100 Ferrara (FE)
phone +39 0532 209370, fax +39 0532 212266
infotour@provincia.fe.it
www.comune.fe.it

Hotel Duchessa Isabella
Via Palestro, 70
44100 Ferrara (FE)
phone +39 0532 202121
info@duchessaisabella.it
www.duchessaisabella.it

Hotel Annunziata
Piazza Repubblica, 5
44100 Ferrara (FE)
phone +39 0532 201111
info@annunziata.it
www.annunziata.it

Ristorante Quel Fantastico Giovedì
Via Castelnuovo, 9
44100 Ferrara (FE)
phone +39 0532 760570
closed: Wednesday

Ristorante Antica Trattoria Volano
Viale Volano, 20
44100 Ferrara (FE)
phone +39 0532 761421
anticatrattoriavolano@interfree.it
closed: Friday

Salumificio Mario
Via Aria Nuova, 51
44100 Ferrara (FE)
phone +39 0532 209476

Pastificio Ricci
Via Pomposa, 135
44100 Ferrara (FE)
phone +39 0532 62663
pastificioricci@tin.it

florence (tuscany)

Informazioni Turistiche
Via Cavour, 1/r
50100 Florence (FI)
phone +39 055 290832, fax +39 055 2760383
infoturismo@provincia.fi.it

Piazza della Stazione, 4
phone+39 055 212245, fax +39 055 2381226
turismo3@provincia.fi.it

Hotel The Westin Excelsior
Piazza Ognissanti, 3
50123 Florence (FI)
phone +39 055 27151
excelsiorflorence@westin.com

Hotel Continentale
Vicolo dell'Oro, 6/r
50123 Florence (FI)
phone +39 055 27262
continental@lungarnohotels.com

Ristorante Enoteca Pinchiorri
Via Ghibellina, 87
50122 Florence (FI)
phone +39 055 242777
ristorante@enotecapinchiorri.com
www.enotecapinchiorri.com
closed: Sunday and Monday; Tuesday and Wednesday for lunch

Trattoria Del Fagioli
Corso Tintori, 47
50122 Florence (FI)
phone +39 055 244285
closed: Saturday and Sunday

Trattoria Alla Vecchia Bettola
Viale V. Pratolini, 3/7
50124 Florence (FI)
phone +39 055 224158
closed: Sunday and Monday

Marchesi de' Frescobaldi
Località Castello di Nipozzano
50100 Florence (FI)
phone +39 055 8311050
info@frescobaldi.it
www.frescobaldi.it

Frescobaldi Wine Bar
Via de' Magazzini, 2
50100 Florence (FI)
phone +39 055 284724
www.frescobaldi.it

foggia (puglia)

Informazioni Turistiche
Via Perrone, 17
71100 Foggia (FG)
phone +39 0881 723141, fax +39 0881 725536
aptfoggia@pugliaturismo.com

Hotel Mercure Cicolella
Viale XXIV Maggio, 60
71100 Foggia (FG)
phone +39 0881 566111
info@hotelcicolella.it

Hotel White House
Via Monte Sabotino, 24
71100 Foggia (FG)
phone +39 0881 721644

Ristorante Il Ventaglio
Via G. Postiglione, 6
71100 Foggia (FG)
phone +39 0881 661500
closed: Sunday night and Monday (in the summer Saturday and Sunday)

Ristorante Rotarott'
Località La Torretta, Zona Incoronata
71100 Foggia (FG)
phone +39 0881 810009
closed: Sunday night and Monday

Nunzio Ninivaggi
Via Torino, 36
70022 Altamura (BA)
phone +39 080 3115852
www.ilpanedinunzio.it

Pr.Ali.Na
Zona Industriale
73020 Melpignano (LE)
phone +39 0836 43439833
pralina@pralinasrl.it
www.pralinasrl.it

forlì (emilia–romagna)

Informazioni Turistiche
Piazza XC Pacifici, 2
47100 Forlì (FC)
phone +39 0543 712435, fax +39 0543 712755
iat@comune.forli.fo.it

Hotel Masini
Corso Garibaldi, 28
47100 Forlì (FC)
phone +39 0543 28072
info@hotelmasini.com

Hotel Ramada Encore
Viale Vittorio Veneto, 3/e
47100 Forlì (FC)
phone +39 0543 22038
reservation@ramadaencoreforli.com

Ristorante Casa Rusticale dei Cavalieri Templari
Viale Bologna, 275
47100 Forlì (FC)
phone +39 0543 701888
closed: Sunday and Monday

Trattoria Locanda al Gambero Rosso
Via G. Verdi, 5
47026 San Piero in Bagno (FC)
phone +39 0543 903405
locanda.gamberorosso@libero.it
www.bagnodiromagnaturismo.it/locanda.gambero.rosso
closed: Monday (January-February on Tuesday, Wednesday and Sunday night)

Cantine Braschi
Via Roma, 37
47025 Mercato Saraceno (FC)
phone +39 0547 91061

Vini pregiati Celli
Via Carducci, 5
47032 Bertinoro (FC)
phone +39 0543 445183

Associazione per la valorizzazione della piadina romagnola
Via Roverella, 1
47023 Cesena (FC)
phone +39 0547 361711

Dimensione Pasta
Via Campo di Marte, 54
47100 Forlì (FC)
phone +39 0543 552188

La piadina del fratelli Lucchi
Via Cervese, 1105
47023 Cesena (FC)

Casa Romagna
Corte Dandini 3
47023 Cesena (FC)
phone +39 0547 613594

Caseificio Pascoli
Via Rubicone destra, 220
47039 Savignano sul Rubicone (FC)
phone +39 0541 945732

genoa (liguria)

Informazioni Turistiche
Stazione Piazza Principe
Piazza Acqua Verde
16100 Genova (GE)
phone/fax +39 010 2462633
iat.principe@apt.genova.it

Aeroporto Cristoforo Colombo
Via Pionieri e Aviatori d'Italia
phone +39 010 6015247
iat.aeroporto@apt.genova.it

Hotel Bristol Palace
Via XX Settembre, 35
16121 Genova (GE)
phone +39 010 592541
info@hotelbristolpalace.com

Hotel Jolly Marina
Via Molo Ponte Calvi, 5
16124 Genova (GE)
phone +39 010 25391
genova-marina.jollyhotels.com

Hotel City
Via San Sebastiano, 6
16123 Genova (GE)
phone +39 010 5545
city.ge@bestwestern.it

Locanda di Palazzo Cicala
Piazza San Lorenzo, 16
16123 Genova (GE)
phone +39 010 2518824
palazzocicala@mentelocale.it
www.palazzocicala.it

Ristorante La Bitta nella Pergola
Località Foce, Via G. Casaregis, 52/r
16129 Genova (GE)
phone +39 010 588543
labittanellapergola@libero.it
closed: Sunday night and Monday (in July also Sunday for lunch)

Ristorante Edilio
Corso A. De Stefanis, 104/r
16139 Genova (GE)
phone +39 010 880501
closed: Sunday night and Monday (in July also Sunday for lunch)

Trattoria Maxelà
Vico Inferiore del Ferro, 9
16100 Genova (GE)
phone +39 010 2474209
closed: Saturday and Sunday for lunch

Enoteca Migone
Piazza San Matteo, 4/r
16100 Genova (GE)
phone +39 010 2473282

Forno Patrone
Via Ravecca, 72/r
16100 Genova (GE)

Bisanti
Via Pre, 27
16100 Genova (GE)

Il Primo Piatto
Via Pal. Fortezza, 51/r
16100 Genova (GE)
phone +39 010 6459729

gorizia (friuli–venezia giulia)

Informazioni Turistiche
Via Roma, 5 (Palazzo della Regione)
34170 Gorizia (GO)
phone +39 0481 3862225,
fax +39 0481 386277
arpt-go1@regione.fvg.it

Albergo Castello di Spessa
Via Spessa, 1
34070 Capriva del Friuli (GO)
phone +39 0481 808124
info@castellospessa.com
www.castellospessa.com

Hotel Alla Transalpina
Via Caprin, 30
34170 Gorizia (GO)
phone +39 0481 530291

Hotel Euro Diplomat
Corso Italia, 63
34170 Gorizia (GO)
phone +39 0481 82166

Ristorante Rosenbar
Via Duca d'Aosta, 96
34170 Gorizia (GO)
phone +39 0481 522700
rosenbar@activeweb.it
closed: Sunday and Monday

Ristorante Majda
Via Duca d'Aosta, 71-73
34170 Gorizia (GO)
phone +39 0481 30871
closed: Tuesday and Saturday for lunch (in the summer Saturday for lunch and Sunday)

Trattoria Alla Luna
Via Oberdan, 13
34170 Gorizia (GO)
phone +39 0481 530374
closed: Sunday night and Monday

Enoteca Regionale La Serenissima
Via Battisti, 26
34072 Gradisca d'Isonzo (GO)
phone +39 0481 99598
www.vignetochiamatofriuli.com

Cantina Produttori Cormons
Via Vino della Pace, 31
34071 Cormons (GO)
phone +39 0481 61798
info@cormons.com
www.cormons.com

La Golosa
Viale 24 Maggio 3°
34170 Gorizia (GO)
phone +39 0481 530408

gragnano (campania)

Informazioni Turistiche
Via San Carlo, 9
80100 Naples (NA)
phone +39 081 402394
info@inaples.it

Piazza del Gesù Nuovo, 7
phone +39 081 5223328

Stazione Mergellina
phone +39 081 7612102

Grand Hotel la Medusa
Via Passeggiata Archeologica, 5
80053 Castellammare di Stabia (NA)
phone +39 081 8723383
info@lamedusahophonecom

Hotel Grillo Verde
Piazza Imbriani, 19
80058 Torre Annunziata (NA)
phone +39 081 8611019
hgv@hotelgrilloverde.it

Trattoria O' Pignatiello
Via A. De Gasperi, 207
80053 Castellammare di Stabia (NA)
phone +39 081 8715100
closed: never

Storico Pastificio Garofalo
Via dei Pastai, 42
80054 Gragnano (NA)
phone +39 081 8011002

Le Antiche Tradizioni di Gragnano
Via Vittorio Veneto, 167
80054 Gragnano (NA)
phone +39 081 813643

Caseificio La Verde Fattoria
Località Moiano
Via Sala, 15
80069 Vico Equense (NA)
phone +39 081 8023095
salvaalba@tin.it

grosseto (tuscany)

Azienda di Promozione Turistica (APT)
Viale Monterosa, 206
58100 Grosseto (GR)
phone +39 0564 462611, fax +39 0564 454606
info@lamaremma.info
www.grosseto.turismo.toscana.it

Bastiani Grand Hotel
Piazza Gioberti, 64
58100 Grosseto (GR)
phone +39 0564 20047
info@hotelbastiani.com

Hotel della Fortezza
Piazza Cairoli
58018 Sorano (GR)
phone +39 0564 632010
fortezzahotel@tin.it

Hotel Granduca
Via Senese, 170
58100 Grosseto (GR)
+39 0564 453833
info@hotelgranduca.com
Agriturismo Pian dei Casali
Località Pianetti
58050 Montemerano (GR)
phone +39 0564 602625
info@piandeicasali.it
www.piandeicasali.it

Ristorante Canapone
Piazza Dante, 3
58100 Grosseto (GR)
phone +39 0564 24546
closed: Sunday

Ristorante Lorena
Via Mameli, 23
58100 Grosseto (GR)
phone +39 0564 22695
closed: Sunday night and Monday

Ristorante Terzo Cerchio
Piazza Castello, 2
58040 Istia d'Ombrone (GR)
phone +39 0564 409235
terzocerchio@virgilio.it
closed: Monday

Ristorante Da Caino
Via Canonica, 3
58050 Montemerano (GR)
phone +39 0564 602817
caino@dacaino.it
closed: Wednesday, Thursday for lunch

Salumeria Giovannino
Via Roma, 76
58017 Pitigliano (GR)
phone +39 0564 616108

Orbetello Pesca Lagunare
Via Leopardi, 9
58015 Orbetello (GR)
phone +39 0564 860288
info@orbetellopesca.it
www.orbetellopesca.it

imperia (liguria)

Ufficio di Informazione e di Accoglienza Turistica (IAT)
Viale Matteotti, 37
18100 Imperia (IM)
phone +39 0183 660140, fax +39 0183 666247
infoimperia@rivieradeifiori.it
www.aptrivieradeifiori.it

Relais San Damian
Strada Vasia, 47
18100 Imperia (IM)
phone +39 0183 280309

Hotel Croce di Malta
Località Porto Maurizio, Via Scarincio, 148
18100 Imperia (IM)
phone +39 0183 667020
info@hotelcrocedimalta.com

Ristorante Agrodolce
Calata Cuneo, 25
18100 Imperia (IM)
phone +39 0183 293702
closed: Wednesday

Trattoria Da Clorinda
Via Garessio, 98
18100 Imperia (IM)
phone +39 0183 291982
closed: Monday

Tenuta Giuncheo
Località Giuncheo
18033 Camporosso (IM)
phone +39 0184 288639
info@tenutagiuncheo.it
www.tenutagiuncheo.it

Alessandri
Via Costa Parrocchia
18028 Ranzo (IM)
phone +39 0182 53458

La Baita
Località Gazzo
18020 Borghetto d'Arroscia (IM)
phone +39 0183 31083
labaitagazzo@katamail.com

Le Streghe di Triora
Corso Italia 50
18010 Triora (IM)
phone +39 0184 94278

Azienda Agricola Maccario
Via S. Bernardo 23
18035 Dolceacqua (IM)
phone +39 0184 206013

Ufficio di Informazione e di Accoglienza Turistica (IAT)
Piazza Santa Maria di Paganica, 5
67100 L'Aquila (AQ)
phone +39 0862 410808, fax +39 0862 65442
presidio.aquila@abruzzoturismo.it

Via XX Settembre, 8
phone +39 0862 22306, fax +39 0862 27486
iat.aquila@abruzzoturismo.it
www.regione.abruzzo.it

Albergo Diffuso
67020 Santo Stefano di Sessanio (AQ)
phone +39 0862 8999116
info@sextantio.it
www.sextantio.it

Hotel Parco delle Rose
Località Paganica, S.S. 17 bis
67016 L'Aquila (AQ)
phone +39 0862 680128
hotelpdr@inwind.it

Hotel Duomo
Via Dragonetti, 10
67100 L'Aquila (AQ)
phone +39 0862 410893

Ristorante Elodia
Località Camarda, S.S. 17 bis del Gran Sasso, 37
67010 L'Aquila (AQ)
phone +39 0862 606219
elodia@tin.it
closed: Sunday night and Monday

Ristorante La Grotta di Aligi
Viale Rendina, 2
67100 L'Aquila (AQ)
phone +39 0862 65260
closed: Sunday

Cooperativa Altopiano di Navelli
Località Civitaretenga
67020 Navelli (AQ)
phone +39 0862 959163

Azienda Agricola Papaoli
Piazza Palazzo, 20
67100 L'Aquila (AQ)
phone +39 0862 27237

Antica Azienda Agricola Peltuinum
Via Peltuino, 19
67020 Prata d'Ansidonia (AQ)
phone +39 0862 62413
info@peltuinum.it

Cooperativa Campo Imperatore
Strada Provinciale, 1
67020 Calascio (AQ)
phone +39 0862 930345

Azienda Agricola La Mascionara
Località Porcinari
67013 Campotosto (AQ)
phone +39 340 2334530

Gabriella Costantini
Via Benedetta, 3
67020 Santo Stefano di Sessanio (AQ)
phone +39 0862 954253

Amalia Cardelli
Via F. Corridoni
67100 L'Aquila (AQ)
phone +39 0862 24659

Informazioni Turistiche
Frazione Gionghi, 73
38046 Lavarone (TN)
phone +39 0464 783226, fax +39 0464 783118
apt.altipiani.lavarone@trentino.to

Hotel Caminetto
Frazione Bertoldi
38046 Lavarone (TN)
phone +39 0464 783214
hophonecaminetto@cr-surfing.net

Ristorante San Colombano
Via Vicenza, 30 (S.S. 46 Est)
38068 Rovereto (TN)
phone +39 0464 436006
sancolombano1@tin.it
closed: Sunday night and Monday

Caseificio Sociale di Lavarone
Via Marconi, 5
38046 Lavarone (TN)
phone +39 0464 783106

Caseificio Sociale di Predazzo e Moena
Via Fiamme Gialle, 48
38037 Predazzo (TN)
phone +39 0462 501287
www.puzzonedimoena.com

Azienda Agricola Paternoster
Via Castel Thun, 6
38010 Vigo di Ton (TN)
phone +39 0462 657282

Informazioni Turistiche
Corso Vittorio Emanuele, 24
73100 Lecce (LE)
phone +39 0832 248092, fax +39 0832 310238
aptlecce@pugliaturismo.com
www.pugliaturismo.com

Hotel Patria Palace
Piazzetta G. Riccardi, 13
73100 Lecce (LE)
phone +39 0832 245111
info@patriapalacelecce.com

Hotel Delle Palme
Via di Leuca. 90
73100 Lecce (LE)
phone +39 0832 347171
hdellepalme@tiscalinet.it

Trattoria Osteria degli Spiriti
Via Battisti, 14
73100 Lecce (LE)
phone +39 0832 246274
info@osteriadeglispiriti.it
closed: Sunday night

Trattoria Cucina Casareccia (Le Zie)
Via Col. A. Costadura, 19
73100 Lecce (LE)
phone +39 0832 245178

Il Giardino del re
Via del Salesiani, 33
73100 Lecce (LE)
phone +39 083 6802540

Al di Vino Bicchiere
Via Santa Maria del Paradiso, 4
73100 Lecce (LE)
phone +39 320 4515594

Sapori del Salento-Stefanico srl
Via Madonna di Fatima, 6
73039 Tricase (LE)
phone +39 0833 544759

Calogiuri
Via Leonardo da Vinci
73023 Lizzanello (LE)
phone +39 0832 651729

lecco (lombardy)

Informazioni Turistiche
Via N. Sauro, 6
23900 Lecco (LC)
phone +39 0341 362360, fax +39 0341 286231
info@aptlecco.com

Hotel Don Abbondio
Piazza Era, 10
23900 Lecco (LC)
phone +39 0341 366315

Hotel Alberi
Lungo Lario Isonzo, 4
23900 Lecco (LC)
phone +39 0341 350992
info@hotelalberi.lecco.it

Ristorante Cermenati
Corso Matteotti, 71
23900 Lecco (LC)
phone +39 0341 283017
closed: Monday

Osteria Olga
Località Maggianico, Via Poncione, 7
23900 Lecco (LC)
phone +39 0341 422030
www.osteriaolga.it
closed: Saturday for lunch and Sunday

Da Ceko il Pescatore
Piazza Era, 8
23900 Lecco (LC)
phone +39 341 284101

Cademartori
Via Vittorio Veneto, 13
22040 Introbio (LC)
phone +39 0341 980324
info@cademartori.it
www.cademartori.it

Carozzi formaggi
Via Provinciale, 60
22040 Ballabio (LC)
phone +39 0341 530455
info@carozzi.com
www.carozzi.com

Invernizzi & Rota
Viale Trieste, 63
22040 Pasturo (LC)
phone +39 0341 955218

Cascina Coldognetta Project Food 2000
Via A. De Gasperi, 19
22040 Moggio Valsassina (LC)
phone +39 0341 996872
info@cascinacoldognetta.com
www.cascinacoldognetta.com

L'Abbinamento sapori e sapere
Via Metauro, 3
20052 Monza (MI)
phone +39 039 736381

livorno (tuscany)

Informazioni Turistiche
Piazza Cavour, 6
57126 Livorno (LI)
phone +39 0586 204611, fax +39 0586 896173

Hotel Gran Duca
Piazza Micheli, 16
57123 Livorno (LI)
phone +39 0586 891024
granduca@granduca.it

Hotel La Vedetta
Via della Lecceta, 5
57128 Montenero Sud (LI)
phone +39 0586 579957
info@hotellavedetta.it

Ristorante Da Galileo
Via della Campana, 20
57122 Livorno (LI)
phone +39 0586 889009
closed: Sunday night and Monday

Ristorante Cantina Nardi
Via L. Cambini, 6/8
57100 Livorno (LI)
phone +39 0586 808006
closed: Sunday; open only for lunch

Ristorante Gambero Rosso
Piazza della Vittoria, 13
57027 San Vincenzo (LI)
phone +39 0565 701021
closed: Monday and Tuesday

Strada del Vino Costa degli Etruschi
Località San Guido, 45
57020 Castagneto Carducci (LI)
phone +39 0565 749768
www.lastradadelvino.com

Tenuta San Guido
Località Capanne
57020 Castagneto Carducci (LI)
phone +39 0565 762003

Fabbrica Liquori Borsi
Via Garibaldi, 5
57020 Castagneto Carducci (LI)
phone +39 0565 766017
borsi@infol.it, www.borsiliquori.it

lodi (lombardy)

Informazioni Turistiche
Piazza Broletto, 4
26900 Lodi (LO)
phone +39 0371 421391, fax +39 0371 421313
info@apt.lodi.it
www.apt.lodi.it

Hotel Concorde Lodi Centro
Piazzale Stazione, 2
26900 Lodi (LO)
phone +39 0371 421322
lodi@hotel-concorde.it

Hotel Anelli
Viale Vignati, 7
26900 Lodi (LO)
phone +39 0371 421354
albergo.anelli@libero.it

Ristorante Tre Gigli all'Incoronata
Piazza della Vittoria, 47
26900 Lodi (LO)
phone +39 0371 421404
tregigli@libero.it
closed: Sunday night and Monday

Ristorante Isola Caprera
Via Isola Caprera, 14
26900 Lodi (LO)
phone +39 0371 421316
info@isolacaprera.com
closed: Tuesday night and Wednesday

De Toma
Corso Vittorio Emanuele, 32
26900 Lodi (LO)
phone +39 0371 420786

La Bottega Casearia
Corso Umberto, 20
26900 Lodi (LO)
phone +39 0371 424979

Angelo Croce
Via C. Battisti, 73
20071 Casalpusterlengo (LO)
phone +39 0377 84236

Caseificio Zucchelli
Cascina Marmorina, 18
20080 Orio Litta (LO)
phone +39 0377 804232

lucca (tuscany)

Azienda di Promozione Turistica (APT)
Piazza Santa Maria, 35
55100 Lucca (LU)
phone +39 0583 919931, fax +39 0583 469964
info@lucca.turismo.it
www.lucca.turismo.toscana.it

Hotel Ilaria e Residenza dell'Alba
Via del Fosso, 26
55100 Lucca (LU)
phone +39 0583 47615
info@hotelilaria.com

Hotel Villa Agnese
Viale A. Marti, 177
55100 Lucca (LU)
phone +39 0583 467109
info@villagnese.it

Locanda l'Elisa
S.S. 12r, Via Nuova per Pisa
55050 Massa Pisana (LU)
phone +39 0583 379737
info@locandaelisa.it

Ristorante La Mora
Località Ponte a Moriano, Via Sesto
di Moriano, 1748
55029 Sesto di Moriano (LU)
phone +39 0583 406402
info@ristorantelamora.it
www.ristorantelamora.it
closed: Wednesday

Ristorante La Buca di Sant'Antonio
Via della Cervia, 1/5
55100 Lucca (LU)
phone +39 0583 55881
la.buca@lunet.it
closed: Sunday night and Monday

Ristorante Osteria Al Ritrovo del Platano
Località Ponte di Campia
55027 Gallicano (LU)
phone +39 0583 766142

Azienda Agricola Alle Camelie
Pieve di Compito
55065 Capannori (LU)
phone +39 0583 55505

Fattoria Maionchi
Località Tofori
55065 Capannori (LU)
phone +39 0583 978194
villa-maionchi@luinet.it

Fattoria Vigna del Greppo
Via del Molinetto, 24
55015 Montecarlo (LU)
phone +39 0583 22599

Consorzio Garfagnana Produce
Via Vittorio Emanuele
55032 Castelnuovo di Garfagnana (LU)
phone +39 0583 65169

**Associazione Castanicoltori
della Garfagnana**
Piazza O. Dini, 4
55032 Castelnuovo di Garfagnana (LU)
phone +39 0583 641363

macerata (marche)

Informazioni Turistiche
Piazza della Libertà, 12
62100 Macerata (MC)
phone +39 0733 234807
iat.macerata@regione.marche.it

Hotel Claudiani
Vicolo Ulissi, 8
62100 Macerata (MC)
phone +39 0733 261400
info@hotelclaudiani.it

Hotel Arcadia
Via Padre Matteo Ricci, 134
62100 Macerata (MC)
phone +39 0733 235961
arcadia@gestionihotels.it

Ristorante Le Case
Località Mozzavinci, 16-17
62100 Macerata (MC)
phone +39 0733 231897
ristorantelecase@tin.it
www.ristorantelecase.it
closed: Sunday night and Monday

Ristorante Al Teatro
Via Umberto I, 7
62024 Matelica (MC)
phone +39 0737 786099
nenny-s@tin.it
closed: Wednesday

Enoteca Simoncini
Galleria del Commercio, 14
62100 Macerata (MC)
phone +39 0733 260576

Fazi Battaglia
Via Roma, 117
60031 Castelplanio (AN)
phone +39 0731 813444

Tenuta di Tavignano
Località Tavignano
62011 Cingoli (MC)
phone +39 0733 617303
tavignano@libero.it

**Belisario-Cantina Sociale di Matelica
e Cerreto d'Esi**
Via A. Merloni, 12
62024 Matelica (MC)
phone +39 0737 787247
www.belisario.it

Casa Francucci
Località Rio, 4
62032 Camerino (MC)
phone +39 0737 6366775

La Marca
Via G. Leopardi, 59
62032 Camerino (MC)
phone +39 0733 557803
info@anticagastronomia.it
www.anticagastronomia.it

mantua (lombardy)

Informazioni Turistiche
Piazza A. Mantegna, 6
46100 Mantua (MN)
phone +39 0376 328253, fax +39 0376 363292
aptmantova@iol.it
www.aptmantova.it

Hotel Rechigi
Via P.F. Calvi, 30
46100 Mantua (MN)
phone +39 0376 320781
info@rechigi.com
www.rechigi.com

Hotel San Lorenzo
Piazza Concordia, 14
46100 Mantua (MN)
phone +39 0376 220500
hotel@hotelsanlorenzo.it
www.hotelsanlorenzo.it

Il Cigno Trattoria dei Martiri
Piazza Carlo d'Arco, 1
46100 Mantua (MN)
phone +39 0376 327101
closed: Monday and Tuesday

Ristorante Aquila Nigra
Vicolo Bonacolsi, 4
46100 Mantua (MN)
phone +39 0376 327180

informazioni@aquilanigra.it
www.aquilanigra.it
closed: Sunday and Monday

Trattoria Due Cavallini
Via Salnitro, 5
46100 Mantua (MN)
phone +39 0376 322084
closed: Tuesday

Le Tamerici
Frazione Pietole
Via Romana, 80
46030 Virgilio (MN)
phone +39 0376 281005
letamerici@tin.it

Salumificio Lusetti
Via Nazionale Cisa, 36/b
46029 Suzzara (MN)
phone +39 0376 522166
info@lusetti.it

Re Carlo Alberto
Via G. Romano, 6
46100 Mantua (MN)
phone +39 0376 221764

La Rinascita
S.S. Goitese, 311
46044 Goito (MN)
phone +39 0376 688248

marsala (sicily)

Informazioni Turistiche
Via XI maggio, 100
91025 Marsala (TP)
phone/fax +39 0923 714097

Delfino Beach Hotel
Via Lungomare, 672
91025 Marsala (TP)
phone +39 0923 751076
delfino@delfinobeach.com

Hotel President
Via Nino Bixio, 1
91025 Marsala (TP)
phone +39 0923 999333
direzione@presidentmarsala.it

Ristorante Bacco's
Via Trieste, 5
91025 Marsala (TP)
phone +39 0923 737262
ristorantebaccos@libero.it
closed: Monday (open in the summer)

Trattoria Garibaldi
Via Rubino, 35
91025 Marsala (TP)
phone +39 0923 953006
closed: Saturday for lunch and Sunday night

Pasticceria Alhoa
Via Mazzini
91025 Marsala (TP)
phone +39 0923 715460

Cantine Florio
Via V. Florio, 1
91025 Marsala (TP)
phone +39 0923 781111
www.cantineflorio.com

Rallo
Via V. Florio, 2
91025 Marsala (TP)
phone +39 0923 721633

Fratelli Buffa
Lungomare Florio, 31
91025 Marsala (TP)
phone +39 0923 982444
info@cantinebuffa.it

matera (basilicata)

Azienda di Promozione Turistica (APT)
Via De Viti De Marco, 9
75100 Matera (MT)
phone +39 0835 331983, fax +39 0835 333452
info@aptbasilicata.it

Albergo Locanda di San Martino
Via San Martino, 22
75100 Matera (MT)
phone +39 0835 256600
info@locandadisanmartino.it
www.locandadisanmartino.it

Albergo La Casa di Lucio
Via San Piero Caveoso, 66
75100 Matera (MT)
phone +39 0835 312798
www.lacasadilucio.com

Sassi Hotel
Via San Giovanni Vecchio, 89
75100 Matera (MT)
phone +39 0835 331009
hotelsassi@virgilio.it

Hotel Del Campo
Via Lucrezio angolo Via Gravina
75100 Matera (MT)
phone +39 0835 388844
info@hoteldelcampo.com

**Ristorante Casino del Diavolo,
da Francolino**
Via La Martella, 48
75100 Matera (MT)
phone +39 0835 261986
info@casinodeldiavolo.com
www.casinodeldiavolo.com
closed: Monday

Ristorante Le Botteghe
Piazza San Pietro Barisano, 22
75100 Matera (MT)
phone +39 0835 344072
closed: Sunday night

Agriturismo Matinelle
Località Matinelle, Strada Provinciale
75100 Matera-Gravina (MT)
phone +39 0835 307343
www.lematinelle.com

Il Buongustaio
Piazza Vittorio Veneto, 1
75100 Matera (MT)
phone +39 0835 331982

Pasta Fresca La Spiga d'Oro
Via G. Racioppi, 3
75100 Matera (MT)
phone +39 0835 389318

Viola
Contrada Santamaria
75010 Gorgoglione (MT)
phone +39 0835 560500
pmviola@tiscali.it

milan (lombardy)

Informazioni Turistiche
Via G. Marconi, 1
20100 Milan (MI)
phone +39 02 72524301, fax +39 02 72524350
aptinfo@libero.it

Stazione Centrale Galleria di Testa, 1
phone +39 02 72524360
turismo@regione.lombardia.it
www.inlombardia.it

Hotel Excelsior Gallia
Piazza Duca d'Aosta, 9
20124 Milan (MI)
phone +39 02 67851
sales@excelsiorgallia.it

Hotel The Gray
Via San Raffaele, 6
20100 Milan (MI)
phone +39 02 7208951
info.thegray@sinahotels.it

Hotel Regency
Via Arimondi, 12
20155 Milan (MI)
phone +39 02 39216021
regency@regency-milano.com

Ristorante Il Luogo di Aimo e Nadia
Via Montecuccoli, 6
20147 Milan (MI)
phone +39 02 416886
info@aimoenadia.com
www.aimoenadia.com
closed: Saturday for lunch and Sunday

Trattoria Tagiura
Via Tagiura, 5
20100 Milan (MI)
phone +39 02 48950613
closed: Sunday

Ristorante Savini
Galleria Vittorio Emanuele II
20121 Milan (MI)
phone +39 02 72003433
savini@thi.it
closed: Sunday

Antico ristorante Boeucc
Piazza Belgioioso, 2
20121 Milan (MI)
phone +39 02 76020224
closed: Saturday and Sunday for lunch

Antica Trattoria della Pesa
Viale Pasubio, 10
20154 Milan (MI)
phone +39 02 6555741
closed: Sunday

Da Berti
Via Algarotti, 20
20100 Milan (MI)
phone +39 02 6694627

Al Less
Via Redi angolo Via Jan
20100 Milan (MI)
phone +39 02 36533440

Pasticceria Sant'Ambroeus
Corso Matteotti, 7
20100 Milan (MI)
phone +39 02 76000540

Cova pasticceria
Via Montenapoleone, 8
20100 Milan (MI)
phone +39 02 76000578

modena (emilia–romagna)

Ufficio di Informazione e di Accoglienza Turistica (IAT)
Via Cudari, 12
41100 Modena (MO)
phone +39 059 206660, fax +39 059 206659
iatmo@comune.modena.it
www.comune.modena.it

Hotel Real Fini
Via Emilia Est, 441
41100 Modena (MO)
phone +39 059 2051530
booking@hrf.it

Hotel Canalgrande
Corso Canalgrande, 6
41100 Modena (MO)
phone +39 059 217160
info@canalgrandehophoneit

Ristorante Fini
Piazzetta San Francesco, Rua Frati Minori, 54
41100 Modena (MO)
phone +39 059 223314
ristorante.fini@hrf.it
closed: Monday

Hosteria Giusti
Vicolo Squallore, 46
41100 Modena (MO)
phone +39 059 222533
closed: Monday and at night

Osteria Francescana
Via Stella, 22
41100 Modena (MO)
phone +39 059 210118
closed: Saturday for lunch and Sunday

Antica salumeria Giuseppe Giusti 1598
Via Farini, 75
41100 Modena (MO)
phone +39 059 222533

Azienda Agricola Galli
Via Albareto, 452
41100 Modena (MO)
phone +39 059 251094

Consorzio Produttori Aceto Balsamico Tradizionale di Modena
Via Granaceto, 134
41100 Modena (MO)
phone +39 059 23698
www.balsamico.it

La Divina Pastella
Stradella Scartazzetta, 33
41100 Modena (MO)
phone +39 059 469896

modica (sicily)

Informazioni Turistiche
Via Capitano Bocchieri, 33
97100 Ragusa (RG)
phone +39 0932 621421, fax +39 0932 623476
info@ragusaturismo.com

Hotel Bristol
Via Risorgimento, 8/b
97015 Modica (RG)
phone +39 0932 762890
hotelbristolmodica@virgilio.it

Hotel Mediterraneo Palace
Via Roma, 189
97100 Ragusa (RG)
phone +39 0932 621944
medpalace@mediterraneopalace.it

Ristorante Fattoria delle Torri
Vico Napolitano, 14
97015 Modica (RG)
phone +39 0932 751286
peppebarone1960@libero.it
closed: Monday

Ristorante Duomo
Via Capitano Bocchieri, 31
97100 Ragusa (RG)
phone +39 0932 651265
ristorante-duomo@inwind.it
www.ristoranteduomo.it
closed: Sunday night and Monday

Rizza
Corso Umberto I, 128
97015 Modica (RG)
phone +39 0932 752515

Antica Dolceria Bonajuto
Corso Umberto I, 159
97015 Modica (RG)
phone +39 0923 941225

Caffè dell'Arte
Corso Umberto I, 114
97015 Modica (RG)
phone +39 0932 943257

Casa del Formaggio
Via Marchesa Tedeschi, 5
97015 Modica (RG)
phone +39 0932 946192

Valle dell'Acate
Contrada Bidini
97011 Acate (RG)
phone +39 0932 874166
info@valledellacate.com
www.valledellacate.com

montalcino (tuscany)

Informazioni Turistiche
Costa del Municipio, 1
53024 Montalcino (SI)
phone/fax +39 0577 849331
info@prolocomontalcino.it

Hotel Vecchia Oliviera
Via Landi, 1
53024 Montalcino (SI)
phone +39 0577 846028
info@vecchiaoliviera.com

Hotel Bellaria
via Osticcio, 19
53024 Montalcino (SI)
phone +39 0577 849326
hotelbellaria@tin.it

Ristorante Castello Banfi
Località Sant'Angelo Scalo, Poggio alle Mura
53024 Montalcino (SI)
phone +39 0577 816054
banfi@banfi.it
www.castellobanfi.com
closed: for lunch; Sunday and Monday

Ristorante Osteria del Vecchio Castello
Località Pieve di San Sigismondo, Poggio alle Mura
53024 Montalcino (SI)
phone +39 0577 816026
osteriavecchiocastello@virgilio.it
closed: Tuesday

La Fortezza
Piazzale Fortezza
53024 Montalcino (SI)
phone +39 0577 849211

Azienda agricola Claudia Ferrero
Podere Pascena
53020 Montalcino (SI)
phone +39 0577 844170
claudiaferrero@tin.it

Fattoria dei Barbi
Località Pedernovi, 170
53024 Montalcino (SI)
phone +39 0577 841111
www.fattoriadeibarbi.it
www.museodimontalcino.it
www.museodelbrunello.it

montefalco (umbria)

Informazioni Turistiche
Piazza IV Novembre, 3
06123 Perugia (PG)
phone +39 075 5736458, fax +39 075.5739386
info@iat.perugia.it

Hotel Villa Pambufetti
Via della Vittoria, 20
06036 Montefalco (PG)
phone +39 0742 379417
info@villapambuffetti.it

Ristorante Coccorone
Largo Tempestivi
06036 Montefalco (PG)
phone +39 0742 379535
info@coccorone.com

Enoteca Federico II
Piazza del Comune, 1
06036 Montefalco (PG)
phone +39 0742 378902
coccorone@libero.it
www.coccorone.it

Azienda Agricola Scacciadiavoli
Località Cantinone
06036 Montefalco (PG)
phone +39 0742 371210
scacciadiavoli@tin.it

Val Di Maggio A. Caprai
LocalitàTorre
06036 Montefalco (PG)
phone +39 0742 378802
www.arnaldocaprai.it

Enoteca norcineria Mondi
Piazza del Comune, 10
06036 Montefalco (PG)
phone +39 0742 378804

Agricola Trevi
Località Torre Matigge, Via Fosso Rio
06036 Montefalco (PG)
phone +39 0742 391631

Agriturismo Camiano Piccolo
Località Camiano Piccolo, 5
06036 Montefalco (PG)
phone +39 0742 379492
camioano@bcsnet.it

montepulciano (tuscany)

Informazioni Turistiche
Piazza del Campo, 56
53100 Siena (SI)
phone +39 0577 280551, fax +39 0577 270676
incoming@terresiena.it
www.siena.toscana.it

Hotel San Biagio
Via San Bartolomeo, 2
53045 Montepulciano (SI)
phone +39 0578 717233
info@albergosanbiagio.it

Hotel Villa Poggiano
Via di Poggiano, 7
53045 Montepulciano (SI)
phone +39 0578 758292
info@villapoggiano.com

Ristorante La Grotta
Località San Biagio, 15
53045 Montepulciano (SI)
phone +39 0578 757479
ristorante.lagrotta@tiscali.it
closed: Wednesday

Ristorante Diva e Maceo
Via di Gracciano nel Corso, 90/92
53045 Montepulciano (SI)
phone +39 0578 716951
closed: Tuesday

Fattoria Le Capezzine
Località Valiano
53040 Montepulciano (SI)
phone +39 0578 724304
capezzine@avignonesi.it
www.avignonesi.it

Caseificio Cugusi
S.S. per Pienza, Via della Boccia, 8
53045 Montepulciano (SI)
phone +39 0578 757558
formaggicugusi@libero.it

mortara (lombardy)

Informazioni Turistiche
Via Fabio Filzi, 2
phone +39 0382 22156, fax +39 0382 32221
27100 Pavia (PV)
info@apt.pv.it
www.apt.pv.it

Hotel San Michele
Corso Garibaldi, 20
27036 Mortara (PV)
phone +39 0384 98614
info@albristosanmichele.it

Ristorante Guallina
Località Guallina Est, Via Molino Faenza, 19
27036 Mortara (PV)
phone +39 0384 91962
guallina@guallina.com
closed: Tuesday

Alla corte dell'oca
Via Sforza, 27
27036 Mortara (PV)
phone +39 0384 98397
info@cortedelloca.com
www.cortedelloca.com

Martignac
Cascina San Giorgio, Via Marconi, 44
27020 Sartirana Lomellina (PV)
phone +39 0384 800014
www.martignac.it

naples (campania)

Informazioni Turistiche
Via San Carlo, 9
80100 Naples (NA)
phone +39 081 402394
info@inaples.it

Piazza del Gesù Nuovo, 7
phone +39 081 5223328

Stazione Mergellina
phone +39 081 7612102

Grand Hotel Vesuvio
Via Partenope, 45
80121 Naples (NA)
phone +39 081 7640044
info@vesuvio.it

Hotel San Francesco al Monte
Corso Vittorio Emanuele, 328
80135 Naples (NA)
phone +39 081 4239111
info@hotelsanfrancesco.it

Ristorante Ciro a Santa Brigida
Via Santa Brigida, 73
80132 Naples (NA)
phone +39 081 5524072
www.cirosantabrigida.it
closed: Sunday

**Ristorante Pizzeria
L'Europeo di Mattozzi**
Via Campodisola, 4
80133 Naples (NA)
phone +39 081 5521323
closed: Saturday and Sunday

Ristorante Al Poeta
Piazza S. Di Giacomo, 134
80123 Naples (NA)
phone +39 081 5756936
closed: Monday

Antica Pasticceria Carraturo
Via Casanova, 97
80100 Naples (NA)
phone +39 081 5545364

Scaturchio
Piazza San Domenico Maggiore, 19
80100 Naples (NA)
phone +39 081 5517031

Prencipe Antico Caffè
Piazza Municipio, 20
80100 Naples (NA)
phone +39 081 5523020

norcia (umbria)

Informazioni Turistiche
Piazza IV Novembre, 3
06123 Perugia (PG)
phone +39 075 5736458, fax +39 075 5739386
info@iat.perugia.it

Hotel Salicone
Viale Umbria
06046 Norcia (PG)
phone +39 0743 828076
info@bianconi.com

**Agriturismo Casale
nel Parco dei Monti Sibillini**
Località Fontevena, 8
06046 Norcia (PG)
phone +39 0743 816481
agriumbria@casalenelparco.com

Ristorante Taverna de' Massari
Via Roma, 13
06046 Norcia (PG)
phone +39 0743 816218
info@tavernadeimassari.com
closed: Tuesday (open from July to September)

Ristorante Dal Francese
Via Riguardi, 16
06046 Norcia (PG)
phone +39 0743 816290
closed: Friday (open from July to September)

La Madia Regale
S.S. Sellanese km 22, Località Ponte Sargano
06040 Cerreto di Spoleto (PG)
phone +39 0743 91703
info@lamadiaregale.it
www.lamadiaregale.it

Salumificio Ciliani
Frazione Savelli
06046 Norcia (PG)
phone +39 0743 829040

Cooperativa Agricola Il Castelluccio
Località Castelluccio, Via della Bufera, 17
06046 Norcia (PG)
phone +39 0743 821166

noto (sicily)

Informazioni Turistiche
Piazza XXVI Maggio
96017 Noto (SR)
phone +39 0931 836744, fax +39 0931 573779

Hotel La Fontanella
Via Rosolino Pilo, 3
96017 Noto (SR)
phone +39 0931 894735
info@albergolafontanella.it

Hotel Villa Mediterranea
Località Lido di Noto, Viale Lido
96017 Noto (SR)
phone +39 0931 812330
info@villamediterranea.it

Ristorante Masseria degli Ulivi
Contrada Porcari
96017 Noto (SR)
phone +39 0931 813019
www.masseriadegliulivi.com
closed: Wednesday (except in the summer)

Trattoria del Crocifisso
Via Principe Umberto, 46
96017 Noto (SR)
phone +39 0931 571151
closed: Wednesday

Consorzio Produttori Mandorla di Noto
Via XX settembre, 119
96017 Noto (SR)
phone +39 0931 836893
consorzio.mandorla@gastrozone.com

Giuseppe Carbone
Via XX settembre, 119
96017 Noto (SR)
phone +39 0931 836893

Caffè Sicilia
Corso Vittorio Emanuele, 125
96017 Noto (SR)
phone +39 0931 835013

Caffè del Ponte
Piazza E. Pancali, 23
96100 Siracusa (SR)
phone +39 0931 64312

Cooperativa Interprovinciale Elorina
Contrada Belliscala
96017 Noto (SR)
phone +39 0931 857068

Solaria
Via Roma, 86
96100 Siracusa (SR)
phone +39 0931 463007

nuoro (sardinia)

Informazioni Turistiche
Piazza Italia, 19
08100 Nuoro (NU)
phone +39 0784 30083, fax +39 0784 33432

Hotel Cualbu
Viale del Lavoro, 21
08023 Fonni (NU)
phone +39 0784 57054
hotelcualbu@tiscalinet.it

Hotel Su Gologone
Località Sorgente Su Gologone
08025 Oliena (NU)
phone +39 0784 287512
gologone@tin.it

Trattoria Il Rifugio
Via A. Mereu, 28-36
08100 Nuoro (NU)
phone +39 0784 232355
www.il-rifugio.net
closed: Wednesday

Azienda Agricola Fratelli Rubanu
Località Cherbos
08027 Orgosolo (NU)
phone +39 0784 402106
rubanugiuseppe@tiscali.it

Cooperativa Pastori
Regione Golloi
08022 Dorgali (NU)
phone +39 0784 96517

Spirito di Vino
Viale Repubblica, 134
08100 Nuoro (NU)
phone +39 0784 260544

Società Cooperativa Vitivinicola di Jerzu
Via Umberto I, 1
08044 Jerzu (NU)
phone +39 0782 70028

oristano (sardinia)

Informazioni Turistiche
Piazza Eleonora, 19
09170 Oristano (OR)
phone +39 0783 36831
enturismo.oristano@tiscalinet.it

Hotel Mistral Due
Via XX Settembre, 34
09170 Oristano (OR)
phone +39 0783 210389
hmistral@tiscali.it

Ristorante Cocco & Dessì
Via Tirso, 31
09170 Oristano (OR)
phone +39 0783 300720
coccoedessi@tiscali.it
closed: Sunday night and Monday (except in
August)

Ristorante Il Faro
Via Bellini, 25
09170 Oristano (OR)
phone +39 0783 70002
info@ristoranteilfaro.net
closed: Sunday

Cooperativa Pescatori e Molluschicultori
Via Cima, 5
09072 Cabras (OR)
phone +39 0783 290848

Fratelli Manca
Via Bovio, 30
09072 Cabras (OR)
phone +39 0783 290848

Tradizioni Nostrane
Via Carducci, 20
09072 Cabras (OR)
phone +39 0783 391161

**Cantina Sociale Cooperativa
della Vernaccia**
Località Rimedio, Via Oristano, 149
09170 Oristano (OR)
phone +39 078 333155

Tremontis Essenzia Dumeti
Zona Industriale
09070 Paulilatino (OR)
phone +39 0785 566029

Salvatore Troncia
Via G. Deledda, 7
09090 Masullas (OR)
phone +39 0783 991736

Hotel Mistral
Via Martiri di Belfiore
09170 Oristano (OR)
phone +39 0783 212505
hmistral@tiscalinet.it

orvieto (umbria)

Informazioni Turistiche
Piazza Duomo, 24
05018 Orvieto (TR)
phone +39 0763 341772, fax +39 0763 344433
info@iat.orvieto.tr.it
www.iat.orvieto.tr.it

Hotel Villa Ciconia
S.S. 71, Via dei Tigli, 69
05018 Orvieto Scalo (TR)
phone +39 0763 305582
villaciconia@libero.it

Hotel Palazzo Piccolomini
Piazza Ranieri, 36
05018 Orvieto (TR)
phone +39 0763 341743
piccolomini.hotel@orvienet.it

Albergo Filippeschi
Via Filippeschi, 19
05018 Orvieto (TR)
phone +39 0763 343275
albergofilippeschi@tiscalinet.it

Ristorante I Sette Consoli
Piazza Sant'Angelo, 1/a
05018 Orvieto (TR)
phone +39 0763 343911
closed: Wednesday

Trattoria L'Asino d'Oro
Vicolo del Popolo, 9
05018 Orvieto (TR)
phone +39 0763 344406
closed: Monday

Enoteca Regionale
Via Ripa Seranica, 1 - Palazzo San Giovanni
05018 Orvieto (TR)
phone +39 0763 393529

Vinosus
Piazza Duomo, 15
05018 Orvieto (TR)
phone +39 0763 341907

Tenuta Le Velette
Località Le Velette, 23
05018 Orvieto (TR)
phone +39 0763 29090
levelette@tin.it

Fattoria di Titignano
Località Titignano
05018 Orvieto (TR)
phone +39 0763 308022
info@titignano.com
www.titignano.com

padua (veneto)

Informazioni Turistiche
Piazza del Santo
35100 Padua (PD)
phone +39 049 8753087

Galleria Pedrocchi
phone +39 049 8767927
infopedrocchi@turismopadova.it

Hotel Grand'Italia
Corso del Popolo, 81
35131 Padua (PD)
phone +39 049 8761111
info@hotelgranditalia.it

Hotel Methis
Riviera Paleocapa, 70
35138 Padua (PD)
phone +39 049 8725555
info@methishophonecom
www.methishophonecom

Hotel Donatello
Via del Santo, 102-104
35123 Padua (PD)
phone +39 049 8750634
info@hoteldonatello.net

Ristorante Antico Brolo
Corso Milano, 22
35139 Padua (PD)
phone +39 049 664555
closed: Monday

Osteria Dal Capo
Via degli Obizzi, 2
35100 Padua (PD)
phone +39 049 663105
closed: Monday for lunch and Sunday

Ristorante Bastioni del Moro
Via Bronzetti, 18
35138 Padua (PD)
phone +39 049 8710006
closed: Sunday
info@bastionidelmoro.it

Ristorante Dotto di Campagna
Località Torre, Via Randaccio, 4
35129 Ponte di Brenta (PD)
phone +39 049 625469
risdotto@hotelsagittario.com
closed: Sunday night and Monday

La Fattoria in città
Via P. Maroncelli, 130
35100 Padua (PD)
phone +39 347 0174342

I Sapori di corte
Via Lusore, 23
35010 Borgoricco (PD)
phone +39 049 5798408

Angelo Rasi
Riviera Paleocapa, 7
35100 Padua (PD)
phone +39 0498 719797

Tomanin
Piazza Vittorio Emanuele
35044 Montagnana (PD)
phone +39 0429 81195

Attilio Fontana Prosciutti
Via Campana, 8
35044 Montagnana (PD)
phone +39 0429 81010
info@fontanaprosciutti.it
www.fontanaprosciutti.it

palermo (sicily)

Informazioni Turistiche
Piazza Castelnuovo, 34
90100 Palermo (PA)
phone +39 091 583847, fax +39 091 586338
info@palermotourism.com

Salita Belmonte, 1
phone +39 091 6398011, fax +39 091 6375400
info@aziendaturismopalermomonreale.it

Grand Hotel Villa Igea
Salita Belmonte, 43
90142 Palermo (PA)
phone +39 091 6312111
villa-igea@amthotels.it

Hotel Principe di Villafranca
Via G. Turrisi Colonna, 4
90100 Palermo (PA)
phone +39 091 6118523
info@principedivillafranca.it

Hotel Residenza D'Aragona
Via Ottavio D'Aragona, 25
90139 Palermo (PA)
phone +39 091 6622222
residenzadaragona@libero.it

Ristorante La Scuderia
Viale del Fante, 9
90146 Palermo (PA)
phone +39 091 520323
closed: Sunday
lascuderia@tiscalinet.it

Trattoria Il Delfino
Via Torretta, 80
90100 Palermo (PA)
phone +39 091 530282
closed: Monday
trattoriaildelfino@virgilio.it

Trattoria Il Mirto e La Rosa
Via Principe di Granatelli, 30
90100 Palermo (PA)
phone +39 091 324353
closed: Sunday
www.ilmirtoelarosa.com

Cappello
Via Colonna Rotta, 68
90100 Palermo (PA)
phone +39 091 489601

Mazzara
Via Generale Magliocco, 15
90100 Palermo (PA)
phone +39 091.321443

Scimone
Località Valdesi, Viale Regina Margherita, 61
90121 Partanna-Mondello (PA)
phone +39 091 584448
www.pasticceriascimone.it

I Peccatucci di Mamma Andrea
Via Principe di Scordia, 67
90100 Palermo (PA)
phone +39 091 334835

Picone
Via G. Marconi, 36
90100 Palermo (PA)
phone +39 091 331300

parma (emilia–romagna)

**Ufficio di Informazione e di Accoglienza
Turistica (IAT)**
Via Melloni, 1/9
43100 Parma (PR)
phone +39 0521 218889, fax +39 0521 234735
turismo@comune.parma.it/turismo
www.turismo.comune.parma.it/turismo

Starhotel Du Park
Viale Piacenza, 12/c
43100 Parma (PR)
phone +39 0521 292929
duparc.pr@starhotels.it

Hotel Verdi
Via Pasini, 18
43100 Parma (PR)
phone +39 0521 293539
info@hotelverdi.it

Ristorante Parizzi
Via Repubblica, 71
43100 Parma (PR)
phone +39 0521 285952
closed: Monday
parizzi.rist@libero.it

Ristorante Salumeria Sorelle Picchi
Via Farini, 12
43100 Parma (PR)
phone +39 0521 233528
closed: Sunday and at night

Ristorante La Filoma
Via XX Marzo, 15
43100 Parma (PR)
phone +39 0521 206181
closed: Tuesday and Wednesday for lunch;
Saturday and Sunday from 7/1 to 8/25
info@lafiloma.com

Consorzio Culatello del Zibello
Piazza Garibaldi, 35
43010 Zibello (PR)
phone +39 0542 99131

La Boutique della Carne
43010 Zibello (PR)
phone +39 0524 99676

Gino Fereoli
Frazione Pilastro, strada Parma, 28
43013 Langhirano (PR)
phone +39 0521 639005
info@fereoligino.it
www.fereoligino.it

Agrinascente
Autostrada A1 ingresso Fidenza
43036 Fidenza (PR)
phone +39 0524 522334

Casa del Formaggio
Via N. Bixio, 106
43100 Parma (PR)
phone +39 0521 230243

Giovanni Davoli
Via San Leonardo, 145/b
43100 Parma (PR)
phone +39 0521 786918

pavia (lombardy)

Informazioni Turistiche
Via Fabio Filzi, 2
27100 Pavia (PV)
phone +39 0382 22156, fax +39 0382 32221
info@apt.pv.it www.apt.pv.it

Hotel Moderno
Viale Vittorio Emanuele, 41
27100 Pavia (PV)
phone +39 0382 303402
info@hotelmoderno.it

Hotel Excelsior
Piazza Stazione, 25
27100 Pavia (PV)
phone +39 0382 28596
info@excelsiorpavia.com

Ristorante Locanda Vecchia Pavia al Mulino
Via al Monumento, 5
27012 Certosa di Pavia (PV)
phone +39 0382 925894
vecchiapaviaalmulino@libero.it
closed: Wednesday for lunch and Monday

Osteria del Naviglio
Via Alzaia, 39/b (p.le San Giuseppe)
27100 Pavia (PV)
phone +39 0382 460392
www.osteriadelnaviglio.it
closed: Monday

Ristorante Villaglori al Sanmichele
Vicolo San Michele, 4
27100 Pavia (PV)
phone +39 0382 20716
closed: Monday; for lunch except Saturday and Sunday

Ristorante Antica Osteria del Previ
Località Borgo Ticino, Via Milazzo, 65
27100 Pavia (PV)
phone +39 0382 26203
closed: never

Azienda Agricola le Fracce
Via Castel del Lupo, 5
27045 Mairano di Casteggio (PV)
phone +39 0383 82526 - 805769
info@le-fracce.it
www.le-fracce.it

Cantina Sociale La Versa
Via F. Crispi, 13
27047 Santa Maria della Versa (PV)
phone +39 0385 278229

La Cantina
Via Cairoli, 19
27100 Pavia (PV)
phone +39 0382 25179

Salumificio Thogan Porri
Località Casa Cucchi, 1
27050 Cecima (PV)
phone +39 0383 551341
www.salamedivarzidop.it

Pasticceria Vigoni
Strada Nuova, 110
27100 Pavia (PV)
phone +39 0382 22103

perugia (umbria

Informazioni Turistiche
Piazza IV Novembre, 3
06123 Perugia (PG)
phone +39 075 5736458, fax +39 075 5739386
info@iat.perugia.it

Etruscan Chocohotel
Via Campo di Marte, 134
06123 Perugia (PG)
phone +39 075 5837314
etruscan@chocohophoneit

Hotel Ristorante Le Tre Vaselle
Via Garibaldi, 48
06089 Torgiano (PG)
phone +39 075 9880447
3vaselle@3vaselle.it
www.3vaselle.it

Hotel Castello dell'Oscano
Località Cenerente, Strada Forcella, 37
06070 Perugia (PG)
phone +39 075 584371
info@oscano.com

Hotel Brufani
Piazza Italia, 12
06121 Perugia (PG)
phone +39 075 5732541
reservationsbrun@sinahotels.it

Albergo Ristorante Giò Arte e Vini
Via R. D'Andreotto, 19
06124 Perugia (PG)
phone +39 075 5731100
hotelgio@interbusiness.it
www.hotelgio.it
closed: Sunday night and Monday for lunch

Ristorante Lungarotti
Corso Vittorio Emanuele, 31
06089 Torgiano (PG)
phone +39 075 9880200
www.lungarotti.it

Museo Perugina
Località San Sisto
06123 Perugia (PG)
phone +39 075 5276796

Geofoods
Via C. Pisacane, 25
06012 Città di Castello (PG)
phone +39 075 8521698
info@geofoods.it
www.geofoods.it

Sandri
Corso Vannucci, 32
06123 Perugia (PG)
phone +39 075 5724112

Alunni
Località Ponte San Giovanni, Via Manzoni, 124
06123 Perugia (PG)
phone +39 075 397265

Enoteca Provinciale
Via U. Rocchi, 18
06123 Perugia (PG)
phone +39 075 5724824

pesaro (marche)

Informazioni Turistiche
Viale Trieste, 164
61100 Pesaro (PU)
phone +39 0721 69341, fax +39 0721.30462
iat.pesaro@regione.marche.it

Via Mazzolari, 4
phone +39 0721.359501, fax +39 0721.33930

Hotel Vittoria
Piazzale della Libertà, 2
61100 Pesaro (PU)
phone +39 0721 34343
vittoria@viphotels.it

Hotel Villa Serena
Strada San Nicola, 6/3
61100 Pesaro (PU)
phone +39 0721 55211
info@villa-serena.it

Ristorante Lo Scudiero
Via Baldassini, 2
61100 Pesaro (PU)
phone +39 0721 64107
info@ristoranteloscudiero.it
www.ristoranteloscudiero.it
closed: Sunday

Trattoria Il Pergolato - Dalla Maria
Località Novilara, Piazzale Cadorna, 5
61100 Pesaro (PU)
phone +39 0721 287210
closed: Tuesday (except in the summer)

Le Trifole
Via de Gasperi 88
61041 Acqualagna (PU)
phone +39 0731 799037

Marini-Azzolini
Viale Risorgimento, 26
61041 Acqualagna (PU)
phone +39 0721 798629
marinitartufi@libero.it
www.publi.it/marini

Salumificio Bartera
Via Rupoli, 7
61038 Orciano di Pesaro (PU)
phone +39 0721 976232

La Baita
Via Nettuno, 27
62012 Civitanova Marche (MC)
phone +39 0733 774231

Bibi
Viale Fiume
61100 Pesaro (PU)
phone +39 0721 31207

pescara (abruzzo)

Informazioni Turistiche
Palazzo Quadrifoglio
Lungofiume Paolucci
65100 Pescara (PE)
phone +39 085 4219981, fax +39 085 4228533
presidio.pescara@abruzzoturismo.it

Piazza I Maggio, 1
phone +39 085 4210188

Hotel Esplanade
Piazza I Maggio, 46
65122 Pescara (PE)
phone +39 085 292141
reservations@esplanade.it

Hotel Ambra
Via Quarto dei Mille
65122 Pescara (PE)
phone +39 085 378247
info@hotelambrapalace

Trattoria Taverna 58
Corso Manthonè, 46
65100 Pescara (PE)
phone +39 085 690724
www.taverna58.it
closed: Saturday for lunch and Sunday

Ristorante La Bandiera
Contrada Pastini, 4
65010 Civitella Casanova (PE)
phone +39 085 845219
marcello.spadone@labandiera.it
www.labandiera.it
closed: Sunday night and Wednesday

Azienda Marramiero
Contrada Sant'Andrea, 1
65020 Rosciano (PE)
phone +39 085 8505766

Azienda Agricola Filomusi Guelfi
Via Guelfi, 11
65028 Tocco da Casauria (PE)
+39 085 98353

Luigi D'Amico "Parrozzo"
Via Pepe, 41
65100 Pescara (PE)
phone +39 085 60627

Pasticceria Caprice
Piazza Garibaldi, 29
65100 Pescara (PE)
phone +39 085 691633

D'Alessandro Enoteca & Dolcezze
Via Trento, 126
65100 Pescara (PE)
phone +39 085 4212673

piacenza (emilia–romagna)

Informazioni Turistiche
Piazza Cavalli
29100 Piacenza (PC)
phone +39 0523 329324, fax +39 0523 306727
iat@comune.piacenza.it

Hotel City
Via Emilia Parmense, 154
29100 Piacenza (PC)
phone +39 0523 579752
info@hotelcitypc.it

Ristorante Antica Osteria del Teatro
Via Verdi, 16
29100 Piacenza (PC)
phone +39 0523 323777
menu@anticaosteriadelteatro.it
www.anticaosteriadelteatro.it
closed: Sunday and Monday

Ristorante Vecchia Piacenza
Via San Bernardo, 1
29100 Piacenza (PC)
phone +39 0523 305462
www.ristorantevecchiapiacenza.it
closed: Sunday

Grossetti Salumi
Località Trevozzo, Via della Fornace, 15
29010 Nibbiano (PC)
phone +39 0523 998856
grossettisalumi@libero.it

Salumificio La Rocca
Via Caneto
29014 Castell'Arquato (PC)
phone +39 0523 805139
info@salumificiolarocca.com,
www.salumificiolarocca.com

Cantine Marchese Malaspina
Contrada Borgoratto, 26
29022 Bobbio (PC)
phone +39 0523 936048
konrad_mala@hotmail.com

Viticoltori Arquatesi
Località Socciso
29014 Castell'Arquato (PC)
phone +39 0523 804441
casabella@enjoy.it

Enoteca Comunale
Palazzo del Podestà, Piazza Municipio
29014 Castell'Arquato (PC)
phone +39 349 8093231

Grande Albergo Roma
Via Cittadella, 14
29100 Piacenza (PC)
phone +39 0523 323201
hotel@grandealbergoroma.it

pisa (tuscany)

Informazioni Turistiche
Piazza Miracoli
56126 Pisa (PI)
phone +39 050 560464
pisa.turismo@traveleurope.it

Hotel Royal Victoria
Lungarno Pacinotti, 12
56126 Pisa (PI)
phone +39 050 940111
mail@royalvictoria.it

Ristorante A Casa Mia
Località Ghezzano, Via Provinciale Vicarese, 10
56100 Pisa (PI)
phone +39 050 879265
ristoranteacasamia@supereva.it
closed: Saturday for lunch and Sunday

Osteria dei Cavalieri
Via San Frediano, 16
56126 Pisa (PI)
phone +39 050 580858
closed: Saturday for lunch and Sunday

Bacchus
Via Mascagni 1
56100 Pisa (PI)
phone +39 050500560
www.bacchusenoteca.com

Norcineria Falaschi
Via A. Conti 18
56027 San Miniato (PI)
phone +39 0571 43190
info@sergiofalaschi.it
www.sergiofaalschi.it

Macelleria Giusti
Via XX settembre 3/24
phone +39 050.815025
56017 San Giuliano Terme (PI)

Cioccolateria De Bondt
Via Turati 22
phone +39 050.501896
56100 Pisa (PI)
www.debondt.it

Antico Pastificio Morelli
Via San Francesco 8
phone +39 0571.459032
56020 San Romano (PI)

Relais dell'Orologio
Via della Faggiola, 12/14
phone +39 050.830361
56126 Pisa (PI)
info@hotelrelaisorologio.com

pistoia (tuscany)

Informazioni Turistiche
Palazzo dei Vescovi, Piazza del Duomo
51100 Pistoia (PT)
phone +39 0573.21622, fax +39 0573 34327
aptpistoia@tiscalinet.it

Albergo La Volpe e l'Uva - Villa Vannini
Via di Villa, 6
51030 Villa di Piteccio
phone +39 0573 42031
info@volpe-uva.it

Ristorante Corradossi
Via Frosini, 112
51100 Pistoia (PT)
phone +39 0573 25683
loriscorradossi@virgilio.it
closed: Sunday

Trattoria La Bottegaia
Via del Lastrone, 17
51100 Pistoia (PT)
phone +39 0573 365602
closed: Sunday for lunch and Monday

Arte del Cioccolato
Via Provinciale 378
51031 Agliana (PT)
phone +39 0574 718506

Amedei
Località La Rotta, Via San Gervasio 29
56025 Pontedera (PI)
phone +39 0587 484849
amedei@amedei.it

Cioccolato & Company
Via Bruceto 4
51010 Massa e Cozzile (PT)
phone +39 0572 911120

Slitti Caffè e Cioccolato
Via Francesca Sud 1268
51015 Monsummano Terme (PI)
phone +39 0572 640240
www.slitti.it

Wine Bar Baldo Vino
Piazza San Lorenzo, 5
51100 Pistoia (PT)
phone +39 0573 21591
closed: for lunch and Sunday

Hotel Patria
Via Crispi, 8
51100 Pistoia (PT)
phone +39 0573 25187
info@patriahophonecom

pordenone (friuli–venezia giulia)

Informazioni Turistiche
Corso Vittorio Emanuele II, 38
33170 Pordenone (PN)
phone +39 0434 21912, fax +39 0434 523814
arpt-pn1@regione.fvg.it

Palace Hotel Moderno
Viale Martelli, 1
33170 Pordenone (PN)
phone +39 0434 28215
info@palacehotelmoderno.it

Hotel Villa Luppis
Località Rivarotta, Via San Martino, 34
33087 Pasiano di Pordenone (PN)
phone +39 0434 626969
hotel@villaluppis.it
www.villaluppis.it

Ristorante Casetta
Località Palse Sud, Via Colombo, 35
33080 Porcia (PN)
phone +39 0434 922720
fab.casetta@inwind.it
closed: Wednesday

Trattoria La Vecia Osteria del Moro
Via Castello, 2
33170 Pordenone (PN)
phone +39 0434 28658
closed: Sunday

Ristorante Novecento
Via C. Menotti, 62
33072 Casarsa della Delizia (PN)
phone +39 0434 86203
www.ristorante900.it
closed: Tuesday

Enoteca La Torre
Via di Mezzo, 2
33097 Spilimbergo (PN)
phone +39 0427 2998

Ristorante Enoteca La Primula
Via San Rocco, 47
33080 San Quirino (PN)
phone +39 0434 91005
info@ristorantelaprimula.it
closed: Sunday night and Monday

Agribene
Località San Leonardo, Via Maniago, 7
33086 Montereale Valcellina (PN)
phone +39 0427 75375
www.newtech.it/agribene

Fantinel
Via Tesis, 8
33090 Tauriano di Spilimbergo (PN)
phone +39 0427 591520
fantinel@fantinel.com
www.fantinel.com

Florutis
Via Gen. Cantore, 13
33094 Pinzano al Tagliamento (PN)
phone +39 0432 950655
www.florutis.it

Cantine Bianchi
Località Prodolone, Piazzale Colloredo, 3
33078 San Vito al Tagliamento (PN)
phone +39 0434 80431

potenza (basilicata)

Informazioni Turistiche
Via del Gallitello, 89
85100 Potenza (PZ)
phone +39 0971 507622, fax +39 0971 507601
info@aptbasilicata.it

Grande Albergo
Corso XVIII Agosto, 46
85100 Potenza (PZ)
phone +39 0971 410220
grandealbergo@tin.it

Albergo La Primula
S.S. 407 Est, Località Bucaletto, 61-62/a
85100 Potenza (PZ)
phone +39 0971 58310
info@albergolaprimula.it

Antica Osteria Marconi
Viale Marconi, 233
85100 Potenza (PZ)
phone +39 0971 56900
fr.ank@katamail.com
closed: Sunday night and Monday

Ristorante 2 Torri
Via Due Torri, 6/8
85100 Potenza (PZ)
phone +39 0971 411661
closed: Sunday

Macelleria Tramutola
Via Sabbioneta, 5
85100 Potenza (PZ)
phone +39 0971 442712

Lucana Salumi
Via Gramsci, 127
85100 Potenza (PZ)
phone +39 0971 991003
lucanasalumi@iol.it

Perbacco
Via Napoli, 52
85042 Lagonegro (PZ)
phone +39 097 341636

Cantine del Notaio
Via Roma, 159
85028 Rionero in Vulture (PZ)
phone +39 0972 717111

D'Angelo
Via Provinciale, 8
85028 Rionero in Vulture (PZ)
phone +39 0972 721517

riva del garda (trentino–alto adige)

Informazioni Turistiche
Giardini di Porta Orientale, 8
38066 Riva del Garda (TN)
phone +39 0464 554444, fax +39 0464 520308
info@gardatrentino.it
www.gardatrentino.it

Hotel Du Lac et du Parc
Viale Rovereto, 44
38066 Riva del Garda (TN)
phone +39 0464 551500
info@hoteldulac-riva.it

Feeling Hotel Luise
Viale Rovereto, 9
38066 Riva del Garda (TN)
phone +39 0464 550858
feeling@hotelluise.com

Hotel Europa
Piazza Catena, 9
38066 Riva del Garda (TN)
phone +39 0464 555433
europa@rivadelgarda.com

Ristorante Al Volt
Via Fiume, 73
38066 Riva del Garda (TN)
phone +39 0464 552570
closed: Monday

Ristorante Villa Negri
Via Bastione, 31/35
38066 Riva del Garda (TN)
phone +39 0464 555061
info@villanegri.it
closed: for lunch except Sunday;
Tuesday from November to February

Panesalame
Via Marocco, 22
38066 Riva del Garda (TN)
phone +39 0464 551954

Pisoni
Località Pergolese, Via San Siro, 7b
38070 Sarche (TN)
phone +39 0461 563216

Bertoldi
Viale Trento, 88
38066 Riva del Garda (TN)
phone +39 0464 553076

Pedrotti
Frazione Lago di Cavedine
38073 Cavedine (TN)
phone +39 0461 564123

rome (lazio)

Informazioni Turistiche
Via Parigi, 5
00100 Rome (RM)
phone +39 06 36004399, fax +39 06 419316

Stazione Termini
phone +39 06 47825194

Hotel Hassler Villa Medici
Piazza Trinità dei Monti, 6
00100 Rome (RM)
phone +39 06 600340
booking@hotelhassler.it

Hotel De Russie
Via del Babuino
00100 Rome (RM)
phone +39 06 328881
reservation@hotelderussie.it

Hotel The Inn at the Spanish Steps
Via dei Condotti, 85
00100 Rome (RM)
phone +39 06 69925657
spanishstep@tin.it

Hostaria dell'Orso di Gualtiero Marchesi
Via dei Soldati, 25/c
00100 Rome (RM)
phone +39 06 68301192
info@hdo.it
closed: Sunday for lunch

Ristorante Da Pancrazio
Piazza del Biscione, 92
00100 Rome (RM)
phone +39 06 6861246
dapancrazio@tin.it
closed: Wednesday

Trattoria Giggetto-al Portico d'Ottavia
Via del Portico d'Ottavia, 21
00100 Rome (RM)
phone +39 06 6861105
closed: Monday

Ristorante Il Sanpietrino
Piazza Costaguti, 15
00100 Rome (RM)
phone +39 06 68806471
www.ilsanpietrino.it

Achilli Enoteca al Parlamento
Viale dei Prefetti, 15
00100 Rome (RM)
phone +39 06 6873446
www.enotecaalparlamento.it

Buccone
Via di Ripetta, 19
00100 Rome (RM)
phone +39 06 3612154

Bomprezzi
Via Tuscolana, 904
00100 Rome (RM)
phone +39 06 7610135

sandrigo (veneto)

Informazioni Turistiche
Piazza Matteotti, 12
36100 Vicenza (VI)
phone +39 0444 320854, fax +39 0444 327072
aptvicenza@ascom.vi.it

Piazza dei Signori, 8
phone +39 0444 544122, fax +39 0444 561646

Jolly Hotel Tiepolo
Viale San Lazzaro, 110
36100 Vicenza (VI)
phone +39 0444 954011
vicenza-tiepolo@jollyhotels.com

Hostaria a le Bele
Località Maso Ovest
36078 Valdagno (VI)
phone +39 0445 970270
closed: Monday and Tuesday for lunch

Antica Trattoria Due Spade
Via Roma, 5
36066 Sandrigo (VI)
phone +39 0444 659948
closed: Monday night and Tuesday

Azienda Agricola Capovilla
Via Giardini, 12
36027 Rosà (VI)
phone +39 0424 581222

Carlotto & C.
Via Garibaldi, 30
36078 Valdagno (VI)
phone +39 0445 402170
info@carlotto.it, www.carlotto.it

sauris (friuli–venezia giulia)

Informazioni Turistiche
Località Sauris di Sotto
33020 Sauris (UD)
phone +39 0433 86076, fax +39 0433 866900

Consorzio A.R.T.A. Tur
Via Umberto I
33022 Arta Terme (UD)
phone +39 0438 929411
info@artatur.it

Hotel Pa' Krhalzar
Località Lates, 5
33020 Sauris (UD)
phone +39 0433 86165
www.alberghi.carnia.org/krhalzar

Hotel Schneider
Via Sauris di Sotto, 92
33020 Sauris (UD)
phone +39 0433 86220

Ristorante Kursaal
Località Sauris di Sotto, Piazzale Kursaal, 91/b
33020 Sauris (UD)
phone +39 0433 86202
closed: Sunday night and Monday

Ristorante Alla Pace
Località Sauris di Sotto, 38
33020 Sauris (UD)
phone +39 0433 866310
allapace@libero.it
closed: Wednesday (except in the summer)

Salumificio-Prosciuttificio Wolf
Località Sauris di Sotto
33020 Sauris (UD)
phone +39 0433 86054
info@wolfsauris.it, www.wolfsauris.it

Prosciuttificio Petris & Polentarutti
Località Sauris di Sopra, 66
33020 Sauris (UD)
phone +39 0433 86035

Eliana Solari
Frazione Pesariis, 96
33020 Prato Carnico (UD)
phone +39 0433 695800

scilla e cariddi (calabria)

Informazioni Turistiche
Aeroporto
89100 Reggio Calabria (RC)
phone +39 0965 64329

Stazione Centrale
phone +39 0965 97957

Grand Hotel Excelsior
Via Vittorio Veneto, 66
89100 Reggio Calabria (RC)
phone +39 0965 812211
excelsior@reggiocalabriahotels.it

Ristorante Glauco
Località Chianalea, Via Annunziata, 95
89058 Scilla (RC)
phone +39 0965 754026
closed: Tuesday (except in the summer)

Ristorante La Grotta Azzurra U Bais
Via Lungomare Cristoforo Colombo
89058 Scilla (RC)
phone +39 0965 754889

Ristorante La Pescatora
Località Marina Grande, Via C. Colombo, 32
89058 Scilla (RC)
phone +39 0965 754147

Bouteillerie
Via San Francesco di Paolo, 19
89100 Reggio Calabria (RC)
phone +39 0965 332548

Wine Shop
Via Pio XI, 3
89100 Reggio Calabria (RC)
phone +39 0965 54233

siena (tuscany)

Informazioni Turistiche
Piazza del Campo, 56
phone +39 0577 280551, fax +39 0577 270676
53100 Siena (SI)
incoming@terresiena.it
www.siena.toscana.it

Albergo Relais Riserva di Fizzano
Località Fizzano
53011 Castellina in Chianti (SI)
phone +39 057 77371
www.roccadellemacie.com

Grand Hotel Continental
Via Banchi di Sopra, 85
53100 Siena (SI)
phone +39 0577 44204
reservation.hcs@royaldemeure.com

Hotel Certosa di Maggiano
Strada di Certosa, 82-86
53100 Siena (SI)
phone +39 0577 288180
certosa@relaischateaux.com

Antica Trattoria Botteganova
Via Chiantigiana, 29 (per Montevarchi)
53100 Siena (SI)
phone +39 0577 284230
info@anticatrattoriabotteganova.it
closed: Sunday

Ristorante Osteria Le Logge
Via del Porrione, 33
53100 Siena (SI)
phone +39 0577 48013
osterialelogge@tin.it
closed: Sunday and holidays

Pasticceria le Campane
Via delle Campane, 9
53100 Siena (SI)
phone +39 0577 282290

Enoteca Il Salotto
Via Gracco del Secco, 31
53034 Colle di Val d'Elsa (SI)
phone +39 0577 926983
info@enotecailsalotto.com
www.enotecailsalotto.com

Antica Salumeria Salvini
Località Costafabbri, S.S. 73 Ponente, 46
53100 Siena (SI)
phone +39 0577 394399

Macelleria Dario Cecchini
Località Panzano, Via XX luglio, 11
50020 Greve in Chianti (FI)
phone +39 055 852020

sogliano al rubicone (emilia–romagna)

Informazioni Turistiche
Piazza del Popolo, 11
47023 Cesena (FC)
phone +39 0547 356327, fax +39 0547 356329
iat@comune.cesena.fc.it

Pro Loco di Sogliano al Rubicone
Piazza G. Matteotti, 41
47030 Sogliano al Rubicone (FC)
phone +39 0541 948610

proloco@cittadelrubicone.com
www.cittadelrubicone.com

Hotel Casali
Via B. Croce, 81
47023 Cesena (FC)
phone +39 0547 27485
hotelcasali@iol.it

Meeting Hotel
Via Romea, 545
47023 Cesena (FC)
phone +39 0547 333160
meetinghotel@libero.it

Ristorante Gianni
Via dell'Amore, 9
47023 Cesena (FC)
phone +39 0547 21328
info@ristorantegianni.com
closed: Thursday

Trattoria Osteria Michiletta
Via Fantaguzzi, 26
47023 Cesena (FC)
phone +39 0547 24691
www.osteriamichiletta.it
closed: Sunday

Fossa Pellegrini
Via Le Greppe, 14
47030 Sogliano al Rubicone (FC)
phone +39 0541 948542

Antiche Fosse
Via Pascoli, 4
47030 Sogliano al Rubicone (FC)
phone +39 0541 948687

Casa del Formaggio
Via XX Settembre, 6
47030 Sogliano al Rubicone (FC)
phone +39 0542 948636

Valentini
Località Dogana
47890 Repubblica di San Marino (RSM)
phone +39 0549 908362

sulmona (abruzzo)

Informazioni Turistiche
Corso Ovidio, 208
67039 Sulmona (AQ)
phone/fax +39 0864 53276

Hotel Santacroce
S.S. 17
67039 Sulmona (AQ)
phone +39 0864 251696
meeting@arc.it

Ristorante Gino
Piazza Plebiscito, 12
67039 Sulmona (AQ)
phone +39 0864 52289
marcoallega@virgilio.it
closed: at night and Sunday

Ristorante Clemente
Vico Quercia, 5
67039 Sulmona (AQ)
phone +39 0864.52284
www.ristoranteclemente.com
closed: Thursday

Fabbrica di Confetti Panfilo Rapone
Piazza XX Settembre, 7
67039 Sulmona (AQ)
phone +39 0864 51201
www.conettirapone.it

Confetti Pelino
Via Introacqua, 55
67039 Sulmona (AQ)
phone +39 0864 52741

Enrico Toro
Via Triburtina, 18
65028 Tocco di Casauria (PE)
phone +39 085 880279

Liquorificio Artigianale Luigi Cesaroni
Via L. Dorrucci, 16
67039 Sulmona (AQ)
phone +39 086 451383

taranto (puglia)

Informazioni Turistiche
Corso Umberto I, 113
74100 Taranto (TA)
phone +39 099 4532392, fax +39 099 4520417
infoaptta@libero.it

Albergo Masseria La Brunetta
Via per Chiatona
74016 Massafra (TA)
phone +39 099 8800942
direzione@masserialabrunetta.it
www.masserialabrunetta.it

Hotel Europa
Via Roma, 2
74100 Taranto (TA)
phone +39 099 4525994
info@hoteleuropaonline.it

Ristorante Le Vecchie Cantine
Località Lama, Via Girasoli, 23
74020 Taranto (TA)
phone +39 099 7772589
www.levecchiecantine.it
closed: for lunch and Wednesday

Ristorante Gesù Cristo
Via C. Battisti 10
74100 Taranto (TA)
phone +39 099 7772589
closed: Sunday night and Monday
(open in August)

Nel Regno di Bacco
Via Berardi 56
74100 Taranto (TA)
phone +39 099 4596218

Enoteca del Primitivo
Vico 1 Senatore G. Lacaita, 16
74024 Manduria (TA)
phone +39 099 711523

teramo (abruzzo)

Informazioni Turistiche
Via Carducci, 11
64100 Teramo (TE)
phone +39 0861 244222, fax +39 0861 244357
presidio.teramo@abruzzoturismo.it

Hotel Zunica
Piazza F. Pepe, 14
64010 Teramo (TE)
phone +39 0861 91319
www.hotelzunica.it

Ristorante Duomo
Via Stazio, 9
64100 Teramo (TE)
phone +39 0861 241774
closed: Sunday night and Monday

Ristorante Locanda del Duca d'Atri
Via San Domenico, 54
64032 Atri (TE)
phone +39 0858 797586
closed: Monday

Enoteca Osteria Centrale
Corso Cerulli Irelli, 26
64100 Teramo (TE)
phone +39 0861 243633

Azienda Agricola Barone Cornacchia
Contrada Torri, 20
64010 Torano Nuovo (TE)
phone +39 0861 887412

Confettificio Galiffa
Corso Adriatico, 216
64016 Sant'Egidio alla Vibrata (TE)
phone +39 0861 840120

turin (piedmont)

Informazioni Turistiche
Piazza Solferino
10100 Turin (TO)
phone +39 011 535181, fax +39 011 530070
info@turismotorino.org

Aeroporto Torino Caselle
phone +39 011 5678124
www.turismotorino.org

Grand Hotel Sitea
Via Carlo Alberto, 35
10123 Turin (TO)
phone +39 011 5170171
sitea@thi.it
www.thi.it

Hotel Victoria
Via N. Costa, 4
10123 Turin (TO)
phone +39 011 5611909
reservation@hotelvictoria-torino.com
www.hotelvictoria-torino.com

Ristorante Del Cambio
Piazza Carignano, 2
10123 Turin (TO)
phone +39 011 543760
cambio@thi.it
closed: Sunday

Ristorante Al Gatto Nero
Corso F. Turati, 14
10100 Turin (TO)
phone +39 011 590477
info@gattonero.it
www.gattonero.it
closed: Sunday

Osteria Antiche Sere
Via Cenischia, 9
10100 Turin (TO)
phone +39 011 3854347
closed: for lunch and Sunday

Caffè Al Bicerin
Piazza della Consolata
10100 Turin (TO)
phone +39 011 4369325

Caffè San Carlo
Piazza San Carlo, 156
10100 Turin (TO)
phone +39 011 5617748

Martini e Rossi Vermouth
Località Pessione
10023 Chieri (TO)
phone +39 011 94191

Fabbrica di pastiglie e caramelle Leone
Corso Regina Margherita, 42
10100 Turin (TO)
phone +39 011 484759

Confetteria Stratta
Piazza Carlo Alberto, 191
10100 Turin (TO)
phone +39 011 547920

Pasticceria Baratti & Milano
Piazza Castello, 27
10100 Turin (TO)
phone +39 011 5613060

Panetteria Lampiano
Strada Parrocchiale, 8
10020 Marentino (TO)
phone +39 011 9435060

Consorzio Montagna Viva
Piazza E. Filiberto, 3
10100 Turin (TO)
phone +39 011 5217882

trapani (sicily)

Ufficio Informazioni
Piazza Saturno
91100 Trapani (TP)
phone +39 0923 29000, fax +39 0923 24004
apttp@mail.cinet.it
www.apt.trapani.it

Hotel Crystal
Piazza Umberto, 1
91100 Trapani (TP)
phone +39 0923 20000
reservation.cry@framon-hotels.it

Agriturismo Baglio Fontanasalsa
Località Fontanasalsa, Via Cusenza, 78
91100 Trapani (TP)
phone +39 0923 591001
fontanasalsa@hotmail.com

Ristorante Taverna Paradiso
Lungomare Dante Alighieri, 22
91100 Trapani (TP)
phone +39 0923 22303
closed: Sunday

Trattoria Cantina Siciliana
Via Giudecca, 32
91100 Trapani (TP)
phone +39 0923 28673
www.cantinasiciliana.it
closed: never

Ristorante Tha'am
Via Abruzzi, 32
91010 San Vito Lo Capo (TP)
phone +39 0923 972836
thaam@wooow.it
closed: Wednesday

Ristorante Delfino
Via Savoia, 15
91010 San Vito Lo Capo (TP)
phone +39 0923 3972711
billecifrancesco@virgilio.it
closed: never

Consorzio Sale Natura
Località Paceco, Via F, 6
91027 Nubia (TP)
phone +39 0923 873844

Saline Ettore e Infersa
Contrada Infersa
91025 Marsala (TP)
phone +39 092 3966936
www.cilastour.com

Sosalt
Zona Ronciglio
91100 Trapani (TP)
phone +39 092 323292
www.sosalt.com

trento (trentino–alto adige)

Azienda di Promozione Turistica (APT)
Via Manci, 2
38100 Trento (TN)
phone +39 0461 983880, fax +39 0461 984508
informazioni@apt.trento.it
www.apt.trento.it

Hotel Adige
Frazione Mattarello, Via Pomeranos, 2
38100 Trento (TN)
phone +39 0461 944545
adigehotel@cr-surfing.net

Hotel Buonconsiglio
Via Romagnosi, 16/18
38100 Trento (TN)
phone +39 0461 272888
hotelhb@tin.it
www.hotelbuonconsiglio.it

Hotel Ristorante Villa Madruzzo
Località Cognola, Via Ponte Alto, 26
38050 Cognola (TN)
phone +39 0461 986220
info@villamadruzzo.it
www.villamadruzzo.it
closed: Sunday

Osteria a Le Due Spade
Via don A. Rizzi, 11
38100 Trento (TN)
phone +39 0461 234343
info@leduespade.com
www.leduespade.com
closed: Monday for lunch and Sunday

Ristorante Lo Scrigno del Duomo
Piazza del Duomo, 29
38100 Trento (TN)
phone +39 0461 220030
info@scrignodelduomo.com
www.scrignodelduomo.com
closed: Saturday for lunch and Monday

Grado 12
Largo Carducci, 12
38100 Trento (TN)
phone +39 0461 982496

Consorzio Melinda
Via Trento, 200/9
38023 Cles (TN)
phone +39 0463 671111
melinda@melinda.it
www.melinda.it

Azienda Agricola Valentini
Frazione Rallo, Via Dos Serena, 16
38010 Tassullo (TN)
phone +39 0463 459985

Gastronomia Mattei
Via Mazzini, 46
38100 Trento (TN)
phone +39 0461 238053

treviso (veneto)

Ufficio di Informazione e di Accoglienza Turistica (IAT)
Piazza Monte di Pietà, 8
phone +39 0422 547632, fax +39 0422 419092
31100 Treviso (TV)
iat.treviso@provincia.treviso.it

Hotel Continental
Via Roma, 16
31100 Treviso (TV)
phone +39 0422 411216
continental@sevenonline.it

Relais Villa Fiorita
Via Giovanni XXIII, 1
31050 Monastier di Treviso (TV)
phone +39 0422 898008
fiorita@villafiorita.it
www.sogedinhotels.it

Hotel Al Foghér
Viale della Repubblica, 10
31100 Treviso (TV)
phone +39 0422 432950
htl@alfogher.com
www.alfogher.com

Ristorante Beccherie
Piazza Ancilotto, 10
31100 Treviso (TV)
phone +39 0422 540871
closed: Sunday night and Monday

Trattoria Antica Torre
Via Inferiore, 55
31100 Treviso (TV)
phone +39 0422 583694
info@anticatorre.tv
closed: Sunday

Trattoria Toni del Spin
Via Inferiore, 7
31100 Treviso (TV)

phone +39 0422 543829
closed: Monday and Sunday for lunch

Ristorante Osteria al Bottegon
Viale Burchiellati, 7
31100 Treviso (TV)
phone +39 0422 548345

Ristorante All'Antico Portico
Piazza Santa Maria Maggiore, 18
31100 Treviso (TV)
phone +39 0422 545259
www.anticoportico.it
closed: Tuesday

Consorzio di tutela del vino Prosecco di Conegliano e Valdobbiadene
Via Roma, 7
31053 Pieve di Soligo (TV)
phone +39 038 83028
cpcv@madianet.it
www.prosecco.it

Treviso Doc
Via del Municipio, 1
31100 Treviso (TV)
phone +39 0422 583519

Azienda Agricola Drusian Francesco
Strada Anche, 1
31030 Bigolino di Valdobbiadene (TV)
phone +39 0423 982151
www.drusian.it

Bisol
Località S. Stefano di Valdobbiadene
31040 San Pietro di Barbozza (TV)
phone +39 0423 900138
www.bisol.it

Consorzio tutela radicchio rosso di Treviso
Via Scandolara, 80
31059 Zero Branco (TV)
phone +39 0422 488087
consorzio@radicchioditreviso.it
www.radicchioditreviso.it

Ortofrutta Savi
Via Alzaia sul Sile, 22
31057 Silea (TV)
phone +39 0422 363006
info@cuoretrevigiano.com
www.cuoretrevigiano.com

Agriturismo Mondragon
Località Arfanta, Via Mondragon, 1
31010 Corbanese (TV)
phone +39 0438 933021
info@mondragon.it

trieste (friuli–venezia giulia)

Informazioni Turistiche
Piazza Unità d'Italia, 4/b
34100 Trieste (TS)
phone +39 040 3478312, fax +39 040 3478320
aptour@libero.it
www.triestetourism.it

Albergo Pesek
Località Dolina
34018 San Dorligo della Valle (TS)
phone +39 040 226294
info@hotelpesek.it
www.hotelpesek.it

Grand Hotel Duchi d'Aosta
Piazza Unità d'Italia, 2
34121 Trieste (TS)
phone +39 040 7600011
info@grandhotelduchidaosta.com

Hotel Riviera & Maximilian's
Località Grignano, Strada Costiera, 22
34014 Trieste (TS)
phone +39 040 224551
info@hotelrivieraemaximilian.com

Hotel Colombia
Via della Geppa, 18
34132 Trieste (TS)
phone +39 040 369333
colombia@hotelcolombia.it

Ristorante Harry's Grill
Piazza Unità d'Italia, 2
34100 Trieste (TS)
phone +39 040 660606
closed: Sunday

Antica Trattoria Suban
Via E. Comici, 2
34100 Trieste (TS)
phone +39 040 54368
closed: Monday for lunch and Tuesday

Ristorante Ai Fiori
Piazza Hortis, 7
34124 Trieste (TS)
phone +39 040 300633
info@aifiori.com
closed: Sunday and Monday

Buffet da Bepi
Via Cassa di Risparmio, 3
34100 Trieste
phone +39 040 366858
closed: Sunday and Monday

Ristorante Daneu
Strada per Vienna, 76
34016 Opicina (TS)
phone +39 040 211241
info@hoteldaneu.com
closed: Monday

Pasticceria Pirona
Largo Barriera Vecchia, 12
34100 Trieste (TS)
phone +39 040 636046

Caffè San Marco
Via C. Battisti, 18
34100 Trieste (TS)
phone +39 040 363538

Caffè Tommaseo
Riva 4 novembre, 5
34100 Trieste (TS)
phone +39 040 362666

Parovel
Località Caresana, 81
34018 San Dorligo della Valle (TS)
phone +39 040 231908
info@parovel.com
www.parovel.com

Azienda Agricola Gruden Zbogar
Samatorza, 47
34010 Sgonico (TS)
phone +39 040 229191

Tipica Salumeria Masè Tullio
Via Timeus, 3
34100 Trieste (TS)
phone +39 040 367274

tropea (calabria)

Azienda di Promozione Turistica (APT)
Via Forgiari - Galleria Vecchio
89900 Vibo Valentia (VV)
phone +39 0963 42008, fax +39 0963 44318
www.costadei.net

Hotel Cala di Volpe
Località Santa Domenica, Contrada Torre
Marino
89865 Tropea (VV)
phone +39 0963 669699
info@caladivolpe.it

Hotel Punta Faro
Località Grotticelle
89865 San Nicolò di Ricadi (VV)
phone +39 0963 663139
sephi@tiscali.it

Ristorante Pimm's
Corso Vittorio Emanuele, 2 (l.go Migliarese)
89861 Tropea (VV)
phone +39 0963 666105
closed: Monday (open July and August)

Accademia Tutela Cipolla Rossa di Tropea
Località Santa Domenica, Via Provinciale
88030 Ricadi (VV)
phone +39 0963 669523
accademia@cipollatropea.it

Delizie Vaticane di Tropea
Località Santa Domenica, Via Provinciale
88030 Ricadi (VV)
phone +39 0963 669523
info@delizievaticane.it
www.delizievaticane.it

Fabbrica Liquore di Cedro S. Maria
Via Nazionale, 40
87020 Santa Maria del Cedro (CS)
phone +39 098 55357

Azienda Agrituristica La Spina Santa
Contrada Spina Santa
89035 Bova Marina (RC)
phone +39 0965 761012
laspinasanta@libero.it
www.laspinasanta.com

La Mimosa
Piazza S. Anna, 3
89100 Reggio Calabria (RC)
phone +39 096 5891816

---

udine (friuli–venezia giulia)

Azienda Regionale di Promozione Turistica (ARPT)
Piazza I Maggio, 7
33100 Udine (UD)
phone +39 0432 295972, fax +39 0432 504743
arpt.ud1@regione.fvg.it

Astoria Hotel Italia
Piazza XX Settembre, 24
33100 Udine (UD)
phone +39 0432 505091
astoria@hotelastoria.udine.it
www.hotelastoria.udine.it

Hotel Ambassador Palace
Via Carducci, 46
33100 Udine (UD)
phone +39 0432 503777
info@ambassadorpalacehophoneit

Hotel Principe
Viale Europa Unita, 51
33100 Udine (UD)
phone +39 0432 506000
info@principe-hophoneit

Ristorante Vitello d'Oro
Via Valvason, 4
33100 Udine (UD)
phone +39 0432 508982
info@vitellodoro.com
closed: Monday for lunch and Wednesday
(June-September Sunday and Monday for lunch)

Ristorante Agli Amici
Località Godia, Via Liguria, 250
33100 Udine (UD)
phone +39 0432 565411
agliamici@libero.it
www.agliamici1887.it
closed: Sunday night and Monday

Trattoria alla Colonna
Via Gemona, 98
33100 Udine (UD)
phone +39 0432 510177
closed: Sunday and Monday for lunch

Ristorante Alla Vedova
Via Tavagnacco, 9
33100 Udine (UD)
phone +39 0432 470291
zamaria@libero.it
closed: Sunday night and Monday

Birrificio Udinese
Via Caccia
33100 Udine (UD)
phone +39 0432 510988
birrificioudinese@tin.it

Bottega del Prosciutto
Via Umberto I, 2
33038 San Daniele del Friuli (UD)
phone +39 0432 957043

Prosciutti Coradazzi
Via Kennedy, 128
33038 San Daniele del Friuli (UD)
phone +39 0432 957582
coradazzi@adriacom.it
www.coradazzi.it

La Casa degli Spiriti
Via dei Torriani, 15
33100 Udine (UD)
phone +39 0432 509216

---

urbino (marche)

Informazioni Turistiche
Piazza del Rinascimento, 1
61029 Urbino (PU)
phone +39 0722 2613, fax +39 0722 2441
iat.urbino@regione.marche.it

Hotel San Domenico
Piazza Rinascimento, 3
61029 Urbino (PU)
phone +39 0722 2626
info@viphotels.it

Hotel Mamiani
Via Bernini, 6
61029 Urbino (PU)
phone +39 0722 322309
info@hotelmamiani.it

Ristorante Vecchia Urbino
Via dei Vasari, 3/5
61029 Urbino (PU)
phone +39 0722 4447
info@vecchiaurbino.it
closed: Tuesday

Ristorante San Giacomo
Località Pantiere, 18
61029 Urbino (PU)
phone +39 0722 580646
www.sangiacomodiurbino.com
closed: Monday

Ristorante Villa Federici
Località Bargni, Via Cartoceto, 4
61030 Serrungarina (PU)
phone +39 0721 891510
info@villafederici.it
www.villafederici.it
closed: Monday and Tuesday

Enoteca Magia Ciarla
Via Raffaello, 54
61029 Urbino (PU)
phone +39 0722 328438

Fattorie Marchigiane
Via Cerbara, 81
61030 Montemaggiore al Metauro (PU)
phone +39 0721 187981

---

venice (veneto)

Informazioni Turistiche
Calle Ascensione, San Marco, 71
30124 Venice (VE)
phone +39 041 5297811
info@turismovenezia.it

Aeroporto Marco Polo
phone +39 041 5298711

Hotel Cipriani
Giudecca, 10
30133 Venice (VE)
phone +39 041 5207744
info@hotelcipriani.it

Hotel Danieli
Riva degli Schiavoni, 4196
30122 Venice (VE)
phone +39 041 5226480
danieli@luxurycollection.com

Hotel Quattro Fontane
Lido di Venezia, Via Quattro Fontane, 16
30126 Venice (VE)
phone +39 041 5260227
www.quattrofontane.com

Ristorante Caffè Quadri
Piazza San Marco, 120
30124 Venice (VE)
phone +39 041 5222105
quadri@quadrivenice.com
closed: Monday from November to March

Ristorante Da Fiore
Calle del Scaleter, San Polo 2202/A
30125 Venice (VE)
phone +39 041 721308
reservation@dafiore.com
www.dafiore.com
closed: Sunday and Monday

Trattoria Bancogiro Osteria da Andrea
Campo San Giacometto, San Polo 122
30125 Venice (VE)
phone +39 041 5232061
closed: Sunday night and Monday

Harry's bar
Calle Vallaresso, San Marco 1323
30124 Venice (VE)
phone +39 041 5285777

Caffè Florian
San Marco 56
30124 Venice (VE)
phone +39 041 5202641
www.caffeflorian.it

Rosa Salva
Ponte Ferai, San Marco 951
30124 Venice (VE)
phone +39 041 5210544

Puppa
Calle dello Spezier, Cannaregio 4008
30124 Venice (VE)
phone +39 041 5237947

Pasticceria Marchini
San Marco Spadaria 676
30124 Venice (VE)
phone +39 041 5229109

All'aciugheta
Castello 4357
30124 Venice (VE)
phone +39 041 5224292

vercelli (piedmont)

Informazioni Turistiche
Viale Garibaldi, 90
phone +39 0163 58002, fax +39 0163 257899
13100 Vercelli (VC)

Hotel Cinzia
Corso Magenta, 71
13100 Vercelli (VC)
phone +39 0161 253585
hotelcin@tin.it

Hotel Ristorante Il Giardinetto
Via L. Sereno, 3
13100 Vercelli (VC)
phone +39 0161 257230

giardi.dan@libero.it
www.hrgiardinetto.com
closed: Monday

Ristorante Il Paiolo
Corso Garibaldi, 72
13100 Vercelli (VC)
phone +39 0161 250577
closed: Thursday

Ristorante Bivio
Via Bivio, 2
13030 Quinto Vercellese (VC)
phone +39 0161 274131
ristorantebivio@hotmail.com
closed: Monday and Tuesday

Azienda Agricola Ferraris
Cascina Torrone Cagna
13041 Bianzè (VC)
phone +39 0161 49297

Azienda Agricola Lodigiana
Strada delle Grange, 20
13036 Ronsecco (VC)
phone +39 0161 816001

Il Pastino
Via G. Ferraris, 15
13046 Livorno Ferraris (VC)
phone +39 0161 477563

Antichi Vigneti di Cantalupo
Via M. Buonarroti, 5
28074 Ghemme (NO)
phone +39 0163 840041
www.cantalupo.net

Antoniolo
Corso Valsesia, 277
13045 Gattinara (VC)
phone +39 0163 833612

verona (veneto)

Ufficio di Informazione e di Accoglienza Turistica (IAT)
Via degli Alpini, 9
37100 Verona (VR)
phone +39 045 8068680, fax +39 045 8003638
iatbra@tiscali.it

Aeroporto Villafranca
phone +39 045 8619163
iataeroporto@tiscali.it

Albergo Villa del Quar
Località Pedemonte, Via Quar, 12
37029 San Pietro in Cariano (VR)
phone +39 045 6800681
info@villadelquar.it
www.hotelvilaldelquar.it

Hotel Due Torri Baglioni
Piazza Sant'Anastasia, 4
37121 Verona (VR)
phone +39 045 595044
duetorri.verona@baglionihotels.com

Hotel Gabbia d'Oro
Corso Porta Borsari, 4/a
37121 Verona (VR)
phone +39 045 8003060
gabbiadoro@easyasp.it
www.hotelgabbiadoro.it

Ristorante Il Desco
Via Dietro San Sebastiano, 7
37121 Verona (VR)
phone +39 045 595358
closed: Sunday and Monday (open Monday night in July, August and December)

Osteria La Fontanina
Portichetti Fontanelle Santo Stefano, 3
37129 Verona (VR)
phone +39 045 913305
closed: Sunday and Monday for lunch

Ristorante 12 Apostoli
Corticella San Marco, 3
37100 Verona (VR)
phone +39 045 596999
dodiciapostoli@tiscali.it
closed: Monday and Sunday night

Trattoria Al Calmiere
Piazza San Zeno, 10
37123 Verona (VR)
phone +39 045 8030765
calmiere@libero.it
closed: Sunday night and Monday

Cantina sociale di Valpantena
Via Colonia Orfani di Guerra, 5/B
37034 Quinto di Valpantena (VR)
phone +39 045 550032
info@cantinavalpantena.it
www.cantinavalpantena.it

Agricola Allegrini
Via Giare, 9
37022 Fumane (VR)
phone +39 045 6832011
info@allegrini.it
www.allegrini.it

Masi
Località Gargagnano, Via Monteleone, 2
37020 Sant'Ambrogio di Valpolicella (VR)
phone +39 045 6832511
masi@masi.it
www.masi.it

Cicchetteria Veneta
Via San Michele alla Porta, 4
37100 Verona (VR)
phone +39 045 8004514

Riseria Ferron
Via Saccovener, 6
37063 Isola della Scala (VR)
phone +39 0456 630642
info@risoferron.com
www.risoferron.com

viterbo (lazio)

Ufficio Informazioni
Via Romiti (Stazione Porta Romana)
01100 Viterbo (VT)
phone +39 0761 304795, fax +39 0761 220957
infoviterbo@apt.viterbo.it

Hotel Salus e delle Terme Pianeta Benessere
Via Tuscanese, 26-28
01100 Viterbo (VT)
phone +39 0761 3581
info@grandhoteltermesalus.com

Hotel Niccolò V
Strada Bagni, 12
01100 Viterbo (VT)
phone +39 0761 3501
info@termedeipapi.it

Ristorante Sale e Pepe
Località San Martino al Cimino, Via Abate
Lamberto, 2-4
01030 Viterbo (VT)
phone +39 0761 379242
closed: Tuesday

Trattoria Il Richiastro
Via dela Marrocca, 16
01100 Viterbo (VT)
phone +39 0761 228009
aperto: Sunday for lunch, Friday and Saturday

Ristorante Da Gino al Miralago
Viale Marconi, 58
01010 Marta (VT)
phone +39 0761 870910
closed: Tuesday (open from 7/20 to 8/30)

Emporio Enogastronomico Menghini
Via C. Dobici, 83
01100 Viterbo (VT)
phone +39 0761 340676
www.emporiostrenne.com

Falesco
Zona artigianale Le Guardie
01027 Montefiascone (VT)
phone +39 0761 825669
falesco@leone.it

Azienda Agricola Giovannelli
Località Poggio Nibbio, Strada Provinciale
Valle di Vico km 2,300
01100 Viterbo (VT)
phone +39 0761 379664

SUGGESTED READINGS

SUGGESTED READINGS

FOOD

Apicius, Marcus Gavius. *Cookery and Dining in Imperial Rome*. Ed. Joseph D. Vehling. New York: Dover Publications, 1979.

Artusi, Pellegrino. *Science in the Kitchen and the Art of Eating Well*. Trans. Murtha Baca. Toronto: University of Toronto Press, 2003.

Camporesi, Piero. *The Magic Harvest: Food, Folklore, and Society*. Transl. Joan Krakover Hall. Mallden, MA: Polity Press, 1999.

Capatti, Alberto, and Massimo Montanari. *Italian Cuisine : A Cultural History*. Trans. Aine O'Healy. New York: Columbia University Press, 2003.

WINE

Bastianich, Joseph, David Lynch, and Lidia Matticchio Bastianich. *Vino Italiano: The Regional Wines of Italy*. New York: Clarkson Potter, 2002.

Belfrage, Nicolas. Brunello to Zibibbo: *The Wines of Tuscany, Central, and Southern Italy*. New York: Mitchell Beazley, 2003.

Colombini, Donatella Cinelli, and Stephen Hobley. *A Traveller's Wine Guide to Italy*. Brooklyn, NY: Interlink Publishing Group, 2001.

TRAVEL

Touring Club of Italy. Italy: A Complete Guide to 1,000 Towns and Cities and Their Landmarks. Milan: Touring Club of Italy, 2003.

Touring Club of Italy. Italian Farm Vacations: The Guide to Countryside Hospitality. Milan: Touring Club of Italy, 2003.

ACRONYMS

DOC: *Denominazione di Origine Controllata*—Controlled denomination of origin

DOCG: *Denominazione di Origine Controllata e Garantita*—Controlled and guaranteed denomination of origin

DOP: *Denominazione di Origine Protetta*—Protected denomination of origin

IGP: *Indicazione Geografica Protetta*—Protected geographical indication

IGT: *Indicazione Geografica Tipica*—Traditional geographical indication

PT: *Prodotto Tipico*—Traditional product

VQPRD: *Vini di Qualità Prodotti in Regioni Determinate*—Quality wine produced in specific regions

VSQPRD: *Vini Spumanti di Qualità Prodotti in Regioni Determinate*—Quality sparkling (*spumante*) wine produced in specific regions

VFQPRD: *Vini Frizzanti di Qualità Prodotti in Regioni Determinate*—Quality sparkling (*frizzante*) wine produced in specific regions

PHOTO CREDITS

First published in the United States of America in 2005
by Rizzoli International Publications, Inc.
300 Park Avenue South
New York, NY 10010
www.rizzoliusa.com

© 2005 RCS Libri Spa, Milan

Production: Colophon srl, Venice, Italy

Editorial Direction: Andrea Grandese

Editor in Chief: Rosanna Alberti

Editor: Paola Gaudioso

Design Concept: Stephen Fay

English Translation: Judith Goodman

Editor (English Edition): Julie Di Filippo

Copy Editor (English Edition): Alta Price

2005 2006 2007 2008 2009 / 10 9 8 7 6 5 4 3 2 1

Printed in Italy

ISBN: 0-8478-2741-0

Library of Congress Control Number: 2005903568